TRADE, DISTORTIONS AND EMPLOYMENT GROWTH IN KOREA

By

Wontack Hong

1 9 7 9

KOREA DEVELOPMENT INSTITUTE

Seoul, Korea

BOARD OF DIRECTORS

Chairman	Rhee, Ki Jun
President	Kim, Mahn Je
Directors	Koh, Seung Je
	Kim, Young Hui
	Chong, Byung Hyou
	Chung, Jai Suk
	Cho, Choong Hoon
	Nam, Wook
	Bae,, Sang Wook
Auditor	Kim, Young Joon

The Korea Development Institute was established on March 11, 1971 by President Park Chung Hee. KDI systematically conducts research on policy matters concerning the overall national economy, helps develop the nation's five-year plans, and assists in policy making.

KDI is a non-profit corporate organization operated on an endowment fund. For this reason, its autonomy and independence are guaranteed to the maximum possible extent in the performance of its policy-oriented research activities.

The results of research conducted by KDI will be published and distributed. The contents of report, however, will represent the opinion of the person in charge of the respective research, and shall not be construed as an official opinion of the Institute.

All Rights Reserved by
THE KOREA DEVELOPMENT INSTITUTE
P.O. Box 113, Cheong Ryang, Seoul, Korea

Distributed Outside Korea by
The University Press of Hawaii

ISBN 0-8248-0678-6

FOREWORD

This paper is part of the Korea modernization study which is being undertaken jointly by the Korea Development Institute and the Harvard Institute for International Development with partial financial support from the United States Agency for International Development. The goal of the modernization study is to analyse various aspects of the modernization process of the Korean economy during the last thirty years (1945-76). This paper is part of a larger study on "Aid, Trade and Industrialization in Korea" which was divided among Krueger, Suh and Hong. In order to minimize repetition and overlaps, Krueger undertook an analysis of the role of the foreign sector and aid in Korea's development in general, Suh concentrated on the import substitution aspect and this paper focused on the impact of export promotion on employment growth. It is hoped that this study, as well as the whole KDI series of modernization studies, will make a valuable contribution toward understanding the growth process of Korean economy and will also assist in assessing prospects for other developing countries.

The Council for Asian Manpower Studies also partly financed this research project. The author wishes to thank Messrs. Young Koo Lee, Chan Soo Park, Moon Jong Kim and Miss Myung Soon Rho for their invaluable research assistance. The author alone is, however, responsible for all possible errors and omissions.

Mahn Je Kim
President
Korea Development Institute

TABLE OF CONTENTS

Foreword

CHAPTER 1. INTRODUCTION 1

CHAPTER 2. FACTOR SUPPLY AND FACTOR INTENSITY OF TRADE 5

  1. Growth and Trade in Korea: 1910–77

  2. Factor Supply and Factor Intensity of Trade: 1960–75

CHAPTER 3. TRADE AND SUBSIDY POLICIES: AN OVERVIEW (1953–77) 36

  1. Government Intervention

  2. Economic Development Plans and Economic Policies

  3. Exchange Control and Trade Policies

  4. Export Promotion

  5. Export Plan and Actual Performance

CHAPTER 4. PREFERENTIAL TAX POLICIES 73

  1. Tax Revenue and Tax Exemptions

  2. Income and Corporation Tax

  3. Business and Commodity Tax

v

CHAPTER 5. TARIFF AND NON-TARIFF IMPORT
            RESTRICTIONS 96

   1. Import Tariffs

   2. Non-Tariff Import Restrictions

CHAPTER 6. LOAN ALLOCATION POLICIES *110*

   1. Distribution of Domestic Bank Loans

   2. Export Financing

   3. Distribution of Foreign Capital: Aid, Loans
      and Investments

CHAPTER 7. FACTOR MARKET DISTORTIONS............*146*

   1. Major Sources of Factor Market Distortions

   2. Underpricing of Imported Capital Goods

   3. Bank Loans, Foreign Capital and Government
      Investment

   4. Real Opportunity Cost of Capital Use

   5. Implicit Subsidies on Capital Use

CHAPTER 8. EMPLOYMENT IMPLICATIONS OF TRADE
            AND SUBSIDY POLICIES *206*

   1. Employment Growth in Korea

   2. Subsidies and Composition of Output and Trade

   3. Subsidies and Choice of Techniques

CHAPTER 9. SUMMARY AND CONCLUSION..............*252*

BIBLIOGRAPHY *271*
STATISTICAL REFERENCES *275*
STATISTICAL APPENDIX *277*

TEXT TABLES

2.1.	Industrial Structure of Korea in the Colonial Period	6
2.2.	Commodity Composition of Exports: 1910–35	8
2.3.	Commodity Composition of Imports: 1910–35	10
2.4.	Employment and Gross Output Value of Manufacturing Sectors: 1926 and 1939	11
2.5.	Growth and Changes in the Industrial Structure: 1953–77	14
2.6.	Capital Accumulation and Employment Growth	20
2.7.	Contribution of Commodity Exports to Sectoral Employment: 1960–75	22
2.8.	Commodity Exports and Sectoral Capital Use: 1960–75	23
2.9.	Contribution of Non-Commodity Exports to Sectoral Employment and Capital Use: 1960–75	24
2.10.	Capital Stock Per Worker in Agriculture and Manufacturing	26
2.11.	Changing Factor Intensity of Trade: 1960–75	32
2.12.	Factor Requirements Per $100 Million Exports or Import Replacements: U.S. (1947), Japan (1951) and Korea (1970)	34
3.1.	Internal and External Financial Gap	40
3.2.	Exports and Imports	46
3.3.	Major Export Promotion Schemes	54
3.4.	Export Plan and Actual Performance: 1966	62
3.5.	Export Plan and Actual Performance: 1971	64
3.6.	Export Plan and Actual Performance: 1976	65
3.7.	Export Plan for 1981	67
3.8.	Raw Material Imports for Direct Use in Export Production: 1966–76	68

4.1.	General Government Revenue	74
4.2.	Exemptions of Internal Taxes and Tariffs	76
4.3.	Corporation Tax Rates	81
4.4.	Allowance for the Consumption of Fixed Capital in Manufacturing	86
4.5.	Sectoral Business Tax Rates	88
4.6.	Commodity Tax Rates and Revenue Collected from Selected Commodities	92
5.1.	Aggregated Legal and Actual Tariff Rates	97
5.2.	Weighted Average Sectoral Legal Tariff Rates (Basic Rates)	98
5.3.	Number of Items Subject to Import Controls: 1967–76	105
5.4.	Sectoral Pattern of Import Control	106
6.1.	Ranking of Loan Priorities	113
6.2.	Short-Term Loans for Support of Exports by Deposit Money Banks	121
6.3.	Foreign Currency Loans	126
6.4.	Loans for Exports	128
6.5.	Summary of Foreign Economic Aid and Relief Goods Received: 1945–63	132
6.6.	U.S. Aid: 1953–76	135
6.7.	U.S. Non-Project Assistance	136
6.8.	Imports of Surplus Agricultural Products under U.S. PL 480: 1956–76	137
6.9.	Guarantees of Repayment of Foreign Loans	143
7.1	Major Investment Funds Under Direct Government Control	147
7.2.	Aid-Financed Capital Goods Imports	151
7.3.	Import Content of Gross Fixed Capital Formation	154
7.4.	Legal and Actual Tariff Rates on Capital Goods Imports	156

7.5.	Major Sources of Funds of the Deposit Money Banks	160
7.6.	Major Sources and Uses of Funds: the Bank of Korea and the Korea Development Bank	161
7.7.	Weighted Average Interest Rates on Loans by Deposit Money Bank and the Korea Development Bank	162
7.8.	Loans to Corporation and Individual Sectors	164
7.9.	Balance of Foreign Loans	167
7.10.	Gross Inflow of Foreign Loans	168
7.11.	Weighted Average Real Interest Rates on Private and Government Foreign Borrowings	171
7.12.	Inflow of Foreign Investment	172
7.13.	Industrial Classification of Foreign Investment (Total During 1962–76)	173
7.14.	Government Direct Investment by Sectors	174
7.15.	Estimates of Sectoral Rates of Return to Capital: 1954–75 (Applying 1970 Non-Labor Shares)	180
7.16.	Estimates of Upper Limit for Rate of Return on Capital in Agricultural Sector: 1966–73	183
7.17.	Estimates of Rates of Return on Capital in Manufacturing	184
7.18.	Rates of Return to Fixed Assets in the Manufacturing Sector	188
7.19.	Estimated Real Opportunity Cost of Capital Use in Manufacturing	189
7.20.	Weighted Average Rates of Return on Capital in the Non-Primary Sectors	193
7.21.	Domestic and Foreign Loan Balance	198
7.22.	Loans and (Weighted Average) Real Interest Rates	200
7.23.	Estimated Rate of Interest Subsidy Associated with Domestic and Foreign Loans to the Manufacturing Sector	202
7.24.	Estimated Rate of Interest Subsidy Associated with Domestic and Foreign Loans: Whole Industry	203
8.1.	Population, Employment and Labor Force Participation Rate	207

8.2.	Persons Employed by Industry	208
8.3.	Differences in Urban-Rural Earnings	210
8.4.	An Estimate of Disguised Unemployment in Agriculture	213
8.5.	Changes in Factor Intensity of Commodity Exports Due to Factor Substitutions and Shifts in Composition of Exports: 1966–73	214
8.6.	Estimate of Effective Exchange Rate: Counting Direct Subsidies Only	218
8.7.	Sectoral Share in Total Value Added and in Total Loans	220
8.8.	Production and Trade of Selected Commodities	227
8.9.	Direct and Total Factor Coefficients of Selected Sectors: 1970	228
8.10.	Employment and Capital Use in Manufacturing (Manufacturing Census Data)	233
8.11.	Weighted Average Interest Rates on Loans to the Manufacturing Sector	234
8.12.	Rate of Change in Wage and Rental: 1967–73	236
8.13.	Employment and Capital Use in Selected Manufacturing Sectors	244
8.14.	Differences in Capital Intensity between Small and Large Firms: 1968	246
8.15.	Direct Factor Intensity of Selected Manufacturing Sectors: 1960–75	250

CHAPTER 1

INTRODUCTION

In the absence of external economies, free trade under perfect competition leads to efficient resource allocation and hence one can justify the balanced incentives for export promotion and import substitution so that the marginal cost of earning and saving foreign exchange can be equalized. Experiences of many developing countries indicate that emphasis on import substitution based on a Prebisch type export pessimism usually leads to an overvaluation of the exchange rate. This reduces the export incentives and increases bureaucratic exchange control, and leads to the development of resource-wasting entrepreneurs reaping profits solely from their monopoly position in the small domestic market and from their ability to get investment financing and import capital goods at subsidized prices, and to ever increasing high cost industries as the initial phase of easy import substitution is finished. On the other hand, export promotion usually produces the benefits of expanded market size and economies of scale. It also encourages efficient management practices of the entrepreneurs because of international competition as well as efficient transmission and diffusion of modern production technology. Finally, it makes subsidies more visible than an import substitution policy which helps reduce irrational elements in government policies.[1]

One can hypothesize a variety of effects that the trade strategy may have upon employment and its rate of growth. First, one strategy might

---

[1] See R. Prebisch, "Commercial Policy in the Developing Countries," *American Economic Review Papers and Proceedings*, May 1959, and J. N. Bhagwati and A. O. Krueger, "Exchange Control, Liberalization, and Economic Growth," *American Economic Review Papers and Proceedings*, May 1973.

result in a higher overall rate of economic growth due to superior resource allocation, and faster gowth would presumably entail higher employment. Second, different trade strategies might imply differences in output composition at each point in time. If employment per unit of output is greater in one set of industries than in another, then employment growth would be faster under the strategy that lets the labor-intensive industries grow relatively faster. Third, alternative trade policies could also influence the choice of technique and the capital-labor ratio in all industries.[2]

To some extent, import substitution itself may lead to export expansion, that is, some import substituting industries may become export industries as time passes. Therefore one may not classify alternative trade strategies simply in terms of import substitution or export promotion because the distinction between these two is blurred. On the other hand, the difference in labor intensity of production for exports and import substitution can be very small and hence the trade strategy itself might not affect employment very much. Furthermore, one might find that a particular policy such as granting exporters favored access to imported capital goods and credit, which may not be really essential to the adopted trade strategy, has adverse effects on employment and that a different set of policies could be used to implement the same trade strategy without the adverse employment effects.

Economists have observed that the decision to emphasize import-substitution or export promotion has important ramifications upon virtually every aspect of economic activity. The effects depend not only on which strategy is chosen, but also on the policy instruments used to implement the choice and on the degree of emphasis given to the chosen strategy.[3] Trade and subsidy policies have mostly been analyzed in terms of the advantages and disadvantages of export promotion versus import-substitution. Our study, however, will analyse and investigate the impact of the government policies upon the trade pattern and employment growth in Korea. The scope of this study is fairly narrow in that it will concentrate on only a few major policies such as preferential tax and loan allocation policies which seem to have had the most important impacts on trade and employment in Korea.

Various policies used in implementing the selected trade strategy may also affect the factor proportions in exporting and import-substituting industries. Furthermore government policies not essential to the chosen

---

[2] A. O. Krueger, *Project on Alternative Trade Strategies and Employment*, Project Working Paper No. 1 (New York: NBER, 1976), mimeographed.
[3] See *Ibid*.

trade strategy can influence the sectoral factor intensities. Therefore the objective of this research is not only to ascertain what employment effects are associated with alternative trade strategies, but also to analyze the ways in which government trade and subsidy policies in general are implemented and to analyze the underlying causal relationships to employment.

If one can say that economists interest in commodity market distortions has shifted in recent years toward the problem of factor market distortions, one may further say that the principal component of the distortion analysis has been the study of labor market distortions. Even in analyzing the labor market distortions, Bhagwati observes that the analysis of the Lewis type of imperfection, where wages are equal between sectors but equal the average product in one sector, has not received much attention by theorists so far.[4] Perhaps by pure accident, the Korean experience leads our study to be more concerned with capital market distortions. Further, when considering labor market distortion, the analysis can proceed more readily from the viewpoint of Lewis type distortions.

In a previous study, *Factor Supply and Factor Intensity of Trade in Korea* (KDI Press, 1976), I attempted to compute changing factor intensity in Korea's trade in association with Korea's capital accumulation. I observed increasing capital intensity of Korea's exports and at first tried to explain it mostly in terms of capital accumulation and associated shifts in wage-rental ratio. As a natural sequence, the present study emphasizes factor market distortions. Our empirical analysis is essentially based on a two-factor multi-commodity model with all its familiar defects and limitations. However, the simplicity in our approach seems to have the advantage of amplifying the most important aspects of trade, distortions and employment growth.

While I have tried to give a balanced treatement of various trade policies and at the same time minimize repetition with my previous study and those by C.R. Frank, Jr., K.S. Kim and L.E. Westphal as well as the companion research work by A.O. Krueger and S.T. Suh, I am not sure that I have been entirely successful in doing so.[5]

---

[4] See S. P. Magee, *International Trade and Distortions in Factor Markets* (New York: Marcel Dekker, 1976), pp. v-vi.

[5] C. R. Frank, K. S. Kim and L. E. Westphal, *Foreign Trade Regimes and Economic Development: South Korea* (New York: NBER, 1975), L. E. Westphal and K. S. Kim, *Industrial Policy and Development in Korea* (Washington D.C.: IBRD, 1974), mimeographed, A. O. Krueger, *The Role of the Foreign Sector and Aid in Korea's De-*

Chapter 2 gives a brief description of growth and trade in Korea during 1910–77 and associated shifts in factor supply and factor intensity of Korea's trade. Chapter 3 presents an overview of economic development plans and economic policies as well as a chronology of Korea's trade and balance of payments policies. The following three chapters investigate the major policy measures which had the most important impacts upon the trade pattern and employment growth in Korea. Chapter 4 investigates preferential direct and indirect tax policies, Chapter 5 looks at tariff and non-tariff import restrictions and Chapter 6 examines loan allocation policies. The latter chapter examines the policies relating to the sectoral distribution of domestic and foreign capital with special emphasis on long and short-term export financing. Chapter 7 analyzes factor market distortions in Korea by estimating the interest rates applied to various forms of domestic and foreign loans, the real opportunity cost of capital use and the associated implicit subsidies on capital use. Chapter 8 investigates the employment implications of trade and subsidy policies by analyzing their impacts on output composition and choice of technique. The last chapter contains a summary of our study and some conclusions.

Wontack Hong

January 1979

---

velopment (Seoul: KDI, 1977), mimeographed, and S. T. Suh, *Import Substitution and Economic Development in Korea* (Seoul: KDI, 1977), mimeographed.

CHAPTER 2

FACTOR SUPPLY AND FACTOR INTENSITY OF TRADE

1. Growth and Trade in Korea: 1910–77

A. Colonial Period (1910–45)

Although the main purpose of our study is to analyze the aspects of trade, distortions and employment growth of the Korean economy in the sixties and seventies (1960–77), this section provides a brief overview of growth and trade in Korea during 1910–77.

From the early twentieth century until 1945, Korea was under Japanese colonial rule. During the initial phase, Japan explotied Korea's traditional primary resources. Korea exported mainly rice and other primary products to Japan and imported all kinds of manufactures from Japan. In the latter years of the colonial period, Japan tried to convert the Korean penninsula into a logistical base for creation of the so-called Greater East Asian Coprosperity Sphere. As a result, development of some light and heavy industries as well as extended social overhead capital facilities was begun.

The per capita GNP of Korea is estimated to have been about $80 in 1910–15 (in 1970 prices), around $100 in 1921–30 and about $140 in 1936–40.[1] That is, the per capita GNP seems to have increased by approximately

---

[1] Korea's wholesale price indices from 1911 to 1970 were applied to the output (or trade) statistics for the colonial period in order to get the figures in 1970 prices and then the resulting estimates were converted to 1970 dollars at the exchange rate of 310.6 won per dollar. See Tables B. 1. and B. 2.

Table 2.1. Industrial Structure of Korea in the Colonial Period

	1911	1921	1926	1932	1936	1940
Value Added						
Agriculture	62%	57%	56%	52%	45%	40%
Forestry	5%	4%	4%	4%	6%	6%
Fishing	1%	3%	3%	3%	4%	5%
Mining	1%	1%	1%	2%	4%	5%
Manufacturing	1%	5%	6%	8%	11%	15%
SOC & Service[1]	(30%)	(30%)	(30%)	(30%)	(30%)	(30%)
Employment						
Total Employed Persons (Million)[2]	—	8.0	8.9	8.5	8.8	8.8
Agriculture	—	90%	88%	86%	84%	81%
Fishing (Including Salt)	—	1%	1%	1%	1%	1%
Manufacturing	—	1%	2%	1%	2%	2%
Others	—	8%	9%	12%	13%	16%
Population (Million)[2]	13.8	17.1	18.6	20.0	21.4	23.0
GNP (Million 1970 $)	1,082	1,634	1,946	2,471	3,169	3,383
Per Capita GNP (1970 $)[3]	$77	$94	$102	$120	$144	$143
Exports/GNP	5%	17%	23%	25%	29%	31%[4]
Imports/GNP	13%	18%	24%	26%	37%	43%[4]

Source: Tables B. 1., B. 2. and B. 12.
Notes: [1]The assumption that 30 percent of GNP consists of non-commodity was based on K. Ohkawa's study on Japan, *The Growth Rate of the Japanese Economy Since 1878* (Tokyo: Kinokuniya, 1957).
[2] Excluding Japanese and foreigners.
[3] Taking account of Japanese residents in Korea.
[4] 1939 ratios.

80 percent during the colonial period implying an average annual growth rate of about 2 percent. Population also grew at approximately 2 percent per annum: in 1911 there were about 13.8 million Koreans and by 1940 there were about 23.0 million. In terms of gross output values, the share of agriculture in the total commodity sectors (agriculture, forestry, fishery, mining and manufacturing) declined from about 87 percent in 1911 to about 43 percent in 1940. On the other hand the share of manufacturing increased from about 4 percent in 1911 to about 29 percent in 1940. In terms of value added, the share of agriculture and forestry declined from two-thirds of GNP in the early 1910's to about half in the late thirties while that of manufacturing increased from around 2 percent to around 13 to 15 percent of GNP.[2]

According to the sectoral employment data based on a census of households by occupation, approximately 90 percent of the working population was engaged in agriculture in 1917. However, the proportion of employed persons in agriculture steadily declined to about 80 percent of total employed persons in 1940, while the share of employed persons in service sectors doubled from about 8 percent in 1917 to about 16 percent in 1940. The share of employed persons in manufacturing increased from about 1 percent in 1917 to about 2 percent in 1940. The total number of employed persons increased by only about 10 percent during 1921–40 while that of total population increased by about 35 percent. Therefore, the expansion of the non-agricultural sectors seems to have been achieved largely through sectoral shifts of workers rather than by an absolute increase in total employment.

Korea's commodity exports began to increase rapidly after the eighteen-eighties. However, the annual commodity exports amounted to less than 10 million yen at the dawn of the twentieth century. During the last decade of the Yi dynasty (1901–10) prior to the formal annexation to Japan, the amount of exports almost doubled, to nearly 20 million yen in 1911, which seems to have been equivalent to approximately 5 percent of GNP in value terms. During the Japanese occupation, the volume of commodity exports almost tripled every ten years reaching about one billion yen in 1939 which is approximately one billion dollars in 1970 prices. The gross value of commodity exports was equivalent to between 5 and 10 percent of GNP during 1910–17, but it increased to between 17 and 21 percent during 1921–25 and to around 30 percent of GNP after 1934.

About 70 to 80 percent of Korea's commodity exports went to Japan

---

[2] See Tables B. 1. and B. 2.

Table 2.2. Commodity Composition of Exports: 1910-35

In Million Yen & Percent

	1910	1951	1920	1925	1930	1935
Rice	6.3 (32%)	24.5 (49%)	77.0 (39%)	173.2 (51%)	109.7 (41%)	244.7 (44%)
Other Foodstuffs[1]	6.2 (32%)	6.7 (14%)	22.0 (11%)	27.2 (8%)	24.5 (9%)	24.5 (4%)
Crude Materials[2]	1.9 (10%)	5.9 (12%)	17.0 (8%)	30.0 (8%)	14.5 (6%)	21.5 (4%)
Fish, Fresh & Salted[3]	0.3 (2%)	0.9 (2%)	12.4 (6%)	14.1 (4%)	11.8 (4%)	12.4 (2%)
Minerals	1.4 (8%)	2.2 (5%)	6.9 (3%)	5.1 (2%)	5.8 (2%)	16.7 (3%)
Sea Weed & Fish Oil	0.1 (1%)	0.4 (1%)	1.4 (1%)	4.3 (1%)	5.6 (2%)	9.3 (2%)
Sugar	— (—)	— (—)	— (—)	4.5 (1%)	4.8 (2%)	3.2 (1%)
Cotton Tissues	— (—)	— (—)	— (—)	1.3 (0%)	2.7 (1%)	4.7 (1%)
Raw Silk	— (—)	0.1 (0%)	2.5 (1%)	27.1 (8%)	23.9 (9%)	19.9 (4%)
Wood, Pulp & Paper	0.1 (1%)	0.2 (0%)	5.0 (3%)	4.5 (1%)	5.9 (2%)	12.3 (2%)
Ammonium Sulphate	— (—)	— (—)	0.6 (0%)	— (—)	2.9 (1%)	16.2 (3%)
Cement	— (—)	— (—)	— (—)	0.4 (0%)	1.8 (1%)	3.7 (1%)
Pig Iron	— (—)	— (—)	6.1 (3%)	4.6 (1%)	5.5 (2%)	7.3 (1%)
Copper & Lead	— (—)	— (—)	1.6 (1%)	0.6 (0%)	1.2 (0%)	24.0 (4%)
Rice Bran & Manure	0.4 (2%)	0.9 (2%)	2.6 (1%)	5.5 (2%)	6.8 (3%)	16.9 (3%)
Sub-Total	16.8 (84%)	41.8 (83%)	155.1 (79%)	302.4 (89%)	227.4 (85%)	437.3 (80%)
Manufactures	0.7 (4%)	1.7 (3%)	19.9 (10%)	53.1 (16%)	61.4 (23%)	199.5 (22%)
Total Exports	19.9 (100%)	50.2 (100%)	197.0 (100%)	341.6 (100%)	266.6 (100%)	550.8 (100%)

Source: Table B. 6.
Notes: [1] Consists of Beans, wheat, leaf tobacco, apples, chestnuts and ginseng.
[2] Consists of cocoons, cotton, bulls, hide and furs.
[3] Consists of iron & gold ore, coal and graphite.

proper during 1901–17 and this increased to around 90 percent after 1921.[3] The rest of Korea's exports went mostly to China and other Asian countries. At the same time, more than two-thirds of Korea's total imports were from Japan proper during 1900–29, and they increased further to between 80 and 90 percent of Korea's imports during 1930–39.

The balance of payments was always in deficit in the period from 1886 to 1939, with the exception of 1924 and 1925. The deficit was financed by exports of gold and silver bullion and coins as well as by the net capital inflow. There were significant capital inflows from Japan from 1904 to 1914 (amounting to nearly half of the total import value), from 1917 to 1922 (about 13 percent of total import value), from 1927 to 1930 (about 14 percent of total import value) and from 1935 to 1939 (about 20 percent of total import value).[4] The net capital inflow in other years was insignificant.

Export goods during the colonial period may be classified into three groups; manufactured goods, rice and beans and other primary products. Between 1910 and 1939 about 50 to 60 percent of Korea's commodity exports consisted of rice and beans and, during 1910 and 1924, about 20 percent consisted of other primary products such as bulls, animal hides, fish, cotton, cocoons, iron ore, gold ore, coal, graphite, leaf tobacco, apples, chestnuts, ginseng and wheat. However, with a gradual expansion of the share of manufactures from less than 5 percent of total exports in the early 1910's to more than 20 percent after 1929, the share of other primary products declined to around the 10 percent level after 1926.[5] Raw silk was the single most important manufactured export during 1921–33. Other exports included rice bran, wood, pig iron, cotton tissues, sea weed, pulp and paper and sugar. In the thirties, exports of ammonium sulphate, cement, copper, lead, fish oil, wheat flour and leather were significant. However, since raw silk as well as rice bran, wood, sea weed, fish oil and leather are almost primary products, one can say that Korea remained essentially an exporter of primary goods during the colonial period.

---

[3] "Japan proper" represents Japan itself, Taiwan and the South Pacific colonial islands. See Table B. 5.

[4] However, except for the periods 1904–14 and 1933–35, the net capital inflow from Japan was mostly through the so-called "foreign countries" which implies China and Manchukuo. During 1918–28, there was a significant net capital inflow into Japan from Manchukuo, China, etc. See Tables B. 4. and B. 5.

[5] Exports of manufactures from Korea included reexports of Japanese-made products which seem to have amounted around 5 percent of total manufactures exports. See Table B. 8.

Table 2.3. Commodity Composition of Imports: 1910–35

In Million Yen & Percent

	1901		1915		1920		1925		1930		1935	
Agricultural Products[1]	0.5	(2%)	2.0	(4%)	30.5	(11%)	63.6	(19%)	43.5	(12%)	58.3	(9%)
Cotton & Rubber	0.4	(1%)	0.7	(1%)	1.3	(1%)	3.9	(1%)	7.0	(2%)	22.2	(4%)
Coal & Salt	1.2	(3%)	2.7	(5%)	18.4	(8%)	10.3	(3%)	11.5	(3%)	17.3	(2%)
Food Products[2]	2.8	(8%)	7.3	(13%)	21.0	(8%)	32.7	(10%)	37.8	(11%)	58.2	(9%)
Cotton Yarn & Thread	1.8	(5%)	2.6	(4%)	4.3	(2%)	10.8	(3%)	8.1	(2%)	14.3	(2%)
Textile Fabrics	9.1	(23%)	11.7	(20%)	35.7	(15%)	69.6	(20%)	44.3	(12%)	47.1	(7%)
Textile Products	0.9	(2%)	5.2	(8%)	15.3	(7%)	36.2	(11%)	45.9	(12%)	101.7	(15%)
Wood & Paper Products	1.9	(5%)	3.1	(6%)	8.6	(4%)	16.5	(5%)	14.7	(4%)	29.8	(5%)
Chemicals	0.8	(2%)	1.3	(2%)	3.5	(1%)	5.2	(1%)	6.6	(2%)	12.8	(2%)
Chemical Fertilizer	–	(–)	–	(–)	–	(–)	3.0	(1%)	6.7	(2%)	14.3	(2%)
Petroleum Products	1.3	(3%)	1.8	(3%)	8.9	(4%)	8.7	(3%)	11.0	(3%)	26.1	(4%)
Nonmetallic Mineral[3]	0.7	(2%)	1.3	(2%)	3.8	(2%)	4.7	(2%)	5.9	(2%)	12.1	(2%)
Iron & Steel	1.0	(3%)	2.1	(4%)	9.6	(4%)	7.4	(2%)	16.1	(4%)	42.4	(6%)
Metal Products	0.2	(1%)	0.5	(1%)	1.6	(1%)	2.5	(1%)	4.3	(1%)	7.9	(1%)
Machinery	0.4	(1%)	0.8	(2%)	3.7	(2%)	2.9	(1%)	6.0	(2%)	13.0	(2%)
Transport Equipment	–	(–)	0.3	(1%)	2.9	(1%)	3.2	(1%)	6.4	(2%)	18.5	(3%)
Misc. Manufactures	0.4	(1%)	1.4	(2%)	7.7	(3%)	15.4	(4%)	24.6	(6%)	30.5	(5%)
Sub-Total	23.4	(59%)	44.8	(75%)	176.8	(71%)	303.1	(89%)	300.4	(82%)	526.5	(80%)
Manufactures	21.5	(54%)	39.4	(66%)	126.6	(51%)	225.3	(66%)	238.4	(65%)	428.7	(65%)
Total Imports	39.8	(100%)	59.7	(100%)	249.3	(100%)	340.1	(100%)	367.0	(100%)	659.4	(100%)

Source: Table B.7.
Notes: [1] Consist of rice, barley, wheat, millet, corn, bean, vegetable, fruit and tobacco.
[2] Consist of fishery products, wheat flours, confectioneries, soy, milk, sugar and beverages.
[3] Consist of cement, glass, and porcelain.

Table 2.4. Employment and Gross Output of Manufacturing Sectors: 1926 and 1939

	1926			1939			
	Output (A) (In Million 1970 Dollars)	Labor (In Thousand Persons)	Labor-Output Ratios	Output (B) (In Million 1970 Dollars)	Labor (In Thousand Persons)	Labor-Output Ratios	(B/A)
Food & Kindred	192.0 (45%)	27.0 (33%)	0.14	380.2 (27%)	49.4 (19%)	0.13	2.0
Textiles & Products	116.0 (27%)	17.4 (21%)	0.15	249.3 (18%)	57.8 (22%)	0.23	2.2
Misc. Manufactures	49.8 (12%)	14.3 (18%)	0.29	153.9 (11%)	64.8 (25%)	0.42	3.1
Chemicals	27.6 (6%)	2.4 (3%)	0.09	359.1 (26%)	27.3 (10%)	0.08	13.0
Nonmetallic Mineral	21.7 (5%)	7.4 (9%)	0.34	41.8 (3%)	15.4 (6%)	0.37	1.9
Steel & Metal Products	16.2 (4%)	11.7 (14%)	0.72	136.4 (10%)	18.8 (7%)	0.14	8.4
Machinery	4.4 (1%)	1.0 (1%)	0.23	67.0 (5%)	28.6 (11%)	0.43	15.2
Total	427.7 (100%)	81.1 (100%)	0.19	1,387.8 (100%)	262.0 (100%)	0.19	3.2

Source: Government General of Chosen, *Chosen Sotokufu Tokei Nenpo* (various issues).
Note: Excluding electricity, gas, charcoal manufacturing and sawing. Including Japanese and foreigners.

Being a Japanese colony, the growth of the textile industry was relatively slow and nearly one-third of Korea's imports during 1910–39 consisted of various textile products. Machinery and equipment took less than 5 percent of total imports. Steel and metal products, various chemical products, paper and wood products took about 20 percent of total imports, and imports of food products (such as fishery products, wheat flour, confectionaries, soy, sugar and beverages) amounted to nearly 10 percent. Furthermore, agricultural products (such as barley, wheat, millet, corn, beans, vegetables, fruit and tobacco) took about 10 to 20 percent of total imports during 1919–39. However, except for coal and salt, imports of minerals were negligible.

The most remarkable fact seems to have been that exports of rice (almost entirely to Japan) amounted to about 13 percent of total rice production in Korea during 1915–19, about 22 percent during 1920–24 and about 40 percent of total output during 1925–39. As a result, although the production of rice in Korea increased by nearly 50 percent between 1915 and 1940, the per capita domestic consumption of rice decreased. The increased gross domestic demand for grain was satisfied by imports of low grade millet and beans from China.[6] Therefore, one can justifiably conclude that Korea was intended to serve mainly as a colonial supplier of rice to Japan. Only at the end of the Japanese occupation did investment occur in some light and heavy industries as well as in electricity, transportation and communication facilities.

According to the household occupation census data, the total number of employed persons in manufacturing (including Japanese) was about 164 thousand in 1926 and 209 thousand in 1939. However, according to the factory employment data, the total number of persons employed in manufacturing was only 81 thousand in 1926 and the number increased rapidly to about 262 thousand in 1939. This latter set of employment data seems to be more consistent with manufacturing output data. That is, both employment and gross output tripled bdtween 1926 and 1939 in manufacturing and a constant labor-output ratio of 0.19 was maintained (persons per thousand 1970 dollars of output).[7]

---

[6] See Table B. 9.

[7] The fact that the estimated labor-output ratio for manufacturing in 1939 was only 0.19 while that in 1960 was 0.38 seems to indicate a very low net value added in manufacturing during colonial period. This may also imply that the application of the 1960 ratio of net-value-added/gross-output to pre-1940 manufacturing output data might have exaggerated the estimated share of manufactures in GNP. See Tables B. 1. and 2. 4.

Among the manufacturing sectors, the machinery, chemicals, steel and metal product industries increased most rapidly in the period 1926–39, while food, textile and nonmetallic mineral product industries expanded below the average rate for manufacturing as a whole. In 1939, about 27 percent of total manufacturing output consisted of food, beverages and tobacco while about 19 percent was textile fibres, fabrics and textile products. Chemicals, fertilizer, coal products, rubber products and paper products made up about 28 percent and about 13 percent was metal products and machinery. About two-thirds of the food and kindred products and about four-fifths of the textiles were produced in the south of Korea while about three-quarters of the paper products, chemicals and nonmetallic minerals as well as almost all basic chemicals, chemical fertilizers, iron and steel were produced in the north in 1939. Printing and publishing, wood products, furniture, leather products, rubber products, machinery and transport equipment were mostly produced in South Korea. However, machinery and transport equipments produced in the thirties were not only small in absolute terms (that is, less than 4 percent of total gross manufactures output value) but were also not very sophisticated.

Heavy industries, electrical power resources and mineral deposits were mostly located in the northern part of Korea. The industries in the south were mainly manufacturers of agriculture and light consumption goods. The Korean economy, which was initially designed as a colonial economy dependent on Japan and was then further crippled by the separation of the North from the South, had to industrialize out of the ruins left in the wake of the Korean War (1950–53).[8]

B. Post Korean War Era (1953–77)

The years between 1953 and 1977 fall into two distinct phases of growth. During the initial phase—the decade following the end of Korean War—Korea pursued inward-looking policies and experineced a fairly unimpressive growth peformance. Reconstruction, after the devastation of the Korean War, was not achieved until the end of the fifties. The economy in the fifties possessed all the familiar characteristics of extremely underdeveloped countries. The next phase of growth, from 1962 until 1977, included the First, Second and Third Five Year Plan period. During this

---

[8] In 1940, about 15 percent of total employed persons in manufacturing were Japanese who worked mostly in technical and administrative positions.

Table 2.5. Growth and Changes in the Industrial Structure: 1953–77

	1953	1957	1962	1967	1972	1977p
Agriculture & Forestry	46%	42%	39%	32%	23%	16%
Fishery	2%	2%	2%	2%	2%	3%
Mining & Quarrying	1%	1%	2%	1%	1%	1%
Manufacturing	6%	9%	12%	17%	25%	35%
Electricity, Water & Sanitation	0%	0%	1%	1%	2%	2%
Transportation & Communications	2%	2%	3%	5%	6%	7%
Construction	2%	2%	3%	4%	5%	6%
Wholesale & Retail Trade	11%	13%	15%	15%	18%	17%
Banking & Other Services	8%	8%	9%	8%	8%	6%
Education & Public Administration	17%	14%	12%	10%	8%	5%
Ownership of Dwellings	5%	4%	4%	3%	2%	2%
GNP (In Billion 1970 Dollars)	2.7	3.3	3.9	6.0	9.7	16.9
Per Capita GNP (In 1970 Dollars)	129	143	148	198	291	464
Commodity Exports/GNP[1]	1%	1%	2%	7%	18%	33%
Commodity Imports/GNP[1]	10%	11%	16%	21%	25%	35%
				(In Billion Current Dollars)		
Commodity Imports	0.35	0.44	0.42	1.00	2.52	10.81
Service Imports[2]	0.01	0.01	0.03	0.08	0.19	1.68
Commodity Exports	0.04	0.02	0.06	0.32	1.62	10.05
Service Exports[2]	0.12	0.04	0.10	0.30	0.49	2.69
Official Aid[3]	0.19	0.37	0.22	0.15	0.07	0.00
Foreign Loans	—	—	0.00	0.17	0.63	1.02

Source: The Bank of Korea, *National Income in Korea* and *Economic Statistics Yearbook*.
Notes: [1] Includes freight and insurance.
[2] Total invisible payments or receipts minus investment income and donations.
[3] Including imports financed by properties and claims funds from Japan.

phase the economy expanded rapidly by following aggressive outward-looking policies. A good foundation for industrial modernization had been established by the end of the Third Five Year Plan.

In 1953, which was the year the Korean War ended in a ceasefire, the gross national product amounted to about $2.7 billion and per capita GNP was about $130 in 1970 dollar prices.[9] About 46 percent of GNP was generated by the agricultural sector and about 43 percent by such service sectors as construction, wholesale and retail trade, public administration and defence, ownership of dwellings and education. The manufacturing sector contributed only about 6 percent of GNP and the social overhead sectors such as electricity, water and sanitary services, transportation and communications contributed about 2 percent. According to the national income statistics, the commodity-exports/GNP ratio amounted to less than 1 percent while the commodity-imports/GNP ratio was about 10 percent, and the difference was financed by foreign savings.

The average annual growth rate of GNP during the nine year period following the war (1953–61) was approximately 4 percent and, in 1962, the agricultural and service sectors together still contributed about 83 percent of the GNP. Nearly two-thirds of the working population were engaged in agriculture in 1963. Commodity exports remained negligible throughout the period, usually amounting to less than 1 percent of GNP, while commodity imports, which amounted to more than 10 percent of GNP on the average, were mostly financed by U.S. grants-in aid. Persistently overvalued domestic currency effectively thwarted the export potential of the Korean economy. The industrial policy pursued during this post-war period may be loosely characterized as a policy of import substitution of non-durable consumer and intermediate goods behind a protective wall of tariffs and quotas. However, any kind of whole-hearted and systematic government effort toward rapid economic growth was conspicuously absent.

---

[9] In this paper, we applied the exchange rate of 310.6 won per dollar in order to convert the (national income) figures in constant 1970 won values into 1970 dollar values. We applied the U.S. wholesale price index in converting the trade figures in current dollar values during 1953–62 into those of 1970 constant dollar values, and applied the export or import unit value index constructed by the Bank of Korea to the trade data of 1963–76. This and following sections were mostly excerpted from my *Factor Supply and Factor Intensity of Trade in Korea* (Seoul: KDI Press, 1976). The data were updated and revised, however, notable differences are that we used trade statistics obtained from the I-0 table in this paper instead of those from the Office of Customs Administration and we also used a revised set of sectoral capital and labor coefficients.

The military coup in mid-1961 provided a turning point. After that the military government began systematic efforts to achieve rapid economic growth, and the vigor of its efforts was maintained by the formulation and energetic execution of a series of five-year economic development plans. The average annual growth rate of GNP rose to about 8 percent during 1962–66 and to 10 percent during 1967–71. Even with the oil crisis, Korea was able to maintain about an 11 percent average annual GNP growth rate during 1972–77.

The annual inflow of foreign loans increased from a negligible amount before 1962 to nearly $0.2 billion in 1967 and to as high as $1.0 billion in 1977. The government's direct and indirect tax revenue, which amounted to less than $0.4 billion before 1962, increased to about $0.7 billion in 1967 and to about $1.3 billion by 1972 (all in 1970 prices).[10] The government was able to achieve particularly dramatic gains in the area of export expansion. Commodity exports (in current dollar prices) increased at an average annual rate of more than 40 percent during the period 1962–77, amounting to about $10 billion in 1977.

During 1953–61, non-commodity exports, which amounted to more than twice the value of commodity exports, were dominated by sales of goods and services to the U.S. Army detachments stationed in Korea, under offshore procurement arrangements. Annual sales to the U.S. Army increased steadily from less than $0.1 billion during 1953–61 to more than $0.2 billion after 1967, but their magnitude started to decline since 1973. On the other hand, receipts form exports of transportation, construction, insurance, travel and miscellaneous services increased very rapidly from almost negligible amounts during 1953–61 to more than $2.5 billion in 1977. The rapid expansion in the tonnage of domestic vessels, tourist services, remittances from Korean workers abroad and revenue from overseas construction projects made the greatest contribution to this remarkable increase in non-commodity exports.

Until the early sixties, the major export items were such primary products as metal ores and concentrates, raw materials of vegetable or animal origin, fish, swine and raw silk. By the mid-sixties, however, plywood, clothing and miscellaneous manufactures emerged as the principal export commodities. In 1973, electronic products, footwear, iron or steel plates and sheets and woven synthetic fabrics joined the list of major export commodities.[11]

---

[10] Data from the Bank of Korea, *National Income in Korea*.

[11] In 1961, for example, the only manufactured goods which could be exported in

Machinery and transport equipment made up roughly 10 to 15 percent of total imports during 1953–61, but their share steadily increased to nearly a third of total imports during 1962–71. Progress in import substitution and shifts in the demand pattern resulted in significant changes in the list of major manufactured imports. During the period 1953–61, large quantities of chemical fertilizer, synthetic fibre yarns and thread, yarn of regenerated fibres, petroleum products, printing paper, cement, iron or steel plates and plastic materials were imported. By 1971, however, the progress in import substitution had eliminated all these items except synthetic fibre yarn and thread as well as plastic materials from the list of major import commodities. To give a specific example, remarkable progress in import substitution for fertilizers and refined petroleum resulted in a sharp decrease in the share of chemicals in total commodity imports from more than 20 percent in 1962 to less than 10 percent in 1973. We can also observe the emergence of a new generation of manufactured imports such as woven synthetic fabrics, iron and steel coils, thermionic valves and tubes, transistors, elements of semi-conductors, chemical pulp and synthetic fibres which are mostly used as raw materials for export production.

In 1977, the modernized manufacturing sector contributed about 35 percent of the GNP while the social overhead sectors contributed nearly 10 percent. The once dominant agricultural sector declined to a mere 16 percent of GNP, and even the share of the service sectors was reduced to about 36 percent from 43 percent in 1962. The share of agricultural employment fell to 40 percent in 1977. The Fourth Five Year Plan (1977–81) aims to expand the share of manufacturing in GNP to about 40 percent and that of SOC sectors to 12 percent by 1981. According to the Plan, about half of total manufacturing output and exports in 1981 will consist of so-called heavy and chemical products.

Having enjoyed positive results from an export-oriented growth strategy such as expanded market size, improved skills, technological transfers and the over-all increase in efficiency resulting from international competition it does not seem likely that Korea will abruptly reverse its "outward-looking" industrialization policy in the near future.

---

sizable quantities were raw silk, plywood and cotton fabrics. By the early seventies, however, Korea could list as important export commodities such diversified items as: clothes, thermionic valves and tubes, elements of semi-conductors, integrated circuits, diodes, transistors, footwear, cotton yarn, synthetic fibre yarn, iron & steel plates, twine & ropes, synthetic fibre fabrics, silk fabrics, leather products, knitted fabrics, cement, TV sets, tape recorders, radio receivers, toys, trunks and suitcases.

2. Factor Supply and Factor Intensity of Trade: 1960-75

A. Capital Accumulation and Rising Wage-Rental Ratio

Korea achieved one of the highest growth rates in the world between 1962 and 1977. Over that period, per capita GNP in 1970 dollars rose from about $150 to $460, for an average annual growth rate of nearly 8 percent. Korea's annual commodity exports, which amounted to less than $0.1 billion before 1962, increased at an average annual rate of about 35 percent in 1970 constant prices in this period, and the ratio of gross commodity exports to GNP increased from about 2 to 33 percent.[12] In 1977 about 35 percent of GNP originated in manufacturing, and manufactured products made up more than 90 percent of the total commodity exports. Nearly one third of the total workers in manufacturing were employed for expot-production since 1973.[13]

According to the trade statistics in BOK's input-output tables, comrmodity exports increased about 35 times (in 1970 constant prices) while the estimated number of persons employed directly and indirectly in export production increased about 8.3 times (from 0.15 million to 1.24 million) during 1963-75. This implies average annual growth rates of about 35 percent and 20 percent, respectively, and an export expansion elasticity of employment of about 0.6. The fixed capital stock directly and indirectly employed for export production increased about 37-fold (from $0.104 billion to $3.90 billion) during 1963-75 implying an average annual growth rate of 35 percent and an export expansion elasticity of

---

[12] If we take account of the raw material imports which were directly used for export production, the ratio of "net" commodity exports to GNP may be estimated at about 20 percent in 1977.

[13] There were several attempts to estimate the employment effect of export expansion in Korea: W. Hong, *Factor Supply and Factor Intensity of Trade in Korea* (Seoul: KDI Press, 1976), S. Watanabe, "Exports and Employment: The Case of the Republic of Korea," *International Labor Review*, December 1972, and W. Hong "Capital Accumulation, Factor Substitution, and the Changing Factor Intensity of Trade: The Case of Korea (1966-72)," and D. Cole and L. Westphal, "The Contribution of Exports to Employment in Korea," in Hong and Krueger (ed.), *Trade and Development in Korea* (Seoul: KDI Press, 1975). Watanabe obtained data from exporting firms regarding their labor and input purchases. Cole and Westphal applied the BOK's estimates of labor coefficients and 43-sector input-output tables. Hong constructed his own set of sectoral labor as well as capital coefficients using various census data and applied the 117-sector input-output tables. A major difference may be found in the labor coefficients for the agricultural sectors which are in man-years in Hong's estimate while the others are in terms of number of employed persons.

capital absorption of about 1.0.[14]

K.C. Han has computed the amount of fixed capital stock employed in Korean industries on the basis of the 1968 National Wealth Survey data.[15] The total gross (undepreciated) fixed capital stock in 1968 was estimated by Han to be 4,836.4 billion won, and the total average gross capital-output ratio of 1,60103 was derived for the 1968 Korean economy as a whole. He also estimated the capital-output ratio on a net (depreciated) basis and it amounted to 1.04721. We have adopted Han's estimate of 3,163.5 billion won as the net fixed capital stock in 1968. In order to measure the annual (sectoral) fixed capital stock for the period after 1953, we used Han's net fixed capital stock estimate for 1968 as a benchmark and subtracted (or added) the net annual fixed capital formation for successive years.[16]

The total net fixed capital stock in Korea, excluding the household wealth in the form of dwellings, increased at an average annual rate of 3.5 percent during 1953–61, at 6.7 percent during 1962–66, and at a remarkable 13.0 percent during 1967–76. The net fixed capital stock of all industries (excluding dwellings) amounted to about $19.6 billion in 1976. On the other hand, the total number of employed persons increased at an average annual rate of nearly 4 percent during 1963–76, that is, from about 7.7 million in 1963 to 12.6 million persons in 1976.

Per capita capital stock increased by about 30 percent during the fourteen year period from 1953 to 1966, and it was only after 1966 that it began to increase rapidly. Per capita capital stock increased by nearly 170 percent

---

[14] In Hong, *op. cit.*, factor intensity of trade was computed using commodity trade statistics from the Office of Customs Administration. However, in this paper, the trade statistics in the BOK's input-ouput tables are used and they do not agree with OCA data mainly because of the U.S. offshore military procurements which do not require customs clearance. See Chapter 7, *ibid*, for detailed computational procedures.

[15] K. C. Han, *Estimates of Korean Capital and Inventory Coefficients in 1968* (Seoul: Yonsei University, 1970) and Economic Planning Board, *Report on National Wealth Survey (as of December 31, 1968)*, Seoul, 1972. According to the National Wealth Survey conducted by the Economic Planning Board the total national wealth in the form of fixed capital in 1968 was estimated to be 4,819.8 billion won in gross terms (i.e., price-adjusted but undepreciated acquisition prices) and 2,469.1 billion won in net terms (i.e., depreciated). Excluding the household wealth in the form of dwellings, it also estimated the total fixed capital stock employed in industrial production to be 3,028.3 billion won in gross terms and 1,875.3 billion won in net terms.

[16] We computed the annual net fixed capital formation by subtracting the provision for the consumption of fixed capital stock from the gross value of fixed capital formation. Since these annual fixed capital formation data have been provided by the Bank of Korea, we will call these annual (sectoral) capital stock data the "Han-BOK" data.

Table 2.6. Capital Accumulation and Employment Growth

	Total Fixed Capital Stock (billion 1970 $)		Total Population (million persons)	Total Employed Persons (million)	Per Capita Capital Stock (1970 $)		Capital Per Employed Person (1970 $)	
	gross	net			gross	net	gross	net
1953	4.75	3.29	21.05		226	156		
1954	4.90	3.36	21.27		230	158		
1955	5.09	3.47	21.50		237	161		
1956	5.30	3.59	22.15		239	162		
1957	5.55	3.73	22.82		243	164		
1958	5.79	3.86	23.51		246	164		
1959	6.04	3.99	24.22		249	165		
1960	6.28	4.11	24.95		252	165		
1961	6.56	4.27	25.77		255	166		
1962	6.93	4.50	26.51		261	170		
1963	7.40	4.78	27.26	7.66	272	175	966	624
1964	7.82	5.00	27.98	7.80	280	179	1,003	641
1965	8.37	5.32	28.71	8.21	292	185	1,020	649
1966	9.20	5.91	29.44	8.42	313	201	1,093	702
1967	10.22	6.64	30.13	8.72	339	220	1,172	761
1968	11.61	7.67	30.84	9.16	377	377	1,268	837
1969	13.43	9.06	31.54	9.41	426	287	1,427	962
1970	15.25	10.38	32.24	9.75	473	322	1,564	1,065
1971	17.23	11.71	32.88	10.07	521	356	1,711	1,163

1972	18.96	12.82	33.51	10.56	566	383	1,796	1,214
1973	21.32	14.25	34.10	11.14	625	418	1,914	1,280
1974	23.79	15.73	34.69	11.59	686	453	2,010	1,357
1975	26.58	17.47	35.28	11.83	753	495	2,247	1,478
1976	30.02	19.55	35.86	12.56	837	545	2,390	1,557

Source: Hong, *op.cit.*, the Bank of Korea, *Economic Statistics Yearbook* and *National Income in Korea* (various issues), and Economic Planning Board, *Korea Statistical Yearbook*, *1960 Population and Housing Census of Korea*, *1966 Population Census Report of Korea* and *Korea Population Projection (1975–85)*. See text also for the data source and methodology for computing capital stock series.

Table 2.7. Contribution of Commodity Exports to Sectoral Employment: 1960-75

In Thousand Persons

I-O Trade Data	1960	1963	1966	1968	1970	1973	1975
Primary Sector							
(A) Total Employment	4,680*	4,894	4,956	4,507	5,027	5,616	5,485
(B) Directly Employed for Exports	38	48	47	41	102	101	207
(C) Indirectly Employed for Exports	18	48	57	77	73	116	142
(B+C)/(A)	(1%)	(2%)	(2%)	(2%)	(3%)	(4%)	(6%)
Manufacturing Sector							
(A) Total Employment	477*	610	833	1,176	1,284	1,774	2,205
(B) Directly Employed for Exports	11	27	101	157	246	433	487
(C) Indirectly Employed for Exports	4	12	29	42	73	102	182
(B+C)/(A)	(3%)	(6%)	(16%)	(17%)	(25%)	(30%)	(30%)
SOC & Service Sector							
(A) Total Employment	1,871*	2,158	2,634	3,072	3,434	3,749	4,140
(B) Directly Employed for Exports	0	0	0	0	0	0	0
(C) Indirectly Employed for Exports	5	11	36	53	88	161	220
(B+C)/(A)	(0%)	(1%)	(1%)	(2%)	(3%)	(4%)	(5%)
Whole Industry							
(A) Total Employment	7,028*	7,662	8,423	9,155	9,745	11,139	11,830
(B) Directly Employed for Exports	49	75	148	199	349	534	693
(C) Indirectly Employed for Exports	27	71	122	172	234	380	544
(B+C)/(A)	(1%)	(2%)	(3%)	(4%)	(6%)	(8%)	(11%)

Source: See text and Hong, *op. cit*., Chapter 7. *1960 population census data including age group 12–13. (Others from the 0.1% quarterly sample survey data of the Economic Planning Board.)

Note: Total employment represents total "number" of employed persons while number of workers directly and indirectly employed for export is on "man-year" basis.

Table 2.8. Commodity Exports and Sectoral Capital Use: 1960–75

In Million 1970 Dollars

I-O Trade Data	1960	1963	1966	1968	1970	1973	1975
Primary Sector							
(A) Total Fixed Capital Stock[1]	513	601	777	928	1,125	1,568	2,019
(B) Directly Employed for Exports[2]	14	21	30	37	110	194	305
(C) Indirectly Employed for Exports[2]	6	16	35	60	58	117	132
(B + C)/(A)	(4%)	(6%)	(8%)	(10%)	(15%)	(20%)	(22%)
Manufacturing Sector							
(A) Total Fixed Capital Stock	772[1]	936[1]	1,508[3]	1,919[3]	2,568[3]	4,648[3]	6,615[3]
(B) Directly Employed for Exports	9	21	87	135	262	724	1,658
(C) Indirectly Employed for Exports	6	17	60	93	214	439	883
(B + C)/(A)	(2%)	(4%)	(10%)	(12%)	(19%)	(25%)	(38%)
SOC & Service Sector							
(A) Total Fixed Capital Stock[1]	2,825	3,247	3,859	5,057	7,112	9,877	12,264
(B) Directly Employed for Exports	0	0	0	0	0	0	0
(C) Indirectly Employed for Exports	12	28	58	103	219	491	920
(B + C)/(A)	(0%)	(1%)	(2%)	(2%)	(3%)	(5%)	(8%)
Whole Industry							
(A) Total Fixed Capital Stock[1]	4,110	4,784	5,909	7,667	10,375	14,253	17,473
(B) Directly Employed for Exports	23	43	117	172	372	918	1,962
(C) Indirectly Employed for Exports	23	61	153	255	491	1,046	1,935
(B + C)/(A)	(1%)	(2%)	(5%)	(6%)	(8%)	(14%)	(22%)

Source: See text and Hong, *op. cit*, Chapter 7.
Notes: [1] Han-BOK net fixed capital stock data.
[2] The relatively large amount of capital employed for exports in the primary sector reflects large exports of fishery products which are fairly capital-intensive.
[3] Applying the M & M Census data.

Table 2.9. Contribution of Non-Commodity Exports to Sectoral Employment and Capital Use: 1960–75
In Thousand Persons or Million 1970 Dollars

Sectoral Employment	1960	1966	1975	Sectoral Employment	1960	1966	1975
Primary Sector				Primary Sector			
(A) Total Employment	4,680	4,956	5,485	(A) Total Capital Stock	513	777	2,019
(B) Dir. Empl. for Exp.	0	0	0	(B) Dir. Empl. for Exp.	0	0	0
(C) Ind. Empl. for Exp.	4	47	10	(C) Ind. Empl. for Exp.	1	13	7
(B + C)/(A)	(0%)	(1%)	(0%)	(B + C)/(A)	(0%)	(2%)	(0%)
Manufacturing				Manufacturing			
(A) Total Employment	477	833	2,205	(A) Total Capital Stock	772	1,273	6,615
(B) Dir. Empl. for Exp.	0	0	0	(B) Dir. Empl. for Exp.	0	0	0
(C) Ind. Empl. for Exp.	4	12	13	(C) Ind. Empl. for Exp.	5	20	55
(B + C)/(A)	(1%)	(1%)	(1%)	(B + C)/(A)	(1%)	(2%)	(1%)
SOC & Service							
(A) Total Employment	1,871	2,634	4,140	(A) Total Capital Stock	2,825	3,859	12,264
(B) Dir. Empl. for Exp.	33	65	259	(B) Dir. Empl. for Exp.	91	165	1,181
(C) Ind. Empl. for Exp.	6	18	41	(C) Ind. Empl. for Exp.	13	32	209
(B + C)/(A)	(2%)	(3%)	(7%)	(B + C)/(A)	(4%)	(5%)	(11%)
Whole Industry							
(A) Total Employment	7,028	8,423	11,830	(A) Total Capital Stock	4,110	5,909	17,473
(B) Dir. Empl. for Exp.	33	65	259	(B) Dir. Empl. for Exp.	91	165	1,181
(C) Ind. Empl. for Exp.	13	76	63	(C) Ind. Empl. for Exp.	19	65	271
(B + C)/(A)	(1%)	(2%)	(3%)	(B + C)/(A)	(3%)	(4%)	(8%)

Source: Hong, *op. cit.*, Chapter 7 and The Bank of Korea, *Input-Output Tables of Korea*.

during 1966–76, but due to the rapidly increasing employment the fixed capital stock per employed person only increased by about 120 percent. However, this still implies that a significant overall capital deepening occurred in Korea during 1966–76.

According to the manufacturing census data, the per worker capital stock in manufacturing has steadily and significantly increased since 1966; from $1.8 thousand per worker in 1966, to $2.4 thousand in 1971 and to $3.0 thousand in 1975. However, according to the Han-BOK capital stock data the increase in per worker capital stock in manufacturing was rather small—about 15 percent during 1966–71 (from about $1.53 thousand in 1966 to about $1.76 thousand in 1971)—and after 1972 it started to decline. The enormous difference between these two sets of data, especially for the period after 1971, may be partly attributed to the fact that the census data covers only those establishments with five or more workers while those with less than five workers may use much more labor intensive production techniques. However the main reason for this discrepancy is that the allowance for consumption of fixed capital stock (as estimated by the BOK), which in the seventies took nearly two-thirds of total gross capital formation in manufacturing, has led to a serious underestimation of the magnitude of net fixed capital formation in the manufacturing sector. It is often argued that the fixed capital consumption allowance is simply a legal concept which has little to do with actual depreciation.

According to the Farm Household Survey data, capital stock per man-year input in agriculture was estimated at about $0.24 thousand in 1966 but increased significantly during 1966–75 to $0.59 thousand in 1975.[17] The per farmer (without taking account of underemployment) capital stock estimated on the basis of the Han-BOK capital stock data also more than doubled during 1966–75.

The wage rate for farm employees started to rise significantly after 1967 (from about $200 in 1967 to $450 in 1976 in 1970 prices), as did the wage

---

[17] The Farm Household Economy Survey data covers only privately accumulated capital stock, and public investments in the field of irrigation, paddy rearrangements, soil improvements, etc., are excluded from our (as well as Han's) computation of capital coefficients for agriculture. However, there is an "agricultural service sector" (I-0 sector 110) that includes the activities of the Land Improvement Association which undertakes the irrigation and drainage work, the rural guidance activities of Agricultural and Fishery Cooperative Unions and veterinarian services. The value of land as well as the improvements made on the existing farm land were completely excluded from our computation of fixed capital stock. The original national wealth survey did not include estimates of such values.

Table 2.10. Capital Stock per Worker in Agriculture and Manufacturing

	Agriculture					Manufacturing		
	Capital Output Ratio (k)	Man-Year-Output Ratio[1] (n)	Capital-Man-Year Ratio (k/n)	Land-Output Ratio	Per Farmer Capital Stock[2] (Han-BOK)	Capital Output Ratio (k)	Labor Output Ratio (n)	Capital-Labor Ratio[3] (k/n)	Per Worker Capital Stock[4] (Han-BOK)
1960	—	—	—	—	—	0.39	0.39	1.00	—
1961	—	—	—	—	—	—	—	—	—
1962	—	1.15	—	—	—	—	—	—	1.53
1963	—	—	—	3.48	0.11	0.33	0.33	1.00	1.55
1964	—	—	—	2.64	0.12	—	—	—	1.55
1965	—	—	—	3.10	0.13	—	—	—	1.39
1966	0.29	1.23	0.24	3.27	0.14	0.56	0.31	1.81	1.53
1967	—	—	—	3.16	0.16	0.47	0.29	1.62	1.43
1968	0.38	1.19	0.32	3.16	0.18	0.41	0.25	1.64	1.44
1969	—	—	—	2.72	0.19	0.41	0.22	1.86	1.56
1970	0.41	1.08	0.38	2.75	0.21	0.40	0.20	2.00	1.67
1971	—	—	—	2.38	0.24	0.38	0.16	2.38	1.76
1972	0.42	0.96	0.44	2.64	0.25	0.37	0.16	2.31	1.70
1973	0.51	0.91	0.56	3.64	0.27	0.34	0.13	2.62	1.58
1974	—	0.80	—	4.45	0.31	0.33	0.12	2.75	1.49
1975	0.47	0.68	0.69	4.45	0.35	0.33	0.11	3.00	1.45
1976	—	0.72	—	5.06	0.38	0.32	0.10	3.20	1.31

Source: Economic Planning Board, *Report on Mining and Manufacturing Census (or Survey)*, various issues, Ministry of Agriculture and Fisheries, *Reports on the Results of Farm Household Economy Survey*, and Hong, *op. cit.*, Table 6.3.

Notes: [1] Man-year input per thousand 1970 dollar of output. GNP deflator for agriculture was applied to get 1970 prices for agricultural output.
[2] Includes forestry and fishery and based on Han-BOK capital stock data and EPB's quarterly survey data on economically active population.
[3] Differs slightly from those in Table 8.10. due to roundings in computation of k and n.
[4] Based on Han-BOK capital stock data and EPB's quarterly sample survey on economically active population.

rate for employees in the manufacturing sector (from about $410 in 1967 to about $740 in 1976). On the other hand, the weighted average real interest rates on all types of loans supplied by both banking institutions and curb markets reached their peak in 1967 and then declined steadily and substantially thereafter.[18] Hence, we can conclude that since 1967 there has been rapid and significant capital accumulation and capital deepening in Korea which was accompanied by a fast rising wage/rental ratio.

B. Factor Intensity of Trade

Assuming a small country trading under a constant set of international commodity prices, the original two-good two-factor Rybczynski proposition may be stated as follows: with an increase in per capita capital stock, per capita production of the capital intensive good increases while per capita production of the labor intensive goods decreases.[19] In a two-factor multi-commodity model, we expect the country to be producing a combination of commodities such that the new weighted average capital/labor ratio is higher than the old ratio. We also expect that the country will be exporting a "bundle of exports" with a higher capital/labor ratio than before and importing a "bundle of imports" with a lower capital/labor ratio unless non-unitary income elasticities of demand prevail and these elasticities are such that the changes in demand strongly favor capital intensive goods.[20]

If we do not assume infinitely (price) elastic foreign demand, the increased exports and/or decreased imports of relatively capital-intensive commodities will lower the relative prices of capital intensive goods in varying degrees. After full price-output adjustments, however, we expect a higher wage/rental ratio and higher sectoral capital-labor ratios than before.[21]

If we assume a constant set of international prices and incompelete specialization, there is no room for changes in the wage/rental ratio and

---

[18] See Tables 7.25. and 8.3.
[19] T. N. Rybczynski, "Factor Endowments and Relative Commodity Prices," *Economica*, New Series, November 1955.
[20] See Hong, *op. cit.* Chapter 2, pp. 12–16.
[21] Since the origin of the disturbance was the relative increase in the production of capital-intensive goods, the ex-post increase in sectoral capital intensities will not completely reverse the changes in the output pattern to result in a relative decrease in the production of capital intensive goods.

sectoral capital/labor ratios within the framework of the Rybczynski theorem. However, we may understand the growth process as a disequilibrium sequence. That is, if we presume a Lewis-type dual economy with large amount of disguised unemployment in the rural sector, we may expect rising wage/rental ratios and rising sectoral capital-labor ratios in both the rural and industrial sectors as capital accumulates, even assuming a constant set of international commodity prices. That is, if the (per capita) capital accumulation of the economy is not limited to the industrial sectors, the average product of labor in the agricultural sector will also increase and as a result the wage rates and sectoral capital-labor ratios in the industrial sectors will be driven upward.[22]

Assuming that the economy starts from a state of equilibrium with a given set of international commodity prices, the rising wage/rental ratio would imply an increase in the relative profitability of producing capital intensive goods either for export or for import substituiton. Extra factor supplies available to the economy (if not the already invested capital stock and associated workers) would naturally tend to flow into the relatively more capital intensive sectors.

The rising wage/rental ratio and the associated factor substitutions in both the capital and labor-intensive sectors would slow down the expansion of the capital intensive sectors. However, the greater the rate of increase in the wage/rental ratio and the higher the rate of per capita capital accumulation in the industrial sector, the faster will be the expansion of the capital intensive sectors producing for export and/or import-substitution.

A relative increase in the production of capital intensive goods implies an increased capital intensity of exports and a decreased capital intensity of imports (due to import substitution for capital intensive imports) unless changes in the domestic demand pattern more than offset changes in the output pattern. However, the substitution of capital for labor in every industry (caused by the rising wage/rental ratio) implies increased capital intensity of both export production and import substitution. That is, we expect increased capital intensity of exports due to changes in both the output (and consequently the trade) pattern and factor substitution to

---

[22] The wage which the growing industrial (capitalist) sector has to pay is determined in Lewis' model by what labor earns in the agricultural (subsistence) sector. Hence the rise in average product in the agricultural sector due to agricultural capital formation will cause a rise in the wage rate in the industrial sector. See A. Lewis, "Economic Development with Unlimited Supplies of Labor," *The Manchester School*, May 1954 and G. R. Ranis and J. H. Fei, "A Theory of Economic Development," *American Economic Review*, September 1961.

accompany per capita capital stock increase in the economy. We may also expect a decline in the capital intensity of imports due to changes in the output pattern (i.e., due to increased production of capital intensive goods) but the import competing industries themselves will become more capital intensive due to factor substitution.

Postulating a multi-commodity complete specialization model, Krueger's analysis is as follows.[23] Consider a relatively labor-abundant country which had completely specialized in one labor-intensive commodity and which began accumulating capital more rapidly than the growth rate of its labor force. As capital accumulates relative to labor, the production process becomes more capital intensive, with an increase in the wage-rental ratio but continued complete specialization in the single commodity. As capital continues to be accumulated, the rental on capital continues declining until it is profitable to produce a more capital-intensive commodity. After production of that commodity has begun, continued capital accumulation results in a shift in the composition of output toward the more capital-intensive commodity. At some point, production of the initial commodity ceases. That is, the composition of production shifts until the point where continued production of the more labor-intensive commodity is inconsistent with full employment at the existing wage-rental ratio. The wage-rental ratio would then start increasing and production techniques would begin to use more capital. During the period when both goods are produced the wage-rental ratio is constant, as international prices are given. When production becomes concentrated on the next-higher capital-intensive commodity, the wage-rental ratio starts rising again and continues until it is profitable to produce the next commodity.

There is, then a two-phase progression up the commodity chain. In the phase when only one commodity is produced, the wage-rental ratio increases with capital accumulation but the pattern of production remains unchanged. In the two-good production phase, the wage-rental ratio is constant, but the structure of production is shifting among commodities. Exports of labor-intensive commodities would gradually be replaced by exports of more capital-intensive commodities as the changing factor endowment altered the country's comparative advantage. Whether a commodity is an export or an import substitute would depend on the factor endowment and the demand pattern.

---

[23] A. O. Krueger, *Growth, Distortions, and Pattern of Trade among Many Countries*, International Finance Section, Princeton University, February 1977, pp. 2–11.

The factor intensity (i.e., capital/labor ratio) of Korea's export commodity bundle grew steadily in capital intensity during 1960–75.[24] The ratio of capital to labor, required directly and indirectly for $100 million worth of export production, was about 0.6 in 1960 ($97 million/164 man-years) and increased to about 3.1 in 1975 ($119 million/38 man-years). However, the factor intensity of competitive import replacement did not increase as rapidly as that of exports during this time. Consequently, although competitive imports were much more capital intensive than exports during 1963–68 (for example, 1.6 versus 1.0 in 1966), the difference became smaller subsequently and there seems to have been only slight differences in their factor intensities after 1970. The extent to which Korea's import-competing industries were more capital-intensive was probably due to the protection accorded to those industries. After all, there is no a priori reason why competitive import replacements should be more capital intensive than export production.

The total amount of labor required to produce $100 million worth of exports (in 1970 prices) has steadily decreased from about 164 thousand man-years in 1960 to 97 thousand in 1968, to 67 thousand in 1970 and to 38 thousand in 1973. That is, the (direct plus indirect) labor-output ratios in export production as a whole decreased at an average annual rate of about 10 percent during 1960-73. (about 8 percent during 1960–66, 10 percent during 1966–70 and 17 percent during 1970–73).[25] This trend seems to reflect the rapidly increasing labor productivity in export production due to technical progress, factor substitution and increasing returns to scale on the one hand, and due to shifts in the composition of the export bundle toward less labor intensive comodities on the other. On the other hand, there was no rapid decline in the amount of fixed capital stock used per $100 million of exports, which fluctuated at around $100 million. Taking account of possible technical progress, this (relative) constancy of capital requirements may be explained in terms of shifts in the composition of the export commodity bundle and sectoral factor substitutions both moving in a more capital intensive direction.

The substantial increase in factor intensity of Korea's exports during

---

[24] Since the 1960 and 1963 sets of capital-output ratios in manufacturing seem to have been significantly underestimated, the rise in factor intensity of Korea's exports during 1960–66 must have been smaller than that presented in Table 2.12. (See Hong, *op. cit.* pp. 70–73.)

[25] The labor-output ratios in import competing production decreased at an average annual rate of 8 percent during 1966–73 (9 percent during 1960–66, 3 percent during 1966–70 and 12 percent during 1970–73).

1966–75 was predominantly due to labor-saving factor substitutions in production processes rather than due to shifts in the composition of exports.[26] Of course the estimated effect of shifts in the composition of exports could have been larger if we had employed a more detailed sectoral breakdown, say, 340-sector classification instead of 117-sector classification. On the other hand, the factor intensity of Korea's competitive import replacements became significantly less capital intensive during 1966–75 due to shifts in the import pattern but because of the offsetting increases in sectoral labor-saving factor substitutions we could not find a consistent decline in the capital intensity of competitive import replacements. Instead, the effect of the increase in capital intensity of competitive import replacement sectors seems to have more than offset that of shifts in the import pattern in the seventies. As a whole, both exports and competitive import replacements showed the same tendency toward more capital-intensive commodities and factor substitution was biased toward labor-saving technology.

The capital intensity of Korea's non-competitive non-natural-resource intensive imports, estimated by using the U.S. and Japanese sectoral factor coefficients, was much higher than that of either exports or competitive imports. Therefore, Korea's trade appears to have been consistent with the comparative advantage doctrine of Heckscher-Ohlin especially with respect to exports versus non-competitive (non-natural-resource-intensive) imports and exports versus non-competitive natural resource intensive imports (such as crude oil, timber, raw cotton, raw sugar, crude rubber and wool). That is, the major difference between factor intensitites is reflected not between exports and competitive imports but between both these categories and noncompetitive imports.

Throughout the period 1953–76, around 80 percent of Korea's total trade was conducted with developed countries, mostly with the U.S. and Japan. Between 1967 and 1973 about 70 percent of Korea's total trade was conduced with the U.S. and Japan and about 13 percent with other developed countries. The share of developing countries in total

---

[26] For instance, the direct capital intensity of exports increased by less than 3 percent due to shifts in the composition of exports but increased by about 6 percent due to capital-labor substitutions during 1966–68. The direct plus indirect capital intensity of commodity exports decreased slightly due to shifts in the composition of exports but increased by about 31 percent due to capital-labor substitutions during 1968–70. Although we could observe a significant increase in the capital intensity of Korea's commodity exports due to shifts in the composition of exports (5 percent) during the period 1970–73, our impression is that factor substitution dominated the changes in the factor intensity of Korea's exports. See Table 8.5.

Table 2.11. Changing Factor Intensity of Trade: 1960–75 (Per $100 Million Commodity Exports or Import Replacements)

In Million 1970 Dollars & Thousand Persons

I-O Trade Data	1960	1963	1966	1968	1970	1973	1975
I. Direct Factor Intensity of Exports	(0.47)	(0.58)	(0.78)	(0.86)	(1.08)	(1.73)	(2.86)
Capital Directly Employed	49	45	42	37	43	38	60
Labor Directly Employed	105	78	54	43	40	22	21
II. Indirect Factor Intensity of Exports	(0.83)	(0.85)	(1.25)	(1.49)	(2.07)	(2.69)	(3.47)
Capital Indirectly Employed	49	64	55	55	56	43	59
Labor Indirectly Employed	59	75	44	37	27	16	17
III. Factor Intensity of Imported Inputs	(—)	(—)	(1.63)	(1.88)	(2.75)	(3.50)	(3.38)
Capital Content of Imported Inputs	(—)	(—)	13	15	22	35	27
Labor Content of Imported Inputs	(—)	(—)	8	8	8	10	8
IV. Aggregate Factor Intensity of Exports	(0.59)	(0.71)	(1.00)	(1.51)	(1.48)	(2.13)	(3.13)
Total Capital Employed (I plus II)	97	109	97	91	99	81	119
Total Labor Employed (I plus II)	164	153	97	79	67	38	38
I. Direct Factor Intensity of Imports	(0.34)	(0.70)	(1.40)	(0.98)	(1.05)	(1.57)	(1.72)
Capital Directly Required	36	57	60	42	46	44	43
Labor Directly Required	105	82	43	43	44	28	25
II. Indirect Factor Intensity of Imports	(1.05)	(1.45)	(1.83)	(2.08)	(2.27)	(4.00)	(4.07)
Capital Directly Required	44	61	53	52	50	44	57
Labor Indirectly Required	42	42	29	25	22	11	14

III. Factor Intensity of Imported Inputs	(—)	(—)	(1.75)	(1.77)	(2.11)	(3.91)	(3.67)
Capital Content of Imported Inputs	(—)	(—)	21	23	19	43	33
Labor Content of Imported Inputs	(—)	(—)	12	13	9	11	9
IV. Aggregate Factor Intensity of Imports	(0.54)	(0.94)	(1.58)	(1.46)	(1.55)	(2.60)	(2.75)
Total Capital Required (I + II + III)	79	117	134	117	115	130	132
Total Labor Required (I + II + III)	147	124	85	80	74	50	48

Source: See text.

Note: Factor intensity (figures in the parentheses) is the amount of capital (in million 1970 dollars) required divided by the amount of labor (in thousand persons) required per $100 million worth of exports or import replacements. Factor requirements computed with A matrix (the matrix of domestic and competitive import input coefficients) include those for imported inputs, but the factor requirements computed with A^d matrix (the matrix of domestic input coefficients) represent only the domestic factors actually required.

Table 2.12. *Factor Requirements per $100 Million Exports or Import Replacements: U.S. (1947), Japan (1951) and Korea (1970)*

	Capital(K) (million 1970 $)	Labor(N) (1,000 persons)	Factor Intensity (K)/(N)
Korea (1970)			
Exports	99.0	67.0	1,478
Competitive-Imports	115.0	74.0	1,554
(1947 U.S. Coefficients)	(155.9)	(9.4)	(16,585)
(1958 U.S. Coefficients)	(147.8)	(8.2)	(18,024)
(1965 Japanese Coefficients)	(122.9)	(45.2)	(2,719)
(1970 Japanese Coefficients)	(116.0)	(37.3)	(3,110)
Non-Competitive Imports, Applying			
1947 U.S. Coefficients	182.9	8.9	20,551
1958 U.S. Coefficients	165.2	7.3	22,630
1965 Japanese Coefficients	135.7	33.3	4,075
1970 Japanese Coefficients	130.9	27.3	4,795
Japan (1951)			
Exports	138.6	125.8	1,102
Competitive Imports	133.1	187.6	710
U.S. (1947)			
Exports	255.1	10.1	25,258
Competitive Imports	309.1	9.4	32,883

Source: The Bank of Korea, *Input-Output Table of Korea: 1970*, R. E. Baldwin, "Determinants of the Commodity Structure of U.S. Trade," *American Economic Review*, March 1971, W. Leontief, "Factor Proportions and the Structure of American Trade: Further Theoretical and Empirical Analysis," *Review of Economics and Statistics*, November 1956, "Domestic Production and Foreign Trade: The American Capital Position Re-Examined," *Proceedings of the American Philosophical Society*, September 1953, S. Ichimura and M. Tatemoto, "Factor Proportions and Foreign Trade: The Case of Japan," *Review of Economics and Statistics,* November 1959, and Hong, *op. cit.* See text also.

Note: The U.S. GNP deflator was applied to both Leontief's and Ichimura's data in order to get 1970 dollar figures. If we apply the GNP deflator of Japan (1970 = 100) and its official exchange rate of 360 yen per dollar in 1970 to Ichimura's data, we get about $1,400/worker for the capital intensity of Japan's exports and $900/worker for that of Japan's competitive imports in 1951. Rice and wheat imports were excluded when the U.S. coefficients were applied to Korea's competitive imports. Rice and wheat production in the U.S. are extremely capital-intensive. Major natural resource intensive imports which consist of crude oil, timber, raw cotton, raw sugar, crude rubber and wool were excluded from non-competitive imports in computing factor intensity. Therefore, non-competitive imports in this table represent mainly non-competitive non-natural-resource-intensive imports. In 1970, about 36 percent of total imports were non-competitive imports and half of them consisted of those six major natural resource intensive goods.

trade was less than 20 percent during 1967–73. Imports from developing countries were mostly crude oil, crude rubber and timber. Since 1974 the U.S. and Japanese share has declined to the 50 percent level while exports to Europe and imports from the Middle East have significantly increased. Despite this change Korea still has very little to offer other developing countries and *vice versa,* with the exception of natural-resource intensive goods.

We may observe that the factor proportions employed in both exports and imports themselves alter with capital accumulation. It appears that exports were significantly more labor-intensive than competitive imports in the mid-sixties but that shifts in Korea's trade pattern, as well as different rates of labor-saving factor substitution occurred in various production processes, led to the employment implications of export promotion and import substitution being approximately equal in the early seventies. In theory, there is no reason why the capital intensity of exports from Korea should be lower than that of its competitive imports, and hence attention will have to be focused on these aspects of the trade regime and factor markets that affected employment in both exports and import-substitution.

Government trade and subsidy policies can directly influence the composition of the various subcategories of tradable goods. Policies such as credit subsidization and underpricing of imported capital can also affect the prices of factors of production, thus altering the profitability of alternative activities and the factor proportions used in them. There has been a sharp rise in the wage-rental ratio in Korea since 1966 and there were significant shifts in factor intensity of exports and import replacements. While some of the capital-labor substitutions in Korean industries may be attributed to the increase in per capita capital stock and the associated rise in the wage-rental ratio (that is, to a shift in the basic comparative advantage position) a substantial portion, especially that which occurred in export industries, may have to be attributed to the subsidy on capital use.

CHAPTER 3

TRADE AND SUBSIDY POLICIES: AN OVERVIEW (1953–77)

1. Government Intervention

Government intervention in the commodity market through direct and indirect taxes, tariffs, quotas, export subsidies, and the protection of import-substituting industries can affect the commodity composition of production and trade and may result in very different rates of employment generation than those which would otherwise be realized under free trade. Factor market interventions, including the overvaluation of foreign exchange and implicit subsidization of capital good imports, can affect the choice of techniques within industries as well as the relative profitability of various activities. Thus, they may alter the actual patterns of production, trade, and employment growth.

Some incentive schemes for exports or import substitution may affect the commodity composition of exports or imports, but not have any effect on the techniques chosen for the production of a specific commodity. However, there are other sorts of schemes, especially those concerned with the provision of loans at subsidized interest rates to help finance the acquisition of capital goods, and the provisions governing the importation of capital goods, which can influence the techniques chosen. Such loans will have the most significant effect on firms which produce capital-intensive goods and on firms which can choose capital-intensive techniques of production. Thus, it is those incentives which aim at altering the price of capital goods or services, relative to labor, which should be examined to determine the impact of incentive measures on the choice of techniques.

This chapter presents an overview of the evolution of the major trade and subsidy policies in Korea. It describes the economic development plans, general economic policies, and various trade policies. In particular, it examines export promotion policies, export plans and actual export performance. The following chapters will investigate preferential tax policies, tariff and non-tariff import restriction systems, and policies regulating the distribution of bank loans and foreign capital in Korea. The main objective of these chapters is to evaluate the environment which has determined the pattern of trade and employment growth in Korea.

Among the many interesting retults which emerged from the Bhagwati-Krueger studies of export promotion and import substitution, is the following conclusion, which provides an interesting insight into our subject.[1]

> " . . . countries which have had export-oriented development strategies appear to have intervened virtually as much and as 'chaotically' on the side of promoting new exports as other countries have on the side of import substitution. Yet, the economic cost of incentives distorted toward export promotion appears to have been less than the cost of those distorted toward import substitution, and the growth performance of the counties oriented toward export promotion appears to have been more satisfactory, . . . the lesson is that policy should err on the side of allowing a higher marginal cost of earning than for saving foreign exchange."

In Korea there have been a host of price controls, distribution controls, and other direct interventions which are characteristic of import substitution regimes. Since 1962, however, Korea's export promotion policies have been more powerful and dominant than her import-substitution policies. Their contention implies that the successful growth of the Korean economy was attributable more to export promotion itself than to the presence of a neoclassically efficient allocation mechanism.

2. Economic Development Plans and Economic Policies

In 1954, Robert R. Nathan and Associates prepared a reconstruction

---
[1] J. N. Bhagwati and A. O. Krueger, *op. cit.*, p. 420.

plan for the UNKRA. But the Nathan Report, which envisioned a self-sufficient economy exporting large amounts of rice and minerals *a la* colonial Korea, was simply ignored by the government. The Three-Year Economic Development Plan (1960–62) of the Ministry of Reconstruction emphasized investment in SOC sectors and self-sufficiency in food production and other basic necessities. This was to be achieved through the promotion of agriculture, small and medium sized industries, and selected key industries. The proposed investment program emphasized increasing capital goods production (that is, chemicals, metals, machinery, etc.), and discouraged excessive growth in consumption goods industries in order to achieve a balanced industrial structure. However, due to the student revolution in 1960, the plan did not have a chance to be implemented.

In the fifties, the main concerns of the Korean government were reconstruction and the maintenance of minimum consumption standards. Consequently, there was no systematic effort to achieve long-term economic development. U.S. aid was the main source of finance for the deficit in the government budget, various import demands, and investments in SOC and in some selected import substituting sectors. During this period the Korean government favored more aid to finance the import of investment goods. At the same time U.S. government insisted on more aid to finance the imports of intermediate and consumer goods for stabilization purposes, that is, in order to finance consumption and investment needs in a non-inflationary manner.

Although there were several export promotion schemes, the exchange rate remained overvalued, and the emphasis lay on import-substitution in such basic necessities as flour milling, sugar refining, and textile manufacturing. The import substitution policy was financed by aid funds and included protective tariffs, quotas, and a multiple exchange rate system. In the fifties, the amount of U.S. aid was determined more or less by the estimated need for investment and basic consumption. However, additional foreign exchange earnings and domestic savings were expected to be matched by a reduction in aid which, in effect, eliminated any strong incentive on the part of the Korean government to expand exports or domestic savings. As a result, although there was some progress in reducing the budget deficit and curbing inflation in the late fifties, no major evolution in economic policies occurred.[2]

[2,3] D.C. Cole and P. N. Lyman, *Korean Development* (Cambridge: Harvard University Press, 1971), p. 167–8.

With the beginning of the sixties, the major concern of the government shifted from reconstruction and the maintenance of minimum consumption standards to long-run economic growth. We may quote Cole and Lyman:[3]

> "policy objectives, and the changes that took place in them, were intimately related to time horizons. . . . It was only as the immediate problems became less serious and the prospects for survival improved, as they did in the latter part of the 1950s, that the time perspective became more extended and the people attached increasing importance to the future in relation to the present. Part of the failure of the Rhee government was that it did not adjust to this extension of the time horizon, whereas the miliatry and successor governments, . . . responded to, and stimulated, popular expectations as to the future . . . ."

The First Five-Year Economic Development Plan (FFYEDP) stated that the ultimate course for Korean economy is industrialization through modernization of industries and considered the first plan period (1962–66) as a preparation stage for such an ultimate course.[4] The major objectives were set as follows: 1) attaining self-sufficiency in the production of food, 2) expansion of key industries, electricity and transportation, 3) increased employment, 4) improvement of balance of payments through export expansion, and 5) maximal mobilization of domestic resources and increased foregin capital inflow. Production of coal, cement, fertilizer, steel ingot and refined petroleum were listed as the key industries to be promoted for import substitution. However, the plan did not emphasize a completely self-sufficient industrial structure and accepted the idea of financing imports with increased exports. The major emphasis in trade policies were laid on expanded production of import-substitute goods, especially the agricultural products such as rice and barley, restricted imports of consumer goods, and export promotion through increased payments of export bonus, expanded short-term export financing and income tax exemption on export activities. Faced with serious crop failures in 1962 and 1963, the military government was willing to rely on expansionary monetary policies. When the inflationary financing threatened harmful effects on resource allocation, intensive efforts were made to increase domestic savings by raising tax revenue and by increasing the interest rates on time

---

[4] The government of Korea, *First Five-Year Economic Development Plan (1962–66)*, January 1962, p. 16. (In Korean)

Table 3.1. Internal and External Financial Gap

In Billion Won and Percent

	Government Revenue		National Saving & Investment			External Transactions			
	Total Current Revenue	Transfers from Abroad	Saving: S (GNP minus Consumption)	Gross Investment: I	(S/I)	Receipts from Abroad	(Percentage of Transfers[1])	Current Payments Abroad	(Percentage of Net Borrowing)
1953	5.0	(45%)	4.5	7.7	(58%)	3.9	(61%)	4.8	(17%)
1954	7.3	(30%)	4.3	7.8	(55%)	3.8	(64%)	5.0	(14%)
1955	12.2	(34%)	5.7	13.8	(41%)	8.1	(59%)	11.7	(14%)
1956	23.5	(55%)	−2.1	14.4	(—)	17.8	(80%)	20.3	(−5%)
1957	31.4	(46%)	10.9	30.3	(36%)	20.3	(78%)	24.0	(0%)
1958	34.5	(41%)	10.3	26.7	(39%)	21.3	(73%)	22.4	(−10%)
1959	38.0	(35%)	8.7	23.7	(37%)	21.6	(66%)	22.7	(−4%)
1960	48.7	(36%)	3.5	26.8	(13%)	29.1	(65%)	31.6	(−3%)
1961	61.1	(37%)	11.6	38.8	(30%)	44.4	(58%)	44.6	(−9%)
1962	72.5	(33%)	5.5	45.5	(12%)	50.3	(58%)	59.5	(12%)
1963	83.5	(31%)	30.5	90.3	(34%)	60.7	(55%)	80.5	(23%)
1964	101.2	(31%)	51.9	102.2	(51%)	92.1	(48%)	97.9	(5%)
1965	130.1	(28%)	60.5	122.0	(50%)	132.7	(42%)	130.3	(2%)
1966	174.1	(19%)	122.5	224.5	(55%)	185.0	(33%)	213.1	(13%)

Year									
1967	231.6	(16%)	151.8	281.0	(54%)	238.5	(27%)	290.4	(18%)
1968	325.5	(10%)	218.3	427.9	(51%)	310.1	(22%)	431.9	(28%)
1969	405.5	(8%)	365.2	620.7	(59%)	406.7	(18%)	564.8	(28%)
1970	519.2	(5%)	423.2	704.7	(60%)	492.1	(13%)	685.4	(28%)
1971	609.5	(4%)	458.3	805.4	(57%)	629.5	(11%)	924.2	(32%)
1972	666.4	(3%)	577.3	805.5	(72%)	952.4	(8%)	1,100.7	(13%)
1973	793.6	(2%)	1,089.8	1,288.9	(84%)	1,741.6	(6%)	1,864.8	(7%)
1974	1,217.4	(2%)	1,302.9	2,102.1	(61%)	2,276.4	(5%)	3,096.9	(26%)
1975	1,805.2	(2%)	1,635.9	2,478.4	(66%)	2,990.2	(5%)	3,903.5	(23%)
1976	2,720.3	(3%)	2,708.4	3,038.8	(89%)	4,801.3	(5%)	4,953.1	(3%)

Source: The Bank of Korea, *National Income in Korea*.
Note: [1] Include some factor income.

and savings deposits.[5]

The government also tried to attract more foreign loans and investments by improving its incentive schemes and institutional arrangements. At the same time, the government initiated a vigorous export promotion policy in order to satisfy the foreign exchange requirements of the planned investment projects and to offset the declining trend in U.S. grants-in-aid.

The First Five-Year Plan did not present a well-worked out set of economic policies, and even appeared misguided in view of the poor performance during the first year of the plan and the subsequent inflation. Nevertheless, it did suggest a number of new policies which were subsequently followed and which later provided the real impetus for Korea's rapid growth. These included the encouragement of exports and domestic savings, and the maintenance of realistic, market-oriented interest and exchange rates. It is difficult to assess the importance of these suggestions in bringing about the actual implementation of policy. However, it can at least be said that the tendencies expressed in the Plan were not opposed to the policy directions which were eventually followed.[6]

The basic objectives of the Second Five-Year Plan (1967-71) were to modernize industrial structure by promoting chemical, steel and machine industries; to build the foundation for a self-supporting economy by increasing domestic saving and by promoting exports of labor-intensive consumer goods and import-substitution of foods and capital goods; and to expand employment to absorb disguised unemployment in agricultural sector. Industrialization through export expansion was taken as the unavoidable course of growth for Korean economy. Manufacturing of steel, refined petroleum, aluminum, fertilizer, soda-ash, cement, motor, automobile and ships were listed as key industries for expansion during

---

[5] The main feature of the Korean tax system is the degree of administrative discretion allowed in assessing most types of taxes. Bargaining, compromise, and payoff were common features of the assessment process. These conditions meant that the way to increase tax collections was not to raise tax rates but simply to raise assessments. The main tools used by the government for this purpose were to allocate collection quotas among regions, districts, and individual tax officials, and to maintain a system of rewards and penalties for the collectors who met or failed to meet their quotas. To strengthen the administrative apparatus, the government in 1966 set up a new Office of National Taxation. Because of a growing feeling that the limits of increased revenue through stronger tax enforcement were being reached, some new tax legislation was pushed through the National Assembly in late 1967. The new laws broadened the tax base, raised tax rates, and introduced a number of equity and incentive features into the tax system. Since then, there have been continuous efforts to improve tax administration, to broaden the tax base and to raise tax rates. D. C. Cole and P. N. Lyman, *op. cit.*, p. 176-7.

[6] D. C. Cole and P. N. Lyman, *op. cit.*, p. 218.

the plan period.[7]

It is remarkable that it was during the Second Five Year Plan period, which was a period of unprecedented expansion for labor-intensive light manufacturing goods exports, that the government established a legal foundation to promote the so-called heavy and chemical industries. The government introduced the Machine Industry Promotion Law and Shipbuilding Industry Promotion Law in 1967, the Electronics Industry Promotion Law in 1960, and the Steel Industry Promotion Law and Petro-Chemical Industry Promotion Law in 1970. Each of these laws specified various tax-cum-financial supports for their respective industries. However, these promotion schemes were not properly implemented until the beginning of the Third Five Year Plan period.

The basic objectives of the Third Five-Year Plan (1972–76) were to develop agricultural sector, to improve balance of payments through export expansion and to promote heavy and chemical industries. Essentially, all the five-year plans have emphasized increased domestic savings, export promotion, investment in SOC sectors, selective import substitution of intermediate and capital goods, and self-sufficiency in major food grains. Perhaps the most notable aspect of the Third Five-Year Plan was the emphasis on heavy and chemical industries.[8] Iron and steel, copper, lead, zinc, cement, sheet glass, pulp, working machine, construction machine, farm machine, electrical machine, automobile, shipbuilding, electronics, synthetic rubber, fertilizer and petrochemical industries were listed as the key industries. The plans were annually revised through the Overall Resources Budget (ORB) on the basis of actual perfomance and updated forecasts. One major revision of the Second Five-Year Plan was to expand investments in the power and transportation sectors to accommodate rapid overall growth. The annual revision conducted by the ORB primarily concerned the numerical targets for investment, output, and exports. Consequently, little revision has been made in development priorities.

The basic objectives of the Fourth Five-Year Plan (1977–81) were to achieve a complete self-reliance in investment financing, to achieve a current account surplus, and to shift industrial structure towards so-called heavy and chemical industries as understood of being consisted of steel products, finished metal products, electronics, electrical and non-electri-

---

[7] The Government of Korea, *Second Five-Year Economic Development Plan (1967–71)*, July 1966, pp. 27–31. (In Korean)

[8] The Government of Korea, *Third Five-Year Economic Development Plan (1972–76)*, February 1971, p. 2. (In Korean)

cal machinery, shipbuilding and other transport equipment manufacturing. These goals were believed to be essential to build an economic structure for self-sustaining growth.[9]

Many officials from all parts of the government participated in the formulation of the Second and subsequent Five-Year Plans. Since the various agencies of the government began to suspect that planning might have a significant influence on budgetary and other polices, it was taken more seriously. Thus, the investment program of the plan has come to be accepted as a general guide to the government capital budget, to decisions regarding the approval of foregin investments and loans, and to projections of Korean economic growth.[10] In particular, businessmen began to recognize that subsidies and other promotional schemes would be concentrated on those industrial activities which the government professed to encourage. Consequently, they became more willing to make investment decisions in accordance with the guidance provided by the government. Occasionally there existed mutually inconsistent and contradictory plans and policies, such as the desire to increase domestic savings while simultaneously maintaining negative real interest rates on time and savings deposits during the First and Third Five-Year Plan periods. Despite such exceptions trade and subsidy policies gradually became more systematic by the presentation of long-term vision. Furthermore, with the more or less successful implementation of a series of five-year plans, the Korean people as a whole became more confident of the benefits to be derived from planning and also more optimistic of future economic growth.

On the other hand, the increased tax revenue implied that more funds were available to the government for its investment activities. Furthermore not only did the government increase the aggregate magnitude of savings by raising the interest rates on time and savings deposits in late 1965, but the distribution of bank loans was also kept under virtually complete control. In addition the distribution of foreign loans and investment, whose inflow had greatly expanded since 1966, was also controlled by the government. The government was further able to influence the output and factor markets themselves through tariffs and quotas, exchange rates, indirect taxes, and taxes on factor income. With such powerful tools at hand, the Korean government was able to synchronize its trade and subsidy policies to achieve a more or less well defined set of goals. These

---

[9] Government of the Republic of Korea, *The Fourth Five-Year Economic Development Plan (1977–81)*, December 1976, pp. 10–11.

[10] D. C. Cole and P. N. Lyman. *op. cit.*, p. 218.

systematic efforts soon started to produce positive results, especially with the beginning of the Second Five-Year Plan (1967–71). However, government interference in the commodity market mechanism through tariffs, quotas, and preferential taxes has directly distorted production and trade patterns, as well as those of consumption. Additionally, government interference in factor markets through the distribution of subsidized loans, foreign capital, or direct investment has influenced relative factor prices and hence factor use in production activities.

3. Exchange Control and Trade Policies

In 1940, exports amounted to about 31 percent of estimated GNP, while imports amounted to about 43 percent. Compared to the pre-World War II period, Korea's exports during 1945–53 were negligible. In 1953, for instance, exports amounted to less than 1 percent of GNP. At the same time imports, which were mostly financed by U.S. grants-in aid, amounted to about 10 percent. In response to such an extreme disparity between exports and imports, various forms of import control emerged during 1945–53, and soon these had developed into an extremely complicated system of multiple exchange rates. Import controls were adopted not only as a means of reducing the deficit in the balance of payments but also as a means of promoting import-substitution oriented industrialization.

In October 1946, a uniform tariff rate of 10 percent was imposed by the U.S. Military Government on all imports except those financed by foreign aid.[11] In an attempt to increase revenue and to provide greater protection for domestic industries the tariff system was revised in 1950. Some of the new provisions were: (1) duty free status for imports of food grains, non-competitive capital goods, and those raw materials required for industrial production; (2) a 10 percent tariff on non-competitive unfinished goods and essential goods, whose domestic production fell short of minimum domestic needs; (3) a 20 percent tariff on competitive unfinished goods; (4) a 30 percent tariff on non-competitive finished goods; (5) a 40 percent tariff on competitive finished goods; (6) 50 to 90 percent tariffs

---

[11] U.S. Military Government Law No. 116 promulgated on October 8, 1946. Exchange controls were first introduced by the U.S. Military Government (1945–48) following liberation in 1945. Under the Korean constitution, the laws and decrees issued by the Military Government remain in force until repealed by law.

Table 3.2.   Exports and Imports

In Million Dollars & Percent

	Exports by Country				Imports by Country			
	Total[1]	U.S.A.	Japan	Other DC	Total[5]	U.S.A.	Japan	Other DC
1945[2]	1.4	—	—	—	7.4	67%	—	—
1946[2]	1.0	—	19%	—	52.9	94%	0%	—
1947[3]	2.2	5%	—	30%	179.5	98%	0%	0%
1948[4]	9.0	6%	16%	—	190.6	95%	0%	2%
1949[4]	7.1	4%	16%	2%	125.8	94%	1%	2%
1950[4]	10.9	5%	75%	1%	60.5	82%	2%	0%
1951	15.6	15%	77%	0%	132.7	25%	14%	0%
1952	27.7	73%	21%	0%	215.0	10%	12%	1%
1953	39.6	77%	15%	1%	347.8	23%	16%	2%
1954	24.5	58%	30%	1%	247.9	41%	16%	3%
1955	18.0	41%	40%	7%	341.4	23%	6%	11%
1956	24.6	44%	33%	14%	386.1	23%	5%	16%
1957	22.2	18%	49%	13%	442.2	25%	8%	10%
1958	16.5	17%	59%	14%	378.2	55%	13%	23%
1959	19.8	11%	64%	11%	303.8	49%	11%	28%
1960	32.8	11%	61%	13%	343.5	39%	20%	27%
1961	40.9	17%	47%	8%	316.1	45%	22%	19%
1962	54.8	22%	43%	12%	421.8	52%	26%	12%
1963	86.8	28%	29%	10%	560.3	50%	29%	10%
1964	119.1	30%	32%	14%	404.4	50%	27%	13%
1965	195.1	35%	25%	14%	463.4	39%	36%	10%
1966	250.3	38%	26%	17%	716.4	35%	41%	10%
1967	320.2	43%	26%	14%	996.3	31%	44%	10%
1968	455.4	52%	22%	12%	1,462.9	31%	43%	12%
1969	622.5	50%	21%	13%	1,823.6	29%	41%	14%
1970	835.2	47%	28%	12%	1,984.0	29%	41%	13%
1971	1,067.6	50%	25%	11%	2,394.3	28%	40%	14%
1972	1,624.1	47%	25%	14%	2,522.0	26%	41%	15%
1973	3,225.0	32%	38%	17%	4,240.3	28%	41%	13%
1974	4,460.4	33%	31%	20%	6,851.9	25%	38%	11%
1975	5,081.0	30%	25%	24%	7,274.4	26%	33%	13%
1976	7,715.3	32%	23%	24%	8,773.6	22%	35%	13%
1977	10,046.5	31%	21%	—	10,810.5	23%	36%	—

Source: The Bank of Chosun, *Annual Economic Review of Korea: 1948*, Korean Traders Association, *Trade Yearbook: 1953*, The Bank of Korea, *Annual Economic Review*: 1957 & 1958, Ministry of Reconstruction, *Monthly Reconstruction Survey & Statistics*, October 1957, and Economic Planning Board, *Statistical Yearbook*, 1966 & 1977.

Notes: [1] Includes exports without draft (until 1961) and unclassifiables.
[2] Official exchange rates were applied to convert won to dollar value.
[3] Computed by using parity exchange rage (1948 = 100) based on the wholesale price indix of 1947 (63.17) and the average exchange rate in the dollar market.
[4] The average exchange rate in the dollar market was applied. Exports from Inchon during March to June 1950 were not included.
[5] Total imports include relief goods, and for 1950–54 period, aid from the United Nations.

on semi-luxury goods; and (7) a duty of more than 100 percent on luxury goods.[12] The basic strucutre of these tariff rates reveals the simple logic by which they were determined as well as the arbitrariness of the rates applied. After September 1950, the same tariff rates have also been applied to aid-financed imports. Tariffs upon aid-financed imports became an important source of government revenue during and after the Korean War.

After 1952, tariff exemptions were granted only on imports of machinery and equipment required for select industries. These industries included; electric power, shipbuilding, metal processing, machinery, chemicals, ceramics, petroleum refining, mining (coal and tungsten only), textiles, silk manufacturing, and fishing. For the shipbuilding, machinery and mining industries, tariff exemptions were also extended to imports of required raw materials. As the structure of domestic production had shifted, some further adjustment of tariff rates was made in 1957. However, the basic structure of tariff rates remained the same. Lower rates were preserved for essential raw materials than for finsihed goods, and for noncompetitive capital goods than for competitive consumption goods. In the fifties, the Korean currency was highly overvalued. This was due to the destruction caused by the war, the resultant shortages of various essential goods, and the associated inflation. Nevertheless, the government resisted devaluation as much as possible and simply tried to maximize aid inflows and earnings from the sales of won currency to the U.N. forces in Korea by maintaining a low official exchange rate.[13] Export promotion was not given any serious consideration. Most of the trade and industrialization policies in Korea were designed essentially to overcome the various side-effects of currency overvaluation, which had resulted in inefficiencies of resource allocation. The government bureaucracies, especially the Ministry of Commerce and Industry (MCI) and the Ministry of Finance (MOF), gained powerful controls over the private economy by maintaining a disequilibrium system associated with the currency overvalutaion. It was only in the sixties that a limited movement toward import liberalization and a vigorous export promotion occurred.

A licensing system for imports and exports was introduced in 1946 in order to prevent imports of nonessential goods and exports of essential domestic products. However, the quantity of imports was not controlled.

---

[12] Law No. 67 promulgated on January 23, 1950.
[13] C. R. Frank, K. S. Kim and L. E. Westphal, *Foreign Trade Regimes & Economic Development: South Korea* (New York: NBER, 1975), Chapter 3.

The government began to control both the types and quantities of imports by means of quota system in 1949. After devaluation in August 1955, the import quota system was replaced by a more flexible system of import licensing.[14] In 1956 the system included a list of automatically approved items for which licenses would be issued freely by the Bank of Korea. There was also a list of restricted items that did require individual licenses from the Ministry of Commerce and Industry. Items that were neither restricted nor automatically approved were presumed to be prohibited from import. The aid-financed imports were administered by the Ministry of Reconstruction in accordance with the annual project and non-project assistance programs agreed upon between the government and the USAID mission. Therefore, the MCI had to prepare a quarterly trade program in coordination with the U.S. commodity assistance program.[15] The Ministry of Finance reviewed the demand for and the supply of foreign exchange but the actual implementation of import controls was carried out by the MCI.

All imports, except those procured with FOA aid funds, required licenses which were granted to registered traders in accordance with the commodity quotas announced quarterly by the MCI, and according to the availability of foreign exchange either held by the importer or allocated periodically from the Government's account. A certificate from the BOK showing possession of foreign exchange was a prerequiste to the issuance of an import license. All payments in regard to invisible transactions required the approval of the Ministry of Finance.

All exports also required licenses which were granted only if full payment had been made in advance or if a first-class banker's irrevocable credit had been established. The foreign exchange proceeds of exports had to be deposited in a foreign exchange Export Account in the Bank of Korea (BOK), which could be used to pay for approved imports and services. Exchange held in an Export Account could also be sold to the Bank of Korea at the official rate, be transferred to other account holders at some mutually agreed upon rate or, subject to official approval, be disposed of through other channels. The balance of an Export Account had to be used within 90 days of the date of the credit entry. In addition, an export bonus system provided that a certain percentage of the exchange derived from exports could be held in a retention credit account at the bank. In this manner it could be used for the import of less essential items

---

[14] MCI Notice No. 224 promulgated on September 3, 1955.
[15] C. R. Frank, K. S. Kim and L. E. Westphal, *op. cit.*

which would not otherwise be allowed.[16] The multiple exchange rate system arose from this export bonus system and from the sales of dollar-denominated deposits held by exporters.[17] However, the export bonus system with preferential foreign exchanges was abolished in June 1961.

In the fifties, exchange controls were administered by the Ministry of Finance and by the Bank of Korea, which was the only authorized exchange bank in Korea and the organ through which all exchange transactions had to pass. Exchange control regulations were issued by the Monetary Board in accordance with the Act establishing the Bank of Korea. Other than for officially approved transactions of the governments own foreign exchange account and those applicable for certain types of raw materials and capital goods, few exchange transactions took place at the official rate. In October 1954, the government commenced to sell its foreign exchange to the public at auction, through the Bank of Korea.

In order to provide direct export subsidies, 10.4 million won were included in 1953 government budget. However, due to the controversy as to whether the subsidy should be paid to export traders or to producers, the actual payment did not occur in 1953. In 1954, 3.9 million won was actually paid to traders as export subsidies, but in 1955 the subsidy fund could not be included in government budget due to severe inflationary pressure and heavy military expenditures. Although the Regulation on Export Subsidy Payments was promulgated in 1956, no actual payments were made until 1960.[18] Exporters could apply to the Bank of Korea for subsidy payments only after receipt of the export proceeds.[19] However, with the actual implementation of unified exchange rate system in 1965, the government abolished this system of direct export subsidy payments.

---

[16] International Monetary Fund, *Exchange Restrictions* (Sixth Annual Report), 1955, p. 367. Most goods could be exported freely under an automatic approval procedure, but the exports of certain goods required the authorization of the ministry concerned. The exports of certain specific goods such as raw cotton, raw hides, certain ores, precious metals, minerals, chemicals, bituminous coal, pulp, wood charcoal, and waste paper were prohibited. IMF, *op. cit.*, 1962, p. 220 and *op. cit.*, 1973, p. 293.

[17] MCI Notice No. 69 promulgated on May 31, 1951. See footnote 12 of Table 3.3.

[18] Presidential Decree No. 1199 promulgated on December 17, 1956.

[19] After 1960, an export subsidy of 3 won per dollar was paid on exports of 42 items. The MCI established four specific subsidy rates for exports between August 1 and December 31, 1961: (1) 25 won for new exports and reexports from bonded area; (2) 20 won for exports on a consignment basis, exports to new markets, and 32 commodities listed in the Ministry's order; (3) 15 won for 44 items; and (4) 10 won for residual group of commodities. Under the trade program for the first half of 1962, MCI announced: (1) 25 won for new exports and reexports from bonded factories; (2) 20 won for 17 items; (3) 15 won for 30 items; (4) 10 won for 37 items; and (5) 5 won for 4 items per dollar.

Export credits received preferential treatment in the allocation of bank loans and were managed outside of the loan celings which were part of the price stabilization efforts of the late fifties. Export credits were made at preferential interest rates and the Bank of Korea provided rediscounts on export bills. In assessing the collateral value of export L/Cs, the market exchange rate rather than the official rate was used.

To further export promotion and price stabilization, special foreign exchange loans were provided to exporters during 1952-54 on the basis of their past export performance. These loans could be used for importing essential consumer goods.[20] The export incentive effect of this foreign exchange loan system eventually declined due to the shortage of Korea's own foreign exchange resources (KFX) and due to the availability of foreign exchange auctioned off by the United Nations Command and the Korean government

Only registered traders were allowed to conduct foreign trade. The requirement for gaining the status of registered trader was a certain minimum value of exports or imports. After 1953, the prerequisties for registration as a foreign trader were minimum starting exports of $7,000 and the ability to export more than one hundred thousand dollars worth of goods within a year from the date of registration.[21] During the period 1957 to 1961, however, registration as a foreign trader was allowed not only on the basis of starting exports (amounting to $3,000-$5,000) but also on the basis of starting imports and the ability to export or import a specified amount per annum.[22] However, in September 1961, the prerequistes for registration were again limited to initial export sales in excess

---

[20] Monetary Board decision on November 27, 1952. These loans were also provided to potential export producers to finance their imports of equipment and raw materials.

[21] MCI Notice No. 113 (Regulation on the Procedure of Foreign Trade) promulgated on January 5, 1953. The prerequisite for starting exports was lowered to $5,000 in December 1953 and the additional requirement was changed to exports of ten thousand dollars per annum in March 1954 and then to twenty thousand dollars in March 1955. (MCI Notics No. 164 promulgated on March 29, 1954 and MCI Notice No. 208 promulgated on March 28, 1955).

[22] MCI Regulation on Registration of Traders promulgated on March 15, 1957 allowed registration also on the basis of one hundred thousand dollars of starting imports with the additional requirement of ten thousand dollars of exports per annum. The Presidential Decree No. 1371 promulgated on June 21, 1958 lowered the prerequiste to ten thousand dollars of starting imports and changed the additional requirement to either ten thousand dollars of exports or fifty thousand dollars of imports per annum. The Cabinet Decree No. 38 issued on July 30, 1960 completely relaxed the incidental condition to "any" amount of exports or imports in six month after registration.

of $5,000.[23] Furthermore, after October 1962, even a registered trader could not start importing until he could export more than thirty thousand dollars per annum. This was raised to fifty thousand dollars in 1966.[24] In order to maintain the status of a registered trader after 1962, it was necessary to export a minimum of twenty thousand dollars worth of goods each year. This requirement was raised to one hundred thousand dollars in 1966.

In 1967, the system requiring the registration of traders was changed to one of licensing. Those intending to start new trade enterprises were licensed only on the condition that they received export L/C of at least ten thousand dollars, with the additional requirement that their annual exports remain in excess of one hundred thousand dollars. This minimum was raised to two hundred thousand dollars in 1969 and to three hundred thousand dollars in 1970.[25] By 1976, the prerequisites for a license were raised to a half million dollars of export L/C and the additional requirement was raised to a minimum of a million dollars of exports per annum.[26] This form of licensing system was unusual in that even an importer's license was granted on the basis of export performance.

In the fifties, the government had relied on various quantitative import restrictions in order to offset the adverse effects of the overvaluation of the domestic currency on the balance of payments. A complex structure of multiple exchange rates had also developed, but on balance the structure of incentives during this period was biased against exports. Furthermore, the level of national income and capital formation became increasingly dependent upon imports of intermediate and capital goods. Thus, devaluation for the purpose of relaxing quantitative import restrictions and promoting exports might have led to a decline in the level of GNP and capital formation. As a result, the government resorted to various *ad hoc* measures such as: lower tariff rates and fewer quantitative restrictions on imports of intermediate and capital goods, and import entitlement schemes for exporters in place of devaluation.

The Korean government announced a new exchange system in February 1961, which abolished the previous multiple currency practices and intro-

[23] Cabinet Decree No. 130 promulgated on September 11, 1961 and Cabinet Decree No. 732 promulgated on May 7, 1962.
[24] Cabinet Decree No. 1018 promulgated on October 29, 1962 and Presidential Decree No. 2923 promulgated on July 11, 1966.
[25] Cabinet Decree No. 2979 promulgated on April 4, 1967, Presidential Decree No. 3709 promulgated on January 6, 1969, and Presidential Decree No. 4681 promulgated on February 27, 1970.
[26] Presidential Decree No. 7999 promulgated on February 23, 1976.

duced a flexible rate, called the banking rate. The banking rate consised of two components: a fixed basis rate of 125 won per dollar and a certificate rate which could be varied by the Monetary Board. The certificate rate was fixed initially at 5 won per dollar, making the initial banking rate 130 won per dollar. However, the certificate rate subsequently failed to float.[27]

There were a series of devaluation in the early sixties, and a particular one enforced in the mid-1964 was significant enough to effectively terminate the postwar era of overvalued domestic currency. The Korean "won" was devalued by almost 50 percent in May 1964. The unitary floating exchange rate system was formally put into effect in March 1965. By the end of 1965 the "won" had stabilized at 270 won per dollar. Thereafter, it floated slowly upward under the continued intervention of the Bank of Korea.[28]

Since 1967, the Korea Exchange Bank, whose capital was wholly subscribed by the government and the Bank of Korea, has taken over from the latter all of its international banking and foreign exchange business. The Korea Exchange Bank, the other exchange banks, and the branch offices of foreign banks, were all authorized to deal in foreign exchange. Export earnings in foreign exchange had either to be surrendered to the Korea Exchange Bank or to other exchange banks at the market rate, or be exchanged into equivalent foreign exchange certificates.[29]

If we take 1970 as a base year, the nominal exchange rate during 1953–63 had been substantially lower than the parity exchange rate which is computed on the basis of either the wholesale price index or GNP deflator for Korea, the U.S. and Japan.[30] Since 1964, however, the nominal exchange rate has not deviated much from the parity rate and that deviation was mostly in favor of strengthening the won. Consequently, the official exchange rate has assumed an increased role in promoting exports and import substitution. Quantitative import controls were lessened after the 1964 devaluation. They were further relaxed in 1967 when a switch was made on the MCI system from a positive list of items that could be imported, with or without authorization, to a negative list of items that

---

[27] IMF, *op. cit.*, 1961, p. 221.
[28] See C. R. Frank, K. S. Kim and L. E. Westphal, *op. cit.*, Chapter 3.
[29] With effect from January 16, 1973, traders with an annual export performance of $5 million or more were permitted to retain their export proceeds as foreign exchange deposits with Korean foreign exchange banks, for use for approved payments. IMF, *op. cit.*, 1974.
[30] See Table 8.6 and Hong, *op. cit.*, Table A. 4.

could not be imported without specific government authorization. All commodities could be imported freely (i.e., applications for import licenses were automatically approved) unless they were on the list of restricted or prohibited commodities. However, the (weighted) average legal or actual tariff rates on imports were increased and the import deposit (in won) system, with its tariff equivalent effects, was continued. (See Table 5.1. and 5.2.)

The trade program for KFX financed imports has been prepared by the MCI. Imports financed by foreign grants and loans have been programed separately by the Economic Planning Board (EPB) in consultation with the MCI. Import licenses are issued by the foreign exchange banks. The foreign exchange budget has been based on the principles of increasing the capacity to repay foreign debts, expanding export industries and restricting the imports of nonessential goods without obstructing the efficient supply of raw materials and goods required for stable economic growth.

4. Export Promotion

The export incentives introduced up to 1961 included: a commodity tax exemption, export financing such as financing the collection of export goods, export shipment financing, and export promotion fund financed through a counterpart fund, a foreign exchange deposit system which insured exporters against exchange risk, trade licensing based on export performance, and export bonus with preferential foreign exchanges, the payment of direct export subsidies, discounts on railroad freight rates, and monoploy rights to export specified items to specific areas.

The export incentives introduced between 1961 and 1971 were: the reduction of corporation and income taxes, tariff exemptions of raw material imports for export production, the financing of imports for exports, the organization of exporters associations, business tax exemption, an accelerated depreciation allowance for fixed capital directly used in export production, the creation of a reserve fund out of current taxable income to help defray the cost of developing new foreign markets, tariff exemptions on capital equipment for export production, a wastage allowance, financing for suppliers of U.S. offshore military procurements, a fund to promote export industry, a fund to convert small and medium size firms into export industries, a fund to prepare exports of agricultural and

Table 3.3. Major Export Promotion Schemes

Type of Incentives	Duration
I. Tax Incentives	
1. Commodity Tax Exemption[1]	1950. 4.—
2. Business Tax Exemption	1962. 1.—
3. Reduction of Corporation and Income Taxes by 50% on Earnings from Export[2]	1961. 1.—1972. 12.
4. Accelerated Depreciation Allowance for Fixed Capital Directly Used for Export Production in Mining, Fishing & Manufacturing[3]	1968. 1.—
5. Reserve Fund Deducted from Taxable Income to Develop New Foreign Markets	1969. 8.—
6. Reserve Fund Deducted from Taxable Income to Defray Export or Foreign Investment Losses	1973. 3.—
II. Tariff Incentives	
7. Tariff Exemptions on Capital Equipment for Export Production	1964. 3.—1973. 12.
8. Tariff Payments on an Installment Basis for Capital Equipment Utilized in Export Production	1974. 1.—
9. Tariff Exemptions on Raw Material Imports for Export Production	1961. 4.—1975. 6.
10. Tariff Drawback on Imported Raw Materials Used for export Production[4]	1975. 7.—
11. Wastage Allowance[5]	1965. 7.—
III. Financial Incentives	
12. Financing for Collection of Export Goods	1948. 2.—1955. 7.
13. Export Shipment Financing	1950. 6.—1955. 7.
14. Export Promotion Fund Financed by a Counterpart Fund[6]	1959. 11.—1964. 1.
15. Financing Imports of Materials to be Used in Export Production[7]	1961. 10.—1972. 2.
16. Export Credits (Trade Credits before 1961)[8]	1950. 6.—
17. Financing for Suppliers of U.S. Offshore Military Procurement	1962. 9.—
18. A Fund to Promote the Export Industry[9]	1964. 7.—1969. 9.
19. A Fund to Convert Small and Medium Size Firms into Export Industries[10]	1964. 2.—
20. A Fund to Prepare Exports of Agricultural	

Table 3.3. (Continued)

Type of Incentives	Duration
and Fishery Products	1969. 9.—
21. Foreign Currency Loans[11]	1967. 5.—
22. Financing Exports on Credit	1969. 10.—
IV. Other Promotion Schemes	
23. A Foreign Exchange Deposit System	1949. 6.—1961. 1.
24. Trade Licensing Based on Export Performance	1953. 1.—
25. An Export Bonus with Preferential Foreign Exchanges[12]	1951. —1961. 5.
26 Export Subsidies[13]	1954. —1955. and 1960. —1965.
27 Discounts on Railroad Freight Rates	1958. —
28. Monopoly Rights to Exports of Specific Items to Specific Areas	1960. 4.—
29. Creation of Exporters Associations on Various Export Products[14]	1961. 9.—
30. The Financing of KOTRA	1962. —
31. An Export-Import Link System[15]	1962. 11.—
32. Discounts on Electricity Rates	1965. —1976.
33. Waiver Issuance for Shipping	1965. —
34. A Local L/C System	1965. 3.—
35. Differential Treatment of Traders Based on Export Performance	1967. 2.—
36. Export Insurance[16]	1969. 1.—
37. General Trading Company	1975. 5.—
38. An Export-Import Bank	1976. 6.—

Notes: [1] After January 1962, exporters who have already paid the commodity tax can get either a refund of the amount paid or deduct it from their future tax obligations. Since March 1966, when an imported material is used for export production, the amount of commodity tax already paid is deducted from the tax obligation on future imports of the same material (within a year from the date of payment of the original tax).

[2] In 1961, earnings from exports to foreign countries received a 30% reduction and those from the U.S. offshore military procurement and tourist services a 20% reduction in the corporation tax. After 1962, these earnings have been treated equally and the rate of reduction was raised to 50%. In 1968, there was a change in the procedure of tax computation. That is, the amount of corporation tax on the entire earnings of a firm is first reduced by a proportion equal to the share of its export earnings, then the 50% reduction scheme was applied. Due to the progressive taxation system, this change in the computing procedure enhanced the benefits.

[3] The additional allowance was equivalent to 30 percent of the normal depreciation allowance when the ratio of revenue from exports to total revenue exceeded 50 percent.

Notes to Table 3.3. (Continued)

This additional allowance was 15 percent when the ratio was 20–50 percent. Since June 1971, the formula for the latter case was changed to that of: normal allowance $\times$ (1 + 30/100 $\times$ foreign exchange revenue/total revenue $\times$ 2).

[4] During April 1961-June 1975, importers of materials which were later used for foreign exchange earning activities and yet on which tariffs had already been paid could get a refund or exemption from future tariffs on imports of the same material, within a year of the date of the initial tariff payment.

[5] Since April 1966, the commodity tax was also exempted for the portion of wastage allowance.

[6] To finance direct production costs or to finance the purchase of export commodities.

[7] It financed opening the import L/C on the basis of foreign exchange holdings by banks. The financing was limited mostly to the imports of the raw materials used in export production. However, as did the special foreign exchange loan during November 1952-November 1954, it also financed the import of some essential goods to stabilize domestic prices during June 1967-February 1972.

[8] Provided under less systematic "Regulations of Trade Financing" during June 1950-July 1955. The "New Regulations on Trade Financing" which were effective between July 1955 and February 1961 were replaced by "Regulations on Export Financing" in February 1961. In February 1972, various financing measures for exports such as an export credit (1961.2.–1972.2.), an import credit (1967.6.-1972.2.), advanced export financing (1966.10.–1972.2.), loans to promote domestic production of raw materials to be used in export production (1969. 4.-1972.2.) etc. were unified under a set of regulations on "Export Financing". Since June 14, 1950, export financing (export bills) could get a rediscount from the Bank of Korea, in principle, unlimited by loan ceilings or other plan on loan funds.

[9] Financed production of export goods.

[10] Operated under the title of the Fund to Promote Sundry Export Manufacturing (1969.6.- 1974.4.), the Fund for Concentrated Support of Firms Producing Export Goods in the area of textiles, clothing, electronics products, tableware, glasses, bags, toys, musical instruments, machineries, and special equipments (1971.2.–1974.2.) and the Fund to Convert Plant Facilities for Export Production (1964.2.–1974.2.) until February 1974.

[11] Provided foreign currency loans to finance imports of capital goods for important (export) industries.

[12] Within the limit of specified portion of their foreign exchange earnings exporters were allowed to import popular (luxury) items which were not normally allowed to be imported. The average bonus rate was about 5 percent during 1951 to May 1952, 10 percent during May 1952 to April 1953, and 15 to 18 percent during April 1953 to December 1954, which was applied to 54 to 67 items of export commodities. This bonus system was, suspended between August 1955 and June 1959, temporarily reactivated and then abolished by MCI Notice No. 372 on June 1961. During July 1960 to May 1961, the bonus system was applied to every export item at a uniform rate of 5 percent of foreign exchange earnings.

[13] First paid by 1954 government budget but abolished in 1955 due to severe inflationary pressure and heavy military expenditures. According to the MCI Notice No. 2659, an export subsidy of 3 won per dollar exported was paid on 42 items after October 1960. New export commodities were paid a subsidy of 25 won per dollar between Octo-

Notes to Table 3.3. (Continued)

ber 1961 and 1965. (MCI Notice No. 2745)

[14] Organized by law to assist member firms by providing services in the areas of marketing, advertising, inspection, arbitration, etc. The government provided various special favors to these associations such as the right to allocate (textile) quotas among firms.

[15] Enforced during 1951 to 1953 in order to link the exports of important commodities (such as copper ore, lead ore, iron sulphide, etc.) to the goods necessary for reconstruction. With the exception of powder iron, it was abolished in 1953. During November 1962 and June 1964, imports were linked to the export proceeds of individual export firms. Since December 1965, only a very limited number of items have been subject to the link system.

[16] The Export Insurance Law was promulgated in December 1968 in order to protect exporters from risks. The insurance covers 70 to 90 percent of the loss.

---

fishery products, foreign currency loans to finance imports of capital goods for export production, the financing of exports on long-term credits, the financing of KOTRA, an export-import link system, special discounts on electricity rates, waiver issuance for shipping, a local L/C system, the differential treatment of traders based on export performance, and export insurance.

Not only were the range and variety of export incentives smaller in the fifties, but the scale and intensity of each incentive scheme was also much weaker. For instance, although the export credit system existed in this period, the automatically synchronized short-term export credit system (awarding a specified amount of won per dollar exported) via unlimited rediscounts by the Bank of Korea, and the allocation of large amounts of long-term loans for direct investment in export production became possible only in the sixties. Tariff exemptions on equipment and raw materials imported for export production together with generous wastage allowances were also introduced in the sixties. Of course the consistent overvaluation of the domestic currency in the fifties also weakened the incentive to export.

It is not that the policy makers of the fifties were pessimistic as to the prospect of export based industrialization. Rather they simply could not imagine the possibility of Korea exporting a large amount of rice, as it did in the colonial period, or exporting, on the basis of its very limited experience, significant quantities of manufactured goods. Their major concern was to maximize aid inflows, save foreign exchange, and promote import substitution. However, the bureaucratic procedures of import control allowed only a limited achievement of the goal of industrialization based on import substitution. On the other hand, this is not meant to imply that the policy makers of the sixties started export promotion policies because they could perceive all the advantages of export oriented growth as revealed ex-post. The adoption of an export promotion policy was a natural response to the declining grants-in aid and expanding demand for foreign exchange. They promoted exports, saw the benefits, and consequently adopted an export-oriented growth strategy. This action, in due course, came to be regarded as an unquestionably wise strategy for Korea.

In describing the important policy factors underlying successful export expansion in Korea since 1962, one should not fail to note that the single most important factor has been the leadership, determination, and devotion of President Park to the cause of "nation-building by export". Since December 1962, he has presided over the monthly sessions of the "Expanded Meeting for Export Promotion". These are attended by all high level government officials connected with economic affairs, the directors of all financial institutions and business associations, the presidents of leading export firms and trade associations, and experts on trade. He has tried to identify the problems in export expansion and to provide workable prescriptions for their solution. Not only the Korean exporters always get the immediate and close attention of the president, but the successful ones are regularly honored with merit medals. As a result, anyone who has accumulated wealth via export activities is almost considered a patriot and is assured that he has the blessing of the government. This has an immense psychological impact in a soceity which still carries remnants of traditional Confucianism. This honor and encouragement bestowed on exporters has undoubtedly helped channel the best of the entrepreneurial class in Korea into export activities.

Since the president has been emphasizing export promotion with such an intensity of zeal, the relevant ministers, especially the Minister of Commerce and Industry, are expected to show no less enthusiasm for the cause. The MCI declares the annual export target at the beginning of each year. If there is a possibility the target will not be fulfilled, the MCI officials as well as other officials related with export administration work seven days a week and overtime to expedite the administrative process, to strengthen existing export support schemes, to innovate new subsidy measures, and to exert irresistable pressures on businessmen to accelerate exports even though it may entail losses. If all such efforts fail to achieve the target amount, MCI officials may even try to adulterate export statistics, e.g., by counting advance export receipts or exports without drafts in bonded processing as actual exports. This is why there have been significant differences between the MCI export figures and the BOK's export figures which are based on customs clearances, and reflects the sharp drop in exports in January.[31] Such over enthusiasm for export expansion has apparently caused some losses, but it has kept fuelling the export-oriented growth process in Korea.[32]

With the beginning of the seventies, the Korean government started to scale down its export promotion schemes. The 50 percent reduction of corporation and income taxes on export earnings was abolished in December 1972. The system of tariff exemptions for capital equipment imported for export production was changed to an installment payment system in January 1974. In July 1975, the tariff exemptions on raw material imports for export production were dropped in favor of a tariff drawback system with a three month grace period for actual payment. The discount on the electrical rate was abolished in 1976. On February 4, 1977, the rate of BOK's rediscount on export credits to finance imports of raw materials for export production was lowered from 75 percent to 50 percent of import value. The rate of BOK's rediscount on other short term export credits has been lowered from 100 percent to 90 percent in 1974, to 80 percent in 1976 and to 70 percent in 1977. Even the title "Expanded Meeting for Export Promotion" was changed to "Expanded Meeting of Trade Promotion Committee" in January 1977, in order to indicate to foreign countries that the Korean government no longer em-

---

[31] The export target in 1975 was $6 billion while the actual achievement was $5.1 billion. What happend at the end of 1975 may give an insight into the degree of export pressure in Korea. The MCI started a "60-day Operation" as an all-out export drive in November. It set up an operations center consisting of the MCI minister (chairman), the vice-minister, the assistant ministers in charge of trade, heavy industry, and light industry, the vice-director of the Bureau of Industry Promotion, the assistant ministers in charge of finance and taxation in the Ministry of Finance, the vice-director of the Office of Customs Administration, the President's secretary of economic affairs and the vice-director of the Korea Traders' Association. The committee held meetings twice a week and provided immediate solutions to impediments to export expansion. At the same time, the MCI, the Bureau of Industry Promotion, the Office of Export Inspection, the Exporters Associations, the Office of Customs Administration, the Foreign Exchange Banks, the Korea Electricity Company, KOTRA, and the trading companies organized emergency work forces to undertake export-related businesses on Saturday afternoons and Sunday mornings. An emergency task force for transportation was established and government officers monitored the export performance of 128 major firms on daily basis. The MCI later produced an export figure of $5.43 billion for 1975 which was slightly more than 90 percent of the target amount. See *The Naeway Business Journal*, November 12, 1975.

[32] See Wontack Hong, "Distortions and Static Negative Marginal Gains from Trade," *Journal of International Economics*, June 1976, pp. 299–308.

phasized only export promotion, but also import liberalization and overall trade promotion. Such measures reflect nothing but confidence in Korea's competitive position on the international market and in its export oriented growth prospects. However, there has been no desire on the part of the Korean government to lessen its drive for export expansion. Only supports for export industries which were considered excessive at this stage of development were eliminated. The government continues to introduce various measures which will promote export expansion in the long run. For example, in light of the Japanese experience, the Korean government decided to introduce the system of general trading companies in 1975. Thus, it granted various administrative supports to a dozen select firms which qualified for specialization in international marketing. The need for specialized trading companies grew out of the lack of efficiency of small scale individual salesmanship on the international market and the undesirable tendency of the Korean exporters to depend upon Japanese general trading companies.[33] Another example is the Export-Import Bank. The Korea Export-Import Bank Act was promulgated on July 28, 1969 to support exports on a medium and long-term deferred payments basis. However, its function was undertaken on an extremely limited scale by the Export Credit Department of the Korea Exchange Bank and it was only in July 1976 that the Korea Ex-Im Bank was established by the government, with a moderate paid-up capital amounting to about $100 million. In order to help the expansion of exports of capital goods produced by newly emerging heavy industries, the government decided to expand the paid-up capital to one billion dollars in 1977. Consequently, the Ex-Im Bank developed a new system of financing exports on long-term credit by rediscounting the export bill at the international financial market.[34] Large scale exports on long-term credit are a too capital-intensive

---

[33] MCI Notice No. 10607 promulgated on April 30, 1975 and revised on December 26, 1975. Unlike those in Japan, the Korean general trading companies do not have any connection with the (government controlled) banks and hence can play an extremely limited role as financial intermediaries. Neither do they get any perferential treatment in taxation. So far, the trading companies have been preoccupied with achieving the export targets assigned to them by the MCI in order to maintain their licenses. This they have done mainly by marketing their own products and by taking over small export firms which are in financial trouble rather than promoting sales on behalf of those firms. The so-called general trading companies are still in their infancy and may have to undergo considerable restructuring before they can put their potential economies of scale in international commerce into effect and function as their Japanese counterparts.

[34] For the first time, the Korea Export-Import Bank could resell the export bill in long-term credit amounting to $158 million (earned from exports of ships to the

method of sales for Korea to finance them entirely with domestic capital funds. The following is another example of small improvement. The short term export credits had been provided on the basis of the individual L/C and the value added content of each firm. After February 1976, however, a firm which could export more than $30 million a year could receive advance credits to finance the production and collection of exports on the basis of its export performance during the past two months.

There was no major movement toward import liberalization after 1967 except for a slight lowering of the tariff rates on imports in 1973. The degree of import liberalization in Korea was quite small as of 1977. Thus, as a result of the specific characteristics of Korea's trade policy, the movement toward an export surplus was rapid. However, if the balance of payment position continues to improve in the latter half of the seventies, a simplified export promotion policy may be necessary. This might entail a reduction in export supports and reduced tariff and nontariff import control. It might also be assumed that the exchange rate would assume a more important role in resource allocation. As long as the necessity of massive foreign capital inflows can be economically justified, on the basis of the marked difference between the rate of return on capital in Korea and the cost of foreign borrowing, export surpluses and excessive foreign exchange holdings are an unnecessary waste of resources.

5. Export Plan and Actual Performance

The First Five-Year Plan which was considered fairly ambitious at the time of its initiation amplified the need for foreign exchange and domestic savings. The inflow of U.S. aid which peaked in 1957 at nearly $0.4 billion had already started its irreversible decline. The government tried to attract foreign loans and investments by improving incentive schemes and institutional arrangements. At the same time, the government initiated a vigorous export promotion policy in order to satisfy the foreign exchange requirements of the planned investment projects and to offset the declining trend in U.S. grants-in-aid. Exports received considerable stimulus

---

Scandinavian countries and Canada and sold to the Korea Ex-Im Bank) in June 1977 to a group of ten European banks at the LIBO rate (London Inter-Bank Offered Rate) plus 1.125 percent for a period of 7-8 years. The Ex-Im Bank financing usually covers up to 80-90 percent of the export contract value for a period of 10-20 years and at an interest rate of 7 percent per annum.

Table 3.4. Export Plan and Actual Performance: 1966

In Million Dollars

Commodity	Export Plan Base Year 1960		Export Plan Target Year 1966		Commodity	Actual Exports Target Year 1966	
All Commodities	32.9	(100.0%)	137.5	(100.0%)	All Commodities	250.3	(100.0%)
Food & Live Animals	10.3	(31.1%)	35.8	(26.0%)	Food & Live Animals	47.4	(18.9%)
Other Crude Materials	17.8	(54.1%)	56.1	(40.8%)	Other Crude Materials	48.3	(19.3%)
Manufactured Goods	4.9	(14.8%)	45.7	(33.2%)	Manufactured Goods	154.6	(61.8%)
Cotton Fabrics	2.9	(8.8%)	3.0	(2.2%)	Cotton Fabrics	10.1	(4.0%)
Silk Fabrics	—	(—)	0.8	(0.6%)	Woolen Fabrics	2.2	(0.9%)
Kohemp Fabrics	—	(—)	1.0	(0.7%)	Synthetic Yarn & Fabric	9.5	(3.8%)
Other Textiles	—	(—)	1.0	(0.7%)	Other Textiles	12.7	(5.1%)
Footwear	—	(—)	0.8	(0.6%)	Footwear	5.5	(2.2%)
Straw-Work Good	—	(—)	2.8	(2.0%)	Clothing	33.4	(13.3%)
Handicrafts	0.2	(0.6%)	2.1	(1.5%)	Wigs (& Human Hair)	15.5	(6.2%)
Plywood	—	(—)	2.0	(1.5%)	Plywood	30.2	(12.1%)
Pig Iron	0.5	(1.5%)	0.5	(0.4%)	Steel Sheets	7.1	(2.8%)
Ginseng Products	0.2	(0.6%)	0.6	(0.4%)	Rubber Tire & Tubes	1.3	(0.5%)
Menthol Ball	—	(—)	1.9	(1.4%)	Radio	3.2	(1.3%)
Saccharine	—	(—)	1.1	(0.8%)	Electric Lamps	0.9	(0.4%)
Bismuth	0.4	(1.2%)	1.0	(0.7%)	Cement	0.5	(0.2%)
Copper	0.3	(0.9%)	0.6	(0.4%)	Copper	1.1	(0.4%)
Misc. Manufactures	0.4	(1.2%)	6.2	(4.5%)	Misc. Manufactures	8.9	(3.6%)
Bonded Processing	—	(—)	20.0	(14.5%)	(Bonded Processing)*	(28.8)	(11.5%)

Source: *FFYEDP (1962–66)* and Ministry of Finance, *Foreign Trade of Korea: 1966.*
*Included in manufactured goods in general.

from the adoption of a realistic exchange rate in 1964 and various export promotion measures afterwards. However, the First Five-Year Plan itself did not envision such a rapid expansion of exports, especially of manufactured exports.

The Plan projected an export growth at around 20 percent per annum during 1962–66, i.e., from $65.9 million to $137.5 million. Major export items consisted of such primary products as fish, swine, rice, dried-laver, raw silk, tungsten, anthracite, other mineral ores, etc. Only about one-third of total commodity exports in target year were expected to consist of manufactured goods, and nearly half of these would consist of bonded processing. Expected major manufactured exports as listed in the Plan included kohemp cloth, straw-work good, handicrafts, pig iron, ginseng products, menthol ball, saccharine, bismuth, and copper.

Actually, however, commodity exports expanded at around 45 percent per annum during 1962–66 and about two-thirds of total exports consisted of manufactured goods in target year. Furthermore, quite a few unexpected items emerged as major manufactured exports: clothing, wigs, steel sheets, woolen fabrics, synthetic yarns and fabrics, rubber tires and tubes, radio, etc. About half of total commodity exports in target year consisted of the following six items: textiles, clothing, wigs, footwear, plywood and steel sheets.

The plan considered export promotion as a means to finance necessary import requirements by export revenue as much as possible, but not as a means for so-called "outward-looking" export oriented growth.[35] Most of the policies actually implemented during 1962–66 were not contemplated in the Plan.

The Second Five-Year Plan (1966–71) projected an average annual growth rate of 17 percent for commodity exports, expecting more than one-third of total exports to be consisting of primary goods in 1971. In fact, exports increased by nearly 35 percent per annum during 1966–71 and more than 80 percent of total exports consisted of manufactured goods (i.e., SITC code 5,6,7 and 8) in 1971. Exports of clothing amounted to about $300 million and those of various electronics products such as thermionic valves and tubes and transisters amounted to about $60 million in 1971. Thus, while the plan anticipated the direction of future changes in the structure of industry and trade, it underestimated the extent of those changes.

Although Korea began to intensify its promotion of import sub-

---

[35] See *FFYEDP (1962–66)*, p. 32.

Table 3.5. Export Plan and Actual Performance: 1971

In Million Dollars

	Export Plan				Actual Exports	
Commodity	Base Year 1965		Target Year 1971		Commodity	Target Year 1971
All Commodities	175.1	(100.0%)	550.0	(100.0%)	All Commodities	1,067.6 (100.0%)
Food & Live Animals	29.1	(16.6%)	121.4	(22.1%)	Food & Live Animals	84.9 (8.0%)
Other Crude Materials	39.0	(22.3%)	86.9	(15.8%)	Other Crude Materials	106.2 (10.0%)
Manufactured Goods	107.0	(61.1%)	341.7	(62.1%)	Manufactured Goods	876.5 (82.1%)
Cotton Fabrics	10.5	(6.0%)	37.0	(6.7%)	Cotton Fabrics	31.0 (2.9%)
Woolen Fabrics	2.2	(1.3%)	10.0	(1.8%)	Cotton Yarn	16.2 (1.5%)
Silk Fabrics	2.5	(1.4%)	5.0	(0.9%)	Synthetic Fabrics	16.4 (1.5%)
Synthetic Fabrics	2.2	(1.3%)	5.5	(1.0%)	Synthetic Yarn	22.8 (2.1%)
Other Textiles	14.6	(8.3%)	58.5	(10.6%)	Cordage, Rope, Net	17.2 (1.6%)
Ceramics	0.2	(0.1%)	15.0	(3.7%)	Other Textiles	20.7 (1.9%)
Clothing	24.6	(14.1%)	83.9	(15.3%)	Clothing	304.3 (28.5%)
Wigs	4.3	(2.5%)	10.0	(1.8%)	Wigs	69.9 (6.6%)
Footwear	4.2	(2.4%)	5.7	(1.0%)	Footwear	37.4 (3.5%)
Plywood	18.0	(10.3%)	40.0	(7.3%)	Plywood	124.3 (11.6%)
Steel Plates	10.4	(5.9%)	3.0	(0.6%)	Steel Plates	20.1 (1.9%)
Radio Receiver	1.4	(0.8%)	8.0	(1.5%)	Radio Receiver	5.8 (0.5%)
Plastic Products	0.0	(0.0%)	6.0	(1.1%)	Electronics Products	59.2 (5.6%)
Cement	0.8	(0.5%)	6.4	(1.2%)	Cement	10.6 (1.0%)
Toys	0.0	(0.0%)	10.0	(1.8%)	Handbags, Travel Goods	5.4 (0.5%)
Other Manufactures	11.1	(6.3%)	37.7	(6.9%)	Other Manufactures	115.2 (10.8%)

Source: SFYEDP (1967–71) and the Bank of Korea, Economic Statistics Yearbook.

Table 3.6. Export Plan and Actual Performance: 1976

In Million Dollars

	Export Plan			Actual Exports	
Commodity	Base Year 1970	Target Year 1976	Commodity	Target Year 1976
All Commodities	835.2 (100.0%)	3,588.5 (100.0%)	All Commodities	7,715.3 (100.0%)
Food & Live Animals	79.8 (9.6%)	292.6 (8.2%)	Food & Live Animals	586.6 (7.6%)
Other Crude Materials	108.8 (13.0%)	226.3 (6.3%)	Other Crude Materials	341.6 (4.4%)
Manufactured Goods	646.6 (77.4%)	3,069.6 (85.5%)	Manufactured Goods	6,787.1 (88.0%)
Textiles	84.9 (10.2%)	461.3 (12.9%)	Textiles	954.4 (12.4%)
Clothing	213.6 (25.6%)	697.7 (19.4%)	Clothing	1,845.5 (23.9%)
Wigs	100.9 (12.1%)	327.0 (9.1%)	Wigs	69.5 (0.9%)
Footwear	17.3 (2.0%)	121.5 (3.4%)	Footwear	398.5 (5.2%)
Plywood	91.8 (11.0%)	159.0 (4.4%)	Plywood	337.1 (4.4%)
Ceramics	0.9 (0.1%)	33.9 (1.5%)	Cement	109.9 (1.4%)
Toys & Plastic Goods	12.5 (1.5%)	108.9 (3.0%)	Handbags, Travel Goods	143.0 (1.9%)
Steel Plates	7.6 (0.9%)	69.2 (1.9%)	Steel Plates	158.2 (2.1%)
Other Steel Products	5.8 (0.7%)	14.0 (0.4%)	Other Steel Products	210.6 (2.7%)
Metal Products	12.2 (1.5%)	56.4 (1.6%)	Metal Products	227.4 (3.0%)
Electronics Products	35.9 (4.3%)	452.0 (12.6%)	Electronics Products	766.6 (9.9%)
Electrical Machinery	8.0 (1.0%)	102.4 (2.9%)	Electrical Machinery	145.9 (1.9%)
Machinery	8.4 (1.0%)	67.8 (1.9%)	Machinery	129.2 (1.7%)
Ships	2.5 (0.3%)	100.0 (2.8%)	Ships	278.2 (3.6%)
Precision Instruments	3.5 (0.4%)	35.1 (1.0%)	Precision Instruments	137.3 (1.8%)
Misc. Manufactures	40.8 (4.9%)	263.4 (7.3%)	Misc. Manufactures	875.8 (12.9%)

Source: *FTYEDP (1972–76)* and the Bank of Korea, *Economic Statistics Yearbook.*

stitution in the early sixties, because of its balance of payments problem in financing various investment projects it also had to promote export expansion. The export subsidy policies were not purposely designed to discriminate among industries. However, due to the limited export potential of the primary sector, the share of manufactured products in total commodity exports, which never exceeded the 20 percent level before 1961, steadily increased to more than 80 percent of total commodity exports by 1971. As one of the most densely populated countries in the world, Korea possessed a strong potential for the production of labor-intensive manufactures for export, and this latent potential has been effectively exploited by positive government policies. Export promotion policies gathered momentum as time passed, and as a result people began to identity the period after 1962 as the export-oriented growth phase in Korea's development. However, Korea has also achieved a very significant level of import substitution in such items as cement, fertilizer, refined petroleum, textile yarn and fabrics during this period, which in due course started to emerge as a new generation of exportables. Import substitution and export expansion may proceed together, possibly with some time lags.

The Third Five-Year Plan projected a 28 percent annual growth for commodity exports during 1971-76 and planned to expand the proportion of so-called heavy and chemical products in total exports from about 14 percent in 1970 to about 33 percent in 1976.[36] Exports actually expand at around 45 percent per annum in nominal prices and at around 33 percent in 1970 constant dollar prices in spite of the oil crisis and world-wide recession in 1974-75. The Plan made some preposterous linear extrapolations in export expansion as exemplified by the projection for wigs, while underestimating export potential for clothing and various steel products. As a whole, however, the shifts in export pattern occurred along the line delineated by the Plan. The Plan emphasized that 1972-76 will be a period to lay a foundation for export expansion of heavy and chemical products, and indeed their share in total exports has significantly increased.

The Fourth Five-Year Plan (1977-81) projected a 16 percent annual increase in commodity exports in 1975 constant dollar prices and strongly emphasized a structural shift in commodity composition of exports toward heavy and chemical products. The proportion of heavy and chemical products in total commodity exports was planned to increase from 29 percent in 1975 to 46 percent in 1981 assuming the same weight as the light manufactures exports.

---

[36] *TFYEDP (1972-76)*, p. 24-25.

Table 3.7. Export Plan for 1981

In 1975 Million Dollars

Commodity	Base Year 1975		Target Year 1981	
All Commodities	5,081	(100.0%)	14,165	(100.0%)
Primary Products & Processed Foods	770	(15.1%)	1,130	(8.0%)
Light Manufactures	2,819	(55.5%)	6,520	(46.0%)
Textiles & Clothing	1,817	(35.8%)	3,740	(26.4%)
Footwear	191	(3.8%)	650	(4.6%)
Wood Products	243	(4.8%)	500	(3.5%)
Others	568	(11.1%)	1,630	(11.5%)
Heavy & Chemical Products	1,492	(29.4%)	6,515	(46.0%)
Steel & Metal	367	(7.2%)	1,040	(7.3%)
Machinery	289	(5.7%)	1,415	(10.0%)
Electronics	409	(8.0%)	1,940	(13.7%)
Ships	138	(2.7%)	910	(6.4%)
Petrochemicals	188	(3.8%)	930	(6.6%)
Others	101	(2.0%)	280	(2.0%)

Source: *FFYEDP (1977–81)*, pp. 184–185. (In Korean)

The export promotion measures adopted in Korea since early sixties were concerned only for gross export volume and more or less ignored the value-added aspect of export earnings. As a result, import content of Korea's exports did not show any tendency to decline.[37] The share of imports which are used as intermediate inputs in export production increased steadily from about 14 percent of total commodity imports in 1966 to about 33 percent in 1976. Their import value was equivalent to around 40 percent of the total value of commodity exports during 1966–77. This implies that the apparent domestic value added content of exports was less than 60 percent, although the actual direct import content of exports might have been over-estimated due to the official wastage allowances

---

[37] Balassa argues that the main beneficiaries of the various export promotion measures are industries that rely heavily on imported raw materials, intermediate products and capital goods because such imports enjoy tariff exemptions and wastage allowances as well as financing at preferential interest rates. This is counter to the Government's announced intention of promoting exports with a high domestic content. Bela Balassa, "Trade Policy and Planning in Korea," in *Basic Documents and Selected Papers of Korea's Third Five-Year Economic Development Plan (1972–76)*, edited by S. H. Jo and S. Y. Park, Seoul: Sokang University Press, 1972.

Table 3.8. Raw Material Imports for Direct Use in Export Production: 1966–76

In Million U.S. Dollars

	Imports for Exports (A)	Total Imports (B)	Total Exports (C)	A/B	A/C
1966	101.1	716.4	250.3	14%	40%
1967	135.2	996.2	320.2	14%	42%
1968	212.9	1,462.9	455.4	15%	47%
1969	314.4	1,823.6	622.5	17%	51%
1970	421.1	1,984.0	835.2	21%	50%
1971	555.3	2,394.3	1,067.6	23%	52%
1972	744.0	2,522.0	1,624.1	30%	46%
1973	1,440.2	4,240.3	3,225.0	34%	45%
1974	1,863.2	6,851.8	4,460.4	27%	42%
1975	2,012.9	7,274.4	5,081.0	28%	40%
1976	2,923.0	8,773.6	7,715.4	33%	38%

Source: Ministry of Finance, *Yearbook of Foreign Trade Statistics (1966–69)*, Office of Customs Administration, *Statistical Yearbook of Foreign Trade (1970–72)*, and Korean Traders Association, *Statistical Yearbook of Foreign Trade (1973–76)*.

which leaked out large amount of duty-free imported raw materials to the domestic market.

The government started to promote export expansion early in the sixties in order to reduce the balance of payments deficit. Nevertherless, this policy seems to have been developed in the absence of any concrete ideas as to exactly which industries enjoyed comparative advantages in export production. Most of the subsidy policies did not directly discriminate among industries and did not favor any specific kind of industry. As demonstrated by the First Five Year Plan document, the government did not envision a major role for labor-intensive manufactured exports. However, as export expansion arose along the lines of classical comparative advantage theory, the government quickly started to channel investments into such emerging export sectors as textiles, clothing, plywood, electronics, and wigs. While the government maintained a high effective exchange rate, it seems to have been the private entrepreneurs who played the major role in the determination of sectoral resource allocations for exports.

With the advent of the seventies, but especially in the preparation of the Fourth Five Year Plan (1977–81), the Korean government appears to have discarded this policy. Thus it has started, though very crudely, to project expected future export patterns corresponding to the assumed states of comparative advantage at higher per capita income levels. At the same time it has started to plan investment schedules for such industries as shipbuilding, electronics, machineries, steel and metal products, and petro-chemicals. That is, instead of following the lead of private enterprises in sectoral resource allocation, the government has tried to lead the entrepreneurs according to the expected changes in the Korean comparative advantage. It is generally expected that Korea will soon lose its comparative advantage in relatively unskilled-labor intensive manufactures and will gain comparative advantages in relatively skill intensive and also moderately capital intensive manufacturing.

It seems clear that most of the export promotion policies of the sixties did not systematically favor specific export industries as to "directly" affect the factor intensity of exports. Of course some policies, such as the subsidized financing of capital goods imports, could have "indirectly" affected the factor intensity of exports as well as import substitution. To that extent, some alteration of policies within the same trade strategy could have furthered the employment goal. In the seventies, however, there appeared a major export promotion policy which would directly affect the factor intensity of exports. The objective of achieving a basic structural shift in the composition of Korea's exports during the Fourth Five Year Plan period (1977–81) from the light-industrial products to the so-called heavy and chemical products would imply the channelling of large amount of investment funds into such sectors as machinery, electronics, shipbuilding, steel and metal products, and petrochemicals at subsidized interest rates. As a result, government decisions in selecting specific industries to be promoted as major export sectors will directly affect the factor intensity of exports and employment growth.

According to the Machine Industry Promotion Law, the government can grant an accelerated depreciation allowance, a tax reduction, and financing for the establishment of industrial estates for machine production. Furthermore, it can provide loans from the Machine Industry Promotion Fund to those firms which enhance import substitution and export expansion in the machine industry and also to those who want to purchase machines from domestic producers.[38] Furthermore, the MCI minister can specify the amount of domestic products used in plant construction or modernization in order to discourage imports of domestically producible machines. According to the Shipbuilding Industry Promotion

---

[38] Law No. 1933 promulgated on March 30, 1967 and revised on January 22, 1971 into Law No. 2303.

Law, the government can provide long-term low interest loans through a fiscal fund to those building ships, manufacturing parts or equipment, and expanding shipbuilding capacities. It can also give a bounty to build ships, engines, equipment, and parts for ships.[39] The bounty granted amounts up to 40 percent of total cost of the domestic input material in the case of shipbuilding and up to 10 percent in the case of manufacturing engines, equipment and parts for ships.[40]

According to the Electronics Industry Promotion Law, the government can construct industrial estates for electronics production, establish an Electronics Industry Promotion Fund with an annual government budget, and provide loans to registered electronics manufacturers.[41] According to the Steel Industry Promotion Law, not only can the government invest in a steel mill (with capacity exceeding one million tons), it can also provide the manufacturer with long-term low interest loans using fiscal funds as well as various forms of administrative support.[42] The government can also provide various SOC facilities in addition to the discounts on railway freight rates (up to 30 percent), harbor rental (up to 50 percent), water rates (up to 30 percent), electricity rates (up to 50 percent) and on gas rates (up to 20 percent). Furthermore, a supplier of iron ore to a domestic steel mill is treated like an exporter of the ore. The Petrochemical Industry Promotion Law also provides various types of support including a special depreciation allowance to 40 selected petrochemical manufactures including naphtha cracking, polyethylene and VCM.[43] Government support is usually granted only to manufacturers who operate in a petrochemical industrial estate. The government has also been constructing a huge estate for the electronics industry and another one for the machine industry with all kinds of supporting SOC facilities.[44]

---

[39] Law No. 1937 promulgated on March 30, 1967 and revised into Law No. 2105 on May 19, 1969.

[40] Implementation Decree (Presidential Decree) promulgated on January 1, 1970 and amended into Presidential Decree No. 7834 on September 29, 1975.

[41] Law No. 2098 promulgated on January 28, 1969 and Presidential Decree (Implementation Decree) No. 3879 promulgated on Aprill 11, 1969.

[42] Law No. 2181 promulgated on January 1, 1970 and Presidential (Implementation) Decree No. 5366 promulgated on October 20, 1970.

[43] Law No. 2182 promulgated on January 1, 1970, and Presidential (Implementation) Decree No. 5346 promulgated on December 1, 1970.

[44] The Chang-Won Machine Industry Estate plans to accommodate about a hundred factories by 1981. They should produce about 40 percent of the total machinery output in Korea (about $5 billion in 1975 price) and contribute more than half of total machine exports (about $1.4 billion in 1975 prices). They should also employ more than 100 thousand workers. As of 1977, 22 factories have begun either experimental or regular operations, construction has started on another 22 factories and 17 are in the

After the sixties, Korean entrepreneurs soon learned that generous subsidies and other promotional schemes would be provided for production activities which the government wished to support, while various disincentives would be applied on non-favored activities. As a result, most of the large firms which could successfully accumulate wealth from light manufacturing, including textiles and wearing apparel production, willingly invested in manufacture of steel products, metal products, electrical and nonelectrical machinery, electronic products, shipbuilding, other transport equipment and petrochemical products in the seventies because the government wished to promote these as major export industries in the late seventies and thereafter. Unlike in some developed countries such as the U.S., the transition from light to heavy industries causes relatively less friction and resistance in Korea. This is because in most cases the initiatives for such a transition are frequently undertaken by the very entrepreneurs who had been engaged in light manufacturing.

In Korea, a successful entrepreneur usually owns, possibly as a result of economies of scale in financial operations (a snowballing effect in wealth accumulation), a group of firms involved in various activities extending from import substituting production for the domestic market to exclusively export-oriented production. As the emphasis of the government shifts from simple labor intensive manufactures to skill intensive and more capital intensive manufactures, the entrepreneur begins to adapt to this shift by investing in a new set of projects. This in turn reduces the relative scale of existing production activities and reshuffles workers accordingly. If this does not happen the chances are good that he will soon no longer be a successful entrepreneur in the Korean economy.

In a country where the owners of declining industries and those of rising industries are more or less separated by either an inflexible attitude toward business practices, limited imagination or economies of age, a movement toward free trade causes much more friction and resistance on the part of the declining industries whose survival is at stake. As a result, shifts in the industrial structure and resource allocation are more difficult and tend to take longer than in a country where the same group of entrepreneurs are involved in both declining and rising industries. Korea in the seventies is still far from being a free trade economy. However, it would

---

planning stage. Total investment for these 61 factories is expected to amount to about $1.2 billion. Total output will be about $2.6 billion and total employment should exceed 100 thousand by 1981. Hence the actual exports and output of the Chang-Won Estate may well exceed the original plan. *The Naeway Business Journal*, Seoul, May 7 and May 8, 1977.

be in a much worse situation if the leading entrepreneurs had remained rigidly entrenched in a particular set of industries regardless of shifts in comparative advantage and government policies. This ability of Korean entrepreneurs to adapt in response to changing economic variables and venture into a new field of activities, in addition to the government policies which encourage continuous shifts in production activities, seem to constitute the necessary ingredients for rapid economic growth.

With an average annual growth rate of 10 percent, GNP had doubled every seven years since 1962. The planned annual growth rate of GNP during the period 1977–91 is about 9 percent which, if achieved, will maintain approximately the same rate of GNP increase. If everything proceeds as planned, GNP will have expanded more than 16 times during a 30 year period since 1962, and Korea will have experienced two major transformations in its trade and production structure: first, from primary industries to light industries in the first half of this period, and second, from light industries to heavy and chemical industries in the second half. The kind of transformation one can expect in the near future for Korea is a change in the socio-economic structure with effective public services, welfare activities and an equitable income distribution.

CHAPTER 4

PREFERENTIAL TAX POLICIES

1. Tax Revenue and Tax Exemptions

The government raises its revenue through such mechanisms as direct and indirect taxes, which intentionally or unintentionally distorts commodity and factor markets. It can also distort the markets without direct revenue effects through quotas, licensing and other legal regulations. This chapter investigates the direct and indirect tax system in Korea in order to approximate its influence on output and trade patterns and on employment growth. The following chapter will investigate the tariff and non-tariff import restriction system in Korea.

Even during 1953–61, when there were no systematic efforts toward long-term economic development, the Korean tax system gave some preferential treatment to the key industries which were producing basic necessities. In the sixties, the tax system was repeatedly revised to provide concentrated support for selected key import substituting industries and for export expansion.

Differential indirect taxes, together with tariffs and quotas, constitute the major sources of commodity market distortions. However, differential direct taxes on factor income from specific production activities may also distrot the commodity market through non-neutral influence on sectoral rates of return.[1] On the other hand, accelerated depreciation allowances

---
[1] For instance, wages of crewmen on deep sea fishing vessels, income from raising livestock, forestry income and business income from international air or marine transportation have been completely exempt from all kinds of taxes (except the global in-

Table 4.1. General Government Revenue

In Billion Won (Percentage Ratio to GNP)

	Current Revenue	Indirect Taxes	Direct Taxes On Corporation	Direct Taxes on Households	Transfers from Abroad
1953	5.0 (10%)	1.7 (4%)	0.1 (—)	0.6 (1%)	2.3 (5%)
1954	7.3 (11%)	3.3 (5%)	0.2 (—)	1.1 (2%)	2.2 (3%)
1955	12.2 (11%)	5.2 (4%)	0.3 (—)	1.6 (1%)	4.2 (4%)
1956	23.5 (15%)	6.7 (4%)	0.4 (—)	1.9 (1%)	13.0 (9%)
1957	31.4 (16%)	10.4 (5%)	0.5 (—)	3.9 (2%)	14.3 (7%)
1958	34.5 (17%)	12.6 (6%)	0.5 (—)	4.4 (2%)	14.2 (7%)
1959	38.0 (17%)	16.2 (7%)	0.7 (—)	5.3 (2%)	13.4 (6%)
1960	48.7 (20%)	18.7 (8%)	0.9 (—)	5.5 (2%)	17.3 (7%)
1961	61.1 (21%)	20.0 (7%)	1.7 (1%)	6.7 (2%)	22.3 (8%)
1962	72.2 (21%)	28.7 (8%)	2.1 (1%)	7.0 (2%)	24.2 (7%)
1963	83.5 (17%)	30.9 (6%)	3.3 (1%)	8.9 (2%)	25.9 (5%)
1964	101.2 (14%)	33.9 (5%)	4.5 (1%)	12.1 (2%)	31.4 (4%)
1965	130.1 (16%)	47.1 (6%)	6.3 (1%)	15.9 (2%)	36.2 (4%)
1966	174.1 (17%)	72.3 (7%)	12.0 (1%)	26.0 (3%)	33.6 (3%)
1967	231.6 (18%)	98.7 (8%)	16.5 (1%)	37.0 (3%)	36.9 (3%)
1968	325.5 (20%)	147.7 (9%)	24.8 (2%)	56.2 (4%)	34.0 (2%)
1969	405.5 (19%)	196.9 (9%)	33.4 (2%)	81.6 (4%)	30.7 (1%)
1970	519.2 (20%)	252.1 (10%)	42.7 (2%)	98.9 (4%)	26.9 (1%)
1971	609.5 (19%)	297.9 (9%)	57.1 (2%)	125.2 (4%)	22.6 (1%)

Preferential Tax Policies

1972	666.3 (17%)	342.8 (9%)	55.5 (1%)	121.4 (3%)	20.4 (1%)
1973	793.6 (16%)	440.2 (9%)	52.4 (1%)	157.5 (3%)	14.0 (0%)
1974	1,217.4 (18%)	689.9 (10%)	115.4 (2%)	211.6 (3%)	28.0 (0%)
1975	1,805.2 (20%)	1,103.7 (12%)	154.1 (2%)	276.0 (3%)	34.1 (0%)
1976	2,720.3 (22%)	1,599.4 (13%)	240.6 (2%)	449.8 (4%)	74 0 (1%)

Source: The Bank of Korea, *National Income in Korea*.

Note: The general government revenue includes income from property and government entrepreneurship and current transfers from households and private non-profit institutions. Indirect taxes include custom duties and business tax. Due to differences in classification, the BOK tax data differs from those of the Bureau of Taxation.

Table 4.2. Exemptions of Internal Taxes and Tariffs

In Million Won & Percent

	Direct Taxes		Indirect Taxes[1]		Import Tariffs	
	Collected	Exempted[2]	Collected	Exempted[2]	Collected	Exempted[2]
1966	33,801	2,857 (8%)	33,671	5,789 (15%)	18,007	20,295 (53%)
1967	51,099	2,828 (5%)	49,190	8,185 (14%)	25,413	32,374 (56%)
1968	77,702	2,640 (3%)	75,239	11,365 (13%)	37,881	66,411 (64%)
1969	110,423	4,572 (4%)	102,932	19,315 (16%)	44,724	86,343 (66%)
1970	138,605	9,830 (7%)	141,557	28,508 (17%)	50,924	107,405 (68%)
1971	178,456	12,695 (7%)	172,604	40,567 (19%)	52,188	143,043 (73%)
1972	175,363	9,350 (5%)	186,589	54,848 (23%)	59,106	214,560 (78%)
1973	198,544	16,923 (8%)	229,539	82,352 (26%)	82,371	319,609 (80%)
1974	313,072	25,047 (7%)	383,745	144,555 (27%)	126,698	302,821 (71%)
1975	380,906	27,147 (7%)	568,652	213,771 (27%)	181,004	222,728 (55%)
1976	548,081	82,081 (13%)	769,648	311,763 (29%)	275,512	

Table 4.2. (Continued)

	Direct Tax Exemptions			Indirect Tax Exemptions		Tariff Exemptions		
	Overseas Shipping	Investment Credit	Export Activities	Overseas Shipping	Export Activities	Foreign Capital	Key Industries	Export Production
1966	16	—	701	—	4,907	32	4,781	4,557
1967	196	—	1,662	74	6,899	257	8,447	7,230
1968	103	103	1,464	67	10,376	689	25,386	16,502
1969	215	164	2,431	21	18,049	1,741	33,036	22,551
1970	293	1,883	3,044	300	23,784	1,350	33,830	35,631
1971	853	1,942	5,401	726	36,450	2,383	37,312	54,333
1972	1,599	2,290	3,255	2,042	44,197	4,160	45,797	111,208
1973	1,543	4,009	4,503	4,503	68,689	6,919	55,825	210,788
1974	2,986	540	0	5,586	101,763	6,615	31,267	248,998
1975	1,435	4,885	0	7,624	169,129	3,170	25,487	171,553
1976	5,522	3,381	0	9,543	259,279			

Source: Bureau of Taxation, *Major Taxation Statistics* (mimeographed).
Notes: [1] Indirect tax includes business tax.
[2] Includes other exemptions. (Figures in the parentheses represent ratios to total taxes.)

and investment credits distort factor prices and favor capital intensive production.

The total annual government revenue was equivalent to 10 to 11 percent of GNP during 1953–55 and to between 15 and 22 percent of GNP during 1956–76. The portion of transfers from abroad in total government revenue steadily declined to a negligible amount during 1953–71 while a rapid increase in tax revenue since 1967 has augmented national savings. Korea derives more than two-thirds of its tax revenue from indirect taxes and custom duties. Income tax has never been a major source of revenue. Hence Korea's tax system more closely resembles that of the Western European countries than those of the U.S. or Japan. Local governments are given extremely limited fiscal responsibilities and powers. Government revenue from direct taxes on corporations was negligible before 1961 and never exceeded 2 percent of GNP during 1961–76. The revenue from direct household taxes increased from between 1 and 2 percent of GNP before 1965 to between 3 and 4 percent after 1965. At the same time, the the revenue from indirect taxes and tariffs amounted to about 5 percent of GNP in the fifties and to around 10 percent of GNP in the sixties and thereafter.

According to the data in the BOK's I-O table, while the total amount of indirect taxes collected was only about 7 billion won in 1960, it has increased rapidly to about 62 billion won in 1968 and to about 691 billion won in 1975. Traditionally, the largest amount of indirect taxes has been collected from tobacco, beverages, processed foods and, since 1966, petroleum products. A large amount of taxes was also collected from textile fibres, other chemicals, transport equipment and, since late in the sixties, nonmetallic mineral products and electronic products.[2]

The amount of direct tax exemptions for such activities as foreign exchange earning (until 1973), foreign route navigation and investment was equivalent to around 7 percent of total direct taxes asessed during 1966–75. The indirect tax exemptions for foreign exchange earning activities and foreign route navigation income amounted to only about 6 billion won in 1966 and they have increased rapidly to more than 300 billion won in 1976. The amount of indirect tax exemptions was equivalent to around

---

come tax on profits or dividends). This probably explains the rapid growth of shipping tonnage in Korea from 0.3 million GT in 1963 to about 3 million GT in 1976 as well as the phenomenal expansion of Korean Air Lines.

[2] Although the absolute amount of indirect taxes collected from machinery and basic chemicals was very small, the tax rates on these commodities were approximately equal to or higher than the average rates.

15 percent of total indirect taxes assessed during 1966–71 and to around 27 percent during 1972–76. Custom duty exemptions for export production, key industries and foreign capital amounted to about 20 billion won in 1966, increasing to about 300 billion won in 1974. These amounts were equivalent to about two-thirds of total customs duties assessed during 1969–70 and to around three-quarters for 1971–73. There was a decline in the rate of tariff exemptions since 1974.

Without clearly defining the concept of "key" industries, the government simply designated such industries and granted them preferential tax treatment, tariff exempt equipment imports and favorable loan allocations. Preferential tax measures can be as important as access to low interest loans for a company's savings, investment and growth. However, the rate of direct tax exemptions has been very small, amounting to less than 10 percent of the total direct taxes actually collected. On the other hand, the rate of indirect tax exemptions has been fairly high and tariff exemptions have been much larger than the amounts actually collected. Hence purely on the basis of the relative ratios of tax exemptions to tax collections, one may say that exemptions from indirect taxes and tariffs have been the most important source of preferential tax treatment in Korea. However, the fact that the share of direct taxes in total government revenue has been relatively small may imply that firms have also effectively been receiving preferential treatment in terms of direct taxes.

2. Income and Corporation Tax

Income tax was introduced in 1916, reintroduced in 1949 and gone through frequent revisions since then. A special corporation tax was introduced in 1940 and abolished in 1947. It was then replaced by a corporation tax in 1949. The official objectives of these tax reforms were: (1) to enhance equitable income redistribution, (2) to reduce the tax burden on middle and low income brackets, (3) to provide incentives for investment activities in important enterprises, (4) to promote industrialization in accordance with the government plans and (5) to increase the absolute amount of government tax revenue. In Korea, the tax incentives offered to favored enterprises are mainly in the form of tax reductions (or exemptions), investment credit and accelerated depreciation allowances.

The corporation tax amounted to 30 to 35 percent of the net taxable income during 1954–60, 17 percent in 1961 (22 percent in case of non-open corporations) and 20 to 30 percent during 1962–67 (35 percent on income in excess of 5 million won in 1966). Open Corporations (i.e., publicly held corporations) were subject to a 35 percent tax on income in excess of 5 million won in 1968 and this was reduced to 25 percent in 1969 and then raised to 27 percent after 1972. Non-open corporations (i.e., privately held corporations) were subject to 45 percent tax on income in excess of 5 million won in 1968–71 but the rate was reduced to 40 percent after 1972.

The highest global income tax rate was 40 percent of the aggregate taxable income (real estate income, business income, dividend and interest, wage and salary and other income) in excess of 24,000 won during 1954–56 if the total income exceeded 0.5 million won per year. If total income exceeded 2 million won per year it was 52 percent of the taxable income in excess of 0.4 million won during 1957–58. The global income tax was abolished in December 1958 and was replaced by the schedular income tax. The highest business income tax rate was reduced from 52 percent of total income in excess of 2 million won to 25 percent of total income in excess of 0.36 million won in 1961. This was raised to 30 percent in 1962. This tax rate was again changed to 45 percent of total income in excess of 1.08 million won in 1963 and to 50 percent of total income in excess of 4 million won between 1966 and 1967. Global income tax was reintroduced in November 1967 with the highest rate being 55 percent of total taxable income in excess of 5 million won. This was revised to 65 percent of total income in excess of 45 million won in December 1971 and to 70 percent of total taxable income in excess of 48 million won in December 1974. Although most income is aggregated and taxed at progressive rates, interest income from small deposits, dividend income of small shareholders and capital gains from land sales are taxed at separate flat rates.

According to the income and corporation tax law promulgated in 1949, income of enterprises which are important to national welfare may be exempted from taxation by a presidential decree.[3] In 1960, income from exports was eligible for a 30 percent reduction of income and corporation tax while income from military procurements, service exports and tourist services was eligible for a 20 percent reduction.[4] During 1962–73, all

---

[3] Law No. 33, Article 8, promulgated on July 15, 1949. Law No. 62, Article 11, promulgated on November 7, 1949.

[4] Law No. 568, Article 7, promulgated on December 30, 1960. Law No. 571, Article 12, promulgated on December 30, 1960.

Table 4.3.   Corporation Tax Rates

	1954. 3.31.	1956. 12.20.	1958. 12. 29.		1960. 12. 30.	
			Family Firm	Others	Open Corp.[1]	Non-Open[2]
All Income	35%	32%	22%	30%	17%	22%

	1961. 12.8.		1962. 11.28.		1963. 12.13.		1965. 12.20.	
	Open Corp.	Non-Open	Open Corp.	Non-Open	Open Corp.	Non-Open	Open Corp.	Non-Open
Below 1 million won	20%		20%		25%		20%	
Above 1 million won	20%		25%		30%		30%	
Above 5 million won	—		—		—		35%	

	1968. 11.22.		1968. 11. 29.		1971. 12. 28.		1974. 12. 21.	
	Open Corp.	Non-Open	Open Corp.	Non-Open	Open Corp.	Non-Open	Open Corp.	Non-Open
Below 1 million won	15%	25%	20%	25%	16%	20%	20%	20%
Above 1 million won	20%	35%	30%	35%	20%	30%	20%	30%[3]
Above 5 million won	25%	45%	35%	45%	27%	40%	27%[4]	40%[5]

Source: Korea Law Editing Association, *Korean Statue Chronicle* (in Korean), 1971 and Hong-Moon-Gwan, *A Complete Collection of Revised Tax Laws* (in Korean), 1972, 1974 & 1977.

Notes: [1] Represents publicly held corporations.
[2] Represents privately held corporations.
[3] Base tax of 600,000 won plus 30 percent of income in excess of 3 million won.
[4] Base tax of 1 million won plus 27 percent of income in excess of 5 million won.
[5] Base tax of 1.2 million won plus 40 percent of income in excess of 5 million won.

income from foreign currency earning activities was eligible for a 50 percent reduction of income and corporation tax.[5] Income from international air or marine transportation has been exempt from income or corporation tax since 1953, and income from live-stock breeding was exempted after 1969.[6]

Since 1961, corporations (with more than 50 million won in fixed assets) engaged in petroleum refining, (steel) shipbuilding, and production of fertilizer, motors, copper, iron, steel, electricity or gold mining were completely exempt from the corporation tax for the first four years after beginning operation. They then received a two-thirds exemption for fifth year and a one-third exemption for the sixth year of operation.[7] Income or dividends from such corporations were also eligible for income tax exemptions in the same amounts.[8]

Corporations (with fixed assets worth more than 5 million won) manufacturing viscose and acetate rayon, nylon yarn, fiberboard, concrete piles, sleeper or pile, straw pulp, soda-ash, sodium-hydroxide, formalin, vinyl resin, ethanol, textile machinery, electric machinery, working machinery, automobiles and parts, bicycles and parts, dairy products, processed sea-foods as well as those engaged in smelting and mining of selected minerals were completely exempt from the corporation tax for the first two years. They were two-thirds exempt for the third year and one-third exempt for the fourth year. Income or dividends arising from these activities were also exempt from income tax in the same proportions.[9]

Since 1970, selected petrochemical industries including the naphtha cracking industry have been exempt from income, corporation and business taxes for the first 5 year period after beginning operations.[10] Exemptions were extended in 1973, to selected machine industries which received complete exemption from income and corporation tax for the first 3 years of operation and 50 percent exemption for the following 2

---

[5] Law No. 823, Article 25 and Law No. 821, Article 9 promulgated on December 8, 1961. This direct export subsidization through tax credits was ended on March 3, 1973.

[6] Law No. 263, Article 11, promulgated on December 14, 1952, Law No. 2050, Article 24, and Law No. 2051, Article 8, promulgated on December 17, 1968. (Complete exemption for the first 6 years and one-half exemption for the next 3 years for livestock breeding.)

[7] Law No. 823, Article 21. Coal mining and land reclamation were added in 1962. (Law No. 1186 promulgated on November 28, 1962.)

[8] Law No. 821, Article 8, promulgated on December 8, 1961.

[9] Law No. 823, Article 22, and Law No. 821, Article 8.

[10] Law No. 2151, Article 4, promulgated on January 1, 1970.

years.[11] Shipbuilding firms, with a capacity exceeding 100 thousand DWT, are completely exempt from income, corporation and business taxes for the first 5 years.[12]

Since 1975, those who invested in "important industries" could get either complete exemption from income and corporation tax for the first 3 years and 50 percent exemption for the following 2 years, an 8 percent investment credit or an extra 100 percent special depreciation allowance. The "important industries" included large scale shipbuilding, naphtha cracking plants, selected machine and electronics manufactures, steel manufactures, and fertilizer manufactures, copper, lead and zinc smelting, selected mining and refining and electric power generation.[13] Firms were required to use the amount of the tax exemption either to increase capital, to repay a long-term debt, to invest in facilities or to offset losses brought forward.

The defence surtax, amounting to 0.25 percent of import value and 2 percent of the income or corporation tax, was introduced in 1975 but it is not applied to any activities (or the portion of the activities) which are exempt from tariff and income or corporation tax.[14]

Since 1967, manufacturers in certain industries have been allowed a deduction from income or corporation tax of an amount equivalent to 6 percent of fixed investment in the year in which the investment was completed. These industries are the: shipbuilding (steel), iron and steel, fertiliter, straw pulp, chemical fibre, automobile, electronics, machinery, processed sea-food, dairy and agricultural products and petrochemical industries. This also applied to electric power generation and selected land improvement construction work.[15] Since 1970, investments in large scale iron and steel manufacturing have been eligible for tax credits equivalent to 10 percent of their investment outlay.[16] In 1971, zinc and aluminum refineries, chemical pulp and soda-ash manufactures and mining were included for the investment tax credit.[17]

Corporations in mining, fisheries or manufacturing which get more than

---

[11] Law No. 2637, Article 4, promulgated on December 20, 1973.
[12] Law No. 2637, Article 4. promulgated on December 20, 1973.
[13] Law No. 2678, Article 4, promulgated on December 19, 1974.
[14] Defence Tax Law, Law, No. 2678, promulgated on July 16, 1975.
[15] Law No. 1964, Article 24 and Law No. 1966, Article 11, promulgated on November 29, 1967. This investment credit was limited to investments of |more than one million won.
[16] Law No. 2151, Article 4, promulgated on January 1, 1970.
[17] Law No. 2315, Article 11, promulgated on December 28, 1971. The minimum investment limit was raised to more than 2 million won.

half of total revenue from foreign exchange earning activities have been allowed an extra 30 percent depreciation allowance since 1967 for consumption of fixed capital stock in addition to the ordinary depreciation specified in the corporation tax law. They have been allowed an extra 15 percent if the foreign exchange earnings constituted 20 to 50 percent of total revenue.[18]

Since 1968, equipment used for small and medium industries and mining industries (specified in the decree by the Ministry of Finance) has been eligible for an extra 30 percent special depreciation allowance in addition to the ordinary allowance.[19] Publicly held corporations (the so-called open corporations) which are listed in the Korea stock exchange have also been entitled to an extra 20 percent depreciation allowance since 1969.[20] An extra 20 percent depreciation allowance was extended, in 1970, to firms operating in specified industrial estates such as the Gu-Mi Electronics Industrial Estate, the Ulsan Petrochemical Industrial Estate, and the Chang-Won Machinery Industrial Estate.[21]

According to the Presidential Emergency Decree on Economic Stabilization and Growth passed on August 3, 1972, firms in the specified key industries were entitled to special depreciation allowance of up to 40 to 80 percent in addition to the ordinary allowance during the five year period starting in 1972 and ending in 1976. The industries which got the 80 percent special depreciation allowance were petrochemicals, steel, nonelectrical machines, electronics, shipbuilding and tourist hotels. Electrical machinery, nonmetallic mineral products, textiles, ceramics, deep-sea fisheries, mining and electricity received a 60 percent special depreciation allowance and the chemical industry got a 40 percent special depreciation.[22] Since 1972, those mining, fishing, construction and manufacturing industries not listed above have been entitled to an 80 percent special depreciation allowance for the portion of capital invested in domestically produced equipment.[23] This provision is to be effective even after 1976 for all industries.

---

[18] Presidential Decree No. 3319, Article 44, promulgated on December 20, 1967. Cf. Corporation Tax Law, Implementation Decree, Article 41 & Article 44, and Income Tax Law, Implementation Decree, Article 55.

[19] Presidential Decree No. 3319, Article 44.

[20] Presidential Decree No. 3700 promulgated on January 6, 1969.

[21] Presidential Decree No. 5285 promulgated on August 20.

[22] Presidential Decree No. 15 promulgated on August 2, 1972 and Presidential Decree No. 6395 promulgated on December 8, 1972.

[23] Presidential Decree No. 6392 promulgated on October 18, 1972 and Presidential Decree No. 7464 promulgated in December 31, 1974. Capital equipment with domestic

After 1969, exporters who met specified minimum qualifications could deduct a reserve fund from their current taxable income for development of new foreign markets.[24] In 1973, any licensed exporter could deduct a reserve fund to develop new foreign markets from its current taxable income within the limit of one percent of its total foreign exchange earnings.[25] Furthermore, anyone engaged in foreign exchange earning activities could deduct a reserve fund for export loss from its taxable income within the limit of one percent of total sales in foreign exchange (or less than 50 percent of total income if this amount is smaller). Anyone who obtained permission from the government to invest abroad could also deduct a reserve fund for losses from foreign investment from their taxable income within a limit of 10 percent of the foreign investment.[26] Since 1976, income from overseas construction projects was entitled to a 50 perent exemption from income and corporation tax for the first 6 years.[27]

One may generalize that, until the early seventies, the reduction (or exemption) of income and corporation tax did not directly discriminate among industries or among different production techniques as far as export activities were conerned. Furthermore, it is clear that selective preferential treatment was mostly provided to key import-substituting industries.

The investment tax credit system (amounting to 6 percent of total investment outlay in plant facilities) not only favored the selected industries but also encouraged capital-intensive production techniques. The accelerated depreciation allowance introduced in the late sixties for exporters and other selected industries also favored capital-intensive investments.

The accelerated depreciation allowance was greately expanded in scope and degree in the early seventies and now seems to be having a very biased impact on investments towards the capital-intensive sectors and techniques. Reduction (or exemption) of income or corporation tax has also begun to be applied for selected prospective export industries such as selected machine and electronics manufactures.

The share of net private corporate savings amounted to only about 2

---

product content in excess of 60–65 percent were regarded as domestically produced capital. All other industries have been allowed a 40 percent special depreciation allowance.

[24] Law No. 2125, Article 19, and Law No. 2566, Article 12, promulgated on March 3, 1973.

[25] Law No. 2795, Article 4, promulgated on December 22, 1975.

[26] Law No. 2565, Article 19, and Law No. 2566, Article 12, promulgated on March 3, 1973.

[27] Law No. 2795, Article 4, promulgated on December 22, 1975.

Table 4.4. Allowance for the Consumption of Fixed Capital in Manufacturing
In Million 1970 Dollars & Percent

	Gross Fixed Capital Formation (I)	Consumption of Fixed Capital (D)	D/I
1957	79.8	24.8	31%
1958	75.5	25.1	33%
1959	62.3	24.4	39%
1960	66.7	29.8	45%
1961	66.0	24.8	38%
1962	88.7	32.7	37%
1963	115.4	48.9	42%
1964	113.9	63.1	55%
1965	157.1	72.1	46%
1966	267.7	66.0	25%
1967	265.9	83.1	31%
1968	357.0	131.4	37%
1969	405.2	168.4	42%
1970	414.3	194.9	47%
1971	424.8	212.1	50%
1972	415.9	308.6	74%
1973	767.8	417.1	54%
1974	626.4	441.4	70%
1975	698.3	502.0	72%
1976	940.5	622.2	66%

Source: The Bank of Korea, *National Income in Korea*.

percent of GNP throughout the period 1962–76. Although the absolute amount of direct taxes on corporations has been relatively small, one may argue that the tax system has not been particularly favorable for corporate saving and investment in the sixties. This can be substantiated by observing that preferential tax treatment in the form of accelerated depreciation and tax-free reserves was introduced only on a moderate scale in the late sixties and was not substantially expanded until the early seventies. The fact that the ratio of allowance for the consumption of fixed capital to gross fixed capital formation in manufacturing jumped from around 40 percent during 1962–71 to nearly 70 percent in 1972–76 seems to indicate that the accelerated depreciation allowance really began to have an effect after the 1972 Presidential Emergency Decree. Preferential treatment on retained earnings during 1972–76 also seems to have augmented the incentives for corporate savings and investment.

On the other hand, if we examine the pattern of industrial expansion in Korea, we can observe that preferential tax treatment was neither a necessary nor a sufficient condition for rapid growth of an industry. A fair number of consumer goods industries expanded rapidly without any preferential treatment, while many capital and intermediate goods industries failed to expand for a long period of time in spite of preferential tax treatments. An interesting aspect of Korea's preferential tax system is that it has usually only been allowed for a fixed period of time, moslty for around five years, instead of being granted on a semi-permanent basis. The principle of short-run fixed-term protection may be consistant with the correctly interpreted version of the infant industry argument.

3. Business and Commodity Tax

The business tax was introduced in 1927, abolished in 1942, introduced again in 1949 and has been frequently revised since then. The business tax is formally classified as a direct tax on profits, but since it is collected from an individual or a corporation engaged in taxable business on the basis of gross receipts or sales volume, it may well be calssified as an indirect tax. The business tax is a multi-stage cumulative turnover tax chargeable at flat rates at all levels of production and distribution of goods and services.

Manufacturing businesses were subject to a business tax of between 0.6 and 1.0 percent of their gross receipts during 1954–76. However, some selected industries (group A) which produced so-called basic necessities were subject to very low rates (0.2 to 0.5 percent). The Group A industries included only spinning, weavings, ginning, and manufacturing of rayon, fertilizer and oil before 1956 but threshing, cleaning and milling were added to this group in 1957 and paper manufacturing was added in 1958. In 1961, briquette manufacturing was added while cleaning and milling were dropped. And, in 1967 rice and barley cleaning was again added together with shipbuilding and rolling stock manufactures. In 1971, noodle-making, knitting and pulp manufacturing were added to Group A.

Fishing, mining and construction were exempt from the business tax before 1961, but between 1962 and 1971 fishing was subject to a 0.5 percent tax while mining was subject to a 0.5 percent tax after 1962. The tax rate on construction has continuously increased from 1.0 percent during 1962–

Table 4.5   Sectoral Business Tax Rates

In Percent

	Tax Base	1949 8.13.	1952 6.21.	1954 3.31.	1956 12.31.	1958 12.29.	1960 12.30.	1961 12.8.	1967 11.29.	1971 12.28.	1974 12.21.
Fishing	Receipts	—	—	—	—	—	—	0.5	0.5	—	—
Mining	Receipts	—	—	—	—	—	—	0.5	0.5	0.5	0.5
Manufacturing (A)[1]	Receipts	1.5	0.9	0.45	0.3[2]	0.3[3]	0.2	0.3[4]	0.3[5]	0.5[6]	1.0[16]
Manufacturing (B)[7]	Receipts	3.0	1.8	0.9	0.6	0.6	0.5	0.7	0.7	1.0	1.5[8]
Construction	Receipts	—	—	—	—	—	—	1.0	1.0	1.5	2.0
Electricty & Gas	Receipts	0.1	0.6	0.3	0.2	0.2	0.15	0.3	0.3	0.5	0.5[8]
Transportation	Receipts	0.4	2.4	1.2	0.8	0.8	0.6	0.7[9]	0.7[9]	1.0[9]	1.5[9]
Railroads	Receipts	0.2	1.2	0.6	0.4	—	0.3	—	—	—	—
Banking	Receipts	0.3	1.8	0.9	0.6	0.6	0.5	0.7	0.7	1.0	1.0
Insurance	Receipts	0.07	0.4	0.2	0.2	0.2	0.15	0.3	0.3	0.5	1.0
Mutual Loans	Receipts	0.1	1.8	0.9	0.6	0.6	0.5	—	0.5	—	—
Pawn Shops	Receipts	2.0	12.0	1.0	4.2	4.2	3.0	1.0	1.0	—	—
Trusts	Receipts	0.5	1.8	0.9	0.6	0.6	0.6	—	0.5	—	—
Wholesale (A)	Sales	0.15[10]	0.6[11]	0.3	0.2	0.2	0.15	0.3[12]	0.3	0.5[13]	0.5[17]
Wholesale (B)	Sales	0.25[14]	1.2[15]	0.6	0.4	0.4	0.3	0.7[14]	0.7[14]	1.0[14]	1.0[18]
Wholesale (C)	Sales	—	1.8	0.9	0.6	0.7	0.5	—	—	—	1.0[14]
Retail (A)	Sales	0.4[10]	0.8[11]	0.4	0.3	0.3	0.2	0.5[12]	0.5	0.75[13]	0.5[17]

Retail	(B)	Sales	0.5	1.8	0.9	0.6	0.6	0.5	1.0^{14}	1.0^{14}	1.5^{14}	1.0^{18}
Retail	(C)	Sales	0.4	2.4	1.2	0.8	0.8	0.6	—	—	—	2.0^{14}
Restaurants		Sales	1.0	4.8	2.4	1.7	1.6	1.0	1.5	1.5	2.0	2.5
Inns		Sales	0.6	3.6	1.8	1.3	1.3	0.9	—	—	—	2.5
Entertainment		Sales	0.8	4.8	2.4	1.7	1.6	1.2	2.0	2.0	3.0	3.5

Source: Korean Law Editing Association, *Korean Statute Chronicle* (in Korean), 1971 and Hong-Moon-Gwan, *A Complete Collection of Revised Tax Laws* (in Korean), 1972 and 1974.

Notes: [1] Applied to spinning, weaving, ginning, rayon, fertilizer and oil pressing.

[2] Threshing, cleaning and milling were added

[3] Paper manufacturing was added.

[4] Applied to threshing, spinning, weaving, ginning, rayon, oil pressing, fertilizer, paper and briquette manufacturing.

[5] Rice and barley cleaning, shipbuilding, and electric car manufacturing were added.

[6] Applied to threshing, rice & barley cleaning, noodle-making, ginning, spinning, weaving, knitting, rayon, oil pressing, fertilizer, paper & pulp manufacturing, briquette manufacturing, shipbuilding and rolling stock manufacturing.

[7] Other manufacturing.

[8] Also applied to waterworks.

[9] Includes storage and trasport service agencies.

[10] Wholesale of grains, salt, tobacco, coal, wood & charcoal, petroleum and others specified by the presidential decree.

[11] Wholesale of grain, salt and tobacco.

[12] Wholesale of grains, salt, tobacco, flour, fertilizer, fruit, fresh fish, briquette, and rationed necessities specified by the cabinet decree.

[13] Sales of grains, salt, tobacco, flour, fertilizer, animal feed, fruit, cut sweet potatoes, fresf fish and briquette.

[14] Sales of others.

[15] Sales of coal, wood & petroleum and rationed necessities specified by the presidenfial decree.

[16] Threshing, rice & barley cleaning and briquette manufacturing were still subject to a 5 percent business tax. Animal feed manufacturing was added to the 1971 group A list. (See footnote 6.)

[17] Flour, fertilizer, and animal feed were droped from the group A list.

[18] Sales of flour, fertilizer, animal feed and books.

71, to 1.5 percent during 1972–74 and to 2 percent after 1975.[28] Among the service industries banking, wholesale and retail were subject to relatively lower tax rates while other services such as restaurants, hotel and entertainment were subject to significantly higher rates.[29]

Sales of self-produced minerals, as well as self-produced agricultural and fishery products by producers who have not established a regular place of business were exempted from business tax since 1949. Sales of other mineral products became subject to the business tax after 1962. The businesses which were exempted from the income and corporation tax were automatically exempted from the business tax during 1949–56.[30]

Businesses who earn foreign currency by either exporting goods and services, supplying military procurements or providing tourist services have been exempt from the business tax since 1962. In addition, businesses engaged in overseas shipping, international air transportation, newspaper publishing, communications and in production of salt, peat or measuring instruments have been exempted from the business tax since 1962.[31]

The business tax system gave relatively preferential treatment to the major textile sectors but, as we will see later, this was more than offset by heavy commodity taxes. Export activities have been uniformly exempted from the business tax since 1962 while the selective preferential treatment has been limited to a small number of businesses which produce so-called basic necessities.

The business tax revenue amounted to about 4 to 8 percent of total tax revenue during 1958–66, 9 to 11 percent during 1967–74 and about 17

---

[28] Electricity (including water services after 1972) has been subject to a 0.3 to 0.5 percent tax on its gross receipts after 1954. The transportation business was subject to a 0.6 to 1.5 percent tax during 1954–76 but the railway business has been exempt from tax since 1961.

[29] In order to reduce the wholesale and retail cost of basic necessities, the business tax on sales of grains, salt, tobacco, flour, fertilizer, animal feed, fruit, cut sweet potatoes, fresh fish and briquettes was discounted by 50 percent after 1972.

[30] Law No. 48, Article 3, promulgated on August 13, 1949. The article 3 was revised to include public enterprises or similar groups according to Law No. 417 promulgated on December 31, 1956. Article 12 of Law No. 48 stated that businesses important for the national welfare could be exempted from tax by a presidential decree, but this article was repealed on December 8, 1961.

[31] Law No. 822, Article 9, revised on December 8, 1961. The law was revised to limit the exemptions only to native businessmen or corporations on December 31, 1968. (Law No. 2060, Article 10.) Law No. 1965 revised on November 29, 1967, enforced since January 1, 1968, and revised as Law No. 2121 on July 28, 1969. Business Tax law, Articles 7 and 10 and Implementation Decree, Articles 34 and 38. Publication became a non-taxable business by Law No. 2318, Article 9, promulgated on December 28, 1971.

percent of total tax revenue in 1975–76.[32]

The selective commodity tax was introduced in 1940 during the Japanese rule and has since gone through a series of revisions. Commodity taxes were collected from manufacturers and other sellers on the basis of either the quantity or the factory-door price. For imported goods, they were calculated either by the quantity or declared value of goods released from bond. In 1974, the ad valorem rates on 57 types of taxable commodities ranged from 2 percent on paper to 200 percent on jewelry.

Relatively high (20 to 100 percent of sales price) commodity sales tax rates were applied to the following items in the fifties: coffee, cocoa, soft drinks, imported leather products, rubber products, special cosmetics, resins, TV sets, radios, refrigerators, electric fans, lighting fixtures, high-quality watches, cameras, binoculars, jewels, billiard and golf equipment, phonographs, pianos, fur products and passenger cars. Except for radios, all these commodities continued to be subject to high tax rates in the sixties, and antlers, molasses, sugar, special plywood, high quality furniture, nutrition preparation in liquid form, air conditioners, automatic washers, electric cleaners and electric ovens were added to this group of high commodity tax items. The rates on electric refrigerators, automatic washers, air-conditioners, electric cleaners, electric ovens, billiard and golf equipment and fur products were further raised to between 50 and 100 percent in the late sixties. The rest of the items were subject to less than a 10 percent commodity tax until 1977.

The textile tax was introduced in 1943 and abolished in 1954. During 1954–69, this tax was included in the general commodity tax, and after 1970 it was again collected separately either from the manufacturers, the purchasers or the importers. The tax rate on taxable textile products varied from 10 percent to 70 precent.

Among the textile products raw wools, semi-processed yarn, imported woolen yarn, fabrics and specific clothes were subject to between a 10 and 70 percent tax on their sales value. Other textile products were subject to a 10 to 20 percent tax. However, the rates for cotton yarn (more than 40 count), worsted yarn, miscellaneous yarn, imported tire cord and worsted cloth were raised to between 24 and 30 percent after 1970.

Since 1961, commodities which are used as raw materials for other manufactures which are exempted from the commodity tax have also

---

[32] Office of National Tax Administration, *Statistical Yearbook of National Tax*, and the Bank of Korea, *Economic Statistics Yearbook*.

Table 4.6. Commodity Tax Rates and Revenue Collected from Selected Commodities

In Million Won & Percent

I-O Sector Classification	1957	1959	1962	1965	1968	1971	1974
18. Sugar	— (6w)[1]	568 (6w)[1]	426 (18w)[2]	1,149 (35w)[2]	4,235 (35w)[2]	7,748(40%)	14,122(40%)
19. Sodium Glutamin Acid	0 (10%)	0 (10%)	—(—)	—(—)	—(10%)	755(10%)	1,414(10%)
20. Coffee & Cocoa	—(30%)	1 (30%)	—(—)	5(50%)	9(50%)	249(50%)	1,671(50%)
22. Soft Drinks	7 (2.2w)[1]	14 (2.2w)[1]	48 (3w)[1]	74 (5w)[1]	268(10%)	1,442(15%)	4,099(20%)
24. Cotton Yarn	216 (10%)	344 (10%)	783(10%)[3]	1,219(10%)[3]	1,863(10%)	1,976(10%)[4]	3,569(10%)[4]
28. Art. Silk Yarn (& Rayon)	101 (10%)	187 (10%)	122(10%)	212(10%)	343(10%)	828(12%)	1,193(12%)
Other Chemical Yarn	111 (25%)	4 (25%)	592(15%)	991(20%)	3,685(10%)	4,872(24%)	10,128(24%)
39. Ordinary Plywood	—(—)[5]	10 (5%)[5]	37 (5%)[5]	111(10%)[5]	419(10%)	963(10%)	1,821(10%)
44. High-Quality Paper	4 (2%)[6]	14 (2%)[6]	55 (2%)	38 (5%)	129 (5%)	298 (5%)	1,473 (5%)
Other Paper	—(—)	—(—)	—(—)	159 (2%)	351 (2%)	702 (2%)	1,367 (2%)
48. Rubber & Products	0 (20%)	—(20%)	—(20%)	447(20%)	521(20%)	890(20%)	2,765(20%)
49–50. Chemicals	2 (5%)	4 (5%)	—(5%)	612(10%)	1,244(10%)	1,953(10%)	5,402(10%)
53. Nutrition Prep. (liquid)	1 (5%)	1 (5%)	—(5%)	128(30%)	593(30%)	1,171(30%)	1,927(30%)
57. Synthetic Resins	—(20%)	—(20%)	3(40%)	504(30%)	601(10%)	1,138(10%)	4,325(10%)

Preferential Tax Policies

61. Cement	4 (2%)	21 (2%)	97 (5%)	292 (5%)	808 (5%)	1,665 (5%)	3,525 (5%)
83. TV Sets (small-size)	– (50%)	– (–)	– (–)	75 (30%)	509 (40%)	2,985 (50%)	13,782 (35%)
84. Air Conditioners	– (–)	– (–)	– (–)	15 (30%)	381 (50%)	962 (65%)	2,171 (50%)
Refrigerators & Parts	0 (20%)	0 (20%)	– (–)	10 (30%)	561 (50%)	538 (65%)	6,188 (50%)
Electric Fans	– (50%)	– (50%)	– (–)	23 (20%)	315 (20%)	550 (20%)	1,331 (20%)
Electric Ovens	– (–)	– (–)	– (–)	– (–)	7 (50%)	41 (50%)	1,262 (50%)
Passenger Cars	35 (100%)	12 (100%)	– (–)	21 (10%)	1,075 (10%)	4,465 (30%)	7,985 (30%)
(Movie) Film, Imported	– (50%)	– (50%)	– (–)	– (–)	332 (50%)	466 (30%)	1,346 (30%)
Sub-total (S/T)	481 (84%)	1,180 (94%)	2,163 (72%)	6,085 (84%)	18,249 (81%)	36,657 (83%)	92,866 (87%)
Total Tax Revenue(T)	575	1,255	2,968	7,639	22,573	44,154	106,971

Source: Association of Tax Officials, *National Tax Code* (in Korean), 1976, and Office of National Tax Administration, *Statistical Yearbook of National Tax* (1966–76).

Notes: [1] Won per 600g.
[2] Won per one kg.
[3] Cotton yarn of less than 40 count. (20 percent for 40–60 count and 25 percent for more than 60 count.)
[4] 24 percent for cotton yarn of more than 40 count.
[5] Includes special plywood.
[6] Includes imported manufactures of high quality paper and other paper.

been exempted from this tax.[33] In 1967, commodities sold in foreign currency to foreigners and commodities used as raw materials for petroleum products (which were subject to the petroleum tax) were exempted from the commodity tax.[34] Commodities directly used as raw materials for textile products (which were already subject to the textile tax) were exempted from the commodity tax in 1970. Furthermore, the excess resulting from the difference between the legally certified average wastage allowance and the actual wastage of raw material used for export production were also exempted from this tax.[35]

The petroleum product tax was introduced in 1961 and revised in 1964 and 1967. Gasoline was subject to a 25 to 30 percent commodity tax during 1950–56 and to a 60 percent tax during 1957–58. Other petroleum products were subject to a 10 to 30 percent tax before 1959.[36] Since 1959, tax rates varied from 100 to 300 percent for gasoline (based on the delivery price or import price), from 20 to 40 percent for diesel oil, 0 to 30 percent for kerosene, 10 to 20 percent for heavy oil and 5 to 10 percent for Bunker C and other oil. Petroleum products exported, or used by airplanes, overseas shipping vessels or deep sea fishing vessels are exempted from the petroleum tax. Raw materials used either for export products or directly for production of other products which were already subject to commodity tax or for other taxable petroleum products were also exempt from this tax.[37]

Most of the commodity (and textile) taxes seem to have been introduced for either revenue purposes or to curb so-called "luxurious" consumption

---

[33] Law No. 824, Article 11, promulgated on December 8, 1961. Fishing net and rope as well as materials used for atomic energy were also exempted from this tax. Exports and commodities for special use such as military supplies and donations to the government have been exempted from the commodity tax since 1950. Law No. 124, Article 13, promulgated on April 10, 1950.

[34] Law No. 1967 revised on November 29, 1967, enforced since January 1, 1968, and revised as Law No. 2115 on January 1, 1970: Commodity Tax Law, Article 11 and Implementation Decree, Articles 11, 13 and 14. In 1969, materials used for construction of tourist hotels and foreigner's residences (by the government housing company) were also exempted from the commodity tax. Law No. 2096, Article 11, revised on January 28, 1969.

[35] Law No. 2155, Article 11, promulgated on January 1, 1970.

[36] Prior to 1961, petroleum tax was included in the commodity tax.

[37] Law No. 1648, Article 7, promulgated on July 8, 1964. Petroleum products used for overseas shipping or deep-sea fishing vessels and those used for production of fertilizer, pesticides, and medicine were exempted from the petroleum product tax by Law No. 1969, Article 7, which was revised on November 29, 1967. Petroleum products directly used for other products which were subject to the commodity tax were also exempted from taxation by this revision.

patterns. Hence it is not surprising to observe large amounts of commodity taxes collected for such items as sugar, TV sets, refrigerators, soft drinks, passenger cars and nutrition preparations. However, it may not be so easy to understand the intention behind collecting commodity taxes from less than 60 items and furthermore such large amounts of taxes from cotton yarn, chemical fibre yarn, plywood, rubber products, chemicals, synthetic resins and cement.

Commodity tax revenue amounted to between 15 and 20 percent of the total government tax revenue before 1962 and after 1962 it contributed 9 to 13 percent. The textile tax yielded 2 to 3 percent of the total government tax revenue during 1970-76 while the petroleum tax revenue amounted to about 5 to 8 percent during 1962-73 and 9 to 12 percent in 1974-76.

In 1976, the government decided to include all indirect taxes in a value added tax system and implement it at a rate of 13 percent with a 3 percent flexible band by July 1, 1977.[38] Goods or services for export and overseas air or marine transportation services (including materials and services supplied to these sectors) are subject to a zero percent value added tax.[39]

---

[38] Value Added Tax Law (Law No. 2934) promulgated on December 22, 1976. The value added tax system was implemented on July 1, 1977 as scheduled. The tax rate was adjusted downward, however, from the originally planned 13 percent to 10 percent, so as to reduce its impact on general price increases.

[39] Sales of unprocessed food material, water, briquettes, anthracite, educational, medical and health services, books, magazines, newspapers, and mass communication services are exempt from the value added tax. This implies that those engaged in these activities cannot claim reimbursements of value added taxes already paid and hence already included in the prices of materials and services they are purchasing for their activities.

CHAPTER 5

TARIFFS AND NON-TARIFF IMPORT RESTRICTIONS

1. Import Tariffs

Import restrictions in Korea were introduced first to reduce the balance of payment deficits and then to protect domestic industries. Protection of the home market through tariff and non-tariff import restrictions may be justified on the basis of the infant industry argument. Those industries in which costs are initially high and yet are subject to increasing returns due to internal or external economies, imperfect knowledge, or learning by doing, may be regarded as infant industries. However, in the actual execution of import controls, this concept of infant industry seems to have been used in the vaguest possible way in Korea. Instead of selecting an infant industry and protecting it, any protected industry seems to have been regarded as an infant industry. Furthermore, many protected industries have developed to the point where they can compete in world market on the basis of basic comparative advantages, and yet most of them still operate behind a wall of protection. This chapter investigates the tariff and non-tariff import restrictions in Korea in order to evaluate their impacts upon the trade pattern and employment growth.

According to the data on tariffs actually collected or exempted and those on commodity imports, the average legal tariff rate (including special tariffs) for all commodity imports was around 24 percent during 1968–73. However, because of tariff exemptions on materials for export production, key industry and foreign investment projects (whose imports have been rapidly increasing) the average rate of tariffs actually collected was only

Table 5.1. Aggregated Legal and Actual Tariff Rates

In Billion Won & Percent

	Commodity Imports[1] (A)	Tariffs Collected			Tariffs Exempted (C)	Total Legal Tariffs (B + C)	Tariff Rates	
		Total (B)	General Tariff	Special Tariff			Actual (B/A)	Legal (B + C/A)
1962	55.5	6.8	6.7	0.1	—	—	12%	—
1963	74.8	6.7	6.4	0.3	—	—	9%	—
1964	89.1	8.5	6.6	1.9	—	—	10%	—
1965	119.0	12.8	8.5	4.3	—	—	11%	—
1966	197.2	17.6	12.2	5.4	20.3	37.9	9%	19%
1967	263.0	24.9	16.5	8.4	32.4	57.3	9%	22%
1968	390.8	36.9	28.2	8.7	66.4	103.3	9%	26%
1969	509.3	41.4	32.3	9.1	86.2	127.4	8%	25%
1970	602.6	50.9	37.8	13.1	107.4	158.3	8%	26%
1971	815.4	52.2	40.0	12.2	143.0	195.2	6%	24%
1972	954.6	59.1	48.4	10.7	216.6	275.7	6%	29%
1973	1,650.2	82.4	78.1	4.3	319.6	402.0	5%	24%
1974	2,783.3	126.7	123.9	—	302.8	429.5	5%	15%
1975	3,388.4	181.0	177.1	—	222.7	403.7	5%	12%
1976	4,229.3	275.5	270.4	—	—	—	7%	—

Source: The Bank of Korea, *National Income in Korea* and *Economic Statistics Yearbook*; Office of National Tax Administration, *Statistical Yearbook of National Tax*; and Bureau of Taxation, *Major Taxation Statistics*(various issues).
Note: [1] Include freight and insurance.

Table 5.2. Weighted Average Sectoral Legal Tariff Rates (Basic Rates)

I-O 43 Sector	1958	1959–60	1961	1962	1964–67	1968–72	1973–74	1975
1. Rice, Barley & Wheat	13%	25%	13%	10%	14%	18%	16%	0%
2. Other Agriculture	10%	13%	16%	12%	11%	17%	13%	5%
3. Forestry	10%	11%	10%	10%	10%	10%	10%	7%
4. Fishery	—	—	—	—	28%	39%	37%	36%
5. Coal	10%	10%	10%	10%	10%	10%	10%	0%
6. Other Minerals	0%	0%	0%	0%	1%	6%	5%	0%
7. Processed Foods	33%	46%	53%	58%	37%	35%	12%	11%
8. Beverages	100%	100%	180%	180%	180%	150%	150%	150%
9. Tobacco	100%	100%	250%	250%	224%	95%	126%	150%
10. Textile Fibres	20%	20%	20%	40%	30%	64%	52%	47%
11. Textile Fabrics	—	—	—	—	75%	98%	81%	80%
12. Textile Products	—	—	—	—	49%	89%	75%	77%
13. Lumber & Plywood	—	—	—	—	12%	16%	25%	25%
14. Wood & Furniture	75%	60%	71%	81%	80%	91%	76%	75%
15. Paper & Products	24%	15%	20%	13%	10%	10%	11%	15%
16. Printing	0%	0%	0%	0%	0%	0%	0%	0%
17. Leather & Products	60%	60%	60%	60%	75%	68%	61%	60%
18. Rubber Products	50%	50%	60%	60%	41%	51%	44%	38%
19. Basic Chemicals	20%	23%	24%	30%	23%	24%	24%	21%
20. Other Chemicals	19%	25%	27%	36%	26%	47%	45%	27%
21. Chemical Fertilizer	10%	10%	9%	9%	5%	0%	0%	0%
22. Petroleum Products	10%	10%	18%	18%	18%	20%	20%	20%

23. Coal Products	15%	15%	15%	15%	20%	5%	5%	5%
24. Nonmetallic Minerals	25%	34%	15%	15%	17%	29%	26%	22%
25. Iron & Steel	10%	10%	10%	10%	10%	12%	11%	18%
26. Steel Products	14%	15%	25%	20%	16%	28%	28%	19%
27. Nonferrous Metal	21%	19%	20%	18%	12%	25%	22%	16%
28. Metal Products	28%	31%	34%	40%	33%	45%	40%	40%
29. Machinery	12%	13%	12%	20%	16%	20%	15%	18%
30. Electrical Machinery	26%	32%	22%	31%	21%	29%	28%	33%
31. Transport Equipment	18%	20%	17%	100%	32%	38%	15%	17%
32. Misc. Manufacturing	29%	47%	38%	40%	19%	55%	55%	52%
42. Scrap	10%	10%	10%	10%	21%	7%	6%	6%
1–4. Agriculture	11%	15%	14%	11%	13%	15%	13%	3%
5–6. Mining	10%	9%	9%	4%	2%	6%	5%	0%
7–32. Manufacturing	20%	20%	22%	25%	20%	34%	26%	23%
All Commodities	16%	18%	19%	21%	17%	26%	20%	12%

Source: Table B. 16.
Note: Weights are actual amount of import during each period.

about 8 to 9 percent from 1966 to 1970 and it declined further to about 5 to 6 percent since 1971. The average legal tariff rate was reduced to 15 percent in 1974 and to 12 percent in 1975.[1]

We also computed the weighted average (basic) legal tariff rates applying the actual individual import volume as weights. About 80 percent of commodities imported were covered in our computation. The average legal tariff rate on all commodity imports was around 16 to 21 percent during 1958–67, raised to about 26 percent in 1968–72, but was lowered to 20 percent in 1973–74 and to 12 percent in 1975.[2]

The legal tariff rates on primary goods were relatively low: the rates on minerals were much lower than those on agricultural products during 1962–74, but the rates on both agricultural and mineral products were very similar before 1962 and after 1975. On the other hand, the tariff rates on manufactured goods were very high throughout the period 1958–75 and reached their peak of 34 percent in 1968–72.

Among manufactured goods, the legal tariff rates on beverages and tobacco; textile fibers, fabrics and products; wood and furniture products; leather and leather products; rubber products; and miscellaneous manufactures were extremely high, mostly ranging between 50 and 200 percent throughout the period 1958–75. The rates on non-basic chemicals, metal products, electrical machinery, processed foods, and transport equipment were also relatively high (ranging around 30 to 50 percent), though the rates on the latter two items were substantially lowered after 1973. The legal tariff rates on electrical machinery were close to the average rate on all manufactured goods and those on non-electrical machinery were lower than the average rate.[3] The fact that there was no fundamental change in sectoral basic tariff rates during 1958–75 seems to suggest that, unlike the preferential tax treatment, the tariff protection system in Korea was not consistent with the infant industry doctrine of fixed term protection.

---

[1] This was partly due to generally lowered legal tariff rates and partly to a sudden increase in tariff exempt imports of crude oil which had been subject to a 5 percent tariff during 1968–74. Due to the oil crisis, the import value of crude oil and related products increased from about $3.0 billion in 1973 to about $1.0 billion in 1974 and $1.3 billion in 1975.

[2] The 1967 tariff reform slightly lowered the simple arithmetic average tariff rate on all imports. However, substantial shifts in the import pattern tended rather to raise the weighted average legal tariff rate for the period 1968–72.

[3] The legal tariff rates on printing and publishing, chemical fertilizers, coal products and minerals were very low; for the most part close to zero percent. The rates on paper and paper products, iron and steel, coal, forestry products, agricultural products and scraps were also fairly low.

The legal tariff rates on such products as textiles, leather, rubber and wood products, which constitute Korea's major export commodities, were around 60 to 80 percent and the rates on such capital goods as machinery and transport equipment were also fairly high. Since the tariff rates on raw materials were relatively low and they escalated in proportion to processing stages, the effective tariff rates on finished consumer goods must have been extremely high.

The tariff law has allowed duty free imports of basic plant facilities and equipment for important industries since 1949.[4] On the basis of this law, imports of machinery for export production received a tariff exemption from 1964 until 1974 when the tariff exemption system was changed into a deferred payment system on an installment basis.[5] Capital goods imported for foreign investment projects were also exempted from tariffs after 1960.[6]

After 1961, raw materials directly used for export production were imported duty free.[7] In administering the technically estimated raw material requirements, the government usually grants a wastage allowance to cover the fraction of inputs which may be defective or may be wasted in the production process. The approximate wastage allowance rates were as follows: 5 to 10 percent for synthetic resin, 10 percent for leather, 10 to 15 percent for natural and synthetic rubber, 5 to 20 percent for steel products, 10 to 30 percent for textile products, 20 to 40 percent for paper, 30 to 50 percent for human hair and 50 percent for veneer logs. The wastage allowances granted seem to have significantly exceeded the genuine wastage, especially in the late sixties. In the seventies, the government has attempted to reduce the wastage allowances to make them closer to the real wastage rate. This effort has been reflected in the falling wastage allowance rates for most items in the seventies.[8]

The raw materials which have been imported duty free and have not actually been wasted in the export production process can be legally resold in the domestic market or can be used to produce goods for domestic

---

[4] Tariff Law Article 33, No. 3 promulgated on November 23, 1949.
[5] Ministry of Finance Decree No. 345 promulgated on March 2, 1964 and Office of Customs Administration Notice No. 42 promulgated in March 1974.
[6] Law No. 532, Article 27, promulgated on January 1, 1960.
[7] Law No. 600, Article 33, promulgated on April 10, 1961, which was revised on December 5, 1963 to exclude materials specified by the decree of the Ministry of Finance, and then revised to Law. No. 1976 Article 32 on November 29, 1967 by adding a condition that products manufactured with duty free imported raw material should be exported or sold in foreign currency in the country within a year of the import date.
[8] See Table B. 18.

consumption. Since imports of such raw materials are generally subject to import controls or high tariff rates, the wastage allowance frequently generated large profits to exporters and created an artificial incentive to employ imported intermediate goods reducing the domstic value added content of exports. However, it also causes an understatement of the domestic value added content of exports in trade statistics.

There were a series of substantial devaluations in the period 1960–64 which were accompanied by the introduction of unified exchange rate system. However, due to the existence of various quantitative import restrictions, the profit margin (import premium) from import activities at the unified exchange rate differed widely among commodities. In order to reduce these extreme differences in profit margins from importing, the government introduced a special tariff law in 1964. According to the law, the Ministry of Finance had authority to apply a special customs tariff to any import commodity which it deemed nonessential. This allowed for an additional tax of 70 or 90 percent of the differential between the estimated wholesale value of the commodity and the import price.[9] The 902 items included in the group which was subject to a 90 percent extra tax on the profit margin were those which had been subject to the basic 40 percent or higher tariff rate (which was the arithmetic average of basic legal tariff rates on all commodities in 1963). The 90 percent group also included 69 items which were classified as luxury goods. The 1,153 items included in the other group, which was subject to a 70 percent extra tax on the profit margin, were selected from the remaining import goods. Machines for important industries were not subject to this special import tariff. The total amount of revenue collected through this special tariff system amounted to about 27 percent of total custom duties actually collected and to about 9 percent of total legal tariff obligations during 1966–72. This special tariff system was repealed in 1973.[10] Since the 1967 tariff reform, the government has been able to alter import duty rates administratively by up to 50 percent.

There is another important form of import restriction which has tariff-

---

[9] Temporary Special Tariff Law (Law No. 1488) promulgated on December 13, 1963. In July 1961, a law was promulgated under which the Minister of Finance could impose special customs duties to restrict the import of nonessential and luxury goods. These duties would be imposed on the basis of the CIF value of the import converted at a 130 won per dollar rate. The Minister was empowered to classify goods for this purpose into four categories, subject to rates of 100, 50, 30 and 10 percent respectively. Four items were assigned to the 50 percent duty category, 14 items to the 30 percent category and 16 items to the 10 percent category. IMF, *op. cit.*, 1961, p. 222.

[10] Law No. 5569 promulgated on March 3, 1973.

equivalent effects. The Monetary Board decision in October 1961 required advance deposit of 100 won per dollar on the value of imports and this was revised to 77 percent of the import value in October 1962. After August 1963, a 100 percent advance deposit was required for general imports, and a payment guarantee by a financial institute was required for imports of raw materials for exports and imports for government operated enterprises. After November 1966, a partial advance deposit was required for imports of raw materials for exports, but those imports which were financed by aid funds, foreign investment or public foreign borrowing were not subject to advance deposit requirements.[11]

After 1968, a fairly complicated system of advance import deposits was enforced. The advance import deposit requirements were as follows: 150 percent for import items subject to a customs duty in excess of 49 percent and for nonessential or luxury items, 100 percent for government imports and for import items subject to custom duties at rates ranging from 30 percent to 49 percent, and 30 percent for others. Advance deposits for KFX imports of raw materials for exports ranged between zero and 30 percent depending on the commodity and the status of the export production, that is, whether the latter was covered by an export contract, bonded warehouse transaction, or an export L/C.[12] After 1971, raw material imports for export use required a 10 to 30 percent advance deposit.[13] The deposit rates on raw material imports for export use were raised to 100 percent in 1972, but were lowered again to 15 percent in 1974, and to 10 percent in November 1975. The import deposit for capital equipment for export production and for government imports has been 100 percent since 1972. That for general imports has been 110 percent and that for

---

[11] Ministry of Finance Notice No. 418 promulgated on Novermber 12, 1966.
[12] Ministry of Finance Notice No. 439 promulgated on July 3, 1968. Machinery and parts imports financed by AID Program Loans were subject to a 10 percent advance deposit until February 1972. The deposit rate was raised to 200 percent in 1969 on imports of non-essential goods from countries within ten days shipping distance from Korea. Imports from this specified area, which were subject to basic tariff rates between 30 percent to 49 percent but not regarded as non-essential luxury goods, required a 150 percent deposit except for 13 items which were regarded as having a significant impact on the domestic price level. Since 1970, the advance deposit requirements have been uniformly applied, irrespective of the origin of the imports.
[13] Ministry of Finance Notice No. 494 promulgated on June 8, 1971. D/A or D/P imports were exempt from advance depsoit requirements during 1968–71 and since 1975. Goods which had been exempt from an import deposit (such as iron scrap, timber, copper ore, and insecticides) were included in 1972 and are required to make a 5 to 20 percent import deposit.

non-essential luxury goods has been 200 percent.[14]

2. Non-Tariff Import Restrictions

The series of devaluations in the early sixties were accompanied by a gradual relaxation of direct trade controls and, in 1967, the so-called "positive" list system was altered to a "negative" system, whereby all commodities not listed were automatically approved for import (AA items).

Automatically approved items consisted mainly of essential consumer goods which were not produced domestically and certain raw materials and capital goods. Prohibited items were mainly luxury goods, items prohibited for public health or moral reason and some domestically produced goods. Restricted items in the negative list required individual licenses.

Under the negative system, more than half of the 1,312 basic (5-digit) SITC import items became AA commodities. There were around 70 prohibited import items during 1967-76. However, the number of quota items has decreased steadily from more than a hundred in 1967-68 to zero in 1976.[15]

The number of items imported under the export-import link system was very small before 1969, but it has increased to around 20 items since 1970. On the other hand, the number of items which require recommendations from MCI or other appropriate ministries has steadily increased from about 300 items in 1967 to about 623 items in 1976. The importers of these items must acquire approval to import, and frequently, must also get approval for the quantity of imports from MCI or other appropriate authorities. Although this system is more flexible than a quota or link system, the government can still effectively control the

---

[14] Advance deposits for imports of capital equipment financed with domestic loans in foreign exchange were, for imports for export industries, 30 percent for imports from countries within ten days shipping distance and 10 percent for imports from other countries and, for other imports financed by such loans, 30 percent. In 1969, advance import deposit requirements on KFX imports of machinery and facilities for the export industry were eliminated for imports from countries of more than ten days shipping distance. *IMF Exchange Restrictions* (*20th Annual Report*), 1969, p. 272. and *ibid.*, 1970, p. 296.

[15] Eligible applicants for some quota items were limited to suppliers of domestic raw materials for export industries.

Table 5.3. Items Subject to Import Controls: 1967–76

	Prohibited Imports		Quota Imports		Linked Imports		MCI Recommendation Req.		Other Restricted Items		Total[1]	
	1/2	2/2	1/2	2/2	1/2	2/2	1/2	2/2	1/2	2/2	1/2	2/2
(Number of Items Based on 5-digit 1,312 Basic SITC Codes)												
1967		104		110		6		163		174		557
1968	78	76	158	66	1	3	52	34	259	376	548	555
1969	77	77	58	68	0	0	56	53	386	395	577	593
1970	78	72	64	65	21	20	78	82	371	357	612	596
1971	69	70	42	44	26	30	60	62	370	370	567	576
1972	67	69	31	29	53	49	109	112	372	388	632	647
1973	66	70	25	25	22	21	135	138	383	397	631	533
1974	69	68	24	24	18	21	161	162	376	383	648	658
1975	68	69	24	21	26	20	164	184	354	369	636	663
1976	61	60	0	0	19	18	221	164	402	450	703	692
(Amount of Imports in Million Dollars)												
1967	—		24.7 (2%)		45.0 (5%)		174.8 (18%)		45.3 (5%)		996.2 (100%)	
1968	—		63.9 (4%)		—		52.4 (4%)		451.0 (31%)		1,468.2 (100%)	
1969	—		91.2 (5%)		—		198.2 (11%)		679.7 (37%)		1,823.6 (100%)	
1970	—		103.3 (5%)		25.0 (1%)		381.5 (19%)		460.1 (23%)		1,984.0 (100%)	
1975	—		113.6 (2%)		476.3 (7%)		2,198.1 (30%)		992.1 (14%)		7,274.4 (100%)	

Source: Korean Traders Association, *Trade Yearbook*, Ministry Finance, *Foreign Trade of Korea* (1967–69), Office of Customs Administration, *Statistical Yearbook of Foreign Trade* (1970–74) and Korean Traders Association, *Statistical Yearbook of Foreign Trade* (1975–76).

Note: [1] Represents total number of restricted items and total amount of commodity imports.

Table 5.4. Sectoral Pattern of Import Control: 1967, 1972 & 1976

Number of Items & Percent

	1967 (2/2)		1972 (1/1)		1976 (2/2)	
	Prohibited, Linked & Quota Items	Recommendation Required	Prohibited, Linked & Quota Items	Recommendation Required	Prohibited, Linked & Quota Items	Recommendation Required
Total	220 (100%)	337 (100%)	151 (100%)	481 (100%)	78 (100%)	614 (100%)
Agriculture & Forestry	2 (1%)	40 (12%)	7 (5%)	45 (9%)	0 (0%)	55 (9%)
Fishery	0 (0%)	1 (0%)	1 (1%)	2 (0%)	1 (1%)	3 (0%)
Mining	2 (1%)	1 (0%)	3 (2%)	5 (1%)	0 (0%)	17 (3%)
Food Products	8 (4%)	48 (14%)	9 (6%)	63 (13%)	6 (8%)	74 (12%)
Yarns & Fabrics	46 (21%)	7 (2%)	19 (13%)	34 (7%)	6 (8%)	36 (6%)
Textile Products	37 (17%)	9 (3%)	19 (13%)	24 (5%)	22 (28%)	26 (4%)
Wood & Furniture	9 (4%)	11 (3%)	2 (1%)	13 (3%)	4 (5%)	11 (2%)
Paper & Products	15 (7%)	8 (2%)	8 (5%)	14 (3%)	4 (5%)	22 (4%)
Rubber Products	10 (5%)	2 (1%)	7 (5%)	2 (0%)	3 (4%)	4 (1%)
Chemicals	16 (7%)	52 (15%)	10 (7%)	75 (16%)	2 (3%)	91 (15%)
Nonmetallic Products	9 (4%)	8 (2%)	1 (1%)	13 (3%)	0 (0%)	21 (3%)
Basic Metals	3 (1%)	22 (7%)	6 (4%)	29 (6%)	0 (0%)	53 (9%)
Metal Products	14 (6%)	26 (8%)	12 (8%)	28 (6%)	2 (3%)	37 (6%)
Machinery	0 (0%)	13 (4%)	4 (3%)	30 (6%)	0 (0%)	34 (6%)
Electrical Machinery	2 (1%)	21 (6%)	16 (11%)	12 (2%)	12 (15%)	15 (2%)
Transport Equipment	0 (0%)	12 (4%)	1 (1%)	18 (4%)	1 (1%)	21 (3%)
Other Manufactures	47 (21%)	56 (17%)	26 (17%)	73 (15%)	13 (17%)	94 (15%)

Source: Korean Traders Association, *Trade Yearbook*.

amount of imports of each commodity group by imposing annual import ceilings on the basis of estimated import needs and the overall balance of payments situation. More than half of the items which require approval have been subject to annual import ceilings. In licensing imports from specified countries, Korea's balance of trade position with the country is also taken into account.

In 1967, the yarns and fabrics, textile products and chemical sectors had the largest number of prohibited, linked and quota items. The chemicals, food and agricultural products sectors had the largest number of items requiring recommendation. There was no change in this pattern until 1976 except that the metal product sector has had a larger number of prohibited imports, linked and quota items than the chemicals sector since 1969, and the electrical machinery sector has had a larger number of such items than the metal products sector since 1972.

The commodities subject to quantitative import controls were mostly non-primary goods. The official objectives of quantitative controls were to prevent imports of luxury goods and protect domestic industries on the one hand, and to reduce overall balance of payment deficits by controlling the less urgent imports without causing inflationary pressure on the other. In principle, imports of finished consumption goods have not been allowed. In order to protect domestic industries, other (non-consumption good) imports competing with domestic products such as intermediate input materials for domestic consumption have been allowed to fill the estemated gap between domestic supply and demand (at the prevailing "domestic price" instead of the estimated gap at international prices). The quantitative control of non-competitive intermediate and capital good imports seems to have been influenced entirely by the overall balance of payment conditions. Imports of raw materials for exports were normally approved automatically, irrespective of their classification. However, some quantitative restrictions were frequently applied when there were influential domestic suppliers of these raw materials. This generated conflicts between export producers who wanted to use low priced (and high quality) imported raw materials and domestic producers of high priced (and allegedly poor quality) raw materials.

Since the prices of many domestically produced import-competing goods were higher than international market prices, the quantitative import controls have generated implicit premium to imports and, in spite of the existence of the Temporary Special Tariff Law (1964–73), the amount of such premium seems to have been larger the larger the overall balance of payment deficits and the associated cut in imports through quantitative restrictions.

It is generally believed that most of the import-competing industries have been over-protected by tariff and quantitative import restrictions. For instance, the protection of import-competing goods such as textiles began in the fifties and has continued into the seventies. The fact that those products which are now Korea's major export items, such as textiles, are still protected by severe (tariff and) quantitative import restrictions may reflect pressure from the manufacturers who are afraid of conspicuous consumption of foreign goods by the well-to-do. It probably also reflects the desire of the government to prevent even a small amount of foreign exchange "waste" on what are considered to be non-essential imports. However, this strong protection of major export industries may actually be regarded as redundant. Furthermore, the over-protection of domestic-market-oriented goods seems to have caused all kinds of undesirable side-effects such as inefficiency and monopolistic exploitation.

With a realistic exchange rate and the negative list system in force since 1967, imports are now subject to less quantitative restrictions than they were in the fifties and early sixties. However, imports of approximately half of the basic SITC (4-digit) items are still under government control and, on certain import items, the government still maintains a system which allocates exchange among the end-users according to their production capacities which not only promotes excess capacity but often forces a proportional expansion of firms in an industry. For instance, the gross sales and profits of coffee and liquor manufactures depend on the amount of imported coffee beans and alcohol allocated to each producer and hence either the maintenance of the *status quo* or the emergence of a sharer is determined by government officials.

The development of consumer goods industries in the fifties and early sixties is largely owing to the tariff and non-tariff import control system. Although non-tariff import restrictions were first introduced to restrain balance of payment deficits, they began to serve as one of the principal tools for the government in promoting industrialization in the fifties. To accelerate investment, capital good imports received preferential treatment and, to raise the utilization rate of existing capacities, intermediate good imports also received preferential treatment. As a result, non-tariff import restrictions mainly served to encourage allocation of available domestic resources to protected consumer good sectors. Since the intermediate and capital goods imports were subject to less quantitative controls, import substitution for these goods could not be as profitable as for consumption goods and hence import substitution of intermediate and capital goods was very slow. It might sound paradoxical, but Korea's relative failure in promoting intermediate and capital goods industries in the fifties and early sixties seems to have positively contributed to rapid export expansion in the late sixties and seventies. That is, the manufacturers of export goods were relatively free to use low cost imported intermediate and capital goods instead of high cost domestic products. This factor, combined with low cost labor helped achieve successful export expansion in Korea.

In the mid-seventies, however, the government's emphasis has clearly shifted to an active development of various intermediate and capital goods industries both for domestic consumption and exports. Should these industries fail to achieve efficiency in terms of international competitiveness because of abuse of tariff and non-tariff protection measures, Korea may face a Latin American style problem in the near future. The impact of high cost of intermediate and capital goods may be more serious than high cost consumer goods, and the adverse effect may spread over the entire production activities in Korea either for domestic consumption or for exports. However, if Korea is successful in producing a wide range of intermediate and capital goods on a competitive basis in international markets without requiring excessive subsidies over a prolonged period, the most difficult step in industrialization will be over and Korea will no longer be classiffed as an underdeveloped economy. Therefore, the need for more rational and cautious policies on tariff and non-tariff import restrictions may become more urgent in the late seventies.

CHAPTER 6

LOAN ALLOCATION POLICIES

1. Distribution of Domestic Bank Loans

During 1953–76, interest rates on bank loans (and savings) were usually kept at an extremely low level compared with those on curb market loans. Although low interest rates raise the present value of the yield from real investments relative to their costs, the volume of such investments was restricted from expanding by credit ratioing to the point where return on investment would be bid down or costs bid up to generate an equilibrium. As a results, there was always a huge excess demand for bank loans in Korea, and hence preferred financing for favored industries served as one of the most powerful tools in pursuing government strategy for sectoral investment, growth and exports. Monetary policy in a low interest rate system essentially takes the form of a direct control that involves fairly arbitrary quantitative quotas or ceilings. The government bureaucracies, especially the Ministry of Finance, gained powerful control over the private economy by maintaining a disequilibrium system associated with the low interest bank loans.

The banking system of Korea was developed on the basis of the Bank and the Bank of Korea Laws promulagted in 1950.[1] In 1950 Korea had a central (Bank of Korea) and four city banks, but the Korea Reconsrtuction Bank (later the Korea Development Bank) was added in 1954 and

---

[1] The Bank of Korea Law is Law No. 138 promulgated on May 5, 1950, revised in 1962, 1963 and 1968 (as Law No. 2042). The Bank Law is Law No. 139 promulgated on May 5, 1950, revised in 1962, 1966 and 1969 (as Law No. 2095).

the Agricultural Bank (later become the Agricultural and Fishery Cooperatives) and a city bank were added in 1958. The Korea Development Bank initially provided long term loans to key industries with government fiscal funds, but its function expanded after 1961 with the introduction of foreign loans as an additional source of funds. After 1961 it was also empowered to handle common stocks and bonds of major industries.

As of 1977, the Korean government operates eleven specialized banks (the Bank of Korea, Korea Development Bank, Medium Industry Bank, Korea Exchange Bank, Korea Trust Bank, Citizens National Bank, Korea Housing Bank, Land Bank of Korea, Export-Import Bank of Korea, Agricultural Cooperatives and Fishery Cooperatives) and as the majority stock holder, indirectly manages the five nation-wide commerical banks.[2] Only the ten small local banks and various investment and mutual savings finance companies are operated independently, although they are also subject to strict formal and informal regulations.

Korean monetary and financial policies were developed with the major concerns being on inflation and development financing. The control of the aggregate money supply was more or less geared to control inflation, and the sectoral credit rationing was the principal tool of development financing. Since the (real) interest rates on savings and loans were fixed at extremely low rates before 1965, the activities of financial institutions were heavily dependent on the rediscounts of the Bank of Korea and were also subject to such direct measures as a loan ceiling system (by industry and by loan funds) and a loan priority system. In Korea, business has always been heavily dependent on bank credits and curb loans. The curb loans were allocated on a free market basis at high interest rates but their magnitude was relatively small and they carried all the inefficiencies inherent in most operations of an informal sector.

In 1951, the Monetary Board introduced "Temporary Regulations on the Uses of Funds in Financial Institutions" which allowed loan expansion within the limit of "quarterly loan ceilings" imposed by the Monetary Board and also granted priority to reconstruction activities.[3] In December 1953, the Monetary Board issued a table of loan priorities, and in 1955 financial institutions were required to obtain prior consent from the Monetary Board before making a loan exceeding one million won or before making a loan to the public sector.[4]

---

[2] The Korea Trust Bank was integrated into a city bank and named the Seoul Trust Bank in 1976.

[3] Monetary Board decision of February 1, 1951.

[4] Monetary Board decision on December 20, 1953 and on August 4, 1955. Public

One can observe that, during 1953–58, the primary and SOC sectors and selected manufacturing sectors received preferential loan treatment. The Loan Priority Ranking Table (Table 6.1) reflects the state of Korea's industrial development in the fifties.

With the objective of achieving more efficient management of loan funds available to the financial sector (in accordance with the government plans for financial stabilization and economic development) the Monetary Board passed the "Regulations on the Uses of Funds in the Financial Sector" on December 30, 1958. According to this Regulation, the financial institutions had to allocate loans on the basis of the Loan Priority Ranking Table. Loans for operating funds had to be provided for a term of less than one year and those for equipment for a term of less than 3 years, within the limit of 70 percent and 50 percent of necessary funds, respectively.[5]

In 1962, the Monetary Board removed the quarterly loan ceilings on loans for trade and military procurements in foreign currency.[6] According to the revision made on February 15, 1962, financial institutions had to give special preferences on loans to foreign exchange earning or import substituting businesses. They also had to give preferences to businesses which produce basic daily necessities and businesses which contribute significantly to the growth of GNP or employment. They were obliged to give lowest priority to businesses which produce nonessential consumption goods, luxury goods, entertainment and restaurant services.[7]

In 1964, the governor of the Bank of Korea was given the authority to specify which industrial sectors were to be promoted and then each financial sectors were to be promoted and then each financial institute was obliged to concentrate its loans in these specified industries. Moreover, since 1965, more than 30 percent of the net increase in total loans had to be

---

sectors consisted of agricultural sector, government monopoly sector, government-owned enterprises, fishery sector, local government, textbook publication and salt manufacturing.

[5] However, the limit on loans which required prior consent by the Monetary Board was raised from one million won to three million won on February 19, 1959. The three million won limit "for a loan" was changed to read "for loans to the same person" on November 5, 1959. That is, if a financial institute intended to make loans exceeding three million won to the same person (*cumulative*), it had to obtain prior consent from the Monetary Board.

[6] Loans to purchase aid-financed imports and loans based on installment savings were not subject to the quarterly loan ceilings after 1961. The Loan Priority Ranking Table was not mentioned in Regulations after June 16, 1960.

[7] The Monetary Board laid out more specific instructions on March 7, 1964 and on June 16, 1964.

Table 6.1. Ranking of Loan Priorities[1]

Class A Funds

Primary & SOC Sectors

    Agriculture, Forestry, Fishery, Mining, International Trade, Cargo Handling, Salvaging, Government Monopolies (Salt & Tobacco), Electricity,[2] Water & Sewer Service,[3] Construction,[3] Transportations[3] and Warehousing.[3]

Manufacturing Sectors

Food[3]	:	Starches, Canned Food, Frozen Food (For Export)[4]
Textiles	:	Cotton Yarn,[2] Cotton Fabrics,[2] Silk,[2] Silk Fabrics,[2] Woolen Fabrics, Chemical Fiber Fabrics, Knitwear.
Chemicals	:	Fertilizer, Insecticides, Carbide, Glycerin, Alcohol,[2] Sheet Glass, Paper, Cement, Bricks, Dyes,[3] Special Type Rubber[3] Drugs,[3] Leather,[3] Paints,[3] Sulphuric Acid,[3] Fire-Proof Material,[4] Rubber Products.[4]
Metal Product[3]	:	Iron or Copper Wire, Nails, Rolled Steel, Basic Metal.[4]
Machinery[3]	:	Pumps, Farm Machines, Motors, Textile Machines, Electrical Equipment, Measuring Instruments, Vehicles, Shipbuilding, Working Machine,[4] Industrial Machines,[4] Power-Using Machine,[4] General Machines,[4] Communication Equipment.[4]
Others[3]	:	Saw Mill Products, Cement Products, Military Procurements, Textbooks, Mintage, Batteries, Briquettes,[2] Handicrafts for Exports, Smelting.

Class B Funds

Funds not included in either Class A or Class C group.[5]

allocated to small and medium industries.[8] In 1965, the Monetary Board allowed the governor of the Bank of Korea to regulate the magnitude of loans by financial institute and by type of funds, but the quarterly loan ceiling system was formally abolished. Loans for equipment purchases could be provided for a term of less than 5 years after 1962 and this was raised to 8 years in 1972.

---

    [8] After 1964, differential interest rates were applied on BOK's rediscounts of commercial bills: 10% on Class A funds and 11.5% on Class B funds.

Table 6.1. (Continued)

Class C Funds

Primary & SOC Sectors[6]

    Flower or Fruit-Culture, Charcoal Manufacturing and Highway Transportation.

Service Sectors

    Wholesale & Retail Trade,[7] Small Scale Transportation & Storage, Entertainment, Hotels, Restaurants, Other Miscellaneous Personal Services, Leasing.[4]

Manufacturing Sectors

    Brewing, Cosmetics, Clothing, Toys, Office Equipment,[2] Kitchen Equipment, and Wooden Articles. Soft Drink,[4] Confectionary,[4] Meat,[4] Leather Footwear,[4] Ornaments,[4] Sports Goods,[4] Seasonings,[4] Furniture,[4] Jewelry.[4]

Notes: [1] Monetary Board Decision on December 20, 1953.
[2] Shifted to Class B funds on August 4, 1955 or on December 29, 1955.
[3] Added to Class A funds from Class C funds on August 4, or December 29, 1955.
[4] Added on March 7, 1964 and amended on June 16, 1964.
[5] Ice-Manufacturing, Marine Transportation Equipment and Warehousing were shifted from Class A to Class B funds on December 29, 1955. Tourist services were added to Class B funds (from Class C) on December 30, 1958.
[6] Shifted or added to Class C funds on August 4, 1955.
[7] Except the loans for super-market chains to improve the distribution system. (Stabilization No. 1200-26 promulgated by the MOF on January 10, 1974.)

In order to reinforce and supplement the Regulation on the Uses of Funds, the Ministry of Finance issued standing rules on loan criteria. For instance, according to the standing rules issued in January 1974, each financial institute has to give preference to loans for the energy sector, food grain sector, industries utilizing domestic resources and waste materials and other sectors which the government wants to support. The first article of these MOF standing rules specified that loans for capital equipment can only be for domestically produced equipment and the funds for importing foreign capital goods must be financed either by foreign borrowing or by (KFX) foreign currency loans. In the last article the Ministry of Finance urged non-bank financial institutions to follow the standing rules and Regulation on the Uses of Funds in their loan activities.

The financial stabilization program, which was implemented after 1957, allowed bank loans to increase within the limit of the net increase in time and savings deposits. Only since the September 1965 interest reform have more indirect forms of control such as adjustments of interest rates and reserve requirements as well as open market operations begun to be applied. At the same time the loan ceiling system has been (officially) repealed. However, the real and nominal interest rates were reduced to the pre-1965 level after the August 3 Presidential Emergency Decree in 1972. This was intended to reduce the burden on businessmen who were lucky enough to have bank loans by lowering the bank interest rates and by freezing the repayment obligation on existing curb loans. As a result, the rate of (net) increase in time and savings deposits started to decline after 1973. As a consequence the government intensified both its direct controls on loan allocations and its efforts to tincrease time and savings deposits through unorthodox means. These included making bank loans to a firm conditional on its opening time deposits equivalent to a specified proportion of the loan amount. This raised the effective real interest rates on loans to businessmen without raising interest rates on time and savings deposits.

The Government created the National Investment Fund (NIF) at the end of 1973 by pooling all kinds of funds under government control (which included the 1.3 billion won KDI endowment fund) and by issuing NIF bonds.[9] Total DMB Loans financed by NIF funds amounted to about 20) billion won in 1974 (at 9 percent), 53 billion won in 1975 (at 12 percent) and 121 billion won in 1976 (at 14 percent).[10] The NIF loans were allocated to the Export-Import Bank, the electricity sector, the primary sector and the important manufacturing sectors. The important manufacturing sectors were the steel, nonferrous metal, chemicals, machinery and shipbuilding industries.

In the fifties and early sixties, the expansion of the money supply was caused mainly by the deficit financing of the government budget. During 1965–67, a major cause of the expanded money supply was the inflow of foreign commercial cash loans which were provided in order to take advantage of extreme interest rate differentials. However, the rapidly growing (short-term) export credits financed by the rediscounts of the Bank of Korea and the development financing for major industries led the monetary expansion thereafter.[11] A remarkable fact is that bank credits

---

[9] NIF Law (Law No. 2635) promulgated on December 14, 1973.
[10] The Bank of Korea, *Monthly Economic Statistics*.
[11] One may add the increasing subsidies to farmers in the form of dual pricing of rice and fertilizer, which was financed by government borrowing from the Bank of Korea, as another major cause of the monetary expansion.

have never been allowed for household consumption activities in Korea except for small remunerations of the Citizens National Bank and housing loans by the Korea Housing Bank. Consumption loans have been almost entirely handled by the informal sector.

It should be noted here that although most of the regulations on bank loans were promulagted by the Monetary Board, the Ministry of Finance (not infrequently on the basis of suggestions or pressure from the Ministry of Commerce and Industry) is actually responsible for the policy measures and the Monetary Board simply takes care of the formalities. Although the Monetary Board has nominal independence, its decisions have never been inconsistent with those of the Ministry of Finance.

The ranking of industrial sectors for priority in loan allocations, as well as the specification of types of business to receive preferential treatment (such as export of import substituting business) were both too gereral and too comprehensive to be a real help to the decision-makers in financial institutions. Since the coverage of eligible industries and businesses was so wide, the financial institutions were always short of funds to meet the demand of the priority industries and preferred businesses. As a result, making the choice for loan allocation among the industries has been subject to direct guidance and control by government officials. In early 1977, apparently in an attempt to enhance the efficiency in loan allocations, the Ministry of Fiannce announced its intention to change what one might call the positive system (i.e., listing priority ranking and preferred types of businesses) to a negative system which lists industries and type of businesses that should not receive loans (such as sugar refiners and ice-cream and seasoning manufacturers for domestic consumption). This allows financial institutions to use their own discretion in al.ocating loans to unlisted industries and businesses. However, due to a flagrant disparity between interest rates on bank loans and those on curb loans, this formal shift in the system is unlikely to reduce government interference and to enhance efficiency in the financial sector. Only by gradually restoring the basic functions of the market mechanism, can one expect a lessening of the disequilibrium in financial sector. The existence of various subsidized loans may be justifiable, but an excessive arbitrariness in resource allocation should be avioded to the extent possible.

Except during a brief period in the late sixties (1965–71), the government has almost always maintained negative real interest rates on time and savings deposits since the end of the Second World War. A few economists argue that a person does not necessarily save less in response to lower interest rates. However, a negative interest rate can never be conducive to enhancing savings propensity. Furthermore, a wide disparity between the interest rates on bank deposits and those on curb loans seems to have greatly reduced the incentive for individual households to save through financial institutions and has forced them instead to depend on imperfect informal financial markets. This has caused a tremendous efficiency loss in mobilizing potentially available investment resources.

2. Export Financing

A. Short-Term Export Financing

The short-term export financing system was developed in Korea with the objective of providing direct support for production and collection (domestic purchase) of exportables. It includes both producers of export goods and exporters who have received an irrevocable export L/C and have concluded contracts to export goods on a D/P, D/A or consignment basis or through bonded warehouse transactions. It is also intended to provide financing for imports or domestic purchase of raw materials for export production on the basis of the value of the imports or the amounts of drafts issued with local L/C.[12]

Short-term loans for export activities were provided under the Finance Regulation during 1948–50 and under the Regulation of Trade Financing during 1950–55. From 1955 to 1960 they were provided under the Trade Financing Regulation and then according to the Regulations on Export Finance after 1961. There were also a number of subsidiary regulations relating to: export promotion fund loans financed by counterpart funds during 1960–63, export industry promotion fund loans during 1964–69, import credits during 1967–72 and domestic raw material financing during 1971–72. The latter regulations were unified into a new Regulation on Export Financing established in 1972.

During 1948–50, commercial banks could provide loans to finance collection of export goods (which were recommended by the MCI) within a limit of 50 percent of the acquistition cost for a period of less than 60 days. The Chosun Exchange Bank could also provide loans on the basis

---

[12] The repayment terms were usually 90 days for L/C basis transactions with a possible extension of up to 30 to 60 days, 120 days for D/P basis, and 180 for D/A, consignment or bonded transactions. Raw material import financing was usually subject to a higher rate of interest.

of B/L within a limit of 75 percent of the shipping value after obtaining permission from the Ministry of Finance.[13] After 1950, loans for exports could be provided by commercial banks within a limit of 80 percent of L/C value (and 90 days) at an interest rate of 9.86 percent per annum which could get a full rediscount at the same interest rate from the Bank of Korea without being subject to quarterly loan ceilings.[14] The interest rate on export loans by commercial banks was raised to 16.43 percent on October 10, 1951, but the interest rate applied to BOK's rediscounts was kept lower than this rate (i.e., 12.78 percent).

Short-term loans for export were handled by both the BOK and commercial banks until 1955, but after that they were handled only by the commercial banks.[15] The interest rate applied to BOK's redicount was further lowered to 6.57 percent in 1955 and a loan ceiling of 100 million won was introduced on June 2, 1955. After 1957, however, export loans could be provided within the limit of the total export value estimated by the bank.[16] The interest rate on BOK's rediscount was revised to 7.3 percent in 1959 and to 10.22 percent in 1960.

During 1960–73, medium term (maximum one year) export loans were supplied to manufacturers of export commodities or to export traders within a limit of 75 percent of the production or gathering costs. These were financed by counterpart funds.[17] The interest rate applied was 10 percent per annum of which 1 percent was collected by the BOK, 7 percent by the concerned commercial bank and the remaining 2 percent was added to the fund. Loans exceeding 2 million won required approval by the BOK, and the BOK itself allocated the funds among the commercial banks.

The Trade Financing Regulation was replaced by the Regulation on Export Finance in 1961.[18] According to the new regulation, the governor

---

[13] Finance No. 587 promulgated on February 5, 1948. Total short-term export loans amounted to 0.24 million won in 1948 and 0.23 million won in 1949. Korea Trader's Association, *Trade Yearbook, 1950*, p. 416.

[14] Regulations on Trade Financing promulgated by the Monetary Board on June 14, 1950. The interest rate was raised to 12.78 percent on April 1, 1951. The BOK started to determine separate interest rates to be applied for export credits after June 1, 1951.

[15] Trade Financing Regulation promulgated by the Monetary Board on July 21, 1955. The interest rate was revised to 13.87 percent on August 4, 1955.

[16] Decision by the Monetary Board on March 30, 1957.

[17] Rules on Export Promotion Fund Loans financed by the Counterpart Fund promulgated on November 5, 1959 by the Monetary Board.

[18] Regulation promulgated by the Monetary Board on February 1, 1961. According to the Monetary Board decision on July 6, 1961, the 90-day limit could be extended within the limit of an extra 45 days should there be an unavoidable delay in L/C delivery dates.

of the BOK could determine the limit of a loan on the basis of the L/C value and related expenses and, within a set limit, each financial institute could provide loans to licensed export traders who obtained L/C or export contracts with foreign traders for a term not exceeding 90 days. Since 1964, loans could also be provided to manufacturers who received orders from an export trader, and since 1965 domestic deliveries of raw materials to producers of export goods was considered to be export performance, thus making suppliers of domestic raw materials for exports eligible for credit financing.[19] In the case of bonded processing or re-exports, loans could be provided only for the value-added portion.[20] Suppliers of export products or of raw materials for export production could receive loans on the basis of the so-called "local L/C" issued by the licensed export trader.

Suppliers to the U.S. Forces under offshore procurement arrangements could also receive export loans after 1962, and in 1970, the benefit was extended to deepsea fishery and overseas construction projects which earn foreign exchange.

The short-term loans for export financing were provided at an interest rate of 13.8 to 9.13 percent per annum during 1960–63, 8.03 to 6.5 percent during 1963–67, 6 percent during 1967 to 1973 and 7 to 9 percent since May 1973. The financial institutes could obtain rediscounts from the BOK on export loans they provided for foreign currency earning activities at an interest rate of 10.22 to 5.48 percent during 1960–63, 4.38 to 4.5 percent during 1963–64 and 3.5 percent per annum since June 1964.[21]

The governor of the BOK set the limit for short-term export loans, per dollar exported, as (figure in parenthesis represents the prevailing exchange rate): 150 won on February 1, 1961 (130 won), 200 won on February 8, 1965 (255 won), 220 won on January 16, 1969 (267.84 won), 240 won on January 8, 1970 (303.60 won), 260 won on January 21, 1971 (371.45 won), 295 won on September 16, 1971 (370 won), 290 won on February 1, 1972, 350 won on March 2, 1972 (381.20 won), 380 won on November 12, 1974 (399 won) and 420 won on December 7, 1974 (483 won).

During 1964–69, a manufacturer producing export commodities could

---

[19] Revision on June 18, 1964 and revision on April 15, 1965.
[20] Revision by the Monetary Board on March 5, 1964.
[21] The Bank of Korea, *Monthly Economic Statistics*. Since 1972, the traders importing raw materials for export production could get export loans within the limit of 90 percent of import cost and within the limit of a quarter of the previous year's export performance and related raw material imports. However, the interest rate applied on bills for raw materials imported for export processing was higher than those applied to other export loans, i.e., 9 percent by commercial banks and 6.5 percent by BOK in its rediscounts. (The Monetary Board decision on February 25, 1972.)

get a loan of 120 won per dollar exported for three months (at an interest rate of 14 precent and BOK rediscount rate of 10.5 percent) with a loan ceiling of 5 million won from the Export Industry Promotion Fund.[22] Agricultural and fishery cooperatives and foreign exchange banks provided export preparation loans to finance the collection of nine agricultural and fishery items specified by the governor of the BOK (such as dried laver, cuttlefish and mushrooms).[23]

In order to promote orderly imports, price stabilization and export expansion, a special foreign currency loan fund was established by the BOK in 1952. Loans were provided to importers on the basis of their "export" performance. These loans were limited to $100,000 for a term of 60 to 90 days at an interest rate of 7.3 percent. The interest rate on loans to finance imports of raw materials for export production, ships and parts, and machinery for export production was 5 percent.[24] Due to the auction system of KFX introduced in 1954, the acquistition of foreign currency became easier and the foreign currency loans were abolished in November, 1954.

According to the Trade Finance Regulation promulagted by the Monetary Board in 1955, commercial banks could provide domestic currency loans to importers within a limit of 80 percent of the import value estimated by the BOK at an interest rate of 16.43 percent for a period of 90 days.[25]

After the devaluations early in 1961, the domestic currcney loans for import financing were abolished. However, in order to encourage a quick recovery from the recession which followed the military coup on May 16, 1961 foreign currency loans for import financing were reintroduced.[26]

---

[22] The Monetary Board decision on July 3, 1964.
[23] Regulation on Management of Agricultural and Fishery Products Export Preparation Fund. The limit on a loan was 70 to 80 percent of the total necessary expenses for a 90 to 240 day term at an interest rate of 12 percent between June 1969 and June 1970 and 6 percent thereafter. These loans amounted to 120 won per dollar exported at an interest rate of 26 percent (with the same 26 percent rediscount rate applied by the BOK) in 1966, and these were raised to 200 won per dollar exported in 1967, 220 won in 1969, and 260 won in 1971.
[24] Decision by the Monetary Board on November 27, 1952. The loan ceiling of $100,000 was removed on March 5, 1953. This preferential treatment was extended to anyone recognized as an "end-user" by the responsible minister at the time. Although these loans were rapaid in foreign currency, the importers had to deposit a won currency equivalent at the official exchange rate when they received the loans.
[25] However, a loan ceiling of 25 million won was imposed on August 4, 1955. The interest rate applied on BOK's rediscounts was 6.57 percent. After 1959, these import loans were limited to the total value of imports estimated by the commercial bank.
[26] These loans were financed with the foreign currency owned by banks according to the Regulation of Deposits in Opening Import L/C with Bank-Owned Foreign Ex-

Table 6.2. Short-Term Loans for Support of Exports by Deposit Money Banks

In Billion Won & Percent

	Total DMB Loans (A)[1]	Export Loans (B)[2]	(B/A)	Net Increase in Money Supply (M)	Net Increase in Bank Notes Issued (N)	Net Increase in Export Loans (B')	(B'/M)	(B'/N)
1961	32.1	0.8	2%	—	—	—	—	—
1962	43.2	1.6	4%	5.0	2.7	0.8	16%	30%
1963	49.1	2.7	5%	2.5	1.1	1.1	44%	100%
1964	53.1	2.5	5%	7.0	6.1	−0.2	−3%	−3%
1965	72.1	4.6	6%	16.7	7.3	2.1	13%	29%
1966	102.7	4.9	5%	19.5	11.3	0.3	2%	3%
1967	178.0	16.7	9%	37.9	21.6	11.8	31%	55%
1968	331.2	24.5	7%	54.9	27.7	7.8	14%	28%
1969	563.0	35.1	6%	74.1	34.2	10.6	14%	31%
1970	722.5	55.9	8%	55.6	29.0	20.8	37%	72%
1971	919.4	80.2	9%	50.4	27.9	24.3	48%	87%
1972	1,198.0	108.4	9%	161.4	58.2	28.2	17%	48%
1973	1,587.5	224.1	14%	210.9	108.6	115.7	55%	107%
1974	2,427.8	360.2	15%	215.4	100.9	136.1	63%	135%
1975	2,905.5	339.2	12%	236.1	106.3	−21.0	−9%	−20%
1976	3,522.1	461.8	13%	362.3	175.4	122.6	34%	70%

Source: The Bank of Korea, *Economic Statistics Yearbook*.
Notes: [1] Excluding remunerations of the Citizens National Bank.
[2] There are slight differences between these figures and the short-term export loan data in Table 6.4. which were also tabulated by the Bank of Korea but unpublished in its statastical yearbook.

Beginning in 1967, foreign exchange banks provided domestic currency loans either to finance imports of raw materials to be used in foreign currency earning activities or for imports of materials and equipment specified by the governor of the BOK.[27]

The regulation on import financing for exports was absorbed into the Export Financing Regulation on February 25, 1972 together with the Regnlation on Advanced Export Financing (promulgated on October 20, 1966) and Regulation on Domestically Produced Raw Material Financing (promulgated on November 26, 1971)[28].

Since exports have increased rapidly and steadily and since short-term export credit is provided automatically at a fixed proportion of the export amount, the net annual increase in export credit has also expanded rapidly. The average annual increase in export credit was equivalent to 16 percent of the increase in the money supply and 34 percent of that in bank notes issued during 1962–69. During 1970–76, however, the annual increase in export credit was equivalent to around 40 percent of the annual increase in the money supply and around 90 percent of the annual increase in bank notes issued on the average (excluding 1975).

A number of economists and policy makers in Korea seem to believe that the short-term export credit system financed by the unlimited rediscount of the BOK has eliminated the flexibility in the monetary policy. They argue that a rapid increase in exports results in a rapid increase of the money supply. Should the government try to control the rate of increase in the money supply, the non-export sectors are subject to an unduly harsh squeeze in credit supply which is likely to cause slower growth of the whole economy. If such an expansion of the money supply occurred without squeezing the credit supply to the non-export sectors, there would be, they seem to believe, an export-led inflationary pressure. However, there are also economists who argue that financing of rapidly expanding

---

change promulgated by the Monetary Board on October 12, 1961 and revised on October 26, 1962. An interest rate of 6 percent was applied, but the interest could be paid in domestic currency.

[27] Regulation on Import Financing promulgated by the Monetary Board on June 29, 1967. These loans were limited to the total CIF import value and 140 won per dollar of imports, respectively, and the loan period was for 90 to 135 days. The latter loans were to achieve stability in domestic commodity prices and hence were provided for such items as: timber, pulp, wool, scrap iron, crude oil, paper, cement, pig iron, iron and steel sheets, engines, special machinery, equipment and parts for motor vehicles.

[28] The interest rate applied on import loans by the commercial banks was 6 percent before 1971 and 9 percent thereafter. The BOK's rediscount rate was 5 percent before 1970, 3.5 percent in 1970 and 6.5 percent during 1971–72.

export activities may not necessarily result in inflation if the government adopts more flexible and liberal import policies.

B. Long-Term Financing for Export Industries

In 1965, the Medium Industry Bank (MIB) began to provide long-term loans on the basis of an MCI Notice to selected small and medium enterprises for the purpose of encouraging industries to specialize in or transfer into export production[29]. The loan funds were supplied by the government budget under the title of Funds to Promote Industries to Specialize in Export Production. The MCI Notice specified 13 eligible sectors to receive concentrated support for specialization in export production: raw silk, silk fabrics, radio and electrical equipment, canned sea-food or mushrooms, woolen products, plywood, cotton fabrics, leather products, sundry goods, pottery, rubber products, clothing, and handicrafts. But only the last four sectors received loans in the beginning. The loans were to finance new plant facilities or to repair and expand existing facilities, and the firms were required to finance more than 50 percent of the total cost with their own funds. The loan amount was limited to less than 10 million won per firm at an interest rate of 11 percent per annum repayable in five years (including a one year grace period).[30]

In 1969, loans were provided to firms manufacturing the following: silk fabrics, clothing, plywood, leather products, rubber footwear, radio and electronic equipment, pottery, plastic products, canned sea-food, mushrooms, tableware, sundry goods, wigs and handicrafts (including toy, wood products, sports goods, clothing accessories and gross-root wallpaper.[31] The loan ceiling was 30 million won for equipment funds (for a period of 8 years with a grace period of 3 years) and 20 million won for operating funds (for a period less than two or three years) if a firm was

---

[29] MCI Notice No. 1,995 promulgated on July 10, 1965.
[30] MCI Notice No. 4,160 promulgated on March 2, 1967; MCI Notice No. 4,614 promulgated on December 30, 1967; and MCI Notice No. 4,692 promulgated on February 20, 1968. In 1967, 200 million won were distributed to those industries specified in MCI Notice No. 1,995. The raw silk, canned sea-food, mushroom and plwood industries were excluded as were those firms that had already received an MIB equipment loan or export specialization loan in 1966. In 1968, 200 million won was distributed among these industries with a limit of 10 million won per recipient. The number of eligible firms was expanded by reducing the self-financing requirement from 50 percent to 30 percent.
[31] MCI Notice No. 4,382 promulgated on January 20, 1969.

considered by the MCI minister to deserving of support.[32]

In 1970, the distribution of loans for export specialization was limited to six sectors only: clothing, silk fabrics, electrical equipment, plastic products, tableware and pottery.[33] However in 1971, the eligible sectors included: clothing (excluding sewn goods), electronic products, pottery, tableware, sundry goods (toys, sporting goods, and furnitures only) and other sectors recommended by the competent minister.[34] The eligible firms were those which exported more than $100 thousand in 1970 ($50 thousand in the case of electronic products) and planned to export more than $200 thousand in 1971 or those which exported $50 thousand in 1970 (no export requirements for toy production) and planned to export more than $300 thousand in 1971.[35]

In order to promote exports of sundry goods the Medium Industry Bank also provided loans to firms exporting clothing accessories, toys, musical instruments, furniture, wood products, sporting goods, travel goods, handicrafts, artificial flowers, stationery and glasses.[36] In 1971, the Medium Industry Bank also provided loans to manufacturers of such products as adhesive tape, woven lables, buttons, shirt pins, and various plastic products.[37]

In order to concentrate government support for export promotion, the MCI selected "export specialization industries" and "strategic export industries" in 1972.[38] Those selected as export specialization industries were: raw silk, ginseng, silk fabrics, ramie products, wallpaper, pottery, tile and handicraft manufactures. Those selected as strategic export industries included manufactures of: electronic products, shipbuilding, rolling stock, steel and metal products, bicycles and parts, sewing machines, plastic products, footwear, leather products, clothing, tuna fish,

---

[32] MCI Notice No. 4,160 promulgated on July 14, 1969. Furthermore the eligibility requirement of having exported $300 thousand in the year prior to the loan application was reduced to $100 thousand.

[33] MCI Notice No. 5,703 promulgated on February 23, 1970.

[34] MCI Notice No. 6,187 promulgated on February 15, 1971.

[35] The expansion in the number of eligible enterprises in 1971 was coupled with a reduction in the interest rate for equipment loans to 10 percent per annum. MCI Notice No. 6,612, No. 8,260, No. 8,263 and No. 8,290.

[36] These loans were limited to 10 million won for equipment and 5 million won for operating funds. MCI Notice No. 5,687 promulgated on February 14, 1970, and MCI Notice No. 8,260 promulgated on January 14, 1972.

[37] MCI Notice No. 6,731 promulgated on May 1, 1971, and MCI Notice No. 7,451 promulgated on October 11, 1971.

[38] MCI Notice No. 8,263 promulgated on January 21, 1972, which replaced the original MCI Notice No. 1,995 promulgated in 1965.

and sundry goods.[39]

In 1971, the Korea Development Bank provided domestic currency loans to the following export industries: toys, electronics, plating, packing, textiles, metal products, machinery, plastic products, footwear, tire and tubes, leather products, pottery and sundry goods. Each loan was to be for more than 5 million won with a term of less than 5 years at an interest rate of 14 percent per annum. Recipients of these loans were obliged to export more than 3 times the loan amount in 2 years and more than 2 times annually for 3 years thereafter. After 1972, these KDB loans were reduced to insignificant amounts.

The Regulations on Export Industry Equipment Financing introduced in 1973 allowed equipment loans to manufacturers of export commodities or manufacturers of raw materials used in export production for a term of less than 8 years with a grace period of 2 to 3 years at an interest rate determined by the Federation of Financial Institutes.[40] A committee on export industry equipment financing was established in the BOK including related government and BOK officials. The governor of the BOK had the authority to determine the aggregate and sectoral magnitude of equipment loans to be assigned to each commercial bank for distribution (taking account of the overall financial stabilization plan and the funds availability in the financial institutions).[41]

C. Foreign Currency Loans for Imports of Capital Equipment

The government began to provide foreign currency loans through foreign exchange banks in 1967 in order to finance the importation of capital equipment and raw material to be used in export industries recommended by the MCI minister (including bonded processing and suppliers of the U.S. Forces under offshore procurement arrangements). These loans were also provided for import substituting industries and for government planned investment projects on the basis of the recommendation of the competent minister.[42] Foreign currency loans were provided mostly

---

[39] MCI Notice No. 7,050 promulgated on June 30, 1971. The total value of these loans was $17.75 million in 1971.

[40] Monetary board decision on February 9, 1973.

[41] Loans provided under this Regulation, at an interest rate of 12 percent per annum, totalled approximately 35 billion won in 1973, 56 billion won in 1973, 56 billion won in 1974, 61 billion won in 1975 and 77 billion won in 1976. The Bank of Korea, *Monthly Economic Statistics*

[42] Regulations on Foreign Currency Loans promulgated on May 18, 1967 by the Monetary Board and revised for the 6th time on February 1, 1968 (Articles 1, 2 and 3). This foreign currency loan replaced the import usance financing.

Table 6.3. Foreign Currency Loans

In Million Won

	Commercial Banks	Foreign Bank Branches	Specialized Banks	Total	(Total In Million Dollars)
1967	4,281	—	25,861	30,142	(111)
1968	8,509	—	46,141	54,650	(198)
1969	8,282	1,837	57,042	67,161	(234)
1970	4,954	4,982	91,460	101,396	(327)
1971	3,151	10,337	143,827	157,315	(455)
1972	2,324	14,798	85,663	102,785	(262)
1973	13,906	30,723	83,503	128,132	(322)
1974	34,454	48,792	111,563	194,809	(480)
1975	126,546	52,993	164,089	343,628	(710)
1976	137,915	60,143	148,091	346,149	(717)
1977	141,163	202,375	163,741	507,279	(1,050)

Source: The Bank of Korea, *Monthly Economic Statistics* (various issues).

Notes: Comercial banks are comprised of five nation-wide commercial banks, ten local banks and the banking accounts of the Korea Trust Bank. Specialized banks are comprised of the Korea Exchange Bank, the Medium Industry Bank, the Citizens National Bank, the Korea Housing Bank, the credit service section of the Agricultural and Fisheries Cooperatives.

with government held KFX, but the branches of foreign banks stationed in Korea have also provided loans since 1969.

Foreign currency loans for export industries were provided for a term of less than two and one half years at an interest rate of 6.5 percent per annum, and the loans for the others were provided for a term of less than 5 years for equipment imports and less than 2 years for raw material imports, both at an interest rate of 7.5 percent per annum.[43] The loan amount was limited to less than 70 percent of the import bill and, in the case of small and medium industries, to less than one hundred thousand dollars.[44] In 1969, the maximum amount of such loans was raised to 100

---

[43] Articles 8 and 11.

[44] The Regulation promulgated as of May 18, 1967 allowed loans up to 50 percent of the import value in the case of short-term equipment loans and up to 80 percent in the case of long-term equipment loans. On May 1, 1968, procedures covering imports for export industries with foreign currency loan funds were announced: 33 industries were made eligible for loans amounting to 30 percent of the value of imports from countries less than ten days shipping distance and 70 percent of the value of imports from other countries.

percent of the total import value for imports from countries more than ten days shipping distance from Korea.

On June 15, 1968, procedures were announced which regulated the use of machinery imported with foreign currency loans; the end-users of such machinery were required to export up to 900 percent of the imported value of the machinery within five years with 300 percent required within two years from the date of customs clearance and 200 percent each year for the following three years.[45]

In January 15, 1970 amendment to the Regulations on Foreign Currency Loans eliminated the limitations on interest rates (Article 11) and changed the term for loans to finance imports of plant equipment for export production to less than 5 years with a grace period of two and one half years (Article 8).[46] This amendment also allowed the governor of the BOK flexibility in determining the amount of a loan for raw materials imports for export production within the limit of their import value (Article 6). In 1972, for example, foreign currency loans were provided at an interest rate of 9.5 percent per annum (based on the decision of Monetary Board on December 16, 1971) to help import plant facilities and equipment for 16 selected sectors (electronics, bicycles, clothing, socks, sweaters, cotton fabrics, knitted goods, woolen fabrics, footwear, plastic goods, tire, and tubes, iron and steel products, pottery and tile, sundry goods, deep-sea fisheries and others) through the Korea Exchange Bank, the Korea Development Bank and other foreign exchange banks. The foreign currency loans provided by foreign bank branches were not subject to restrictions on sectoral allocation. The Korea Exchange Bank was allowed by the Monetary Board on December 16, 1972 to extend the repayment period of a loan by 50 percent if it is deemed necessary.

Total foreign currency loans by a financial institute are, in principle, limited to the extent of the institute's excess holdings of foreign currency. However, this restriction is exempted for loans to government managed enterprises, public enterprises and enterprises which can contribute to the improvement of the balance of payments. The coverage of foreign currency loans was extended in 1973 to include loans to develop foreign supply sources of important raw materials.[47] The interest rates on foreign currency loans was usually determined on the basis of the floating Eurodollar rate plus a 2 to 3 percent surcharge. On January 31, 1974, the Bank

---

[45] IMF, *op. cit.*, 1969, p. 274.

[46] The Regulation was revised again on February 9, 1973 to allow equipment loans for a period up to 8 years with a grace period of 3 years.

[47] Monetary Board decision on August 16, 1973.

Table 6.4. Loans for Exports

	1961	1962	1963	1964	1965	1966	1967	1968
								In Billion Won
Short-Term Loans (A)[1]	0.8	1.8	2.7	2.5	4.6	4.9	16.6	23.4
Export Credit	0.8	1.8	1.8	1.9	3.9	3.6	13.1	19.4
Suppliers in Foreign Currency[2]	—	—	0.9	0.5	0.7	1.2	3.4	3.6
Long-Term Loans (B)	—	—	—	0.2	0.6	1.1	3.7	10.6
Small & Medium Industries[3]	—	—	—	0.2	0.6	1.1	1.8	2.8
Foreign Currency Loans	—	—	—	—	—	—	1.9	7.8
Total Bank Loans (C)	52.3	67.5	76.7	84.8	108.9	230.4	230.4	397.6
A/C	2%	3%	4%	3%	4%	3%	7%	6%
B/C	—	—	—	0%	1%	1%	2%	3%

	1969	1970	1971	1972	1973	1974	1975	1976
Short-Term Loans (A)[1]	38.4	57.4	80.1	106.8	222.2	359.5	462.9	582.5
Export Credit	29.7	48.9	68.5	91.7	203.5	267.9	324.6	457.0
(Production & Collection)	(11.9)	(19.3)	(29.4)	(36.4)	(71.1)	(79.7)	(114.1)	(187.3)
(Raw Material Purchase)	(0.1)	(0.8)	(4.3)	(14.8)	(41.3)	(47.3)	(118.8)	(162.5)
(Raw Material Imports)	(17.7)	(28.7)	(34.8)	(40.6)	(92.1)	(141.0)	(91.7)	(107.2)
Supplier in Foreign Currency[2]	5.3	4.5	6.9	9.1	10.2	50.2	97.0	75.7
Agr. & Fishery Export Preparation	3.4	4.0	4.9	6.1	7.6	41.1	41.4	49.8
Long-Term Loans (B)	13.6	25.6	57.1	72.3	155.1	247.0	290.1	311.3
Small & Medium Industries[3]	3.3	4.2	5.0	5.2	6.6	9.8	8.9	9.1
Export on Credit	—	—	0.4	1.5	4.1	4.3	29.9	556.2
Foreign Currency Loans	10.3	21.4	51.7	65.6	100.2	166.6	178.9	179.0
Export Industry Equipment					44.2	66.3	72.3	67.0

Total Bank Loans (C)	659.1	851.4	1,077.0	1,437.1	1,906.0	2,853.5	3,483.3	4,464.8
A/C	6%	7%	7%	7%	12%	13%	13%	13%
B/C	2%	3%	5%	5%	8%	9%	8%	7%

Source: The Bank of Korea.
Notes: [1] Includes short-term loans from export industry promotion funds.
[2] Includes loans to suppliers of U.S. offshore procurements and services for military use abroad.
[3] Consists of loans by funds to convert facilities for export production, funds for concentrated support of firms producing exportables, funds to promote specialization in export production, funds to promote sundry goods manufacturing for export and those to support the export industry in general.

of Korea introduced a floating interest rate system under which interest rates for all foreign currency loans can fluctuate in accordance with six-month average Euro-dollar rates but the rates may not rise beyond a maximum which is set by the Monetary Board.

D. The Magnitude of Total Bank Loans for Exports

According to the BOK data on loans for exports, the share of such short-term loans in total KDB and DMB loans has increased from about 3 percent in 1961–66 to about 6 to 7 percent in 1967–72 and to between 12 and 13 percent in 1973–76. At the same time the share of long-term loans for export production has increased from about 1 to 3 percent in 1965–70, to between 8 and 9 percent in 1973–76. It seems that loans for exports were mostly on a short-term basis in the sixties but long-term loans for investment in export production began to increase rapidly in the early seventies so that nearly 40 percent of loans for exports were on a long-term basis by the mid-seventies. Total loans for exports amounted to about 3 to 5 percent of total KDB and DMB loans in 1962–66, 8 to 12 percent in 1967–72 and to around 21 percent in 1973–76.

According to these BOK data, long-term loans for exports were mostly loans by the small and medium industry export promotion fund and foreign currency loan funds. Hence one may approximate the magnitude of long-term loans for export production given the volume of Medium Industry Bank loans and (KFX) foreign currency loans. However, since all DMB and KDB loans have been allocated among industries according to the Regulations on Loan Funds which gave preferential treatment to export businesses, it may not be possible to adequately approximate the "long-term" financial support for export production in Korea on the basis of these two types of loans alone.

3. Distribution of Foreign Capital: Aid, Loans and Investments

A. Allocations of Foreign Grants-in-Aid

Most of Korea's imports in the fifties were financed from three sources: the U.S. bilateral assistance program, won redemptions from the United Nations Command (UNC) and grants-in aid from the United Nations

Korea Reconstruction Agency (UNKRA).[48] Foreign aid financed imports of food and essential raw materials and also financed about three-quarters of the total gross investment in the fifties.

The "non-project" aid dollars as well as government held foreign exchange were allocated by lottery at the official exchange rate or by competitive bidding in terms of won-deposits, purchase of national bonds or payments of additional tax. Industrial "end-users" and traders with a past record of importing usually got preferential treatment. Such complicated methods of allocating foreign exchange in the fifties created an effective exchange rate for most imports that was substantially above the official rate.[49]

The allocation of project assistance funds was made at the counterpart deposit rate which was almost the same as the official exchange rate.[50] The official exchange rate was applicable to government transactions and won sales to the UNC. As a result, the government resisted devaluation of the official exchange rate. Only because of great pressure from the United States, which used its leverage to delay release of aid funds, did devaluation of about 300 percent occur in 1953 and 1955.

The U.S. aid agency naturally influenced the allocation of aid funds for both investment projects and raw materials imports. They have even had a significant voice in decisions about long-term domestic credits derived from aid-generated counterpart funds. To quote Cole and Lyman[51]:

> Trade policies have clearly been one of the most important tools for resource allocation. In the 1950s Korea employed what Kindleberger has called a disequilibrium system to influence resource allocation. This consisted of a highly overvalued exchange rate that kept down the basic cost of imports; low tariffs or tariff exemption on favored imports such as capital and intermediate goods, accompanied by an extensive set of controls for allocating these goods to producers and other users; and finally high tariffs and/or prohibition on practi-

---

[48] The won advance to UN forces for local currency expenditures were repaid in dollars by the UNC at the official exchange rate, which amounted to $62 million in 1952, $122 million in 1953 and $38 million in 1954. The Bank of Korea, *Monthly Research Review*, December 1959.

[49] For a more detailed description on the multiple exchange rate system, see C. R. Frank, Jr., K. S. Kim and L. E. Westphal, *op. cit.*, Chapter 3.

[50] There was a separate exchange rate for depositing won revenue arising from the sales of aid imports into the Counterpart Fund Special Account. It was based on the "Agreement on Aid between the United States and the Republic of Korea" which became effective in December 1948.

[51] D. C. Cole and P. N. Lyman, *op. cit.*, p. 187.

Table 6.5. Summary of Foreign Economic Aid & Relief Goods Received: 1945-63

In Thousand U.S. Dollars

CY	Total	U.S.A.				CRIK		
		GARIOA	ECA & SEC	PL 480¹	ICA²	SUN	SKO	UNKRA²
1945	4,934	4,934	—	—	—	—	—	—
1946	49,496	49,496	—	—	—	—	—	—
1947	175,371	175,371	—	—	—	—	—	—
1948	179,593	179,593	—	—	—	—	—	—
1949	116,509	92,703	23,806	—	—	—	—	—
1950	58,706	—	49,330	—	—	—	9,376	—
1951	106,542	—	31,972	—	—	—	74,448	—
1952	161,327	—	3,824	—	—	10,299	145,235	1,969
1953	194,170	—	232	—	5,571	8,365	150,422	29,580
1954	153,925	—	—	—	82,437	14,049	36,142	21,297
1955	236,707	—	—	—	205,815	4,950	3,761	22,181
1956	326,705	—	—	32,955	271,049	24	307	22,370
1957	382,892	—	—	45,522	323,267	—	—	14,103
1958	321,272	—	—	47,896	265,629	—	—	7,747
1959	222,204	—	—	11,436	208,297	—	—	2,471
1960	245,394	—	—	19,913	225,237	—	—	244

Loan Allocation Policies 133

1961	199,245	—	44,926	154,319
1962	232,310	—	67,308	165,002
1963	216,483	—	96,828	119,659

Source: The Bank of Korea, *Economic Statistics Yearbook: 1961 & 1964.* (Original Source: Economic Cooperation Administration for GARIOA and ECA, Office of Supply for SEC and CRIK, UNKRA for UNKRA, and United States Operations Mission to Korea for ICA and PL 480.)

Notes: [1] Although a portion of the proceeds from sales of surplus agricultural commodities imported under the U.S. Public Law 480 is used by the U.S. Government and this portion cannot be regarded as foreign aid received, it is included here to show the total imports under the same law.

[2] Includes technical assistance and administrative expenses of the aid agency.

cally all imports that competed with domestic production. This system gave the government some very powerful tools for controlling the expansion of industrial capacity and the levels of operation and profitability of existing capacity . . . Because most of the imports in the 1950s were financed by foreign aid, the aid agencies were also involved in initial allocation decisions on capital goods imports and in subsequent adjustments of import controls to provide protection for new or expanding industries.

Since most of the major investments either for reconstruction or for new projects during the fifties and early sixties were financed with foreign aid, the decisions on these aid projects were a major factor in setting the investment pattern. On the other hand, since private domestic savings were negligible, the Korean Reconstruction Bank was formed in 1954 to provide long-term loans to key industries and the Agricultural Bank was established in 1958 to channel funds to agriculture and fisheries. However, both banks depended mainly on aid-generated conterpart funds for their financing. In this way aid inflows supported both the foreign and the domestic costs of most investment projects. By controlling both sources of financing, and also by manipulating import restrictions or domestic price ceilings to affect the profitability of different production activities, the government and the aid authority had a powerful set of tools for channeling investment activity. The influence of USAID on investment patterns continued even in the sixties, but their relative significance diminished in proportion to the declining size of U.S. grants-in-aid.

The aid authority favored investment in the final processing industries rather than in the more capital-intensive intermediate goods industries, and it insisted upon a mix of imports involving less capital goods than the Korean government wished. In order to forestall inflation, it wanted to put a large share of the limited resources into intermediate goods imports that would keep existing production facilities running, satisfy consumer demand and avoid the credit expansion and increased domestic spending likely to accompany new investment activity. In any case, the Korean government, which wanted to raise the level of foreign aid, argued repeatedly not only for more investment goods but also for more intermediate goods and food imports to restrain inflation, but it was not willing to raise the exchange rate.[52]

As the level of aid started to decline after 1957, with foreign exchange earnings remaining small, the reduced supplies of imports forced cut-

---

[52] *Ibid.*

Table 6.6.   U.S. Aid: 1953–77

In Million Dollars & Percent

BOK Data	AID (ICA) Assistance		PL 480 Aid	Total U.S. Aid
	Project	Non-Project		
1953				5.8 (0%)
1954	10.2 (1%)	72.3 (4%)		82.4 (4%)
1955	97.5 (5%)	108.4 (5%)		205.8 (10%)
1956	85.4 (4%)	185.7 (9%)	33.0 (2%)	304.0 (14%)
1957	92.7 (4%)	230.5 (10%)	45.5 (2%)	358.8 (16%)
1958	63.9 (3%)	201.7 (8%)	47.9 (2%)	313.5 (12%)
1959	43.6 (2%)	164.7 (6%)	11.4 (0%)	219.7 (8%)
1960	50.9 (2%)	174.7 (6%)	19.9 (1%)	245.5 (9%)
1961	36.1 (1%)	118.2 (4%)	44.9 (2%)	199.3 (7%)
1962	16.6 (1%)	148.4 (5%)	67.3 (2%)	232.3 (8%)
1963	11.0 (0%)	108.6 (3%)	96.8 (3%)	216.5 (6%)
1964	6.0 (0%)	82.3 (2%)	61.0 (2%)	149.3 (4%)
1965	4.9 (0%)	67.0 (2%)	59.5 (1%)	131.4 (3%)
1966	5.1 (0%)	60.2 (1%)	38.0 (1%)	103.3 (2%)
1967	5.7 (0%)	47.0 (1%)	44.4 (1%)	97.0 (2%)
1968	6.6 (0%)	43.4 (1%)	55.9 (1%)	105.9 (2%)
1969	13.3 (0%)	19.2 (0%)	74.8 (1%)	107.3 (1%)
1970	3.9 (0%)	17.0 (0%)	61.7 (1%)	82.6 (1%)
1971	5.2 (0%)	12.4 (0%)	33.7 (0%)	51.2 (1%)
1972	4.5 (0%)	0.6 (0%)	— (—)	5.1 (0%)
1973	2.3 (0%)	— (—)	— (—)	2.3 (0%)
1974	1.0 (0%)	— (—)	— (—)	1.0 (0%)
1975	1.2 (0%)	— (—)	— (—)	1.2 (0%)
1976	1.7 (0%)	— (—)	— (—)	1.7 (0%)
1977	0.9 (0%)	— (—)	— (—)	0.9 (0%)

Source: The Bank of Korea, *Economic Statistics Yearbook* and *National Income Statistics Yearbook*.

Note: Figures in the parentheses represent percentage ratios of U.S. aid to GNP (all in terms of 1970 dollar prices). Project assistance includes technical, defence & development grants.

backs in both production and new investment, causing stagnation. Competition for import quotas of aid goods became more intense and much of the industrial investment was guided by the desire to qualify for larger import quotas, even if the existing capacity was not fully utilized.

The magnitude of U.S. aid was equivalent to between 10 and 16 percent

Table 6.7. U.S. Non-Project Assistance

In Million Dollars & Percent

	1954–61		1962–66		1967–71	
Total	1,255.5	(100%)	436.2	(100%)	143.9	(100%)
Agricultural Products	275.6	(22%)	34.4	(8%)	15.2	(11%)
Minerals	28.2	(2%)	6.6	(2%)	1.1	(1%)
Others*	33.4	(3%)	14.2	(3%)	5.8	(4%)
Manufactured Products	918.4	(73%)	381.1	(87%)	121.8	(85%)
Food Products	30.4	(2%)	9.9	(2%)	0.0	(0%)
Textile Products	107.5	(9%)	17.7	(4%)	8.0	(6%)
Misc. Manufactures	92.5	(7%)	56.3	(13%)	30.2	(21%)
Chemical Products	560.6	(45%)	266.4	(61%)	72.7	(51%)
Nonmetallic Mineral	15.3	(1%)	0.0	(0%)	—	(—)
Steel & Metal	39.8	(3%)	25.6	(6%)	1.4	(1%)
Machinery	72.3	(6%)	5.1	(1%)	9.5	(7%)

Source: Table B. 4.
*Include ocean freight, military surplus commodities, fishery supplies, construction materials and other unclassifiable goods.

Table 6.8. Imports of Surplus Agricultural Products under U.S. PL 480: 1956–76

In Million Dollars & Percent

	PL 480 (Grants-in Aid)			PL 480 Title I (Loans)			
	Total	Wheat	Cotton	Total[1]	Wheat	Cotton	Rice
1956	33.0	23%	25%				
1957	45.5	3%	4%				(59%)[2]
1958	47.9	63%	1%				
1959	11.4	32%	61%				
1960	19.9	93%	4%				
1961	44.9	45%	48%				
1962	67.3	39%	46%				
1963	96.8	58%	33%				
1964	61.0	41%	50%				
1965	59.5	48%	50%				
1966	38.0	30%	70%				
1967	44.4	18%	77%				
1968	55.9	49%	44%				
1969	74.8	42%	52%	78.7	19%	—	75%
1970	61.7	53%	44%	45.9	1%	—	86%
1971	33.7	53%	47%	68.9	30%	14%	45%
1972	—	—	—	184.2	40%	6%	44%
1973	—	—	—	60.4	35%	24%	28%
1974	—	—	—	—	—	—	—
1975	—	—	—	84.0	—	—	100%
1976							

Source: The Bank of Korea, *Economic Statistics Yearbook* (for grants-in-aid data) and USAID-Korea (for loan data).

Notes: [1] Includes corn.
[2] Grants-in aid in 1957.

of GNP during 1955–58 and to around 8 percent during 1959–61. However, its magnitude rapidly declined from about 8 percent of GNP at the beginning of the first five year plan period to about 2 percent at the end of the period. The magnitude of U.S. aid was further reduced to 1 percent of GNP during the second five year plan period and decreased to a negligible amount after 1972. It was completely terminated in 1978. One may say that although the Korean economy was heavily affected by the inflow of U.S. aid during 1954–61, its influence declined rapidly during 1962–66 and became negligible thereafter. Since 1967, the foreign capital inflow has been dominated by foreign loans and investments instead of grants-in aid.

During 1954–61, nearly two-thirds of the U.S. aid was for non-project assistance which financed imports of various raw materials and finished consumer, intermediate and investment goods. The remaining one-third was for project assistance and surplus agricultural products under PL 480. The amount of project assistance was fairly large during 1954–62, but became negligible thereafter. However, both the PL 480 grants-in-aid and the non-project assistance continued in significant amounts until 1971. The capital goods imported under non-project assistance were distributed to selected businessmen and the raw material imports were distributed mostly to the so-called "end-users" who possessed the production facilities. Although the imports financed by aid dollars were subject to customs duties and various forms of taxes, the aid dollars were sold, in principle, on the basis of the official exchange rate which was about half of the estimated parity rate (or black market rate) during 1953–61. Hence it was this distribution mechanism which was frequently accused of being the source of corruption in Korea in the fifties.

The total U.S. non-project assistance during 1954-61 amounted to about $1.3 billion. About 45 percent of it was allocated for financing chemical product imports, 24 percent for agricultural and food products and 9 percent for textile products. The aid-financed imports of chemical products consisted mainly of fertilizer and refined petroleum, while the imports of agricultural and food products consisted mainly of raw cotton, wheat, barley, raw sugar, raw rubber, tallow, lumber and logs.[53] Imports of textile products were made up almost exclusively of rayon yarn and worsted yarn. The non-project assistance also financed imports of a significant quantity of machinery and equipment, steel and metal products (such as iron and steel shapes and nonferrous metals), minerals (such as bituminus coal and nonmetallic minerals) and various other manufactures such as paper, pulp, flat glass and cement.

There were no basic shifts in the composition of non-project assistance during 1962–66 except that the amount of aid allocated for machinery became very small. About 61 percent of total non-project assistance during 1962–66 was allocated for chemical products, 10 percent for agricultural and food products, 6 percent for steel and matal products, 4 percent

---

[53] Other chemical products included dyestuffs, medical supplies, pesticides, synthetic plastic, explosives and coaltar pitch.

for textile products and 13 percent for various miscellaneous manufactures. During 1962–66, the quantity of aid-financed imports of textile fibres declined significantly, imports of fertilizer and refined petroleum continued to take a large portion of non-project assistance, and there were significant increases in imports of paper products, rubber products, various chemicals and nonferrous metal products. Imports of fertilizer continued from 1967 to 1969 but during 1967–72 most of the non-project assistance was allocated to paper products, chemicals, rubber products, textile fibres and machinery.

Since 1956, the PL 480 grants-in-aid provided such surplus U.S. agricultural commodities as wheat, cotton, barley, sorghum, corn, tallow, tobacco and rice, amounting to around $50 million a year during 1956–71. During 1959–71, more than 90 percent of PL 480 aid consisted of wheat and cotton. The distribution of aid-financed wheat and cotton nourished the flour milling and cotton textile industries which were the major growth industries in the fifties and early sixties. The flour milling industry remained a domestic-comsumption-based industry but the cotton textile industry was developed into a major export sector in the sixties. The PL 480 Title I loans were introduced in 1969 and they mostly financed the importation of rice, wheat and cotton. The PL 480 grants-in-aid terminated in 1971 and the inflow of U.S. surplus agricultural products began to be financed by long-term loans and KFX only. By 1975, the PL 480 loans only financed rice imports. Wheat and cotton which have an extensive market in Korea have had to be imported with KFX and other foreign loans since 1974.

The amount and composition of U.S. non-project assistance and PL 480 grants-in-aid seem to have been-determined on the basis of the estimated needs for various basic necessities for subsistence and reconstruction. The massive inflow of such aid-financed imports helped keep the prices of various necessities at a relatively low level and also helped maintain a domestic consumption pattern which could not be achieved without such aid-inflow. One may say that the direction of import substitution in the fifties and early sixties was heavily influenced by the pattern of U.S. non-project assistance and PL 480 grants-in-aid, since there was always pressure on the Korean government to undertake import substitution to maintain the aid-supported consumption pattern while the U S. project assistance helped such effort for self-sufficiency.

The two major finished commodity items imported with aid funds were fertilizers and petroleum products. Other important items were rayon yarn, worsted yarn, paper, pulp, tires and tubes, dyestuffs, medical supplies, explosives, pesticides, plastic, cement, iron and steel shapes, flat glass and nonferrous metals. Cotton cloth and cotton yarn were also imported with aid funds during 1954–55, but since the cotton textile industry had a long history of development in Korea, its recovery from the war damages was very quick and there were no aid-financed imports of cotton textiles after 1956. Import substitution for such items as cement, plate glass and explosives, started in the late fifties while that of other items occurred in the sixties. Such import substituting industries were supported by allocation of aid funds and KFX for their imports of capital goods and raw materials and were protected by strict import restrictions.

In the fifties, part of the capital goods imports were financed by project assistance which was sold at official exchange rates, and the rest were financed by auctioned foreign exchange (non-project assistance funds and KFX) which, while more expensive, made it possible to dispense with much of the time consuming red tape. The subsidies which had been associated with project assistance was very much reduced with the introduction of a unified exchange rate system in the early sixties and the absolute amount of project assistance itself became negligible after 1963. The non-project assistance continued financing imports of capital goods and raw materials in the sixties, but its magnitude also became negligible after 1969. The important items of raw material imports financed with non-project assistance funds included raw rubber, non-metallic minerals, animal hides, bituminous coal (none in the sixties) abaca, pulp, lumber and logs and coaltar pitch (none in the sixties).

The aid-financed imports of various finished goods helped maintain a relatively lower level of domestic prices for those commodities but did not discourage production expansion. Any import substituting efforts for such commodities were encouraged by the government and U.S. aid authority by allocating KFX and aid funds for necessary capital goods and raw materials and through protection measures after establishment.

One can easily observe that the list of aid-financed import commodities corresponds almost exactly with the list of major import substituting investments in the fifties and sixties. One may conclude that, from the end of the Korean War until the late sixties, the U.S. aid first financed imports of various finished products and raw materials which were felt to be necessary to maintain an adequate consumption pattern in Korea and second financed the import substitution for these goods in order to eliminate the need for (aid-financed) imports.

The local currency revenue from the sales of aid financed imports were transferred to the Korean government as counterpart funds. During 1954–

61, more than a third of the counterpart funds (excluding revenues from PL 480 program which were used mostly for defence expenditures) were used for direct military support: about half of them were distributed for investments in the agricultural, mining, manufacturing, and transportation sectors, and about 10 percent of them were spent for health, education and social welfare. The amount of counterpart funds steadily decreased during 1962–73 and, furthermore, the funds have almost entirely been spent for military and public administration expenditures since 1962.

B. *Allocation of Foreign Loans and Investments*

Faced with the prospect of declining U.S. grants-in-aid, the first serious efforts to attract foreign loans and investment were made in 1960. The Foreign Capital Inducement Promotion Law allowed foreign direct or joint investment, capital and technology inducement and foreign cash loans.[54] Foreign investment business (as well as royalty earning from technology inducement) was entitled to complete exemption from income and corporation tax for the first five years, a two-third exemption for the following 2 years and a one-third exemption for the next year.[55] Capital equipment imported for foreign invested businesses were also exempted from tariffs.[56] The wage earnings of foreign managers and technicians were completely tax exempt for the first three years and half exempt for the following five years.[57] Furthermore, the Law granted income tax exemption on interest earnings arising from foreign loans for the first five years and half exemption for the following three years. This was amended to a complete income tax exemption without specifying a time limit in 1963.[58]

In order to meet the high investment requirements of the three Five-Year Plans, the government continuously amended old laws and adopted

---

[54] Law No. 532 promulgated on January 1, 1960.
[55] Article 19 and Article 20 of Law No. 532. The law was further clarified and supplemented by a Special Law on Capital Goods Inducement on a Long Term Settlement Basis, Law No. 1114, promulgated on July 31, 1962 and revised into Law No. 1317 on April 11, 1963. All these regulations were incorporated into the new Foreign Capital Inducement Law (Law No. 1802) promulgated on August 3, 1966. The income arising from Foreigner's share in a foreign investment project continued to receive exemption from income and corporation tax for the first five years, but the exemption was reduced to one-half (instead of two-thirds) for the following three years (instead of two years).
[56] Article 27 of Law No. 532.
[57] Article 23 of Law No. 532.
[58] Article 25 of Law No. 532. Law No. 1317 promulgated on April 11, 1963, which was integrated into Law No. 1802 on August 3, 1966.

new laws to encourage an inflow of foreign loans and investment. The government has also provided guarantees of repayment and repatriation to foreign lenders and investors since 1962. The guaranteeing institutions were the Korea Development Bank and the Bank of Korea and they received government authorization on a case-by-case basis.[59] No limits were placed on conversion and remittance of legitimate profits and dividends and up to 20 percent of the original capital invested could be repatriated each year; two years after the commencement of operations in Korea.

While the amount of bank (savings and) loans increased greatly following the interest rate reform in 1965, they still could not meet the full range of needs for loan funds. The commercial banks were neither accustomed nor equipped to enter into longer term financing except when directly ordered by the government. They also could not satisfy working capital needs. The main long-term lending institution was the Korean Reconstruction Bank which depended on the limited government fiscal funds and repayments of past loans. Private enterprises, in the absence of well developed institutional arrangements for equity financing, and in light of the shortage of long-term loan finances and high interest rates on short-term funds, were very much inclined to look abroad to finance their capital expansion needs. On the other hand, not only did the government open the doors to external credit from private sources in order to fill the gap in the domestic financing institutions, but it also continued to improve policies that encouraged private lending from abroad. Since the restoration of normal diplomatic and commercial relations with Japan in 1965, the government has also tried to increase the inflow of Japanese capital.[60]

According to the Foreign Capital Inducement Law promulgated in 1966, the EPB minister could approve the inflow of foreign investments to businesses if the inflow would contribute significantly to the improvement of the balance of payments position and development of key industries, public enterprises and projects sepcified in the economic development plan.[61] When authorizing foreign capital inducement, the EPB minister had to seek the opinion of the competent minister who, in turn, was required to transmit his opinion to the EPB in less than fifty days. When

---

[59] Law on Repayment Guarantee of Foreign Loan, Law No. 1115, promulgated on July 31, 1962, which was replaced by the Foreign Capital Inducement Law in 1966.
[60] D. C. Cole and P. N. Lyman, *op. cit.*, p. 181.
[61] Law No. 1802 promulgated on August 3, 1966, which replaced the Foreign Capital Inducement Promotion Law of 1960 and the Special Law on Capital Goods Inducement on a Long Term Settlement Basis of 1962.

Table 6.9. Guarantees of Repayment of Foreign Loans

In Billion Won

	Commercial Banks	Specialized Banks	KDB[1]	Total Guarantees
1962	3	—	2	5
1963	4	—	18	22
1964	10	—	38	48
1965	12	1	62	75
1966	40	1	103	144
1967	50	98	143	291
1968	126	223	175	524
1969	225	342	300	866
1970	319	455	424	1,198
1971	436	564	600	1,600
1972	422	662	611	1,695
1973	585	778	787	2,150
1974	789	1,063	1,311	3,163
1975	1,448	1,270	1,480	4,198
1976	2,165	1,484	2,512	6,161

Source: The Bank of Korea, *Monthly Economic Statistics*.
Note: [1] Includes guarantees for KEB (Korea Exchange Bank) foreign exchange.

applications for authorization compete with each other in the same business field, the competent minister was required to recommend the most appropriate recipient.

Private foreign loans were generally first agreed to by Korean borrowers and foreign lenders, who then sought approval from the Korean government for the issuance of a guarantee. While the Korea Development Bank actually guaranteed the repayment in won, and the Bank of Korea assured convertibility of the won into foreign exchange, the Economic Planning Board had the dominant voice within the administration on which projects should be approved. Finally, all such guarantees required the formal approval of the National Assembly, which, while often complaining loudly about specific projects, generally was brought around to granting the approval by various inducements.[62]

In 1966, the government allowed repayment guarantees of foreign private loans by the commercial banks within the limit of their net worth

---

[62] D. C. Cole and P. N. Layman, *op. cit.*, p. 181.

or time deposits and allowed the Bank of Korea to guarantee convertibility of the won into foreign exchange on the basis of the assurance of foreign exchange repayment issued by the commercial banks.[63] The approval of private loans increased rapidly after the government introduced this system of repayment guarantees by the commercial banks that bypassed the need for review and approval by the National Assembly; a process which required much maneuvering and often payoffs by the borrower. With the introduction of the system of commercial bank guarantees, the government repayment guarantees are limited to loans to large scale key national industries which are regarded as difficult for a commercial bank to guarantee. The Minister of Finance has to seek the opinion of banking institutions on matters relating to cash loan contracts or capital goods inducement contracts before transmitting his opinion to the EPB minister. However, the commercial banks, which are all controlled by the government, frequently did not scrutinize the proposed investment before agreeing to guarantee the borrower's repayments.[64] Since very few foreign borrowings could be acquired without a repayment guarantee, the foreign loan guarantees gave the government, and particularly the Economic Planning Board which assumed the main responsibility for approval, a means of controlling the kinds of investment and loans being undertaken.

On October 12, 1972, a set of criteria was announced for the inducement of foreign investment in industrial projects which gave highest priority to export-oriented and import substituting industries. In accordance with these criteria, foreign investment was acceptable in 209 lines of activity (that is, 138 export-oriented industries and 71 import-substituting industries). Foreign investment in 29 industries which were regulated by law, such as cigarette and ginseng, was prohibited and foreign investment in such fields as mining, airlines, marine transportation, railroads and electric power was restricted. For the manufactures of electronic products and machinery, foreign participation were, with certain exceptions, allowed only on a fifty-fifty venture basis.[65]

---

[63] Korea Traders Association, *Foreign Trade Yearbook: 1967*, p. 114, and Regulation on Foreign Repayment Guarantee and Exceptional Measure on Foreign Repayment Guarantee promulgated by the Monetary Board on January 25, 1966.

[64] Due to frequent failures of the repayment-guaranteed enterprises to fulfill their obligations, the Law amended on April 12, 1973 included the following punitive provision. That is, when a government repayment guaranteed enterprise is a juridical person, the directors and executive officers are jointly and severally liable for compensation of all damages inflicted on the government. See Law No. 2598, Article 32.

[65] IMF, *op. cit.*, 1973, **p.** 295 and *op. cit.*, 1975, p. 297.

In the earlier period when U.S. aid was the main source of savings, the government and the aid authority controlled the allocation of aid and domestic credit throughout the economy and thereby exerted a strong direct influence over both the public and private sectors. However, in the late sixties private domestic savings and private foreign capital inflows have assumed a dominant role in the financing of investment and production in the private sector, especially in manufacturing. Foreign government loans and World Bank loans have gone increasingly to public investment in the SOC sectors and to government-owned manufacturing enterprises such as fertilizers and oil refining. The government has retained control over the approval of foreign private loans, but the approval process is relatively more flexible and expeditious than that previously associated with grant aid projects.[66]

---

[66] D. C. Cole and P. N. Lyman, *op. cit.*, p. 195.

CHAPTER 7

FACTOR MARKET DISTORTIONS

1. Major Sources of Factor Market Distortions

Various government policies often make capital relatively cheep and induce the adoption of capital intensive (imported) technology and/or the undertaking of capital intensive production. Such production may be profitable to the subsidized private entrepreneur but may imply a loss for the country as a whole when calculated in terms of real opportunity costs of capital. Moreover, the net effect of these policies may be to reduce employment opportunities and to retard the growth of GNP. This chapter investigates the extent of factor maket distortions in Korea by estimating the real interest rates on various loans, the real opportunity cost of capital and the implicit subsidies on capital use in Korea.

The reduction of income-taxes on some selected production activities improves the profitability of such activities and hence affects the employment growth through shifts in the output mix. Although the wages received by crewmen on deepsea fishing vessels as well as income accruing from raising livestock, forestry, overseas shipping and air transportation have all been exempt from income taxes in Korea, the share of outputs from these sectors in gross national produce has been relatively small. Investment credits, accelerated depreciation allowances and income tax reductions (or exemption) for selected major industries can also generate distortions, but are not believed to have been really significant in absolute magnitude in Korea. Total corporation tax revenue itself usually amounted to less than 10 percent of total government revenue and the rate of

Table 7.1. Major Investment Funds Under Direct Government Control

In Billion Won & Percent[1]

	Type of Funds		Gross Domestic Capital Formation	Major Sources of Funds			Net Annual Foreign Borrowing
	Net Increase in KDB & DMB Loans	Gov't Investment		Net Increase in Time & Savings Deposit	Net Increase in Bank Notes Issued	Implicit Gov't Revenue Surplus[2]	
1962	15 (33%)	18 (20%)	46	7 (15%)	3 (7%)	— (—)	9 (20%)
1963	9 (10%)	17 (17%)	90	1 (1%)	1 (1%)	— (—)	20 (22%)
1964	8 (8%)	24 (20%)	102	2 (2%)	6 (6%)	— (—)	6 (6%)
1965	24 (20%)	46 (20%)	122	16 (13%)	7 (6%)	— (—)	−2 (−2%)
1966	41 (18%)	54 (19%)	225	40 (18%)	11 (5%)	19 (8%)	28 (12%)
1967	81 (29%)	98 (23%)	281	59 (21%)	22 (8%)	38 (14%)	52 (19%)
1968	167 (39%)	143 (23%)	428	127 (30%)	28 (7%)	90 (21%)	122 (29%)
1969	262 (42%)	142 (20%)	621	196 (32%)	34 (5%)	103 (17%)	158 (25%)
1970	193 (27%)	160 (20%)	705	125 (18%)	29 (4%)	121 (17%)	193 (27%)
1971	226 (28%)	255 (32%)	805	132 (16%)	28 (3%)	146 (18%)	295 (37%)
1972	361 (45%)	201 (16%)	806	203 (25%)	58 (7%)	63 (8%)	148 (18%)
1973	469 (36%)	335 (16%)	1,289	303 (24%)	109 (8%)	133 (10%)	123 (10%)
1974	947 (45%)	618 (25%)	2,102	236 (11%)	101 (5%)	189 (9%)	820 (39%)
1975	630 (25%)	784 (26%)	2,478	460 (19%)	106 (4%)	317 (13%)	913 (37%)
1976	982 (32%)		3,039	631 (21%)	175 (6%)	629 (21%)	152 (5%)

Sources: Bank of Korea, *Economic Statistics Yearbook* and *National Income in Korea*.

Notes: [1] Figures in the parentheses represent percentage ratio to gross domestic capital formation.

[2] The difference between government investment & loans and government deficit financing (i.e., net borrowings from the Bank of Korea, government bonds issued, net foreign borrowings and foreign aid).

direct tax exemption amounted to less than 10 percent on the average during 1966–76. The reduction of income tax by 50 percent for business activities earning foreign currency (which was effective until 1973) significantly benefited export production in general, but did not directly discriminate among industries.

In terms of money value, the annual net increase in the amount of loans by the deposit money banks (DMB) and the Korea Development Bank (KDB) during 1967–76 was equivalent to about 35 percent of annual gross domestic capital formation on the average. At the same time the annual government investment was equivalent to about 20 percent of the annual gross domestic capital formation. In other words, the government was able to directly influence the allocation of funds equivalent to more than half of the gross domestic capital formation during 1967–76. The annual net foreign borrowing, which was also subject to government control, amounted to about 25 percent of gross domestic capital formation from 1967 to 1975.

In this chapter, therefore, we are going to concentrate on what seem to have been the most important sources of factor market distortions in Korea in terms of the absolute magnitude of subsidies involved. These are: (1) bank loans whose interest rates are much lower than the curb market rate, (2) foreign loans which cost much less than those acquired domestically and (3) direct government investments which can be regarded as subsidies to selected industries from the viewpoint of the entire national economy. Since every financial institution is tightly controlled by the government in Korea, the allocation of bank loans may be regarded as government subsidies. However, although the inflow of foreign loans and investments has been controlled by the government, one may not regard them literally as "government" subsidies.

On the other hand, currency overvaluation or tariff exemptions on imported capital goods can lead to relatively low prices for (imported) capital goods. Therefore, we will also try to approximate the magnitude of such implicit subsidies on factor use and the fraction of capital goods that were imported.

When capital is provided at an interest rate which is less than its real opportunity cost in the country some form of capital rationing must exist between firms. If every firm intending to invest in a plant receives a lump sum allocation of subsidized credit and is forced to borrow the additional funds at the prevailing curb interest rate, the choice of technique may not be affected at all. But such a uniform lump sum allocation system does not exist in Korea. On the other hand, if some selected firms are able to obtain all the capital they wish at subsidized prices, while others are confronted with higher prices, the effect on the choice of technique can be highly significant. That is, those who can finance their entire investment expenses at subsidized interest rates are likely to use highly capital intensive technology (unless they can smuggle out subsidized loans to the curb market or use them for other unauthorized projects) while others who have to rely exclusively on curb loans will use much less capital intensive production techniques. One can also presume that these offset each other as far as the factor intensity of the whole national economy is concerned.

If those who obtained loans at subsidized interest rates had been free to use the funds however they pleased, they would more likely have tended to use less capital intensive methods of production, reflecting higher opportunity costs of capital. That is, the distortions in factor markets need not result in any distortions in actual industrial factor use. In most cases, however, the domestic or foreign loans in Korea were earmarked for specific projects. There was, at least in principle, no option but to use the borrowed funds at subsidized interest rates for specified projects or to give up the idea of using bank or foreign loans altogether. Hence the legal interest rate itself (plus some unavoidable associated costs) may be regarded as the opportunity cost of a bank loan. Of course the irregular practice of smuggling out loan funds for other unauthorized activities does not seem to have been uncommon. Judging from the actual pattern of industrial capital formation in Korea, however, one may assume that such irregular practices were rather limited in absolute magnitude and were more or less exceptional.

In Korea, a would-be entrepreneur who intends to build a factory either with a bank loan or with a foreign loan usually does not obtain all the necessary funds for the project at a subsidized interest rate. He knows that he has to finance some portion (say, ten or twenty percent) of the necessary capital with his own funds which can command the curb interest rate. If a would-be investor knows that he will either be able to get a loan at a subsidized interest rate to build a factory or will be rejected completely, then he is in effect confronted with having some fixed amount of capital at a subsidized price and it may pay him to propose more capital-using techniques than if he had to finance the whole project with capital obtained at curb market prices. After all, since either a bank loan or a foreign loan is provided at a very subsidized interest rate, even a project with fairly excessive capital intensity can be profitable. Furthermore, although an entrepreneur cannot obtain unlimited loans from the government (i.e., banks or foreign loan sources) or the curb market, the amount he can get from the curb market usually depends on his overall credit picture which is favorably influenced by the amount of subsidized credits he obtains from the government. Therefore, we may well assume that entrepreneurs choose the factor combinations in production on the basis of the weighted average price of capital (i.e., the weighted average price of subsidized loans and curb market loans). In this paper, we asume that sectoral factor intensities are determined on the basis of the average wage rate and weighted average interest rate on capital use.

One of the most familiar themes in development economics is that wages paid by the modern manufacturing industry are higher than the marginal social cost of labor, while capital tends to be under-priced, which together tend to make the private profitability of capital-intensive project exceed their social profitability. Most literature on labor markets in developing countries suggests that either labor legislation or trade union activities are the major sources of the above-opportunity-cost wage rates. In Korea, wage differences cannot be explained by the existence of powerful labor unions or by government legislation. The apparent differences between rural and urban wages may reflect an imperfectly-functioning labor market coupled with structural distortions. It is also possible that higher urban wages may mostly reflect the higher costs associated with urban living in such areas as housing, transportation and public service fees.

We will first examine the implicit subsidies on capital use in the form of low-priced imported capital goods. Then we will estimate the magnitude and interest rates for domestic and foreign loans and the associated subsidies on capital use by estimating the real opportunity cost of capital use in Korea. However, we will not attempt to investigate labor market distortions, assuming that deliberate government policies do not cause very significant distortions. We will simply keep the possibility in mind that the labor price could have been higher than its real opportunity cost due to a Lewis-type dualism.

2. Underpricing of Imported Capital Goods

A. Aid-Financed Capital Goods Imports

Most of Korea's imports were financed by U.S. grants-in aid between 1953 and 1961 which may be called an era of currency overvaluation.

Table 7.2. Aid-Financed Capital Goods Imports

In Million 1970 Dollars

	1954–61		1962–66		1967–71	
Total Project Assistance	523.6	(24%)	58.6	(2%)	30.1	(0%)
Agriculture & Forestry	30.0	(1%)	2.0		3.9	
Fishery	5.4		0.3		—	
Mining	7.3		8.4		1.1	
SOC Sectors	303.8	(14%)	27.1	(1%)	0.3	
Service Sectors	84.7	(4%)	14.3		24.8	
Manufacturing	92.4	(4%)	6.5		—	
Food Products	2.3		0.1		—	
Textile Products	5.8		—		—	
Misc. Manufactures	19.1	(1%)	2.0		—	
Chemical Products	47.7	(2%)	4.3		—	
Nonmetallic Mineral Products	2.3		—		—	
Steel & Metal	3.7		—		—	
Machinery	11.6		0.2		—	
U.S. Non-Project Machinery Imports	92.3	(4%)	6.1	(0%)	9.7	(0%)
Gross Fixed Capital Formation	2,224.0	(100%)	3,046.0	(100%)	9,102.0	(100%)

Source: Tables B.14. and B.15.
Note: U.S. wholesale price index for machinery and equipment (1970 = 100) was applied to the U.S. project and non-project machinery imports in order to get 1970 dollar figures. Gross fixed capital formation data are from Table 7.3.

About a quarter of the total U.S. aid during 1954–61 was project-assistance for specific investment projects. The absolute amount of project assistance was negligible after 1962. The share of capital goods in total non-project assistance was about 6 percent during 1954–61, but their share also became insignificant in the sixties (except the machinery imports which amounted to several million dollars in 1969 and 1970). About two-thirds of the capital goods imports financed by non-project assistance during 1954–61 consisted of various types of industrial machinery and the rest were electrical machinery and transport equipment such as generators, electrical apparatus and auto spare parts.

During the period 1954 to 1961, about 58 percent of the total U.S. project assistance ($304 million in 1970 prices) was allocated to SOC sectors (electricity, water, transportation and communications), 16 percent to service sectors (health, sanitation, housing and education), 9 percent to fertilizer production, 9 percent to other manufacturing and 6 percent to agriculture and forestry. Although the amount of project assistance was much smaller from 1962 to 1966, the distribution pattern was similar to that of the previous period except that a significant amount was allocated to mining and construction rather than fertilizer production. During 1967–71, not only was the absolute amount of project assistance small ($30 million) but the distribution pattern was also different: 82 percent to service sectors, 13 percent to agriculture and none to manufacturing.

The total value of imports financed by U.S. project assistance during 1954–61 amounted to about $524 million in 1970 prices and the imports of machinery and equipment financed by non-project assistance amounted to $92 million. This was equivalent to 24 percent and 4 percent, respectively, of total gross fixed capital formation.[1]

Therefore one may say that not only did U.S. aid financed most of Korea's imports between 1954 and 1961 but it also directly financed nearly 30 percent of the total gross fixed capital formation. Furthermore, since the parity exchange rate (1970 = 100) was approximately twice the size of the official exchange rate during 1953–60, and since the official exchange rate was applied to the U.S. project assistance, the magnitude of the implicit subsidy on imported capital goods may be approximated by taking the amount of aid-financed capital good imports for 1954–61 (i.e., an amount equivalent to about 24 percent of gross fixed capital formation). However, only about 18 percent of the U.S. project assistance

---

[1] The total value of imports financed by project assistance during 1962–66 amounted to about $59 million which was equivalent to only about 2 percent of total gross fixed capital formation during the period.

was allocated to the manufacturing sector during 1954–61 (and only about 11 percent was allocated during 1962–66). The share of capital goods in total non-project assistance was only about 6 percent during the (first) period. Therefore, as far as the manufacturing sector is concerned, the subsidy element associated with underpriced imported capital goods seems to have been relatively small during 1954–61 (and 1962–66). We now turn to another major source of implicit subsidy on capital use: the underpricing of imported capital goods due to tariff exemptions.

B. *Tariff Exemptions on Capital Good Imports*

During 1953–66, about one third of gross fixed capital formation was in the form of (electrical and non-electrical) machinery and transport equipment compared with more than 40 percent for the period 1967 to 1976.

According to the BOK's input-output tables, the import content of fixed capital formation in the form of machinery and equipment was as high as 73 percent in 1963 and 71 percent in 1973. A familiar form of subsidy on capital use is the importation of capital goods at favorable exchange rates. The underpricing of imported capital goods may inhibit the establishment of domestic capital goods industries and at the same time reduce the employment opportunities by lowering the ratio of capital to labor costs.

In the fifties, imports of capital goods were mostly financed by U.S. project assistance and partly by non-project assistance. Although capital goods were also, in principle, subject to customs duties, official exchange rates were applied to project assistance imports and hence the imported capital goods were underpriced to the extent that the domestic currency was overvalued. In the sixties, however, an increasing number of imports were financed with non-aid funds. In addition, the repeated devaluation of the unified exchange rate also eliminated the excessive overvaluation of domestic currency. Hence the source of subsidy on imported capital goods consisted mainly of tariff exemptions and subsidized financing of the imports by domestic or foreign loans.

The weighted average legal tariff rate on nonelectrical machinery was about 14 percent during 1964–67, 20 percent during 1968–72 and 15 percent during 1973–74. Since the weighted average legal tariff rate on all commodities for the same periods was about 17 percent, 26 percent and 20 percent respectively, the rates on nonelectrical machinery were, on the average, about 20 percent lower than the average rate for all commodities.

Table 7.3. Import Content of Gross Fixed Capital Formation

In Billion Won & Percent

I-O 56 Sector Classification	Gross Fixed Capital Formation		
	Total Inputs	Imported Inputs	Import Content
37–39. Machinery & Equipment			
1960	4.5	2.2	49%
1963	20.6	15.0	73%
1966	83.6	59.2	71%
1968	161.2	115.9	72%
1970	207.7	130.6	63%
1973	433.2	309.0	71%
1–56. All Goods & Services			
1960	24.9	5.3	21%
1963	56.9	15.3	27%
1966	206.3	59.5	29%
1968	405.1	118.1	29%
1970	688.1	133.3	19%
1973	1,186.0	315.4	27%

Source: The Bank of Korea, *Korean Input-Output Tables.*

The weighted average legal tariff rate on electrical machinery was about 21 percent during 1964–67, 29 percent during 1968–72 and 28 percent during 1973–74 (that is, about 25 percent higher than the average rate for all commodities). For transport equipment it was about 32 percent during 1964–67, 38 percent during 1968–72 and 15 percent during 1973–74. This implies extremely high rates before 1972 and below average rates after 1973. (See Table B.16.) This change was mostly attributable to rapidly increasing duty free imports of railway locomotives, aircraft and steel vessels on the one hand and a drastic decline in motor vehicle imports on the other.

Due to various forms of tariff exemptions granted for imports of raw materials and capital goods, tariff duties actually collected amounted to only about 10 percent of the total import value before 1968. This declined to between 6 and 9 percent during 1969–72 and to about 4 percent after 1973. According to the tariff law promulgated in 1949, basic plant facilities and equipment for important industries, specified by the Minister of

Finance, could be imported duty free.[2] On the basis of this law, the Ministry of Finance allowed tariff exemptions on machinery for export production in 1964.[3] After 1974, however, the tariff exemption system was replaced by tariff payments on an installment basis within a period of three years. This means that capital goods for export production are subject to around 20 percent tariff rates over a three year period.[4] As a result, although total machinery and equipment imports increased by about 60 percent in 1974, the absolute value of tariff exemptions increased by only about 7 percent in current won values. On the other hand, capital goods imported for foreign investment project have been exempted from tariffs ever since 1960.[5]

Since a large number of capital goods were imported duty free for either export production (until 1974), key industries or foreign investments, the rate of tariffs actually collected from machinery imports amounted to only around 4 to 5 percent during 1966–74 while that from electrical machinery amounted to about 8 to 12 percent before 1971 and was reduced to between 3 and 4 percent after 1973. Tariffs actually collected from transport equipment amounted to about 7 to 11 percent before 1971 and 4 to 5 percent after 1972.

The legal as well as actual tariff rates on non-electrical machinery imports were much lower, on the average, than those on all commodities while the rates on electrical machinery and transport equipment were higher than those on all commodities. However, the legal as well as actual tariff rates on all capital goods as a whole (that is, non-electrical machinery, electrical machinery and transport equipment) were very close to those on all commodities. That is, the weighted average legal tariff rate on all capital goods was about 21 percent during 1964–67, 27 percent during 1968–72 and 18 percent during 1973–74. The rate on all commodities was about 17 percent during 1964–67, 26 percent during 1968–72 and 20

---

[2] Tariff Law Article 33, No. 3 promulgated on November 23, 1949. Replaced by Tariff Law Article 28, No. 1 on November 29, 1967.

[3] Ministry of Finance Decree No. 345 promulgated on March 2, 1964 which was replaced by Decree No. 446 on March 18, 1967. Recommendation by the Minister of Commerce and Industry was required in order to qualify for tariff exemption. According to the Office of Customs Administration Notice No. 5 promulgated in February 1972, those firms which imported dury free machinery (or parts) must export more than 60 (or 90) percent of the total products of the concerned plant.

[4] Tariff Law (Law No. 1976) Article 36 promulgated on November 29, 1967 and enforced by Office of Customs Administration Notice No. 42 promulgated in March, 1974 and Ministry of Finance Notice No. 593 promulgated on January 14, 1974.

[5] Foreign Capital Inducement Law, Law No. 532, Article 27, promulgated on January 1, 1960.

Table 7.4. Legal and Actual Tariff Rates on Capital Goods Imports

In Million Dollars & Percent

	Machinery				Electrical Machinery			
	Total Imports	(Legal Rate)	Tariffs Collected	Tariffs Exempted	Total Imports	(Legal Rate)	Tariffs Collected	Tariffs Exempted
1966	96.4	(17%)	4.4 (5%)	11.4 (12%)	26.1	(24%)	3.1 (12%)	3.3 (12%)
1967	142.6	(19%)	8.8 (6%)	18.0 (13%)	47.6	(28%)	6.6 (14%)	6.7 (14%)
1968	268.7	(20%)	9.9 (4%)	43.2 (16%)	92.3	(29%)	9.0 (10%)	17.5 (19%)
1969	291.6	(17%)	12.3 (4%)	37.9 (13%)	111.1	(29%)	10.2 (9%)	22.7 (20%)
1970	290.7	(19%)	18.6 (6%)	37.3 (13%)	129.5	(31%)	14.3 (11%)	25.6 (20%)
1971	325.2	(17%)	13.4 (4%)	43.7 (13%)	164.8	(22%)	13.7 (8%)	23.9 (14%)
1972	333.7	(19%)	12.4 (4%)	50.4 (15%)	225.5	(20%)	13.7 (6%)	31.7 (14%)
1973	517.6	(14%)	17.1 (3%)	58.2 (11%)	388.2	(15%)	13.3 (3%)	44.7 (12%)
1974	669.2	(16%)	35.9 (5%)	74.1 (11%)	538.2	(13%)	21.6 (4%)	50.7 (9%)

	Transport Equipment				All Commodity Imports			
	Total Imports	(Legal Rate)	Tariffs Collected	Tariffs Exempted	Total Imports	(Legal Rate)	Tariffs Collected	Tariffs Exempted
1966	50.0	(26%)	3.8 (8%)	8.8 (18%)	716.5	(19%)	69.4 (10%)	62.6 (9%)
1967	121.4	(20%)	12.1 (10%)	12.3 (10%)	996.2	(23%)	126.2 (13%)	96.6 (10%)

Year												
1968	162.5	(43%)	14.0	(9%)	55.8	(34%)	1,464.1	(28%)	140.2	(10%)	256.7	(18%)
1969	180.2	(35%)	13.2	(7%)	51.3	(28%)	1,825.9	(24%)	150.1	(8%)	298.1	(16%)
1970	157.8	(43%)	17.9	(11%)	51.3	(32%)	1,985.0	(26%)	183.4	(9%)	344.6	(17%)
1971	179.2	(25%)	12.1	(7%)	32.5	(18%)	2,395.0	(22%)	154.5	(6%)	377.0	(16%)
1972	190.5	(24%)	9.2	(5%)	36.9	(19%)	2,522.0	(22%)	138.8	(6%)	394.4	(16%)
1973	265.7	(24%)	12.9	(5%)	51.6	(19%)	4,241.5	(18%)	184.3	(4%)	582.4	(14%)
1974	642.4	(10%)	23.8	(4%)	41.2	(6%)	6,844.6	(12%)	288.5	(4%)	528.0	(8%)

Source: Based on the taped trade statistics of the Office of Customs Administration. Cf. Table 5.1.
Note: Tariff rates computed on the basis of OCA taped data, ONTA, *Statistical Yearbook of National Tax* and those computed on the basis of BOK's input-output tables are slightly different from each other.

percent 1973–74. The rate of tariffs actually collected on all imported capital goods deviated from that on all commodities by 3 to 5 percent during 1966–69.[6] They were identical in 1970, 1971, 1973 and 1974. That is, the actual tariff rate on all capital goods was a little lower than those on all commodities until 1969 (i.e., around 7 percent as opposed to 9 percent), but the rates became almost identical and have even moved together since 1970.

In any case, the "less important" industries, which supply the domestic market only, had to pay 18 to 27 percent legal tariff rates on imported capital goods, while the key or export industries were able to get complete tariff exemptions. The absolute value of tariff exemptions on capital goods imports was about $30 to 50 million per annum during 1966–67, about $100 to 135 million per annum during 1968–72 and around $140 to 150 million per annum during 1973–74 in 1970 prices. These exemptions were equivalent to approximately 5 percent of the annual gross fixed capital formation in Korea. While the absolute magnitude of tariff exemptions was by no means small, we will find that the interest subsidy associated with loans was large enough to make tariff exemptions look relatively insignificant.[7]

As a whole, one may say that the legal or actual tariff rates on capital goods were similar to the average legal or actual rates on all commodity imports. Although the non-electrical machinery imports received preferential treatment, the relative amount of the subsidy on capital goods imports as a whole, which was provided through the preferential tariff exemption system, does not seem to have been really large. Therefore, we now have to examine the financing of the acquisition of capital goods in order to identify the major source of subsidy on capital use.

---

[6] The difference was about 3 percent in 1966 (7 percent versus 10 percent), 4 percent in 1967 (9 percent versus 13 percent), 5 percent in 1968 (5 percent versus 10 percent), 2 percent in 1969 (6 percent versus 8 percent) and 1 percent in 1972 (5 percent versus 6 percent).

[7] The tariff exemptions on electronics products were mostly for raw material used in export production i.e., exemptions on intermediate inputs rather than those on capital equipment. However, the amount of tariff exemptions on capital goods presented here does include such tariff exemptions on intermediate electronics products (which are classified as electrical machinery and equipment in the 43 sector I-O table). Since the imports of electronics intermediate input materials significantly increased after 1968, to make up nearly half of the total electrical machinery and equipment imports in 1973–74, the tariff exemption figures may be regarded as upper limits and the tariff rates actually collected from electrical machinery and equipment (exclusive of electronics products) must have been much higher than the figures presented in Table 7.4.

3. Bank Loans, Foreign Capital and Government Investment

A. Bank Loans

Before 1965, the real interest rates on time and savings deposits were negative in most years. As a result the major sources of loan funds at the deposit money banks had been deposit money and borrowings from the government and BOK. Since the drastic increase in interest rates on time and savings deposits in September 1965, the absolute magnitude of DMB loan funds has increased very rapidly with time and savings deposits becoming the major source of DMB funds. In terms of money value, the annual net increase in DMB loans was equivalent to between 9 and 16 percent of gross domestic fixed capital formation during 1962–66 (except in 1964), but it increased to around 35 percent after 1966. Although the absolute amount of demand deposits and borrowings from the government also increased continuously, their relative share in total DMB loan funds rapidly declined after 1966. On the other hand, due to the ever-increasing short-term export credits which were financed by the rediscounts of the Bank of Korea, the relative share of the DMB borrowings from the BOK increased steadily after 1968. It is interesting to note that sub-loan funds from foreign sources increased significantly after 1967. The foreign liabilities of the DMB have increased from about 13 billion won in 1967 to about 843 billion won in 1976.

Before 1965, more than 20 percent of total DMB loans was for equipment purchases. However, investment in equipment began to be financed largely by foreign borrowings after 1965 and as a result the share of long-term equipment loans declined to about 12 percent of total DMB loans between 1965 and 1971. From 1972 to 1976, however, the share of these loans increased to around 17 percent.

The main sources of loan funds of the Korea Development Bank have been: (1) government funds, (2) counterpart funds, (3) foreign loan funds, (4) foreign currency deposit funds and (5) loans from the deposit money banks. In value terms, the net annual increase in KDB loans was equivalent to around 5 percent of annual gross domestic fixed capital formation during 1962–76. About 80 percent of the KDB loans were for equipment purchases. It is notable that the share of the counterpart funds decreased rapidly after 1966 while the share of foreign loan funds in KDB

Table 7.5. *Major Sources of Funds of the Deposit Money Banks*

In Billion Won & Percent

Year-End Balance	Major Sources of Funds for DMB				
	Demand Deposits	Borrowings from BOK	Borrowings from Gov't	Time & Savings Deposits	Foreign Liabilities
1961	19.3 (49%)	3.1 (8%)	11.3 (29%)	5.4 (14%)	—
1962	26.9 (48%)	1.5 (3%)	15.9 (28%)	12.2 (22%)	—
1963	26.2 (43%)	4.4 (7%)	17.7 (29%)	12.8 (21%)	—
1964	28.6 (41%)	7.6 (11%)	19.0 (27%)	14.5 (21%)	—
1965	48.0 (46%)	6.9 (7%)	18.7 (18%)	30.6 (29%)	—
1966	50.9 (34%)	6.1 (4%)	22.8 (15%)	70.1 (47%)	0.0 (0%)
1967	77.0 (30%)	12.0 (5%)	28.1 (11%)	128.9 (50%)	12.9 (5%)
1968	117.5 (26%)	18.9 (4%)	37.8 (8%)	255.5 (57%)	18.6 (4%)
1969	167.7 (22%)	35.2 (5%)	65.1 (8%)	451.5 (59%)	48.7 (6%)
1970	213.4 (20%)	90.2 (9%)	93.3 (9%)	576.3 (55%)	73.8 (7%)
1971	268.9 (20%)	111.6 (8%)	101.8 (8%)	708.7 (53%)	144.5 (11%)
1972	412.4 (23%)	179.3 (10%)	116.0 (6%)	911.5 (51%)	178.3 (10%)
1973	539.4 (23%)	280.0 (12%)	126.5 (5%)	1,214.4 (53%)	149.6 (6%)
1974	656.9 (19%)	666.5 (19%)	147.8 (4%)	1,450.6 (42%)	519.4 (15%)
1975	868.6 (20%)	672.7 (15%)	172.8 (4%)	1,910.6 (44%)	732.8 (17%)
1976	1,147.0 (21%)	686.2 (13%)	205.8 (4%)	2,541.1 (47%)	842.5 (16%)

Source: The Bank of Korea, *Monetary Statistics in Korea: 1960–73* and *Monthly Economic Statistics* (various issues).

Table 7.6. *Major Sources and Uses of Funds: the Bank of Korea and the Korea Development Bank*
In Billion Won & Percent

Year-End Balance	Bank of Korea			Korea Development Bank		
	Bank Notes Issued	Loans for Exports	Other Loans	Loan Fund Type		
	Total (Inc.)	Total (Inc.)	Total (Inc.)	Counterpart Fund[1]	Foreign Loan Fund[1]	Industrial Fund
1957	9 (1)			3.0 (100%)	—	—
1958	12 (3)			5.5 (52%)	—	5.1 (48%)
1959	13 (1)			8.3 (58%)	—	5.9 (42%)
1960	15 (2)			9.5 (60%)	—	6.3 (40%)
1961	18 (3)			9.1 (50%)	—	9.1 (50%)
1962	21 (3)			13.6 (60%)		9.1 (40%)
1963	22 (1)			15.4 (59%)		10.6 (41%)
1964	28 (6)	1 (—)	9 (—)	16.5 (55%)	0.1 (0%)	13.4 (45%)
1965	35 (7)	3 (2)	16 (7)	16.5 (49%)	0.1 (1%)	17.0 (50%)
1966	47 (11)	4 (1)	21 (5)	16.4 (36%)	1.0 (2%)	28.1 (62%)
1967	68 (22)	8 (4)	24 (3)	13.5 (26%)	2.0 (4%)	36.8 (70%)
1968	96 (28)	14 (4)	33 (9)	15.9 (24%)	2.3 (3%)	48.2 (73%)
1969	130 (34)	32 (18)	35 (2)	14.5 (15%)	3.3 (3%)	78.2 (81%)
1970	159 (29)	48 (16)	72 (37)	13.4 (10%)	12.9 (10%)	102.6 (80%)
1971	187 (28)	72 (24)	72 (0)	12.3 (8%)	36.5 (23%)	108.6 (69%)
1972	245 (58)	100 (28)	113 (41)	10.8 (5%)	27.2 (11%)	201.0 (84%)
1973	354 (109)	217 (117)	106 (−7)	9.6 (3%)	36.1 (11%)	272.8 (86%)
1974	455 (101)	308 (91)	379 (273)	8.9 (2%)	66.2 (17%)	309.8 (80%)
1975	561 (106)	380 (72)	416 (37)	9.0 (2%)	104.0 (23%)	348.0 (75%)
1976	736 (175)	461 (81)	335 (−81)	8.8 (2%)	174.3 (33%)	351.3 (66%)

Source: The Bank of Korea, *Economic Statistics Yearbook*.
Notes: [1] Includes foreign currency deposit fund.

loans grew substantially.

The net annual increase in BOK loans and discounts which was usually negative prior to 1963, amounted to between 2 and 9 percent of annual gross domestic fixed capital formation during the period 1963-75 (except in 1974). The steady increase in BOK loans and discounts after 1966 was due to the continuously expanding rediscounts for export credits. For instance, about half of the BOK loans and discounts in 1971, 1972, 1974 and 1975 were for exports, and about two-thirds were for exports in 1973 and 1976. Other loans and discounts were for procurement of fertilizer, discounts on commercial bills and for agricultural production loans. The so-called "loans and discounts" of the Bank of Korea consisted of discounts to other financial institutions and were either financed by government fiscal funds or by printing bank notes. It appears that the growth in the supply of bank notes has increasingly taken the form of expanded export credits in Korea. For instance, the absolute value of total loans and

Table 7.7. *Weighted Average Interest Rates on Loans by the Deposit Money Bank and the Korea Development Bank*

Interest Rates	DMB Loans		KDB Loans	
	Nominal	Real	Nominal	Real
1961	13.3%	0.1%	—	—
1962	13.4%	4.0%	8.4%	−1.0%
1963	13.1%	−7.5%	8.3%	−12.3%
1963	13.3%	−21.3%	8.4%	−26.2%
1965	16.2%	6.2%	9.2%	−0.8%
1966	21.4%	12.5%	11.8%	2.9%
1967	21.8%	15.4%	12.5%	6.1%
1968	21.5%	13.4%	12.7%	4.6%
1969	20.7%	13.9%	12.2%	5.4%
1970	17.6%	8.4%	12.5%	3.3%
1971	16.4%	7.8%	12.4%	3.8%
1972	17.7%	3.7%	9.9%	−4.1%
1973	13.9%	7.0%	9.7%	2.8%
1974	14.0%	−28.1%	9.7%	−32.4%
1975	13.6%	−12.9%	11.2%	−15.3%
1976	13.7%	1.6%	11.3%	−0.8%

Source: The Bank of Korea, *Economic Statistics Yearbook* (various issues).
Note: Real interest rate equals nominal interest rate minus the rate of change in the wholesale price index.

discounts furnished by the Bank of Korea increased by 110 billion won in 1973. At the same time, the value of DMB loans for exports, financed through the BOK rediscounts, increased by 114 billion won, which was equivalent to the total net increase in bank notes and coins issued in 1973.

The weighted average (nominal) interest rate on DMB loans increased from about 13 percent in 1961–64 to about 21 percent in 1966–69 and then fell steadily to about 14 percent in 1973–76. The weighted average (nominal) interest rate on KDB loans steadily increased from about 8 percent in 1962–64 to nearly 13 percent in 1966–71 and then it also fell to about 11 percent in 1975–76.

We also computed the weighted average real interest rate by subtracting the rate of change in the wholesale price index from the nominal average interest rate. The real interest rate on DMB loans was either negative or very small before 1965. With a drastic rise in nominal interest rates in September 1965, however, the weighted average real interest rate for DMB loans reached its peak of 15 percent in 1967 and then fell steadily, to less than 2 percent in 1976. The real interest rate on KDB loans was always lower than that of DMB loans but the pattern of changes in weighted average real interest rates of DMB loans and KDB loans were very similar to each other. The interest rate on KDB loans reached its peak of 6 percent in 1967 and then fell steadily, to less than zero percent in 1976.

After the August 3rd Presidential Emergency Decree in 1972, the nominal interest rates on KDB and DMB loans were reduced to the pre–1965 level and those on time and savings deposits were reduced even below the pre–1965 level. Due to substantial inflation associated with the oil crisis, the post–1972 period became very much like the pre–1965 period in terms of real interest rates on loans and deposits and a slow rate of growth for time and savings deposits.

All the KDB loans and 30 to 40 percent of the total DMB loans were so-called "policy loans" which were allocated according to the government investment and financial plan. The remaining 60–70 percent of DMB loans were allocated in accordance with the Regulation on the Use of Loan Funds. Since the Regulation is fairly vague with respect to actual loan management, there existed, at least in theory, some room for discretion by bank officers. In practice, however, even the distribution of non-policy loans was heavily influenced by the government investment policies and various other non-economic considerations.

Since the interest rates on bank loans were less than one-third of the rate applied on curb market loans the selection of industries as well as the selection of individual borrowers were both subject to government

Table 7.8. Loans to Corporations and Individual Sectors

In Billion Won & Percent

	BOK Loans	Bank Loans*	Curb Loans	Gov't Loans	Foreign Loans	Total
			Flow of Funds			
1963	2.8 (—)	12.3 (—)	— (—)	0.1 (—)	8.1 (—)	— (—)
1964	−0.7 (—)	8.0 (—)	— (—)	0.0 (—)	10.2 (—)	— (—)
1965	9.9 (19%)	24.9 (49%)	8.7 (17%)	0.0 (0%)	7.8 (15%)	51.3 (100%)
1966	6.0 (6%)	44.9 (44%)	2.2 (2%)	0.0 (0%)	49.9 (48%)	103.0 (100%)
1967	1.6 (1%)	111.3 (57%)	16.3 (8%)	0.0 (0%)	66.9 (34%)	196.1 (100%)
1968	7.8 (2%)	174.7 (51%)	39.3 (12%)	0.0 (0%)	117.8 (35%)	339.6 (100%)
1969	4.1 (1%)	280.3 (60%)	33.9 (7%)	0.0 (0%)	152.7 (32%)	471.0 (100%)
1970	−2.0 (0%)	248.4 (52%)	69.5 (15%)	9.4 (2%)	150.7 (32%)	476.0 (100%)
1971	2.0 (0%)	295.1 (64%)	36.8 (8%)	5.1 (1%)	124.5 (27%)	463.5 (100%)
1972	2.0 (0%)	334.8 (82%)	−14.2 (−3%)	−1.8 (0%)	86.8 (21%)	407.6 (100%)
			Stock of Funds			
1962	0.5 (—)	67.9 (—)	— (—)	0.3 (—)	0.6 (—)	— (—)
1963	3.3 (—)	80.2 (—)	— (—)	0.3 (—)	8.7 (—)	— (—)
1964	2.6 (2%)	88.2 (72%)	11.7 (10%)	0.3 (0%)	19.0 (16%)	121.8 (100%)
1965	12.5 (7%)	113.1 (65%)	20.4 (12%)	0.3 (0%)	28.0 (16%)	174.3 (100%)
1966	18.5 (7%)	158.0 (57%)	22.6 (8%)	0.3 (0%)	77.9 (28%)	277.3 (100%)
1967	20.1 (4%)	269.3 (57%)	38.9 (8%)	0.1 (0%)	144.8 (31%)	473.2 (100%)
1968	27.9 (3%)	444.0 (55%)	78.2 (10%)	0.1 (0%)	262.6 (32%)	812.8 (100%)
1969	32.0 (2%)	724.4 (56%)	112.1 (9%)	0.1 (0%)	415.3 (32%)	1,283.9 (100%)
1970	30.0 (2%)	972.8 (55%)	181.6 (10%)	9.5 (0%)	566.0 (32%)	1,759.9 (100%)
1971	32.0 (1%)	1,267.9 (57%)	218.4 (10%)	14.6 (1%)	690.5 (31%)	2,223.4 (100%)
1972	34.0 (1%)	1,602.7 (61%)	204.2 (8%)	12.8 (0%)	777.3 (30%)	2,631.0 (100%)

Source: The Bank of Korea, *Flow of Funds in Korea: 1971*, *Economic Statistics Yearbook*: *1973*, and Y. C. Park, *op. cit.* (for curb loan data).
  * Includes insurance & trust loans.

influence. Only insignificant loans seem to have been obtained by direct appeals to the bank officers using various incentive measures. It also seems that fewer irregular practices occurred in selection of industries than in selection of individual borrowers, implying that most of the bank loans were channelled to the industrial sectors which the government was trying to promote.

Due to the chronic shortage of bank loan funds, the use of bank loans has been regarded as a privilege. Consequently it is the use of curb market loans, though relatively small in absolute magnitude, which is based on the market mechanism, however inefficient this market mechanism is.

According to the flow of funds table constructed by the Bank of Korea and Park's estimate of the volume of credit in the informal loan markets, the share of bank loans in total outstanding loans declined from about 52–72 percent during 1964–66 to 55–57 percent during 1967–71. At the same time the share of foreign loans increased from about 16 percent in 1964–65 to more than 30 percent after 1966. The share of curb loans in total outstanding loans was around 10 percent during 1964–72.[8] Although the share of BOK loans (to government controlled corporations) was fairly significant in the mid-sixties, it became insignificant after 1970.

On August 3, 1972, the government issued a Presidential Emergency Decree (for Economic Stability and Growth). One of the policy measures included in the Decree was adjustment of terms and conditions of loans from the curb market in which all enterprises were required to report to government the amounts of such loans.[9] In compliance with this Decree, 40,677 enterprises reported their debts, which totaled 345.6 billion won. Although the reported curb loans included a substantial amount of disguised investment assets of firms, they could not completely cover the existing curb loans. Even Park's estimation (204 billion won in 1972) could not cover the curb loans transacted within the corporate business sector. A reasonable estimation might be that the share of curb market loans in total loans in Korea could have been at least 20 percent during

---

[8] Y. C. Park, *The Unorganized Financial Sector in Korea, 1945–75*, Korea Development Institute, 1976 (Preliminary Draft).

[9] The August 3 Decree froze the existing curb market loans in Korea and forced the lender to postpone the repayment schedule and reduce the interest rate by varying degrees as specified by the decree. Although the decree temporarily disrupted the function of the curb market, it apparently alleviated the burden of many firms as a form of windfall interest subsidies. The decree also gave tax allowances to improve the asset position of firms in general through accelerated depreciation and tax-free reserves on a temporary basis (up to the end of 1976).

1962–72.[10]

B. Foreign Capital

There was no private or government borrowing of foreign capital before 1959, and the inflow of foreign capital between 1959 and 1961 was negligible, amounting to less than $4 million. The government began borrowing more foreign capital (mostly from the U.S.) during the First Five-Year Plan period (1962–66), and by 1966 the loan balance was about $115 million. Private borrowing, mostly from the U.S. and Japan, also amounted to about $160 million by the end of 1966.

During the Second Five-Year Plan period (1967–71), the inflow of foreign public loans (i.e., government borrowing) amounted to about $150 million per annum and that of foreign commercial loans (i.e., private borrowing) amounted to nearly $300 million per annum on the average. These foreign loans came mostly from the U.S. and Japan. The annual private borrowing of foreign capital exceeded $600 million and the annnal government borrowing amounted to nearly $500 million on the average during 1972–76.

If we subtract repayments, the net total debt outstanding at the end of 1976 amounted to about $3.17 billion for government borrowing and $3.18 billion for private borrowing. About 42 percent of the total government borrowing was from the U.S., about 30 percent from international financial institutions and about 20 percent from Japan. Similarly, about 36 percent of total private borrowing was from the U.S. while about 16 percent was from Japan.

About 30 percent of total public loans was for SOC sectors, about 25 percent was for U.S. surplus agricultural product loans, about 10 percent was for service sectors and less than 10 percent was for manufacturing sectors. However, nearly two-thirds of the commercial loans was for the manufacturing sector and about 25 percent was for SOC sectors. The magnitude of public loans for the primary sectors was relatively small. However, there were a substantial amount of commercial loans for the fishery sector between 1959 and 1976.

The commercial loans for manufacturing were concentrated on chemicals, textiles, metals, transport equipment, petroleum refining, and nonmetallic mineral product industries. The public loans for manufacturing were concentrated on metals and chemicals industries. The commercial

---

[10] See Y. C. Park, *op. cit.*, p. 1.

Table 7.9. — Balance of Foreign Loans

In Million Dollars & Percent

	Total	Private Foreign Borrowing				Total[1]	Government Foreign Borrowing			
		U.S.	Japan	Germany			U.S.	Japan	IBRD, IDA, ADB & IFC	
1959	2.1	2.1 (100%)	—	—		—	—	—	—	
1960	2.0	2.0 (100%)	—	—		1.1	1.1 (100%)	—	—	
1961	1.7	1.7 (100%)	—	—		2.1	2.1 (100%)	—	—	
1962	1.5	1.5 (100%)	—	—		8.1	8.1 (100%)	—	—	
1963	19.8	7.2 (36%)	—	10.2 (52%)		32.1	16.9 (53%)	—	12.1 (38%)	
1964	36.0	14.2 (39%)	—	18.3 (51%)		43.0	20.9 (49%)	—	13.9 (32%)	
1965	60.3	21.5 (36%)	4.3 (7%)	23.5 (39%)		53.8	25.1 (47%)	—	16.9 (31%)	
1966	161.7	40.1 (25%)	66.8 (41%)	23.4 (14%)		114.5	63.0 (55%)	17.4 (15%)	16.9 (15%)	
1967	288.7	62.0 (21%)	119.3 (41%)	38.1 (13%)		188.1	114.7 (61%)	30.9 (16%)	16.9 (9%)	
1968	517.1	158.7 (31%)	183.7 (36%)	60.3 (12%)		292.8	197.0 (67%)	44.3 (15%)	24.1 (8%)	
1969	829.3	272.8 (33%)	254.2 (31%)	82.2 (10%)		433.7	308.6 (71%)	63.3 (15%)	32.3 (7%)	
1970	1,039.1	365.6 (35%)	273.5 (26%)	102.2 (10%)		576.7	411.1 (71%)	80.6 (14%)	49.0 (8%)	
1971	1,256.2	446.6 (36%)	314.7 (25%)	104.6 (8%)		886.6	548.7 (62%)	182.6 (21%)	104.1 (12%)	
1972	1,412.4	471.7 (33%)	360.5 (26%)	101.7 (7%)		1,335.1	804.4 (60%)	272.7 (21%)	171.2 (13%)	
1973	1,720.5	614.7 (36%)	372.7 (22%)	122.2 (7%)		1,790.2	955.0 (53%)	412.5 (23%)	293.6 (16%)	
1974	2,125.9	818.7 (39%)	425.3 (20%)	118.8 (6%)		2,120.0	1,003.8 (47%)	530.9 (25%)	438.1 (21%)	
1975	2,766.9	1,056.6 (38%)	540.7 (19%)	144.5 (5%)		2,548.2	1,072.8 (42%)	577.1 (23%)	705.0 (28%)	
1976	3,180.3	1,141.1 (36%)	519.9 (16%)	193.8 (6%)		3,168.4	1,319.2 (42%)	619.0 (20%)	965.9 (30%)	

Source: Tables B. 25. and B. 28.

Note: [1] Includes other sources. All these foreign loans may be regarded as long-term loans because out of 1,282 cases only in 4 cases the sum of grace period and repayment was less than 3 years.

Table 7.10. Gross Inflow of Foreign Loans

In Million Dollars & Percent

Sector	Private Foreign Borrowing			
	1959–66	1967–71	1972–76	Total
Agriculture	—	—	2.7 (0%)	2.7 (0%)
Fishery	41.6 (23%)	47.3 (3%)	65.9 (2%)	154.8 (3%)
Mining	—	1.5 (0%)	3.0 (0%)	4.5 (0%)
Manufacturing	128.4 (72%)	806.8 (58%)	2,126.0 (68%)	3,061.2 (65%)
Textiles	33.4 (19%)	118.0 (9%)	408.8 (12%)	560.2 (12%)
Chemicals	43.7 (25%)	143.3 (10%)	538.8 (17%)	725.8 (15%)
Petroleum	17.0 (10%)	192.0 (14%)	62.3 (2%)	271.3 (6%)
Metals	3.8 (2%)	104.9 (8%)	467.4 (15%)	576.1 (12%)
Nonmetallic Mineral	19.8 (11%)	117.0 (8%)	148.2 (5%)	285.0 (6%)
Machinery	6.8 (4%)	22.8 (2%)	61.9 (2%)	91.5 (2%)
Transport Equipment	2.7 (2%)	43.7 (3%)	366.7 (12%)	414.1 (9%)
Others	1.4 (1%)	65.1 (5%)	71.9 (2%)	138.2 (3%)
SOC Sectors	3.8 (2%)	480.0 (35%)	685.7 (22%)	1,169.5 (25%)
Electricity	2.1 (1%)	269.2 (19%)	340.3 (11%)	611.6 (13%)
Transportation	1.7 (1%)	210.8 (15%)	330.1 (11%)	542.6 (12%)
Communications	—	—	—	—
Water & Sanitary Service	—	—	—	—
Service Sectors	3.8 (2%)	52.0 (4%)	56.5 (2%)	112.3 (2%)
Agricultural Products	—	—	—	—
Unclassifiable	—	—	201.4 (6%)	201.4 (4%)
Total	177.5 (100%)	1,387.6 (100%)	3,151.2 (100%)	4,706.4 (100%)

Table 7.10. (Continued)

In Million Dollars & Percent

Sector	Government Foreign Borrowing						
	1959–66		1967–71		1972–76		Total
Agriculture	—		0.9	(0%)	123.7	(5%)	124.6 (4%)
Fishery	—		4.6	(1%)	13.5	(1%)	18.1 (1%)
Mining	8.7	(7%)	4.4	(1%)	—		13.1 (0%)
Manufacturing	21.7	(18%)	62.1	(8%)	137.2	(6%)	221.0 (7%)
Textiles	3.8	(3%)	5.1	(1%)	—		8.9 (0%)
Chemicals	13.9	(12%)	40.6	(5%)	29.1	(1%)	78.7 (2%)
Petroleum	—		—		—		—
Metals	—		8.3	(1%)	83.3	(3%)	91.6 (3%)
Nonmetallic Mineral	4.0	(3%)	3.0	(0%)	—		7.0 (0%)
Machinery	—		2.8	(0%)	23.3	(1%)	26.1 (1%)
Transport Equipment	—		—		—		—
Others	—		2.3	(0%)	1.5	(0%)	8.7 (0%)
SOC Sectors	70.2	(59%)	250.1	(32%)	725.1	(30%)	1,045.4 (32%)
Electricity	11.9	(10%)	88.2	(11%)	120.4	(5%)	220.5 (7%)
Transportation	42.6	(36%)	117.1	(15%)	468.6	(19%)	628.3 (19%)
Communications	15.6	(13%)	30.7	(4%)	91.0	(4%)	137.3 (4%)
Water & Sanitary Service	0.1	(0%)	14.2	(2%)	445.2	(2%)	59.5 (2%)
Service Sectors	6.7	(6%)	10.9	(1%)	266.6	(11%)	284.2 (9%)
Agricultural Products	—		331.3	(42%)	517.9	(22%)	849.2 (26%)
Unclassifiable	11.7	(10%)	119.1	(15%)	623.8	(26%)	254.6 (23%)
Total	118.9	(100%)	783.4	(100%)	2,407.7	(100%)	3,310.0 (100%)

Source: Economic Planning Board.

loans for SOC sectors were concentrated on electricity and transportation while the public loans were concentrated on the transportation sector.

The weighted average (nominal) interest rate on foreign commercial loans acquired by Korea was about 5 percent during 1959–66 and about 7 percent during 1967–76. The weighted average interest rate on public loans was about 3 percent during 1959–71 and about 4 percent during 1972–76. The weighted average length of the grace period for commercial loans was about 3 years and that for public loans was about 7 years. The average length of the repayment period for commercial loans was about 7 years and that for public loans was about 20 years. (See Table B. 30.)

Since the average annual rate of increase in the U.S. wholesale price was about 1 percent during 1962–66, 3 percent during 1967–71 and about 10 percent during 1972–76, the real weighted average interest rate on foreign commercial loans may be approximated at about 4.4 percent during 1962–66, 3.5 percent during 1967–71, and -2.8 percent during 1972–76 and that on foreign public loans may be approximated at about 1.7 percent for the first period, −0.4 percent for the second and −4.1 percent for the last period. These rates may be regarded as the real interest rates on foreign loans to the Korean economy as a whole.

We may also compute the real interest rates to the individual entrepreneur by taking account of the rate of change in the domestic wholesale price index and the rate of devaluation in Korea.

The average annual rate of increase in the wholesale price index was about 17 percent during 1962–66, about 8 percent during 1967–71 and about 20 percent during 1972–76. The average annual rate of devaluation of won currency with respect to the dollar was about 19 percent during the period 1962–66, about 5 percent during 1967–71 and about 7 percent during 1972–76. Therefore the real average annual interest rate on foreign commercial loans may be approximated as about 8 percent for the period 1962–66, 3 percent for 1967–71 and −6 percent for 1972–76 while that on foreign public loans may be approximated as about 5 percent for the first period, 0 percent for the second and −9 percent for the last period. However, since private entrepreneurs have to go through fairly complicated procedures to get approval for foreign loans, the real effective interest rates to individual entrepreneurs might have been somewhat higher than these figures.

On an arrival basis, the total foreign investment during the period 1962 to 1969 amounted to about $50 million. However, with increased government efforts to promote foreign direct and joint investment, the

Table 7.11. Weighted Average Real Interest Rates on Private and Government Foreign Borrowings

	Nominal Interest Rates on Foreign Loans		Rate of Change in the Wholesale Price Index		Change in Exchange Rate (E)	Real Interest Rate on Foreign Loans		
	Private (A)	Public (B)	U.S. (C)	Korea (D)		Private (A−C)	Public (B−C)	Private (A−D+E)	Public (B−D+E)
1959	5.3%	—	0.2%	2.6%	0.0%	5.1%	—	2.7%	—
1960	5.3%	3.1%	0.1%	10.7%	27.5%	5.2%	3.0%	22.1%	19.9%
1961	5.3%	3.2%	−0.4%	13.2%	100.0%	5.7%	3.6%	92.1%	90.0%
1962	5.6%	5.0%	0.4%	9.4%	2.0%	5.2%	4.6%	−1.8%	−2.4%
1963	5.6%	2.5%	−0.4%	20.6%	0.0%	6.0%	2.9%	−15.0%	−18.1%
1964	5.3%	2.3%	0.2%	34.6%	64.9%	5.1%	2.1%	35.6%	32.6%
1965	5.5%	2.1%	2.0%	10.0%	24.3%	3.5%	0.1%	19.8%	16.4%
1966	5.5%	2.3%	3.3%	8.9%	2.1%	2.2%	−1.0%	−1.3%	−4.5%
1967	5.8%	2.4%	0.2%	6.4%	0.1%	5.6%	2.2%	−0.5%	−3.9%
1968	5.9%	2.4%	2.4%	8.1%	1.4%	3.5%	0.0%	−0.8%	−4.3%
1969	6.1%	2.6%	4.0%	6.8%	3.8%	2.1%	−1.4%	3.1%	−0.4%
1970	6.5%	2.8%	3.6%	9.2%	6.1%	2.9%	−0.8%	5.4%	1.7%
1971	6.6%	3.0%	3.2%	8.6%	11.6%	3.4%	−0.2%	9.6%	6.0%
1972	6.6%	3.3%	4.6%	14.0%	13.2%	2.0%	−1.3%	5.8%	2.5%
1973	7.5%	3.6%	13.1%	6.9%	1.7%	−5.6%	−9.5%	2.3%	−1.6%
1974	8.2%	3.9%	18.9%	42.1%	1.9%	−10.7%	−5.0%	−32.0%	−36.3%
1975	7.3%	4.4%	9.2%	26.5%	19.2%	−1.9%	−4.8%	0.0%	−2.9%
1976	7.0%	4.8%	4.6%	12.1%	0.0%	2.4%	0.2%	−5.1%	−7.3%

Source: The Bank of Korea, *Monthly Economic Statistics* and Tables B. 26. and B. 27.

Table 7.12. Inflow of Foreign Investment

Arrival Basis   In Thousand Dollars

	From U.S.A.	From Japan	Total
1962			3,927
1963			2,000
1964			3,204
1965			21,038
1966			273
1967	97,983	228,739	2,348
1968			13,845
1969			7,030
1970			24,295
1971			34,850
1972			60,703
1973			191,115
1974	28,180	130,614	162,594
1975	11,288	31,747	61,626
1976	28,178	49,220	85,494
Total	157,629	440,320	674,342

Source: Economic Planning Board.

annual inflow increased from about $24 million in 1970 to about $60 million in 1972, and to about $200 million in 1973, coming mostly from the U.S. and Japan. More than half of the total foreign investment, which amounted to $674 million during 1962–76, was concentrated on three sectors: textiles, electronics and hotels. There was also significant foreign investment in chemicals, petroleum refining, machinery, steel and metal products, transport equipment and fertilizer production.

C. *Direct Government Investment*

Government budgetary surplus and deficit financing also influenced resource allocation in the form of direct government investment and low interest rate loans for strategic sectors. Although the government inherited the former Japanese enterprises at the time of independence, it divested itself of most of the manufacturing facilities, retaining mainly monopoly enterprises and public utilities such as power, railroads, and communication. It has however, created new government-owned corporations to

Table 7.13. Industrial Classification of Foreign Investment (Total During 1962–76)

	In Thousand Dollars & Percent
Arrival Basis	
Agriculture	4,006 (1%)
Fishery	4,552 (1%)
Mining	1,315 (0%)
Manufacturing	564,245 (84%)
Food Products	4,990 (1%)
Textile & Wearing Apparel	139,934 (21%)
Wood Products	1,335 (0%)
Fertilizer	31,254 (5%)
Medicine	5,304 (1%)
Chemicals	59,350 (9%)
Petroleum Products	57,738 (9%)
Ceramics	17,439 (3%)
Steel & Metal Products	35,169 (5%)
Machinery & Equipment	39,700 (6%)
Electrical & Electronics	90,935 (14%)
Export Equipment	35,131 (5%)
Misc. Manufactures	46,056 (7%)
Social Overhead & Service	100,224 (15%)
Banking Services	8,048 (1%)
Contruction Serivces	19,252 (3%)
Electricity	4,165 (1%)
Transportation	5,080 (1%)
Hotel Services	63,679 (9%)
Total Foreign Investment	674,342 (100%)

Source: Economic Planning Board.

Table 7.14. *Government Direct Investment by Sectors*

In Billion Won & Percent

	Total	Primary Sectors	Manu- facturing	Sub-Total	SOC & Service Sectors			
					Trans- portation	Communi- cations	Elec- tricity	Others[1]
1963	21.4	4.9 (23%)	4.3 (20%)	12.2 (57%)	6.9 (32%)	1.2 (6%)	1.7 (8%)	1.1 (5%)
1964	18.3	4.2 (23%)	2.4 (13%)	11.7 (64%)	5.3 (29%)	2.4 (13%)	1.3 (7%)	0.8 (3%)
1965	25.0	7.2 (29%)	4.4 (18%)	13.4 (54%)	5.5 (22%)	3.8 (15%)	0.6 (2%)	1.5 (6%)
1966	47.4	14.5 (31%)	7.0 (15%)	25.9 (55%)	9.3 (20%)	6.9 (15%)	0.1 (0%)	2.6 (5%)
1967	53.6	13.0 (24%)	6.3 (12%)	34.3 (64%)	11.5 (21%)	8.8 (16%)	— (—)	3.5 (7%)
1968	101.1	29.5 (29%)	6.3 (6%)	65.3 (65%)	28.6 (28%)	10.5 (10%)	6.6 (7%)	4.2 (4%)
1969	145.2	36.6 (25%)	14.0 (10%)	94.6 (65%)	46.5 (32%)	14.3 (10%)	1.6 (1%)	8.8 (6%)
1970	146.7	36.5 (25%)	13.9 (9%)	96.3 (65%)	39.1 (27%)	16.0 (11%)	1.1 (1%)	10.9 (8%)
1971	161.6	37.7 (23%)	22.0 (14%)	101.9 (63%)	36.2 (22%)	18.9 (12%)	0.4 (0%)	8.6 (6%)
1972	256.2	47.1 (18%)	34.7 (14%)[2]	123.9 (48%)	42.2 (16%)	27.4 (11%)	4.3 (2%)	8.2 (3%)
1973	202.4	54.1 (27%)	18.9 (9%)	129.4 (64%)	53.1 (26%)	24.9 (12%)	5.0 (2%)	8.4 (4%)
1974	336.9	108.7 (32%)	21.2 (6%)	207.0 (61%)	62.8 (19%)	44.6 (13%)	27.6 (8%)	24.8 (7%)
1975	617.8	146.6 (24%)	60.9 (10%)	410.3 (66%)	124.1 (20%)	82.2 (13%)	22.2 (4%)	35.9 (6%)

Source: The Bank of Korea, *Economic Statistics Yearbook* and Ministry of Finance, *Summary of Financial Statistics and Final Report on Revenues and Expenditures* (various issues).

Note: [1] Water services, dams, industrial estate and other construction.
[2] Excluding investment to Korea Development Bank.

pioneer in some of the basic import-substitution industries such as fertilizer, oil refining and steel production. These are all industries in which there are economies of scale, so that in the early stages of development one producer is likely to dominate the market and establish a monopoly position. The government has preferred to control such industries directly, bearing the risk of innovative investment and assuring that production expands to meet domestic needs, rather than trying to regulate private producers and threatening them with competition from imports. As these industries have become better established and there has been room for several enterprises, the government has opened the way to private investors.[11]

Until 1968, government investment and loan activities were dependent on aid funds and deficit financing. Since 1966, however, the government has made an important contribution to total national saving by generating a substantial net revenue surplus each year.

During 1962-76, the annual government direct investment usually amounted to about 30 percent of total government expenditures. This was equivalent to about 20 percent of annual gross fixed capital formation and nearly 6 percent of GNP on the average. Although net government lending (through the BOK, KDB and other deposit money banks) amounted to approximately 6 to 8 percent of total government expenditures in the sixties, it decreased to the 2 to 3 percent level after 1972.

Most of the government direct investments were concentrated on agriculture (including irrigation, land reclamation and flood control), transportation (such as highways, harbor and shipping facilities, and railroads), communications and other SOC sectors (such as electricity, water services, multi-purpose dams, industrial estates, science and technology and education). Until 1973, investment in electricity was mostly financed by long-term domestic and foreign loans. The exceptionally large government direct investment in the manufacturing sector in 1971 and 1972 was due to the construction of a million-ton-capacity steel mill. Government investment in manufacturing has been mainly limited to government owned monopoly enterprises. The government has also made significant investments in forestry, fishery and coal mining.

---

[11] D. C. Cole and P. N. Lyman, *op. cit.*, p. 197.

4. Real Opportunity Cost of Capital Use

In order to estimate the magnitude of subsidies on capital use, we need to have some idea on the real opportunity cost of capital use. For this purpose, we have attempted to estimate the aggregate as well as sectoral rates of return on capital in Korea.[12]

The rate of return on capital is measured in terms of the annual rate at which the future (actual or prospective) net income flows from an investment have a discounted value equal to the value of the invested capital required to bring about these income flows. For prospective investments it is equal to the expected marginal productivity of capital or the marginal efficiency of capital in Keynesian analysis.[13]

If we assume a constant annual rate of return to investment (I) during the lifetime of an invested capital, and if we further assume that the capital does not depreciate during a specified period of time (i.e., lifetime) but completely evaporates after the specified period, then we get the following relationship:

$$I = S_n = \frac{Y}{1+i} + \frac{Y}{(1+i)^2} + \cdots \frac{Y}{(1+i)^n} = \frac{Y}{i}\left[1 - \left(\frac{1}{1+i}\right)^n\right]$$

where Y represents the (constant) amount of annual return to the invested capital and i represents the marginal efficiency of capital.

Let $Y = rI$ where r represents the constant annual rate of return to invested capital during its lifetime. Then we get:

---

[12] The rate of return on invested capital is a widely used concept. It provides a measure of actual performance (that is, a measure of the annual rate at which each unit of capital input generates net return) as well as required performance (that is, the target annual rate against which the performance of prospective or already invested capital inputs can be assayed). The latter is often termed the cost of capital.

[13] One may assume a Keynesian type constant average propensity to save, and understand our exposition in terms of a two-stage model in which the economy first allocates its income between savings and consumption at a certain constant ratio, after which a "maximum rate of return" principle is applied to the allocation of investment among various projects. Then one can avoid the problem of estimating the amount of utility sacrificed by consumers and the discount rates applied to the future consumption. Of course there needs to be nothing optimal about such proportional saving, unless the savings ratio is the familiar golden rule ratio or the saving propensity is adjusted once in a while in the growth process to make it roughly consistent with the intertemporal utility maximization principle.

$$i = r\left[1 - \left(\frac{1}{1+i}\right)^n\right]$$

In order to avoid complications associated with the actual depreciation pattern, we will adopt two extreme approaches. One is to use a (constant) net income flow (i.e., gross income flow minus depreciation) versus a unit of net capital which, being maintained by the depreciation allowance, perpetuates its initial capacity.[14] Another is to use (constant) gross income flow versus non-depreciating gross capital.[15] In each case, the rate of return can be computed by dividing the constant net annual future income flow (Y) by the current value of capital (I) which happens to be identical to the most commonly used laymen's concept of rate of return on invested capital (r). In effect, one can get a set-up in which the one-year rate of return on the invested capital becomes identical to the rate of return in perpetuity.[16]

We estimate the historical rate of return on capital in Korea in this section by dividing the aggregate or incremental amount of national income that can be attributed to capital with the total or incremental stock of capital. Both income and capital stock are valued in units of the same

---

[14] We assume that the fixed capital depreciates at a given simple rate every year and that is made good by investing to that extent. "If the value of the machine per person is M and its life is T periods, we may assume that an investment of (M/T) every year keeps it in continual good health so that it can be assumed that it lasts forever." See A. K. Sen, *Choice of Techniques* (Blackwell: Oxford, 1962), p. 58.

[15] There is no significant difference between this latter measure and the one assuming non-depreciating capital for a fixed period after which the capital is scrapped at zero salvage value. Suppose i = 0.9r, then
$$0.1 = \left(\frac{1}{1+0.9r}\right)^n, \text{ i.e., } (1 + 0.9r)^n = 10$$
implying that
    if $r = 0.3$, $(1.27)^n = 10$ and $n = 10$,
    if $r = 0.2$, $(1.18)^n = 10$ and $n = 14$,
and if $r = 0.14$, $(1.126)^n = 10$ and $n = 20$, approximately.

That is, if we assume 10–20 years for the lifetime of a capital (which does not depreciate during its lifetime) on the average, the difference between the estimated rate of return to capital assuming non-depreciating capital for an infinite period and that assuming non-depreciating capital for a specified period becomes insignificant.

[16] Usually the so-called laymen's estimates deviate from what one may call the theoretical estimates (i) depending on the accounting procedures used such as the fraction of each original investment outlay which is expended for book-keeping purposes and the specific depreciation formula which is used in deriving income over each project's lifetimes. In our net-to-net estimates, we are assuming that the depreciation allowance keeps initial invested capital intact, eliminating any need for expending a fraction of the initial outlay as current expenses each year. Cf. E. Solomon, "Alternative rate of return concepts and their implications for utility regulation," *The Bell Journal of Economics & Management Science*, Spring 1970.

purchasing power. Our estimation procedure relies principally on Korea's national income accounts to determine the income generated by capital and the stock of capital. Input-Output data as well as manufacturing census data are also used.[17] We will first describe the methodological procedures through which we calculate the rate of return on capital.

If we assume a linearly homogenous production function of the Cobb-Douglas form for every industry in Korea, the product of the average value-added of capital and the capital share represents the marginal productivity of capital. However, the rate of return to factors of production in Korea is unlikely to be determined solely according to the neoclassical marginalist principle. Institutional, structural (e.g., a dualistic economic structure) and traditional elements may be more influential determinants of factor returns. However, it is not necessary to assume a Cobb-Douglas production function in order to estimate the rate of return on capital. The return to non-labor factors in the business-accounting sense can indicate how much a unit of capital can earn in Korea under the given pace of technical progress and scale economies, the average quality of entrepreneurship, the existing power structure among factor owners and institutional arrangements, the natural resource endowment and the general business climate. Since the returns to non-labor include returns to physical capital, technical progress, economies of scale, market imperfection and entrepreneurship, what we will call the "rate of return on capital" (average value added of capital times non-labor share in value added) represents the rate of return to all factors but labor. We presume indivisibility among these non-labor factors of production. Our estimates of the rates of return to capital differ from the so-called shadow price or social rates of return on capital which assume a distortion free economy. For instance, our estimates of rates of return may contain an element of monopoly profit which ought not to be reflected in estimates of the social returns.

On the basis of the BOK's national income statistics, we computed various different sets of estimates for sectoral average value added of fixed capital in Korea. We first computed "net" "incremental" value-added/fixed-capital ratios allowing a one-year time lag, $d(Y_t - D_t)/(I_{t-1} - D_{t-1})$, where Y represents gross value added, D the allowance for the consumption of fixed capital stock and I represents the gross fixed capital formation in each sector at 1970 constant "market prices". We also

---

[17] In computing return on capital, we imputed and deducted the labor income that is properly attributable to owners in unincorporated enterprises, family members, and the like.

computed sectoral net-value-added/net-fixed-capital-stock ratios, $(Y-D)_t/K_t$, on the basis of Han-BOK capital stock data without allowing any time lag. We then took the other extreme approach by assuming non-depreciating capital stock. We computed gross incremental value-added/fixed-capital ratios, dY_t/I_{t-1}, as well as gross-value-added/gross-fixed-capital-stock ratios, Y_t/C_t, as estimates for the average value added of fixed capital.

The intention of adopting these two extreme approaches was to approximate the possible "range" of actual rates of return to capital in Korea. Theoretically, we expected that the estimated rates of return to capital based on net-value-added versus net-capital would be lower than those based on a non-depreciating capital assumption. However, presumably due to defects in the data on fixed capital consumption allowances, we got the opposite results. Since the so-called allowance for consumption of fixed capital stock is a legal concept which does not accurately reflect the actual depreciation, the "net" investment figure might have grossly underestimated the real amount of investment.[18] That is, a replacement of depreciated capital stock in legal terms might in effect simply represent a new investment while the "allowance" for depreciation is simply an allowance of tax-free profits.

On the other hand, the value added in market prices contains a variable amount of indirect taxation and it is not clear how one ought to allow for it. One might argue that indirect taxes on a product of a sector are completely shifted to consumers and hence cannot be regarded as the value added of that sector which happens to bear the burden of the government tax levy. In 1970, for example, about two-thirds of the gross value added in the tobacco and petroleum product sectors consisted of indirect taxes. Had the government decided to raise the same amount of tax revenue via some other commodities, the sectoral value added would have been very different. Although one can easily challenge the underlying assumption of zero price elasticity of demand and can argue that the amount actually paid by the consumers should reflect the real utility to them, we also computed sectoral "incremental" gross and net

---

[18] Arithmetically, there was no big difference between "change" in net value added and those in gross value added, while the differences between gross investment and net investment were enormous. For instance, the so-called allowance for the consumption of fixed capital amounted to about 60 percent of gross fixed capital formation in manufacturing during 1970–74. On the other hand, the net value added was (by definition) smaller than gross value added, and yet the net capital stock was much smaller than gross capital stock.

Table 7.15. Estimates of Sectoral Rates of Return to Capital: 1954-75 (Applying 1970 Non-Labor Shares)

	Primary Sector	Manu-facturing	SOC Sector	Service Sector	Primary Sector	Manu-facturing	SOC Sector	Service Sector
Non-Labor Share	0.52	0.58	0.49	0.18	0.53	0.61	0.58	0.20
	(Net Incremental VA/I Ratios at Market Price)				(Gross Incremental VA/I Ratios at Market Price)			
1954-61	291% (5.59)	37% (0.64)	9% (0.19)	63% (3.51)	161% (3.03)	25% (0.41)	10% (0.17)	15% (0.74)
1962-66	292% (5.62)	47% (0.81)	10% (0.20)	31% (1.74)	172% (3.25)	38% (0.63)	12% (0.21)	14% (0.72)
1967-71	43% (0.83)	62% (1.07)	7% (0.14)	28% (1.54)	31% (0.59)	47% (0.77)	8% (0.14)	21% (1.04)
1972-75	27% (0.52)	108% (1.86)	6% (0.13)	14% (0.75)	20% (0.38)	54% (0.89)	8% (0.13)	10% (0.49)
	(Net-VA/Net-K-Stock Ratios at Market Price)				(Gross-VA/Gross-C-Stock Ratios at Market Price)			
1953-61	170% (3.26)	24% (0.42)	5% (0.11)	10% (0.58)	118% (2.23)	18% (0.30)	5% (0.08)	9% (0.44)
1962-66	153% (2.94)	31% (0.53)	7% (0.14)	13% (0.74)	102% (1.93)	23% (0.38)	6% (0.11)	10% (0.51)
1967-71	115% (2.22)	41% (0.71)	7% (0.14)	17% (0.94)	77% (1.46)	31% (0.50)	7% (0.12)	13% (0.64)
1972-75	82% (1.57)	60% (1.03)	6% (1.03)	18% (0.98)	56% (1.05)	39% (0.64)	7% (1.12)	13% (0.65)

Non-Labor Share	0.52	0.46	0.41	0.14	0.53	0.51	0.53	0.16
	(Net Incremental VA/I Ratios at Factor Cost)				(Gross Incremental VA/I Ratios at Factor-Cost)			
1954-61	291% (5.59)	23% (0.49)	6% (0.15)	41% (2.92)	160% (3.02)	17% (0.33)	8% (0.15)	10% (0.62)
1962-66	292% (0.83)	26% (0.57)	6% (0.15)	23% (1.67)	172% (3.24)	26% (0.50)	10% (0.18)	11% (0.69)
1967-71	43% (0.83)	38% (0.82)	5% (0.12)	19% (1.34)	31% (0.59)	31% (0.61)	6% (0.12)	15% (0.92)
1972-75	27% (0.52)	64% (1.39)	5% (0.11)	8% (0.60)	20% (0.38)	36% (0.71)	6% (0.11)	7% (0.42)
	(Net-VA/Net-K-Stock Ratios at Factor Cost)				(Gross-VA/Gross-C-Stock Ratios at Factor Cost)			
1953-61	170% (3.26)	15% (0.32)	4% (0.09)	7% (0.53)	118% (2.22)	12% (0.24)	3% (0.06)	7% (0.41)
1962-66	152% (2.93)	19% (0.41)	5% (0.11)	9% (0.66)	102% (1.92)	15% (0.30)	5% (0.09)	7% (0.46)
1967-71	115% (2.22)	25% (0.54)	5% (0.12)	12% (0.84)	77% (1.46)	20% (0.39)	6% (0.11)	9% (0.57)
1972-75	82% (1.57)	36% (0.79)	5% (0.11)	12% (0.86)	55% (1.04)	26% (0.50)	6% (0.11)	9% (0.58)

Source: Table B. 22. and the Bank of Korea, *National Income in Korea.*

Note: The non-labor share excludes depreciation allowance when we apply "net" capital, and excludes indirect taxes when we apply value added at "factor cost".

value-added/fixed-capital ratios using value added figures at the 1970 constant "factor cost" which excluded indirect taxes.[19]

The annual gross fixed capital stock data which were used in computing gross-value-added/gross-capital-stock ratios were obtained by adding (or subtracting) BOK's data on annual gross fixed capital formation to Han's 1968 gross fixed capital stock data which was dervied from the 1968 National Wealth Survey. The annual net fixed capital stock data were obtained in the same fashion. Those who have an abhorrence toward working with any kind of capital "stock" data, whether in gross value or in net value, may prefer using incremental-value-added/investment ratios to approximate the average value added of fixed capital.

We computed the 1970 sectoral non-labor share in value added on the basis of the data in the 1970 I-O table. The value added may or may not include the depreciation allowance and/or indirect taxes depending on the selected estimate of the value-added/fixed-capital ratio. We also made an adjustment to exclude imputed wages for unpaid family workers and working proprietors, who are abundant in the agriculture and service sectors, from the non-labor share in value added.

A notable finding was that the rates of return on capital in the primary sector were estimated to have been more than a hundred percent for the period 1954–66. This might be attributable to the fact that we excluded the years with negative incremental value-added/fixed-capital ratios (i.e., the poor harvest years) when computing the average annual rate of return on capital in the primary sector. However, even when we computed the rate of return on the basis of net-value-added/net-capital-stock ratios, we obtained more than one hundred percent rates of return for the primary sector during the period 1954–71. Such high average annual rates of return on capital in the primary sector may then be explained by the fact that we have excluded the value of land from total fixed capital stock. If we compute the rate of return on capital in the agricultural sector including land in total fixed capital stock on the basis of the Farm House-

---

[19] Harberger included indirect taxes in his calculation of social rate of return to capital. He argues that "if a given product that sells for 100 pesos is subject to, say, a 10 percent excise tax, and if it is produced by just two factors, labor and capital, then this excise tax on the final product is equivalent to a 10 percent tax on the returns to each of the factors. Thus, for example, if labor's cost share is 60 percent and capital's 40 percent, the 10 pesos of excise revenue to be collected can be treated as taxes of 6 pesos on the labor income involved in the production of the final good and of 4 pesos on the return to capital." A. C. Harberger and D. L. Wisecarver, "Private and Social Rates of Return to Capital in Uruguay," *Economic Development and Cultural Change*, April 1977, p. 431.

Table 7.16. Estimates of Upper Limit for Rate of Return on Capital in Agricultural Sector: 1966-73

	Employed Labor		Total Wage Expenditure (Won)	Wage Rate Per Man-Year (Won)	Labor Inputs (Man-Years)	Total Imputed Wages (W) (Won)
	(Converted Work Days)	(In Man-Years)				
1966	59.48	0.2124	7,835	36,888	0.83938	30,626
1968	45.75	0.1634	10,793	66,053	0.78751	52,017
1970	37.50	0.1339	13,604	101,598	0.76264	77,483
1973	34.26	0.1224	22,523	184,011	0.74990	137,990

	Agricultural* Gross Income (V) (Won)	Non-Labor Income (V-W) (Won)	Fixed Capital (K) (Won)	Land (L) (Won)	Total Fixed Assets (K+L) (Won)	Rate of Return to Capital (V−W)/(K+L)
1966	111,236	80,610	32,963	374,567	407,530	20%
1968	150,776	98,759	54,598	455,731	510,329	19%
1970	213,470	135,987	90,264	601,788	692,052	20%
1973	420,777	282,787	205,879	1,483,676	1,689,555	17%

Source: Ministry of Agriculture & Fisheries, Report on the Results of Farm Household Economy Survey (various issues).
* Including wages for hired labor and rent for farm land. (Sum of agricultural income, wages and rent for farm land.)

Table 7.17. Estimates of Rates of Return on Capital in Manufacturing

Annual Averages	Incremental Value-Added/Investment Ratios			
	At Constant Factor Cost		At Constant Market Prices	
	Gross VA-to-Gross I (A)	Net VA-to-Net I (B)	Gross VA-to-Gross I (C)	Net VA-to-Net I (D)
1954–61	0.33	0.49	0.41	0.64
1962–66	0.50	0.57	0.63	0.81
1967–71	0.61	0.82	0.77	1.07
1972–75	0.71	1.39	0.89	1.86

	Non-Labor Share Excluding Indirect Taxes		Non-Labor Share Including Indirect Taxes	
	Gross (r)	Net (r')	Gross (p)	Net (p')
1954–61	52%	48%	60%	57%
1962–66	52%	48%	59%	57%
1967–71	52%	47%	61%	59%
1972–75	59%	52%	65%	60%

Annual Averages	Value-Added/Capital-Stock Ratios			
	At Constant Factor Cost		At Constant Market Prices	
	Gross VA-to-Gross C (E)	Net VA-to-Net K (F)	Gross VA-to-Gross C (G)	Net VA-to-Net K (H)
1954–61	0.24	0.32	0.28	0.42
1962–66	0.30	0.41	0.38	0.53
1967–71	0.39	0.54	0.50	0.71
1972–75	0.50	0.79	0.64	1.03

	Estimated Rates of Return to Capital (Assuming Non-Depreciating Capital Stock)			
	Excluding Indirect Taxes		Including Indirect Taxes	
	rA	rE	pC	pG
1954–61	17%	13%	25%	17%
1962–66	26%	16%	37%	22%
1967–71	32%	20%	47%	31%
1972–75	42%	30%	58%	42%

hold Economy Survey data, rates of return to capital are 17 to 20 percent during 1966–73. This real rate of return on capital in the agricultural sector seems to be overestimated for a number of reasons. First, the land value in the Farm Household Survey seems to have been underestimated in comparison with the market value. Secondly, social overhead capital stock for agriculture, such as irrigation or dam facilities, was not included. Finally, agricultural income did not exclude the imputed cost of self-produced intermediate inputs. Since the returns to land constitute a very large portion of non-labor income in agriculture, these latter estimates may more closely reflect a possible upper limit for the real rate of return on capital in the primary sector, especially in agriculture and probably in fisheries and mining also.

From the above estimates we can observe that the rate of return on capital has been very high in manufacturing, relatively low in agriculture and services and lowest in the social overhead sectors. Artificially low priced SOC services seem to have enhanced the rate of return in other sectors, especially in the manufacturing sector. In any case, such marked differences in the rate of return on capital among sectors may explain the rapid expansion of manufacturing, the moderate decline in the service sector and the drastic decrease in the share of GNP contributed by agriculture. It may also explain the need for government direct investment in the social overhead sector.

There are several factors accounting for these persistent differences in returns to capital among industries including : (1) different degrees of monopolistic control, (2) different heights of barriers to the movement of capital among industries, (3) different growth rates of demand for each industrial product, (4) imperfect capital mobility generating quasi-rent and (5) varying degrees of difficulty associated with the withdrawal of capital from low return industries.[20] Furthermore, the market prices of social overhead capital (SOC) services usually do not reflect their true utility to society. This is not only because of the extensive existence of external economies associated with SOC sectors but also because the government has somehow traditionally maintained the SOC prices at such a low level that investments in most SOC sectors are quite unprofitable.

We further computed the labor share in the manufacturing sector during the period 1960–75 on the basis of manufacturing census and I-O

---

[20] See B. S. Minhas, *An International Comparison of Factor Costs and Factor Use*, (Amsterdam: North Holland, 1963), pp. 82–83.

data. The labor share in total value added estimated on the basis of manufacturing census data was much smaller than that estimated on the basis of I-O data. As a result, the non-labor shares computed on the basis of manufacturing census data ranged around 60–70 percent during 1960–73, while those computed on the basis of I-O data ranged around 47–65 percent.[21]

On the basis of various sets of estimates for average value added of capital in manufacturing and the non-labor share in manufacturing during 1960–75, which were computed from the I-O data, we made a separate series of estimates for the rates of return on capital in the manufacturing sector. Since there was a slightly increasing tendency in the non-labor share during 1960–75, the rates of return were slightly different from those estimated with the 1970 set of non-labor share data. In any case, the rates of return on capital in the manufacturing sector were much higher than those in other sectors.

We also computed the (gross) value-added/capital-stock ratios on the basis of manufacturing census data only, and the resulting estimates of rate of return to capital were higher than those estimated on the basis of Han-BOK (gross) capital stock data. On the other hand, if we compute the rates of return to fixed assets in the manufacturing sector on the basis of the BOK's Financial Statements Analysis, we get rates of return to fixed capital which are closer to the estimates based on Han-BOK data.

As was mentioned, the rates of return estimated on the basis of net-value-added/net-capital ratios were much higher than those estimated on the basis of gross-value-added/gross-capital ratios. In manufacturing, the former rates were about 40 percent higher than the latter rates. To be on the conservative side, we decided to use the estimates based on gross-value-added/gross-capital ratios to approximate the rate of return on capital in Korea. After all, estimates of capital in net terms are less reliable and gross investment is itself a major vehicle of technical progress.

The estimated sectoral "rate of return on capital" represents the actual rate of return under the given actual conditions in the Korean economy. We may call the difference between the official interest rate on a bank loan and the average rate of return on capital a "subsidy" in the sense that, to an average entrepreneur in Korea, the difference may represent a windfall gain arising from imperfection in the capital market. According

---

[21] In the U.S. labor received approximately four-fifth of the income of manufacturing industries, and the capital the remainder in 1954. G. Stigler, *Capital and Rates of Return in Manufacturing Industries* (Princeton University Press: New Jersey, 1963), p. 6.

Table 7.18. Rates of Return to Fixed Assets in the Manufacturing Sector

In Thousand Won & Percent

	Value Added per Employee[1]	Fixed Assets per Employee	Net Profit in Value Added	Value Added to Fixed Assets	Non-Labor Share[2]	Rates of Return to Fixed Assets
1962	108	137	31.1%	0.788	54%	43%
1963	133	221	35.7%	0.602	55%	33%
1964	201	361	31.6%	0.557	57%	32%
1965	232	387	34.2%	0.600	56%	34%
1966	281	418	31.2%	0.672	59%	40%
1967	304	460	28.1%	0.661	58%	37%
1968	373	763	27.2%	0.489	57%	28%
1969	431	845	18.3%	0.610	55%	28%
1970	538	1,109	14.0%	0.476	53%	25%
1971	522	1,140	5.5%	0.458	51%	23%
1972	691	1,378	19.1%	0.502	53%	27%
1973	853	1,637	35.6%	0.582	58%	34%
1974	1,069	1,865	27.2%	0.573	53%	30%
1975	1,242	2,141	18.9%	0.580	50%	29%
1977	1,699	2,612	20.7%	0.651	50%	33%
1962–66	—	—	32.8%	0.644	56%	36%
1967–71	—	—	18.8%	0.519	54%	28%
1972–76	—	—	24.3%	0.578	53%	31%

Source: The Bank of Korea, *Financial Statements Analysis* (various issues).
Notes: [1] Excludes depreciation and bad debts.
[2] Type V non-labor share. (See Table 7.14.)

Table 7.19. Estimated Real Opportunity Cost of Capital Use in Manufacturing

Annual Averages	Excluding Indirect Taxes		Including Indirect Taxes	
	Based on VA/C-Stock (Type I)	Incremental VA/I (Type II)	Based on VA/C-Stock (Type III)	Incremental VA/I (Type IV)
	Possible Lower Limit	Possible Medium Range		Possible Upper Limit
	(Without Taking Account of Net Working Capital)			
1954-61	13%	17%	17%	25%
1962-66	16%	26%	22%	37%
1967-71	20%	32%	31%	47%
1972-75	30%	42%	42%	57%
	(Taking Account of Net Working Capital)			
1954-61	10%	13%	13%	19%
1962-66	12%	20%	20%	29%
1967-71	17%	27%	26%	39%
1972-75	25%	35%	35%	48%
	(Taking Account of Capital Loss)			
1964-61	9%	12%	12%	18%
1962-66	9%	17%	14%	26%
1967-71	16%	26%	25%	38%
1972-75	17%	27%	27%	40%

Source: Table 7.17. and the Bank of Korea, *Economic Statistics Yearbook*.
Note: Gross-value-added to gross-capital ratios were used assuming non-depreciating capital stock. The type II estimate might be interpreted as representing marginal rate of return on reproducible (but non-depreciating) capital and the type III estimate the average rate of return in manufacturing.

to the BOK's Financial Statements Analysis, an average of 5 percent of the total (gross) value added in manufacturing was directly taxed away by the government during the period 1967–75.[22] Hence we also have to take account of the direct tax element when we estimate the actual amount of subsidy given to an individual entrepreneur. However, from the viewpoint of the entire national economy, the return on capital "before (direct) tax" represents the real opportunity cost of capital in Korea, regardless of the fact that the government takes away part of the return. Tax revenue generated by private investment can be regarded as social returns directly attributable to such an investment. Therefore, we did not subtract direct taxes from return to capital when we estimated the amount of the "subsidy" on capital use. Hence the estimated subsidy in the following section will represent the subsidy to a sector rather than that to individual entrepreneurs in the sector. To estimate the latter, we have to subtract approximatley 10 percent from each estimated rate of return on capital (in manufacturing).[23]

Among the various sectoral rates of return on (fixed) capital estimated in this section we decided to use those for manufacturing to represent the (average) real opportunity cost of (fixed) capital in Korea. Furthermore, in order to be on the conservative side, we took the relatively low rates among those estimates for manufacturing (i.e., the estimates based on gross incremental-value-added/investment ratios and gross-value-added/gross-capital-stock ratios) as the rates of return on (fixed) capital in computing sectoral subsidies on capital use. Since there are four such sets of estimates, two including indirect taxes and the other two excluding them, we took the set estimated at market prices (i.e., including indirect taxes) and incremental ratios as a possible upper limit and the set estimated at factor cost and stock ratios as a possible lower limit for the real opportunity cost of capital in Korea. The other two sets are fairly similar to each

---

[22] See Table B. 19.

[23] There is also a body of rather controversial literature dealing with the incidence of corporate income tax. If it were a tax on pure profits, there should be no attempted shifting through price, output or factor market effects. At two extremes, Hall was unable to find evidence of shifting, while Harberger found that capital bears about 112–120% of the tax burden, so that it distorts the factor market for capital between the corporate and noncorporate sectors. See S. P. Magee, *International Trade and Distortions in Factor Markets* (Marcel Dekker: New York, 1976), p. 94., C. A. Hall "Direct Shifting of the Corporation Income Tax in Manufacturing, *American Economic Review*, May 1964 and A. C. Harberger, "The Incidence of the Corporation Tax," *Journal of Political Economy*, June 1962. We are interested in estimating gross earning of capital regardless of the magnitude of government sharing in the form of direct taxes. In this paper, we assume no shifting of direct taxes.

other, and may be regarded as medium level estimates for the rate of return on capital.

We then made two important adjustments. According to the BOK's Financial Statements Analysis, the ratio of fixed assets to total assets and the ratio of net working capital to total assets in manufacturing averaged 46.1 percent and 9.5 percent, respectively, during 1967–75. This implies that an average firm uses net "working capital" whose money value is equivalent to about 20 percent of the value of its fixed capital[24] However, we have ignored working capital in our computation of the rate of return on (fixed) capital. Therefore, we first deflated the rates of return for 1967–75, which we have estimated in this section, by 1.20 in order to reflect the existence of the net working capital. As a result, the possible real opportunity cost of capital use in Korea (using the Type II estimate in Table 7.19.) was reduced from 32 percent to 27 percent per annum during 1967–71 and from 42 percent to 35 percent during 1972–75. The amount of net working capital for the years 1960–66 was equivalent to about 30 percent of the value of fixed capital. Hence we deflated the rates of return for 1954–66 by 1.30, obtaining 20 percent for the average annual rate of return during 1962–66 and 13 percent for that during 1954–61.

The second adjustment was to take account of capital loss. In the case of embodied technical progress, obsolescence and the associated capital loss reduce the rate of return on capital. To the extent that embodied technical progress occurs at the given set of prices of output, material inputs and labor, the progress may simply enhance the profits (or rents) instead of lowering the market price of old capital stock in order to equate the rate of return on new invested capital to that of the old one.[25] However, the price of capital goods in Korea rose at an average annual rate of about

---

[24] Net working capital represents the difference between current assets and current liabilities. Since we have been using mostly macro-aggregated sectoral output data, we take account of only "net" working capital instead of "gross" working capital in order to avoid double counting of existing working capital in the economy. The size of working capital depends, among other things, on the time lag between payment to owners of current inputs and the receipts of the sales value of the consequent output. The size of the lag will depend not merely on the technical speed of production but also on the marketing lags, i.e., on organizational factors. See A. K. Sen, *Choice of Techniques* (Blackwell: Oxford, 1962), pp. 110–111.

[25] The social equivalent of obsolescence is, of course, not a simple capital loss. It represents, rather, the fact that it is more costly to increase next year's capital stock through this year's saving than it will be to increase the following year's capital stock through next year's saving. See R. M. Solow, *op. cit.*, p. 62. Furthermore, disembodied technical progress, which could be as important as embodied technical progress, does not cause obsolescence.

10 percent during 1956–61, 14 percent during 1962–66, 7 percent during 1967–71 and 12 percent during 1972–76. During these periods the wholesale price index for all commodities rose at an average annual rate of about 11 percent, 17 percent, 8 percent and 20 percent respectively.[26] That is, the relative price of capital stock fell at an average annual rate of about 1 percent during 1956–61, 3 percent during 1962–66, 1 percent during 1967–71 and 8 percent during 1972–76. Therefore, if we take account of capital loss, the rate of return on capital (using the Type II estimate) becomes 12 percent for the period 1954–61, 17 percent for 1962–66, 26 percent for 1967–71 and 27 percent for 1972–75. Since nearly 10 percent of the gross return on capital was taken away from the entrepreneur in the form of direct taxes, the rate of return on capital to individual entrepreneurs was approximately 9 percent during 1962–66 and 18 percent during 1967–75.[27]

The deposit money banks applied the highest (nominal) interest rate on overdue loans (31.2 to 36.5 percent per annum during 1966–72), the second highest rate on overdrafts (25 to 32 percent), and relatively high rates on discounted commercial bills (22 to 28 percent). According to the data collected by the Bank of Korea, the (nominal) curb market interest rates fluctuated within a range of 33 to 62 percent per annum during 1963–76.[28]

We have observed steady increases in the upper limit of the estimated average rates of return on capital (Type IV estimate) from 26 percent during 1962–66 to 38 percent during 1967–71 and an increase in the curb market (real) average interest rate from 40 percent during 1963–66 to 44 percent during 1967–71.[29] If we take the period of 1967–71, the (arithmetic) average real interest rate on non-preferential bank loans (i.e., overdue loans and overdrafts) was 26 percent per annum. If one emphasizes the extreme backward state of financial institutions in Korea, one might argue that the (real) interest rates on non-preferential bank loans or the (real) curb rates would reflect the real rates of return on capital in Korea. This implies that the upper limit estimate (Type IV estimate) might be closer

---

[26] The Bank of Korea, *Economic Statistics Yearbook* (various issues). Wholesale price index for machinery and parts was used for the 1956–61 period.

[27] The share of direct taxes in total non-labor value added in manufacturing averaged about 8 percent during 1967–71 and about 9 percent during 1972–76. See Table B. 19.

[28] If we compute the real curb market interest rates by subtracting the rates of change in the wholesale price index, the average real interest rate for curb market loans was about 40 percent during 1963–66, 44 percent during 1967–71, 19 percent during 1972–76 and about 40 percent during 1963–72. The drastic fall in curb rates during the period 1972–75 seems to have been due to the extremely high rate of inflation in 1974–75 and the Decree on curb loans on August 3, 1972.

[29] However, the former rate continued increasing to 40 percent during 1972–76 while the latter rate fell to 19 percent.

Table 7.20. Weighted Average Rates of Return on Capital in the Non-Primary Sectors

	Rate of Return in Manu-facturing[1]	SOC Sectors		Service Sectors		All Non-Primary Sectors[3]	
		(Non-L Share)	(V/C Ratio)[2] Rate of Return	(Non-L Share)	(V/C Ratio)[2] Rate of Return	Weighted by Gross Capital	Weighted by Net Capital
1954–61	12%	(.44)[4]	4%	(.30)[4]	(.44) 13%	11%	11%
1962–66	17%	(.52)[5]	6%	(.32)[5]	(.51) 16%	13%	13%
1967–71	26%	(.56)[6]	7%	(.27)[6]	(.64) 17%	16%	15%
1972–75	27%	(.60)[7]	7%	(.25)[7]	(.65) 16%	15%	14%[8]

Source and Notes:
[1] Estimates in Table 7.19. which took account of net working capital and capital loss.
[2] Estimates based on gross-value-added/gross-capital-stock ratios at market price in Table 7.15.
[3] Weighted by gross or net sectoral capital stock.
[4] Estimates of the non-labor share obtained from the 1960 I-O Table and adjusted for unpaid workers.
[5] Estimates of the average non-labor share obtained form 1963 and 1966 I-O Tables and adjusted for unpaid workers.
[6] Estimates of the average non-labor share obtained from 1968 and 1970 I-O Tables and adjusted for unpaid workers.
[7] Estimates of the non-labor share obtained from the 1973 I-O Table.
[8] The average rate of return on capital in the non-primary sector estimated by applying the gross incremental value-added/investment ratio in all non-primary sectors at factor cost (obtained from BOK's *National Income in Korea*) and the non-labor share in the sector excluding indirect tax (obtained from Table B. 22.) was 14 percent in 1967–71 and 1972–75. If indirect tax is included, the rate of return becomes 20 percent in each period. (Not adjusted for net working capital or capital loss.)

to the actual rate of return on capital in Korea than the medium range estimate (Type II estimate).

Since the real rate of return in manufacturing seems to have been exaggerated due to artificially low priced SOC outputs, we also estimated the weighted average rate of return on capital in all non-primary sectors applying the gross or net sectoral fixed capital stock as weights. Since there are many different sets of estimates for sectoral rates of return, the specific set selected for the computation in Table 7.20. was based on our subjective judgement of what may be regarded as reasonable estimates. If these figures are taken as a rough approximation of the average rate of return on capital in all non-primary sectors, one can conclude that the rate of return in Korean industries as s whole increased from around 11 percent in 1954–62 to around 15 percent in 1967–75. If we examine the estimated rate of return in agriculture in Table 7.16., it does not seem likely that the rate of return in the primary sector could deviate wildly from these weighted average rates of return in the non-primary sectors.

All of our calculations have related to the historical returns that past investment has generated, and hence the observed rates of return derived from the national income account have been changing over time and are expected to keep changing in the future. One usually expects a decline in the rate of return on capital as economic development takes place (in terms of per worker capital stock), unless technical progress more than offsets the tendency of falling marginal productivity of capital caused by per worker capital accumulation. Regardless of one's opinion about the inevitability of a declining trend in the rate of return on capital in the very long run, some fluctuations can be expected (i.e., rises and falls of the rate of return on capital) in the growth process of an economy. For instance, the continuous rise in the rates of return on capital in Korea during 1953–75 may reflect the effects of rapidly accumulating social overhead capital stock, the internal and external economies of scale, accumulations of skills and other human capital and various forms of technical progress such as the expanding market network associated with the export-oriented growth process. The extended horizon of business activities towards every part of the international market may have significantly contributed to raising the profitability of doing business in Korea. The views which stress sharply limited "absorptive capacity" for investment in underdeveloped countries may be interpreted as suggesting a relatively low rate of return on capital in the earlier phase of industrialization.[30]

---

[30] See R. S. Eckaus, "Absorptive Capacity as a Constraint due to Maturation Processes", in J. N. Bhagwati and R. S. Eckaus, eds., *Development and Planning*, (Cam-

Chenery's estimates of the marginal productivity of capital were 0.17 for countries with a per capita income of less than $200, 0.27 for countries with a per capita income of $200–850 and 0.12 for more developed countries.[31] These results are consistent with the long-run declining trend in the rate of return on capital, allowing a rise and fall of the rate in the growth process.

According to the gross and net capital stock data estimated on the basis of Han-BOK data, about a third of total gross capital stock in 1976 could be dated to the post-1972 period and about two-thirds of it to the post-1968 period. At the same time about half of the total net capital stock in 1976 could be dated to the post-1972 period and more than 80 percent of it to the post-1968 period.[32] Overall productivity increases may largely depend on the rate at which the intrinsic productivity of new capital rises and the extent to which a high rate of investment modernizes the capital stock. Therefore, a substantial portion of the rising rate of return on capital in Korea might as well be attributed to the embodied technical progress associated with capital formation and non-proportional increase in the relative price of new capital stock.

The rising trend in estimated rates of return may also be understood in terms of the rising rate of capital utilization. A study on the utilization of capital equipment in Korean manufacturing suggests that the average growth rates of utilization during 1962–71 were in the range of 7 to 10 percent per annum.[33]

---

bridge, Mass, 1973), pp. 79–83. Y. C. Kim and G. C. Winston also showed that the smaller the per capita income, the smaller the output per unit of capital stock and the lower the utilization rate of capital stock. "The Optimal Utilization of Capital Stock and the Level of Economic Development," *Economica*, November 1974.

[31] Quoted in N. H. Leff, "Rates of Return to Capital, Domestic Savings, and Investment in the Developing Countries," *Kyklos*, Vol. 28, 1975. The average rates of return on capital in manufacturing estimated by Minhas were 16.0 percent in the U.S., 15.8 percent in Canada, 17.9 percent in Japan and 19.1 percent in India during 1949–58. He also quoted the estimates of the UN (which did not make allowances for working capital): for Israel at 22 percent in 1953–54 and for Egypt at 25–30 percent in 1954–55. Somehow he used these estimates as evidence to support his conclusion that average rates of return on capital differ only slightly between the developed and underdeveloped countries. See B. S. Minhas, *op. cit.*, pp. 86–89.

[32] Hong. *op. cit.*, Tables A. 28. and A. 29.

[33] Y. C. Kim and J. K. Kwon "The Utilization of Capital and the Growth of Output in Developing Economy: The Case of South Korean Manufacturing," *Journal of Development Economics*, 4, 1977. Bruton suggested that virtually all the growth of total productivity as conventionally measured simply reflects the improved utilization of capital and that the growth of "pure" technology was virtually nil in Latin American countries. H. J. Bruton, "Productivity Growth in Latin America," *American Economic Review*, December 1967.

In the fifties, the behavior of Korean investors seems to have been typically characterized by a preference for short-term investment projects. This behavior might be attributed to the fact that the rate of return on capital was too low to justify their assuming the greater risk and uncertainty associated with long-term investments. Since late in the sixties, one can observe more frequent shifts by Korean investors to a longer run investment horizon and to high corporate savings ratios. This shift may well be attributed to the experience of high rates of return on capital during 1967–76.

The concept discussed in this section is essentially a one-period or short-run rate of return which, if we wish, can be understood as the rate of return in perpetuity under certain assumptions. In Solow's terms, the rate of return as we have calculated it is the rate of interest paid by the bank on one-year deposits—only the bank is really the complete collection of capital-using production processes in the economy (i.e., manufacturing sector)—and furthermore:[34]

> "... one-period rates of return are the fundamental ones because ... saving-investment decisions come up for consideration every period and can easily be changed or even undone; so that even a long and complicated investment program can probably be duplicated by a series of cleverly-chosen short-term programs."

After analyzing the employment implications of trade and factor market distortions, one may like to consider a small variation around some pre-existing situation. Then the estimated set of average rates of return for a limited time horizon can provide a convenient class of base situations from which one can contemplate possible displacements.

5. Implicit Subsidies on Capital Use

The major sources of loans in Korea were DMB loans, KDB loans, private and government foreign borrowings and curb loans. The DMB loans constitutd about 40–50 percent of total loans (year-end balance) during 1964–75. The share of KDB loans amounted to about 20–30 percent of total loans during 1964–66, but their share was reduced to around 10 percent thereafter. The share of foreign loans was negligible until 1962

---

[34] See. R. M. Solow, *Capital Theory and the Rate of Return* (Amsterdam: North-Holland, 1963), pp. 21–25 and 57–58.

but their share has rapidly increased to about 30–40 percent of total outstanding loans in Korea since 1966. The share of curb loans, admittedly underestimated, amounted to around 11 percent of total loans during 1964–71, and around 7 percent during 1972–75.

In section 3, we estimated the (weighted average) real interest rates on bank loans and those on government and private foreign borrowings. The real interest rate on DMB loans reached its peak of 15 percent in 1967 and then steadily declined to become negative in 1974. The rate on KDB loans was almost always negative except during 1966–71. Taking account of the devaluation effect, the interest rate on private foreign borrowings was estimated to have been about 8 percent during 1962–66, 3 percent during 1967–71 and -6 percent in 1972–76. The interest rate on government foreign borrowings was estimated to have been about 5 percent during 1962–66, about zero percent during 1962–71 and about -10 percent during 1972–76 on the average. In section 4, we estimated the average real rates of return on fixed capital in Korea and found that the (Type II estimate) rate of return (in manufacturing) was about 12 percent in 1954–61, about 17 percent during the First Five Year Plan period, 26 percent during the Second Five Year Plan period and about 27 percent during the Third Five Year Plan period. Therefore, the use of a large amount of (domestic or foreign) borrowed capital at low interest rates in Korean industries implies extremely high rates of return on equity investment. On the basis of the above estimates we can now approximate the total amount on interest rate subsidies associated with bank loans and foreign borrowings in Korea.

The rate of interest subsidy on bank loans or foreign loans was computed by subtracting the real (weighted average) interest rates on these loans from the real (average) rate of return on capital (Type II estimate). The rate of interest subsidy on DMB loans was about 18 percent during 1962–66, 14 percent during 1967–71 and 35 percent during 1972–75 while the rate of interest subsidy on KDB loans was about 24 percent, 21 percent and 41 percent for the same periods. Similarly, the rate of interest subsidy on private foreign borrowings was estimated to have been about 9 percent during 1962–66, 23 percent during 1967–71 and 33 percent during 1972–75 while the rate of interest subsidy on government foreign borrowings was estimated to have been about 12 percent, 26 percent and 37 percent for the same periods.

In order to get some idea on the aggregate magnitude of interest subsidies, we estimated the ratio of the total interest subsidy associated with domestic and foreign loans in the manufacturing sector to the total (gross

Table 7.21. Domestic and Foreign Loan Balance

In Million 1970 Dollars & Percent

	DMB Loans[1]	KDB Loans[1]	Foreign Borrowing[2] Private	Foreign Borrowing[2] Government	Curb Loans[3]	Total
1957	180	152	—	—	—	—
1958	264	175	—	—	—	—
1959	295	229	3	1	—	—
1960	359	234	2	1	—	—
1961	420	260	2	2	—	—
1962	505	274	2	9	n.a.	790
1963	432	242	23	37	n.a.	734
1964	330 (46%)	210 (30%)	42 (6%)	50 (7%)	78 (11%)	710 (100%)
1965	410 (46%)	225 (25%)	69 (8%)	61 (7%)	125 (14%)	890 (100%)
1966	512 (43%)	250 (21%)	179 (15%)	127 (11%)	121 (10%)	1,189 (100%)
1967	792 (45%)	246 (14%)	319 (18%)	208 (12%)	183 (10%)	1,748 (100%)
1968	1,327 (47%)	279 (10%)	557 (20%)	316 (11%)	329 (12%)	2,808 (100%)
1969	2,007 (49%)	357 (9%)	859 (21%)	449 (11%)	416 (10%)	4,088 (100%)
1970	2,196 (46%)	415 (9%)	1,040 (22%)	576 (12%)	585 (12%)	4,812 (100%)
1971	2,498 (44%)	455 (8%)	1,217 (22%)	859 (15%)	631 (11%)	5,660 (100%)

Year					
1972	2,838 (44%)	603 (9%)	1,309 (20%)	515 (8%)	6,502 (100%)
1973	3,435 (45%)	733 (10%)	1,410 (19%)	567 (7%)	7,612 (100%)
1974	4,191 (50%)	774 (9%)	1,466 (17%)	588 (7%)	8,476 (100%)
1975	4,029 (46%)	846 (10%)	1,747 (20%)	598 (7%)	8,829 (100%)
1976	4,456	936	1,919	1,912	n.a.

Source: The Bank of Korea, *Economic Statistics Yearbook* and Tables B. 23. and B. 26.

Notes: [1]Since part of the foreign borrowings have been supplied to DMB and KDB for their sub-loan operations, there are double countings in total amount of loans. The amount of such double-counting seems to have amounted to around 5 percent of total KDB and DMB loans. KDB and DMB loans were deflated by the GNP deflator for the whole industry. The exchange rate of 310.6 won per dollar was applied. Remunerations of CNB were excluded.

[2] Deflated by the U.S. wholesale price index to get 1970 figures.

[3] Obtained from Y. C. Park, *op. cit.* and deflated by the GNP deflator for the whole industry.

Table 7.22. Loans and (Weighted Average) Real Interest Rates

	DMB Loans		KDB Loans		Curb Loans		Private Foreign Borrowing		Year-End Balance Gov't Foreign Borrowing	
	Billion Won	Interest Rate	Billion Won	Interest Rate	Billion Won	Interest Rate	Million Dollars	Interest Rate	Million Dollars	Interest Rate
1957	10.9		9.2				—		—	
1958	15.9		10.5				—		—	
1959	18.3		14.1				2.1	(2.7%)		
1960	24.3		15.9				2.0	(22.1%)	1.1	(19.9%)
1961	32.7	(0.1%)	20.3				1.7	(92.1%)	2.1	(90.0%)
1962	44.8	(4.0%)	24.3	(−1.0%)	—	(—)	1.5	(−1.8%)	8.1	(−2.4%)
1963	49.4	(−7.5%)	27.6	(−12.3%)	—	(31.9%)	19.8	(−15.0%)	32.1	(−18.1%)
1964	49.9	(−21.3%)	31.7	(−26.2%)	11.7	(27.2%)	36.0	(35.6%)	43.0	(32.6%)
1965	67.1	(6.2%)	36.8	(−0.8%)	20.4	(48.9%)	60.3	(19.8%)	53.8	(16.4%)
1966	95.6	(12.5%)	46.6	(2.9%)	22.6	(49.8%)	161.7	(−1.3%)	114.5	(−4.5%)
1967	168.4	(15.4%)	52.4	(6.1%)	38.9	(50.1%)	288.7	(−0.5%)	188.1	(−3.9%)
1968	315.9	(13.4%)	66.4	(4.6%)	78.2	(47.9%)	517.1	(−0.8%)	292.8	(−4.3%)
1969	540.4	(13.9%)	96.1	(5.4%)	112.1	(44.5%)	829.3	(3.1%)	433.7	(−0.4%)
1970	682.1	(8.4%)	129.0	(3.3%)	181.6	(40.6%)	1,039.6	(5.4%)	576.7	(1.7%)
1971	865.0	(7.8%)	157.5	(3.8%)	218.4	(37.8%)	1,256.2	(9.5%)	886.6	(6.0%)
1972	1,125.6	(3.7%)	239.1	(−4.1%)	204.2	(25.0%)	1,412.5	(5.8%)	1,335.1	(2.5%)
1973	1,492.8	(7.0%)	318.5	(2.8%)	246.4	(26.4%)	1,720.5	(2.3%)	1,790.2	(−1.6%)
1974	2,303.9	(−28.1%)	425.7	(−32.4%)	323.6	(−1.5%)	2,125.9	(−32.0%)	2,112.0	(−36.3%)
1975	2,751.6	(−12.9%)	577.8	(−15.3%)	408.4	(14.8%)	2,766.9	(0.0%)	2,548.2	(−2.9%)
1976	3,522.1	(1.6%)	739.9	(−0.8%)	—	(28.4%)	3,180.3	(−5.1%)	3,168.4	(−7.3%)

Table 7.22. (Continued)

In Million 1970 Dollars & Percent

	Total KDB & DMB Loans[2]		KDB, DMB & Curb Loans[2]		Total Foreign Loans[3]		Total Domestic & Foreign Loans	
	Total Loans	Interest Rate	Total Loans	Interest Rate	Total Loans	Interest Rate	Total Loans	Interest Rate
1959	524	(2.2%)	—	—	3	(2.7%)	—	—
1960	593	(2.2%)	—	—	3	(21.3%)	—	—
1961	680	(2.2%)	—	—	4	(90.9%)	—	—
1962	778	(2.2%)	856[4]	(4.5%)[4]	11	(−2.3%)	867	(−4.4%)
1963	674	(−9.2%)	752[4]	(−5.4%)[4]	60	(−16.9%)	813	(−6.3%)
1964	541	(−23.2%)	619	(−16.8%)	92	(34.0%)	711	(−10.2%)
1965	636	(3.7%)	761	(11.1%)	130	(18.2%)	891	(12.1%)
1966	762	(9.4%)	883	(14.9%)	306	(−2.6%)	1,189	(10.4%)
1967	1,038	(13.2%)	1,221	(18.7%)	527	(−1.8%)	1,748	(12.5%)
1968	1,607	(11.9%)	1,936	(18.0%)	873	(−2.0%)	2,809	(11.8%)
1969	2,364	(12.6%)	2,780	(17.4%)	1,308	(1.9%)	4,088	(12.4%)
1970	2,611	(7.6%)	3,196	(13.6%)	1,616	(4.1%)	4,812	(10.4%)
1971	2,953	(7.2%)	3,584	(12.6%)	2,076	(8.1%)	5,660	(11.0%)
1972	3,441	(2.3%)	3,956	(5.3%)	2,546	(4.2%)	6,502	(4.9%)
1973	4,168	(6.3%)	4,735	(8.7%)	2,887	(0.3%)	7,612	(5.5%)
1974	4,965	(−28.8%)	5,553	(−25.7%)	2,923	(−34.1%)	8,476	(−28.7%)
1975	4,875	(−13.3%)	5,473	(−10.2%)	3,356	(−1.4%)	8,829	(−6.9%)
1976	5,392	(1.2%)	5,473	(−10.2%)	3,833	(−6.2%)		

Source: The Bank of Korea, *Economic Statistics Yearbook*, and the Economic Planning Board.
Notes: [1] Excluding the remuneration of the Citizen's National Bank.
[2] GNP deflator of Korea (1970 = 100) and the exchange rate of 310.6 won per dollar were applied in order to get 1970 dollar values.
[3] Private and foreign borrowings were deflated by using the U.S. wholesale price index (1970 = 100).
[4] Applying the 1964 information on curb loans. Curb interest rates are unpublished BOK data.

Table 7.23. Estimated Rate of Interest Subsidy Associated with Domestic and Foreign Loans to the Manufacturing Sector

In Million 1970 Dollars & Percent

	Total Fixed Capital Stock		DMB & KDB Loans					Total Foreign Borrowing				
	Gross (C)	Net (K)	Total Loans	(Subsidy Rate)	Interest Subsidy(S)	S/C	S/K	Total Loans	(Subsidy Rate)	Interest Subsidy(S)	S/C	S/K
1957	972	647	142	(12%)	15	2%	2%	—	(—)	—	—	—
1958	1,047	697	193	(13%)	25	2%	4%	—	(—)	—	—	—
1959	1,110	735	236	(13%)	30	3%	4%	3	(9%)	0	0%	0%
1960	1,177	772	250	(13%)	31	3%	4%	2	(−10%)	0	0%	0%
1961	1,243	813	259	(13%)	34	3%	4%	2	(−80%)	−2	0%	0%
1962	1,331	869	307	(15%)	46	3%	5%	5	(19%)	1	0%	0%
1963	1,447	936	257	(27%)	59	5%	7%	27	(32%)	9	1%	1%
1964	1,560	987	216	(40%)	87	6%	9%	44	(−18%)	−8	−1%	−1%
1965	1,718	1,072	291	(14%)	40	2%	4%	55	(−2%)	−1	0%	0%
1966	1,985	1,273	365	(7%)	27	1%	2%	156	(19%)	29	2%	2%
1967	2,251	1,456	501	(13%)	66	3%	4%	273	(27%)	74	3%	5%
1968	2,608	1,682	819	(14%)	117	4%	7%	419	(27%)	114	4%	7%
1969	3,013	1,918	1,168	(13%)	154	5%	8%	514	(23%)	119	4%	6%
1970	3,428	2,138	1,242	(19%)	233	7%	11%	659	(21%)	138	4%	6%
1971	3,852	2,351	1,437	(19%)	267	7%	12%	824	(16%)	132	3%	6%
1972	4,269	2,458	1,693	(24%)	406	10%	17%	963	(21%)	202	5%	8%
1973	5,036	2,809	2,234	(21%)	475	9%	17%	977	(26%)	254	5%	9%
1974	5,663	2,994	2,843	(55%)	1,575	28%	53%	1,037	(59%)	612	11%	20%
1975	6,361	3,190	2,743	(40%)	1,103	17%	35%	1,286	(27%)	347	5%	11%
1976	7,301	3,508	3,083	(26%)	802	11%	23%	1,478	(31%)	458	6%	13%

Source: Tables 7.19., 7.21., 7.22., B. 34 and B. 35.

Notes: Type II estimates for the rate of return on capital in manufacturing (Table 7.19.) and real interest rates on total loans to manufacturing were applied in computing subsidy rates. In the case of DMB loans, the real interest rate for 1961 was applied to the entire 1957–61 period, and in case of KDB loans, the real interest rate for 1962 was applied to the entire 1957–62 period.

Table 7.24. Estimated Rate of Interest Subsidy Associated with Domestic and Foreign Loans: Whole Industry
In Million 1970 Dollars & Percent

	Total Fixed Capital Stock		DMB & KDB Loans					Total Foreign Borrowing			
	Gross (C)	Net(K)	Total Loans	(Subsidy Rate)	Interest Subsidy(S)	S/C	S/K	Total Loans	(Subsidy Rate)	Interest Subsidy(S)	S/C	S/K
1957	5,550	3,731	332	(11%)	38	1%	1%	—	(—)	—	—	—
1958	5,790	3,862	439	(11%)	50	1%	1%	—	(—)	—	—	—
1959	6,041	3,992	524	(11%)	60	1%	1%	3	(8%)	0	0%	0%
1960	6,278	4,110	593	(11%)	68	1%	2%	3	(−10%)	0	0%	0%
1961	6,555	4,269	680	(11%)	77	1%	2%	4	(−80%)	−3	0%	0%
1962	6,926	4,495	779	(11%)	84	1%	2%	11	(15%)	2	0%	0%
1963	7,339	4,784	674	(22%)	151	2%	3%	60	(30%)	18	0%	0%
1964	7,882	5,001	540	(36%)	194	2%	4%	92	(−21%)	−20	0%	0%
1965	8,365	5,323	635	(9%)	60	1%	1%	130	(−5%)	−7	0%	0%
1966	9,198	5,909	762	(3%)	25	0%	0%	306	(16%)	48	1%	1%
1967	10,217	6,637	1,038	(3%)	33	0%	0%	527	(18%)	96	1%	1%
1968	11,606	7,667	1,606	(4%)	71	1%	1%	873	(18%)	157	1%	2%
1969	13,434	7,667	2,364	(3%)	79	1%	1%	1,308	(14%)	183	1%	2%
1970	15,244	10,374	2,611	(9%)	230	2%	2%	1,616	(12%)	194	1%	2%
1971	17,127	11,709	2,953	(9%)	254	2%	2%	2,076	(8%)	166	1%	1%
1972	18,961	12,823	3,441	(12%)	427	2%	3%	2,546	(10%)	255	1%	2%
1973	21,315	14,253	4,168	(10%)	407	2%	3%	2,877	(15%)	432	2%	3%
1974	23,788	15,729	4,995	(44%)	2,166	9%	14%	2,923	(49%)	1,432	6%	9%
1975	26,578	17,473	4,875	(28%)	1,381	5%	8%	3,356	(16%)	537	2%	3%
1976	30,015	19,553	5,392	(13%)	701	2%	4%	3,831	(20%)	766	3%	4%

Source: Tables 7.20., 7.21., 7.22. B. 34. and B. 35.

Note: Estimates for the average rate of return on capital in all non-primary sectors (Table 7.20.) and the real interest rates on total loans to all industries were applied in computing subsidy rates. In the case of DMB loans, the real interest rate for 1961 was applied to the entire 1957–61 period, and in case of KDB loans, the real interest rate for 1962 was applied to the entire 1957–62 period.

or net) fixed capital stock in the manufacturing sector. The ratio to net stock was around 4 percent on the average during 1957–61 and around 6 percent during 1962–66. Between 1967 and 1971 it reached approximately 14 percent and since 1972 has exceeded 25 percent. The ratio of the interest subsidy to total gross fixed capital stock averaged about 3 percent during 1957–61 and about 5 percent during the First Five-Year Plan period. During the Second Five-Year Plan period it averaged about 9 percent and it was more than 14 percent during the Third Five-Year Plan period. The most remarkable fact is that although the absolute amount of interest subsidies associated with foreign loans was negligible before 1966, it was equivalent to more than half of the total amount of interest subsidies associated with KDB and DMB loans together after 1966. Moreover the ratio of the interest subsidy to (gross) capital stock has been steadily increasing from a moderate 3 to 4 percent before 1962 to more than 14 percent during the Third Five Year Plan period. The ratio of the interest subsidy to gross fixed capital formation increased from around 40 percent during 1962–66, to around 75 percent during 1967–71 and to more than 100 percent after 1972.

Since the real rate of return on capital in the manufacturing sector seems to have been overstated due to underpricing of SOC services, we also estimated the ratio of the total interest subsidy associated with domestic and foreign loans to total (gross or net) fixed capital stock in all industries in Korea (excluding the ownership of dwelling sector). The ratio to gross or net capital stock increased from around 1 to 2 percent during 1957–66 to more than 4 to 5 percent during the Third Five Year Plan period. The ratio of the interest subsidy to gross fixed capital formation increased from around 20 percent 1962–71 to more than 35 percent after 1972.

Some foreign loans were distributed through the KDB and DMB in the form of two-step sub-loan funds. About 3 percent of the total KDB loans were provided with foreign sub-loan funds during 1965–69, 10 percent were provided during 1970–71 and 5 percent during 1972–75. About 1 to 2 percent of total DMB loans were provided with foreign sub-loan funds during 1965–75. There must, therefore, have been some double-counting in our estimation of interest subsidies.

The social rate of return on investment in the U.S. during 1954–57 was estimated to have been around 18 to 20 percent by Eckaus and around 19 to 26 percent by Solow. The private rate of return estimated by Denison for the U.S. in 1957 was about 13 percent. Solow suggested that the social rate of return was high not only relative to private rates of return but also compared with the interest rates at which individuals in the U.S. evince a willingness to save. Therefore, he suggested that rates of interest considerably higher than the current ones in the U.S. might be socially desirable and it would seem to be in society's interest to find ways of making somewhat larger savings.[35]

During 1972–75, the average estimated rate of return on capital in Korea was around 27 percent in manufacturing and around 15 percent for all industries. If our estimates for the average rate of return on capital in manuacturing and the associated rates of interest subsidies on capital use in Korea were anywhere close to accurate, then they also suggest that rates of capital accumulation in Korea should be (and have been) considerably higher than they were and the government should have undertaken measures to enhance savings by raising returns to saving, e.g., by raising the real rate of interest on bank deposits.

In this chapter, we used the rate of return on capital in manufacturing as the real opportunity cost of capital use in Korea. The estimated rates of return on capital in agriculture, SOC and service sectors were substantially lower than those in manufacturing and hence the real opportunity cost of capital for the whole industry might have been exaggerated. However, even if we use the average rate of return on capital for the whole industry as an estimate of the real opportunity cost of capital in Korea, none of our conclusions are affected, except those on the absolute magnitude of interest subsidy associated with loans.

---

[35] R. M. Solow, *op. cit.*, pp. 93–97. The social rate of return on investment in Solow's model is equal to the marginal product of effective capital minus an allowance for depreciation and for obsolescence.

CHAPTER 8

EMPLOYMENT IMPLICATIONS OF TRADE AND SUBSIDY POLICIES

1. Employment Growth in Korea

Most of the literature on employment implications of industrialization in developing countries has been directed toward the following three questions: Is there necessarily a conflict between increasing employment and increasing output? Which goods should be produced (the output composition problem)? How should they be produced (the choice of techniques problem)?[1] Sections 1–3 of this chapter attempt to examine each of these three questions in turn on the basis of the Korean experience.

According to the EPB's Annual Report on the Economically Active Population, the population of 14 years old and over, which represents Korea's potential labor force, increased by nearly 50 percent during 1963–76 implying an average annual growth rate of about 3 percent. During the same period, the total number of employed persons in Korea increased by about 64 percent, implying an average annual growth rate of about 4 percent. The total number of male employed persons increased by about 3.5 percent per annum while that of females increased by nearly 5 percent per annum on the average. As a result, the labor force participation rate of males stayed at around 75–76 percent throughout the period 1963–76 while that of females steadily increased from about 36 percent in 1963 to about 42 percent in 1976.

---

[1] D. Morawetz, "Employment Implications of Industrialization in Developing Countries: A Survey," *Economic Journal*, September 1974, p. 496.

Table 8.1. Population, Employment and the Labor Force Participation Rate

In Thousand Persons & Percent

	Population Over 14 Years	Employed Persons			Labor Force Participation Rate		Unemployment Rate
		Total	Male	Female	Male	Female	
1963	15,085	7,662	4,988	2,674	76%	36%	8.2%
1964	15,502	7,799	5,082	2,717	76%	35%	7.7%
1965	15,937	8,206	5,322	2,884	77%	37%	7.4%
1966	16,367	8,423	5,482	2,941	77%	36%	7.1%
1967	16,764	8,717	5,655	3,062	76%	37%	6.2%
1968	17,166	9,155	5,855	3,300	76%	38%	5.1%
1969	17,639	9,414	6,088	3,326	77%	38%	4.8%
1970	18,253	9,745	6,167	3,578	75%	39%	4.5%
1971	18,984	10,066	6,371	3,695	74%	39%	4.5%
1972	19,724	10,559	6,665	3,894	75%	39%	4.5%
1973	20,438	11,139	6,923	4,216	74%	41%	4.0%
1974	21,148	11,586	7,275	4,311	75%	41%	4.1%
1975	21,833	11,830	7,489	4,341	75%	40%	4.1%
1976	22,549	12,556	7,736	4,820	75%	42%	3.9%
1977	23,339	12,929	8,518	4,803	76%	41%	3.8%

Source: Economic Planning Board, *Annual Report on the Economically Active Population: 1977.*

Table 8.2. Persons Employed by Industry

In Thousand Persons

	Primary Sectors			Manufacturing			SOC & Service		
	Total	Male	Female	Total	Male	Female	Total	Male	Female
1963	4,894	3,053	1,841	610	428	182	2,158	1,507	651
1964	4,878	3,044	1,834	637	435	202	2,284	1,603	681
1965	4,887	3,042	1,845	772	536	236	2,547	1,744	803
1966	4,956	3,057	1,899	833	569	264	2,634	1,856	778
1967	4,905	3,009	1,896	1,021	684	337	2,791	1,962	829
1968	4,907	2,969	1,938	1,170	772	398	3,072	2,110	962
1969	4,939	3,046	1,893	1,232	802	430	3,243	2,240	1,003
1970	5,027	2,969	2,058	1,284	861	423	3,434	2,337	1,097
1971	4,968	2,918	2,050	1,336	870	466	3,762	2,583	1,179
1972	5,400	3,098	2,302	1,445	955	490	3,714	2,612	1,102
1973	5,616	3,266	2,350	1,774	1,090	684	3,749	2,567	1,182
1974	5,634	3,310	2,324	2,012	1,289	723	3,940	2,676	1,264
1975	5,485	3,227	2,258	2,205	1,450	755	4,140	2,812	1,328
1976	5,666	3,268	2,398	2,678	1,657	1,021	4,212	2,811	1,401
1977	5,508	3,254	2,254	2,798	1,702	1,096	4,623	3,170	1,453

Source: Economic Planning Board, *Annual Report on the Economically Active Population: 1978.*

During 1963–76, the annual growth rate of total employment was only about 1 percent higher than that of the total potential labor force. However, there was a rapid transfer of labor from relatively less productive to more productive forms of employment. Moreover there was a significant rise in the absolute level of productivity in the former. The number of employed persons in manufacturing increased about 4.4 times (from 0.6 million in 1963 to 2.7 million in 1976) implying an average annual growth rate of about 12 percent. Total male employment in manufacturing increased by about 11 percent per annum (from 0.43 million in 1963 to 1.66 million in 1976) while female employment increased by about 14 percent per annum (from 0.18 million in 1963 to 1.02 million in 1976). The total number of employed persons in service and SOC sectors increased by about 5.5 percent per annum (about 5 percent for male and 6 percent for female). On the other hand, the total number of employed persons in the primary sectors increased by only about 1.2 percent per annum: about 0.5 percent per annum for males and 2.0 percent for females.

The most remarkable trend in employment was, therefore, an extremely rapid increase in the number of employed persons in manufacturing and a very slow increase in the primary sectors. Another remarkable trend was the more rapid expansion in female employment than in male employment in every industrial sector in Korea.

According to the manufacturing census data, the annual wage rate in manufacturing increased from $373 in 1966 to $569 in 1971 (average growth rate of 9 percent per annum) and to $743 in 1976 (average growth rate of 6 percent per annum) in 1970 prices. On the other hand, possibly due to rapid capital accumulation and technical progress in the agricultural sector, the per worker farm income increased from about $224 in 1966 to $352 in 1971 (average growth rate of 10 percent per annum) and to $513 in 1976 (average growth rate of 8 percent per annum). Hence one may interpret the rapid increase in the wage rate in manufacturing as a result of the capital accumulation in manufacturing and the associated increase in labor productivity and/or the result of a rising minimum wage floor *a la* Lewis via the rising average product of farm workers.

The differences between urban-rural earnings in Korea were equivalent to about 80 percent of rural earnings during the period 1967–71 and about 60 percent during the period 1972–76. This may be partly attributed to extra costs of urban living (i.e., the costs of urban housing, transportation and public utilities). Of course, the per worker earnings figures themselves may be misleading in representing the living standard of a household because the average number of workers in an urban wage earner's house-

210   Trade, Distortions and Employment

Table 8.3. Differences in Urban-Rural Earnings

In 1970 Dollars & Percent

	Per Worker Farm Income		Wage Rate for Farm Employee		Wage Rate in Manufacturing				Differences in Urban-Rural Earnings	
					Census Data		Office of Labor Data			
	A	(dA/A)	B	(dB/B)	C	(dC/C)	D	(dD/D)	C/A	C/B
1962	225	(—)	220	(—)			334	(—)		
1963	256	(14%)	210	(−4%)			308	(−8%)		
1964	255	(0%)	250	(19%)			338	(10%)		
1965	218	(−15%)	190	(−24%)			348	(3%)		
1966	224	(3%)	170	(−10%)	373	(—)			1.7	2.2
1962–66 Av		(1%)		(−5%)				(2%)		
1967	225	(0%)	200	(18%)	405	(9%)	375	(7%)	1.8	1.9
1968	251	(12%)	230	(15%)	449	(11%)	424	(13%)	1.8	1.9
1969	273	(9%)	260	(13%)	495	(10%)	502	(19%)	1.8	1.9
1970	283	(4%)	270	(4%)	532	(7%)	563	(12%)	1.9	2.1
1971	352	(24%)	300	(11%)	569	(7%)	601	(7%)	1.6	2.0
1967–71 Av.		(10%)		(12%)		(9%)		(12%)		
1972	363	(3%)	300	(0%)	563	(−1%)	608	(1%)	1.6	2.0
1973	378	(4%)	350	(17%)	635	(13%)	617	(1%)	1.7	1.8
1974	429	(13%)	380	(9%)	632	(0%)	659	(7%)	1.5	1.7
1975	447	(4%)	412	(9%)	683	(8%)	674	(2%)	1.5	1.6
1976	513	(15%)	451	(10%)	743	(9%)	785	(16%)	1.4	1.6
1972–76 Av.		(8%)		(9%)		(6%)		(5%)		

Source: Ministry of Agriculture & Fisheries, *Report on the Results of Farm Household Economy Survey*, Economic Planning Board, *Report on Mining and Manufacturing Census (or Survey)* and Bank of Korea, *Economic Statistics Yearbook*.
Note: GNP deflator for all industries and the exchange rate of 310.6 won per dollar were applied to get 1970 dollar values.

hold during 1971–75 was only about 1.4 persons while that in rural household was about 2.9 persons.² The latter, unlike the former, usually includes a housewife (and parents as well) who takes care of both farming and household work. We are simply emphasizing the fact that while there were previously significant differences in urban-rural earnings the difference has decreased due to a more rapid rate of increase in average rural earnings in Korea.

According to the Harris-Todaro model, the available industrial labor supply is an increasing function of the urban-rural differences in earnings (allowing for the chance of being unemployed).³ In Korea, the urban-rural differential in earnings has steadily declined, which may have increased the pressure for higher wage increase in the manufacturing sector by reducing the incentives for migration from rural to urban areas.

There was a rapid rise in the real wage income during 1967–71 (about 9 percent per annum) which seems to have been consistent with the rising labor productivity both in the argicultural and industrial sectors. The rapid rise in labor productivity must have continued after 1972 and yet, possibly due to high inflation in 1974–75, the rate of increase in real wages was moderate (abound 6 percent per annum on the average) during 1972–76. Considering the fact that the total value added of manufacturing increased by an average annual rate of more than 20 percent during 1966–76, the rate of increase in the manufacturing wage rate seems to have been slower than the rate of increase in labor productivity in the industrial sector. Hence, the trend of wage movements in Korea seems to have been very conducive to enhancing the share of entrepreneurial profits.

The number of employed persons in manufacturing increased by more than 12 percent per annum and the number in service and SOC sectors increased by about 5.5 percent while the growth rate of the potential labor force was only about 3 percent per annum during 1963–76. In spite of this, the fact that the growth rate of total employment was only about 1

---

[2] Economic Planning Board, *Annual Report on the Family Income and Expenditure Survey* and Ministry of Agriculture and Fisheries, *op. cit.* Urban wage earners do not include only manufacturing employees and their income does not include only wages. Hence there is no direct comparability between the average per worker farm income and average wage rate in manufacturing. There may be more comparability between the wage rate in manufacturing and wage rate for farm employee.

[3] J.R. Harris and M.P. Todaro, "Wages, Industrial Employment and Labor Productivity: the Kenyan Experience," *Eastern Africa Economic Review*, June, 1969, and J. R. Harris, "Migration, Unemployment, and Development: A Two-Sector Analysis," *American Economic Review*, March 1970. Due to possible optimistic expectations and illusions, the average wage rate in manufacturing as a whole may serve as a better index of attraction to rural labor than the average rate of urban unskilled workers.

percent higher than that of potential labor-force may be a matter of serious concern for Korea which might still have a fairly large amount of disguised and seasonal unemployment in rural areas.

According to the EPB's quarterly sample survey on the economically active population, the total number of employed persons (14 and over) amounted to about 8.4 million in 1966, 9.8 million in 1970 and 11.1 million in 1973. Out of this, 4.7 million 4.8 million and 5.3 million in each year, respectively, were employed in the agricultural sectors. The agricultural employment figures are well-known to be biased in an upward direction because of extensive disguised unemployment.[4] The problem is aggravated by the practice of the Economic Planning Board which defines employed persons as "all persons fourteen years and over who worked regularly more than one hour during the refernece week before the survey data for pay or profit, including unpaid family workers and persons who had a job but did not work temporarily."

If we apply the labor-output ratios obtained from the Farm Household Survey to the agricultural output values presented in the input-output tables, and if we assume an eight hour working day and 280 working days a year, we get 3.3 million man-years employed in the agricultural sector in 1970 and 2.9 million man-years in 1973, both of which are less than two-thirds the official agricultural employment figures.[5]

It is possible to consider the difference between the agricultural employment figures and the estimated man-year figures (which were based on labor coefficients obtained from the Farm Household Survey and output values from the input-output table) as a measure of disguised unemployment in the Korean agricultural sector. This amounted to about 0.6 million man-years in 1966, about 1.1 million man-years in 1968, about 1.5 million man-years in 1970 and about 2.4 million man-years in 1973. The

---

[4] The strict interpretation of disguised unemployment is that the marginal productivity of labor, over a wide range, is zero. The disguised unemployment may take the form of a smaller than "normal" number of working hours per head per year. The point is that a considerable part of the agricultural labor force can be removed from the agricultural sector without affecting the agricultural output appreciably. See A. Lewis, "Economic Development with Unlimited Supplies of Labor", *The Manscheter School*, May 1954, and G. R. Ranis and J. H. Fei, "A Theory of Economic Development," *American Economic Review*, September 1961.

[5] Since 1962, the Ministry of Agriculture and Fisheries has conducted annual surveys on 1,200 farm households spread over 80 enumeration districts throughout the country. The surveys include 124 questions concerning the farm household economy. "The Report on the Results of Farm Household Economy Survey" is regarded as the most reliable source of information on the agricultural sector in Korea. It provides estimates of annual labor input on a man-hour basis.

Table 8.4. An Estimate of Disguised Unemployment in Agriculture

	1966	1968	1970	1973
I-O Sectoral Output Value (In Thousand 1970 Dollars)				
1. Rice, Barley & Wheat	1,476,569	1,287,809	1,407,555	1,491,735
2. Other Cereals	81,937	90,281	89,863	84,958
3. Vegetables	500,370	442,997	478,047	374,728
4. Fruits	55,655	74,748	73,657	99,103
5. Industrial Crops	115,402	124,609	121,198	192,504
6. Livestock & Sericulture	331,693	481,565	409,352	481,611
7. Forestry	161,273	163,925	210,635	172,384
Labor-Output Ratios (Man-Year per $1,000 Outputs)				
1. Rice, Barley & Wheat	1.0549	1.0543	0.9563	0.6446
2. Other Cereals	2.4420	2.7719	2.1123	2.1980
3. Vegetables	1.5534	1.4909	1.2653	1.4729
4. Fruits	2.1336	1.6048	1.6733	1.0540
5. Industrial Crops	2.1336	1.6048	1.6733	1.0540
6. Livestock & Sericulture	1.5719	0.8982	0.8053	0.8122
7. Forestry	0.7363	0.7363	0.7363	0.7363
Total Number of Employed Persons (In Man-Year)				
1. Rice, Barley & Wheat	1,557,633	1,357,737	1,346,045	961,572
2. Other Cereals	200,090	250,250	189,818	186,738
3. Vegetables	777,275	660,464	604,873	551,937
4. Fruits	118,746	119,956	123,250	104,455
5. Industrial Crops	246,222	199,973	202,801	202,899
6. Livestock & Sericulture	521,388	432,542	329,651	391,165
7. Forestry	118,745	120,698	155,091	126,926
8. Non-Agricultural[1]	558,474	379,482	381,922	337,265
Total (M)	4,098,573	3,521,102	3,333,451	2,862,957
0.1% Sample[2] (E)	4,695,000	4,582,000	4,826,000	5,260,000
Disguised Unemployment (E-M)	596,427	1,060,898	1,492,549	2,397,043

Source: Ministry of Agriculture & Fisheries, *Reports on the Results of Farm Household Economy Survey 1966–1974*, The Bank of Korea, *Economic Statistics Yearbook: 1976* and Economic Planning Board, *Annual Report on the Economically Active Population: 1974*, and Hong, *op. cit.*, p. 63.

Notes: [1] Represents total labor input (in man-years) on non-agricultural work in the agricultural sector.

[2] Represents the average number of persons who worked regularly for more than one hour, for earnings, during the quarterly survey period (i.e., a week in each quarter).

Table 8.5. *Changes in Factor Intensity of Commodity Exports Due to Factor Substitutions and Shifts in Composition of Exports: 1966–73*

I-O Trade Data	Average	1966	1968	1970	1973	Due to Changes in Composition		
						1966–68	1968–70	1970–73
Direct Factor Intensity of Exports (Capital/Labor Ratios)								
Average								
Applying 1966 Coefficients		**0.78**	0.84	0.81	0.88	2.5%	−1.1%	7.1%
Applying 1968 Coefficients		0.87	**0.86**	0.87	0.90	7.7%	−3.6%	8.6%
Applying 1970 Coefficients		1.11	1.11	**1.08**	1.17	−1.1%	1.2%	3.4%
Applying 1973 Coefficients		1.54	1.59	1.60	**1.73**	0.0%	−2.7%	8.3%
						3.2%	0.6%	8.1%
Due to Factor	1966–68	11.5%	2.4%	7.4%	2.3%	10.3%	—	—
Substitutions	1968–70	27.6%	29.1%	24.1%	30.0%	—	25.6%	—
	1970–73	38.7%	43.2%	48.1%	47.9%	—	—	60.2%
Direct plus Indirect Factor Intensity of Exports (Capital/Labor Ratios)								
Average								
Applying 1966 Coefficients		**1.00**	1.06	1.05	1.09	2.3%	−1.2%	5.0%
Applying 1968 Coefficients		1.12	**1.15**	1.16	1.21	6.0%	−0.9%	3.8%
Applying 1970 Coefficients		1.51	1.54	**1.48**	1.56	2.7%	0.9%	4.3%
Applying 1973 Coefficients		2.05	2.02	2.00	**2.13**	2.0%	−3.9%	5.4%
						−1.5%	−1.0%	6.5%
Due to Factor	1966–68	12.0%	8.5%	10.5%	11.0%	15.0%	—	—
Substitutions	1968–70	34.8%	33.9%	27.6%	28.9%	—	28.7%	—
	1970–73	35.8%	31.2%	35.1%	36.5%	—	—	43.9%

Source: Hong, *op. cit.* and see Chapter 2.

moderate increases in the total number of employed persons in the agricultural sector coupled with rapidly decreasing labor-output ratios in the agricultural subsectors seem to have caused these steady and significant increases in our estimate of disguised unemployment in rural area.[6]

The phenomenal growth of exports was the cause of Korea's rapid employment expansion, especially in manufacturing. However, if we examine the factor intensities of Korea's commodity exports, not only was there some increase in capital intensity due to shifts in the composition of commodity exports but there was also an extremely pronounced increase in capital intensity due to factor subsititution in production processes. For instance, the direct plus indirect capital intensity of exports increased by 2.3. percent due to shifts in the export composition but also increased by as much as 11 percent due to sectoral factor substitutions during 1966–68. The total capital intensity of commodity exports decreased slightly due to shifts in the export composition but increased by about 31 percent due to factor substitutions between 1968 and 1970. While we can observe a significant increase in the capital intensity of Korea's commodity exports due to shifts in export composition (about 5 percent) during the period 1970–73, there were much more significant changes in the factor intensity of Korea's exports due to factor substitution in the production processes (about 35 percent). Some of the sectoral capital-labor substitutions as well as shifts in export composition, may be attributed to the increase in per capita capital stock in Korea and the associated rise in the wage-rental ratio. However, a substantial portion of the factor substitutions may have to be attributed to the subsidy on capital use.

It should be noted that deducing the employment effects of trade and subsidy policies in terms of employment growth would not provide an adequate basis to judge the overall efficiency of such policies. For instance, Korea's exports might have been less capital intensive if there had been no subsidy on capital use, but one might question whether Korea could have expanded its exports so rapidly if it had insisted upon using less capital-intensive production techniques in order to maximize the direct

---

[6] On the other hand, according to the EPB's quarterly 0.1 percent sample survey, the average number of hours worked per week in the manufacturing and service sectors was about 30 percent greater than that in the agricultural sector during 1963–76. The 1970 Population Census (10% Sample) also classified employed persons according to the duration of work. If we convert the employment data into man-year figures, we get an estimate of about 8 million instead of 9.8 million persons for the total number of employed persons in 1970. Hence we may argue that the overall disguised unemployment in Korea in the early seventies was equivalent to at least 1.5 million man-years.

employment effects of export expansion. This is because capital and labor might not be good substitutes for each other in terms of product quality and, moreover, there might be limited foreign demand for extremely labor-intensive goods. One might also argue that once a developing country becomes successful in exporting large amounts of labor-intensive goods, the developed countries will erect sufficiently high barriers against these imports so that the developing country has no other choice but to expand capital intensive exports.[7] The ever-increasing world-wide quota restrictions against Korea's major export items such as cotton textiles, synthetic textile products, wearing apparels, footwear, various electronics products, tablewares such as spoons and forks and canned mushroom substantiate this argument. Slower growth in export earnings might also have resulted in slower growth of the Korean economy as a whole, thus reducing overall employment growth rates.

2. Subsidies and Composition of Output and Trade

It is possible to increase employment with a given stock of capital by changing the product mix. In a closed economy, the scope of such shifts is limited by the domestic demand pattern. However, in an export-oriented economy like Korea's, an increase in both employment and output may be achieved by concentrating on the production and export of labor intensive goods.

If factor prices are identical to their shadow prices, both output and employment can be maximized. However, the existence of various distortions in factor market as well as in the commodity market may lead to a resource allocation which maximizes neither output nor employment. Furthermore, the introduction of employment as a major independent policy goal raises questions about the extent of conflict between employment growth and output growth as well as the appropriate discount rates to be attached to employment and output. Expansion of labor intensive production may raise the employment growth rate, but on the other hand,

---

[7] The quantitative import restrictions can mainly be circumvented by shifts in the structure of production and exports, but also partly by quality improvements. As far as long-run improvements in production technology and management efficiency, as well as an ability to adapt and transform according to changes in circumstances are concerned, Korea seems to benefit from such foreign restrictions against simple quantitative export expansions.

may decrease the total value of output in a given international or domestic demand situation. One may even speculate that expansion of labor-intensive production may lower the future rates of savings or technical progress.[8]

Since the conflict between output and employment is a rather complex problem, we will simply examine the association between the allocation of subsidies (i.e., subsidized loans), sectoral output and trade patterns, and then look at the implications on employment growth.

Across-the-board trade policies can influence the amount of trade. Such policies can make it profitable to produce (and export) a commodity that would otherwise be entirely imported. However, as long as trade interventions are uniform, it should not be possible to observe that some exported commodities are "further away" from the commodities with comparative advantage than others that were not. Thus, if one observes the expansion of capital intensive exports in a labor-abundant country, one must either conclude that effective export subsidies were not uniform or be obliged to refute the applicability of the factor proportions explanation of trade in the particular case.[9]

An appropriate procedure for examining the hypothesis that the trade regime itself influences the employment effect of trade may be to compute the "average effective exchange rate for exports" or the "average effective protection rate", compute the labor requirements of exports or import-substitutes which receive the average rate and then calculate separately the labor requirements for those industries receiving above-average subsidization or protection.[10]

An estimate of average effective exchange rates for exports, including direct subsidies only, can be readily computed by using data on short-term export credits and direct tax exemptions. The subsidy element associated with the short-term export credits can be computed on the basis of the difference between the real interest rate on export credits, whose nominal rate has been around 6 percent per annum, and the real rate of return on capital. They also often compute the effective exchange rate by considering the exemptions of indirect taxes and import tariffs as subsidies for exports. However, most foreign countries provide such exemptions and hence they cannot be regarded as subsidies to the Korean exporters who have to compete against foreign exporters in the inter-

---

[8] See A. K. Sen, *Choice of Techniques*, Oxford: Basil Blackwell, 1968.
[9] See A. O. Krueger, *Alternative Trade Strategies and Employment* (mimeographed), 1976.
[10] *Ibid.*

Table 8.6. Estimate of Effective Exchange Rate: Counting Direct Subsidies Only

	(A) Per Dollar Interest Subsidy	(B) Per Dollar Direct Tax Exemption	(C) Per Dollar Indirect Tax Exemption	(D) Per Dollar Tariff Exemption	(E) Official Exchange Rate
1966	3.7	11.4	23.2	18.2	272.2
1967	13.5	8.8	25.6	22.6	272.5
1968	10.2	5.8	25.0	36.3	276.4
1969	15.2	3.9	29.0	36.2	286.8
1970	19.4	3.7	28.5	42.7	310.6
1971	21.8	5.1	34.1	50.9	346.1
1972	22.7	2.0	27.2	68.5	391.8
1973	18.8	1.4	21.3	65.4	398.4
1974	48.5	0	22.8	55.8	406.0
1975	30.7	0	33.3	33.8	484.0
1976					484.0

	(S = A+B) Subsidy Per Dollar Exported	(S/E) Subsidy Rate Per Dollar Exported	(S+E) Effective Exchange Rate	(F) Effective Parity Exchange Rate (1970=100)	(S + E)/F Deviation from Parity Rate
1966	15.1	6%	287.3	273.0	5%
1967	22.3	8%	294.8	287.4	3%
1968	16.0	6%	292.4	305.5	-4%
1969	19.1	7%	305.9	316.7	-3%
1970	23.1	7%	333.7	333.7	0%
1971	26.9	8%	373.0	358.1	4%
1972	24.7	6%	416.5	397.2	5%
1973	20.2	5%	418.6	371.3	13%
1974	48.5	12%	454.5	422.7	8%
1975	30.7	6%	514.7	504.0	2%
1976	19.2	4%	503.2	538.0	-6%

national market.

The amount of direct subsidies for export activities is estimated to have been equivalent to around 7 percent of the total export value during 1966–76. We may call the sum of subsidies per dollar exported and official exchange rate (won per dollar), the average nominal effective exchange rate. Then we can observe that, between 1966 and 1976, this rate was usually higher than the effective parity exchange rate (1970 = 100), implying that the government maintained an effective exchange rate for exports that was higher than the real effective rate in 1970. The parity rate was computed by averaging the parity rate based on the U.S. wholesale price index (1970 = 100) and that based on the Japanese wholesale price index (1970 = 100).

The above estimates did not include various other forms of direct export subsidies such as discounted rates on transportation, electricity and other public utilities as well as wastage allowance (which, other than wastage allowance, seem to have been insignificant in absolute amount). They also did not include the major indirect subsidies in the form of long-term loans for export industries or government investments for SOC facilities which support export production. Therefore, the estimated figures must have significantly underestimated the total amount of subsidies provided for Korean export activities. In any case, the short-term interest rate subsidies, partial exemptions of direct taxes and wastage allowances are across-the-board uniform export subsidies which do not directly influence the employment effect of exports. One might only say that such subsidies must have been conducive to employment expansion in general because Korea supposedly has comparative advantages in labor-intensive products. However, the allocation of long-term (equipment) loans as well as government investments for export industries were not across-the-board uniform subsidies and hence would more likely have resulted in a biased employment effect of exports.

Until early in the sixties, 75 to 90 percent of the total DMB equipment loans was allocated to the primary sector and only 5 to 15 percent was allocated to the manufacturing sector. However, the share of the primary sector in total DMB equipment loans steadily declined to around 25 percent by the early seventies, while the share of the manufacturing sector increased to more than one third of the total DMB equipment loans. The share of loans to service sectors, in total DMB equipment loans, increased from less than 7 percent before 1966 to around 30 percent thereafter. At the same time the amount of DMB equipment loans to SOC sectors remained negligible. The KDB equipment loans have concentrated

Table 8.7. Sectoral Share in Total Value Added and in Total loans

In Million 1970 Dollars & Percent

	Share in Total Value Added				
	1957 (A)	1962 (B)	1967 (C)	1972 (D)	1975 (E)
GNP[1]	3,266	3,899	5,966	9,735	13,295
Agriculture	42.4%	39.0%	32.4%	22.8%	18.6%
Fishery	1.9%	1.7%	1.9%	2.4%	3.0%
Mining	1.0%	1.6%	1.5%	1.0%	1.0%
SOC Sector	2.9%	4.0%	6.1%	8.0%	9.0%
Service Sector	42.4%	42.8%	41.6%	40.6%	36.3%
Manufacturing	9.3%	11.8%	16.6%	25.2%	32.1%
	100.0%	100.0%	100.0%	100.0%	100.0%
Food Products	39.6%	33.9%	32.0%	27.3%	20.8%
Textiles	25.1%	18.1%	14.4%	16.2%	13.4%
Wearing Apparel	7.1%	8.8%	6.7%	9.6%	15.3%
Leather	1.2%	0.9%	0.5%	0.8%	3.3%
Wood Products	3.3%	2.3%	2.6%	2.4%	1.6%
Paper & Products	0.7%	2.2%	2.4%	2.0%	1.8%
Rubber Products	1.5%	1.9%	1.6%	1.3%	1.3%
Fertilizer	—	0.6%	1.3%	2.1%	1.7%
Other Chemicals	2.7%	4.4%	5.0%	6.2%	6.2%
Petroleum & Coal	0.9%	1.5%	5.8%	8.1%	5.7%
Nonmetallic Mineral	2.5%	3.7%	4.5%	4.2%	3.7%
Basic Metals	1.0%	2.2%	2.4%	2.3%	2.7%
Metal Products	1.3%	1.9%	1.7%	0.9%	1.2%
Machinery	2.0%	4.4%	2.8%	1.2%	1.1%
Electrical Machinery	1.0%	2.0%	3.4%	4.6%	8.9%
Transport Equipment	2.9%	3.6%	5.6%	3.9%	5.9%
Misc. Manufacturing	7.3%	7.7%	7.2%	6.9%	5.4%
	100.0%	100.0%	100.0%	100.0%	100.0%

Table 8.7. (Continued)

In Million 1970 Dollars & Percent

	Share in Total Loans				
	1957–61 (F)	1962–66 (G)	1967–71 (H)	1972–75 (I)	1957–75 (J)
Total Loans[2]	516	786	3,388	6,794	2,665
Agriculture	29.5%	17.8%	6.1%	4.8%	7.5%
Fishery	1.6%	2.5%	2.6%	2.7%	2.6%
Mining	4.1%	2.9%	2(2%	1.5%	2.0%
SOC Sector	8.9%	16.4%	18.9%	17.9%	17.7%
Service Sector	12.6%	15.3%	16.4%	14.2%	14.9%
Manufacturing	41.4%	43.1%	46.2%	48.0%	47.7%
	100.0%	100.0%	100.0%	100.0%	100.0%
Food Products	13.6%	109.%	8.1%	8.5%	8.7%
Textiles	23.6%	24.3%			
Wearing Apparel	0.4%	0.8%	22.3%	23.8%	23.5%
Leather	0.8%	0.6%			
Wood Products	2.8%	3.1%	4.2%	5.1%	4.6%
Paper & Products	4.1%	3.7%	3.3%	4.3%	3.9%
Rubber Products	2.2%	3.1%			
Fertilizer	19.0%	16.6%	29.1%	21.7%	24.4%
Other Chemicals					
Petoleum & Coal	2.7%	4.7%			
Nonmetallic Mineral	8.6%	9.3%	8.4%	6.5%	7.4%
Basic Metals	6.7%	3.9%	6.0%	10.4%	8.3%
Metal Products	2.2%	2.6%			
Machinery	1.9%	3.0%	12.1%	15.1%	13.7%
Electrical Machinery	0.6%	3.2%			
Transport Equipment	5.3%	3.7%			
Misc. Manufacturing	5.8%	6.6%	6.6%	4.9%	5.6%
	100.0%	100.0%	100.0%	100.0%	100.0%

Table 8.7. (Continued)

In Million 1970 Dollars & Percent

	Share in Loans vs. Share in Value Added				
	1957–61 (F/A)	1962–66 (G/B)	1967–71 (H/C)	1972–75 (I/D)	1957–75 (J/A)
Agriculture	0.70	0.46	0.19	0.21	0.18
Fishery	0.84	1.47	1.37	1.13	1.37
Mining	4.20	1.81	1.47	1.50	2.00
SOC Sector	3.07	4.10	3.10	2.24	6.10
Service Sector	0.30	0.36	0.39	0.35	0.35
Manufacturing	4.45	3.65	2.78	1.91	5.13
Food Products	0.34	0.32	0.25	0.31	0.22
Textiles	0.94	1.34			
Wearing Apparel	0.06	0.09	1.03	0.90	0.70
Leather	0.67	0.67			
Wood Products	0.85	1.35	1.62	2.13	1.39
Paper & Products	5.86	1.68	1.38	2.15	5.57
Rubber Products	1.47	1.63			
Fertilizer	7.04	3.32	2.12	1.23	4.78
Other Chemicals					
Petroleum & Coal	3.00	3.13			
Nonmetallic Mineral	3.44	2.51	1.87	1.55	2.96
Basic Metals	6.70	1.77	2.50	4.52	8.30
Metal Products	1.69	1.37			
Machinery	0.95	0.68	0.90	1.43	1.90
Electrical Machinery	0.60	1.60			
Transport Equipment	1.83	1.03			
Misc. Manufacturing	0.80	0.86	0.92	0.71	0.77

Table 8.7. *(Continued)*

In Million 1970 Dollars & Percent

	Share in Total Exports				
	1960	1966	1970	1973	1975
Total Exports[3]	91.1	447.5	1,208.7	3,119.7	3,932.3
Agriculture	12.1%	3.2%	2.4%	1.8%	1.8%
Fishery	4.1%	2.2%	4.2%	3.2%	4.2%
Mining	10.9%	5.6%	3.2%	0.8%	0.9%
SOC Sector	24.4%	10.0%	12.0%	9.5%	9.1%
Service Sector	22.5%	11.7%	9.9%	8.4%	9.5%
Manufacturing	23.8%	50.6%	61.9%	71.4%	74.5%
	100.0%	100.0%	100.0%	100.0%	100.0%
Food Products	24.2%	16.1%	7.3%	5.2%	7.4%
Textiles	23.7%	25.2%	26.4%	20.6%	12.5%
Wearing Apparel	1.6%	12.5%	16.7%	21.2%	22.7%
Leather	1.1%	0.7%	0.4%	0.9%	3.8%
Wood Products	3.8%	14.1%	12.0%	10.9%	5.0%
Paper & Products	1.1%	9.5%	0.5%	0.8%	0.6%
Rubber Products	8.1%	4.4%	2.7%	3.5%	4.7%
Fertilizer	—	—	0.8%	0.2%	0.0%
Other Chemicals	5.4%	0.5%	1.2%	1.6%	1.9%
Petroleum & Coal	—	2.9%	3.7%	1.3%	2.7%
Nonmetallic Mineral	3.2%	2.3%	1.3%	1.6%	2.2%
Basic Metals	4.3%	4.9%	2.4%	6.4%	5.4%
Metal Products	0.5%	2.1%	1.8%	2.4%	2.5%
Machinery	2.7%[4]	1.8%	0.4%	1.6%	0.9%
Electrical Machinery	5.9%[4]	2.7%	6.2%	12.1%	12.3%
Transport Equipment	5.4%[4]	0.7%	0.7%	0.9%	4.0%
Misc. Manufacturing	10.2%	9.2%	16.3%	9.8%	11.3%
	100.0%	100.0%	100.0%	100.0%	100.0%

Source: The Bank of Korea, *National Income in Korea* and *Input-Output Tables of Korea*, and Tables B. 19., B. 20., B. 23. and B. 26.
Notes: [1] Includes foreign sector.
[2] Annual average of total KDB, DMB and foreign loans.
[3] Includes unclassifiable exports.
[4] Mostly re-exports.

on the manufacturing and SOC sectors and the amount of equipment loans to the primary sectors was not only small but was also concentrated in the mining sector. The loans to the service sector amounted to around 10 percent of total KDB equipment loans.

Due to the extreme disparity between the interest rates on bank loans which has prevailed in Korea, and those on curb loans a fairly large portion of the loans for operations seem to have been used for fixed capital formation. Curb loans were relied upon for shortterm operation funds. Therefore it seems most relevant to examine the allocation of the sum of equipment and operation loans in analyzing the employment effect of the interest rate subsidy.

During 1957–75, the share of loans allocated to agriculture and service sectors in total loans (total KDB, DMB and foreign loans) was much smaller than the share of these sectors in GNP while the share of loans allocated to manufacturing and SOC sectors was much larger than their share in GNP. On the other hand, the contribution of agriculture to GNP rapidly declined (from 42 percent in 1957 to 17 percent in 1976) and that of service sectors steadily declined (from 42 percent in 1957 to 35 percent in 1976) while the proportion of GNP arising from manufacturing increased from 9 percent in 1957 to 35 percent in 1976 and that from SOC sectors rose from 3 percent in 1957 to 9 percent in 1976. Hence one can easily detect a close association between the pattern of loan allocations and shifts in the industrial structure. One may say that the expansion of SOC sectors in Korea was mainly due to extensive loan allocations at subsidized interest rates (as well as direct government investments). However, in the case of other sectors, one may prefer to explain the observed shifts in the industrial structure in terms of differences in sectoral rates of return. One may then say that, as a whole, the pattern of loan allocations must have been conducive to or consistent with such a shift in Korea's industrial structure during 1957–76 without implicating inefficiency in the loan allocation pattern itself.

The share of loans allocated to the fishery sector was greater than its share in GNP after 1962, and there was an expansion of this sector from about 2 percent of GNP in 1957 to 3 percent in 1976. Although the share of loans allocated to the mining sector was always greater than its share in GNP there was no expansion of its share in GNP between 1957 and 1976.

Among the manufacturing industries, the food product sector always received a very small amount of loans (in terms of its share in total manufacturing outputs) while the chemicals sector (such as petroleum refining and fertilizer) always received a very large amount of loans during 1957–75. The share of the food product sector in total manufacturing output declined from about 40 percent in 1957 to about 20 percent in 1975 while that of chemicals expanded from about 4 percent in 1957 to about 14 percent in 1975.

Although the share of paper, nonmetallic mineral product, basic metals and metal product sectors in total loans was fairly large throughout the period 1957–75, and their share in total manufacturing output doubled during 1957–62, there was no further expansion in the share of these sectors from 1962 to 1975. Hence the association between loan allocations and output expansion for paper, nonmetallic mineral products, basic metals and metal products seems to have been very weak compared with that of chemicals and food products.

The amount of loans allocated to the textile products, miscellaneous manufactures, machinery and transport equipment sectors has been more or less proportional to their share in total manufacturing output: that of textiles and miscellaneous manufactures was slightly less and that of machinery was slightly larger than their share in total outputs. The share of textiles and wearing apparel in total manufacturing output fluctuated around 26 percent during 1962–75. The share of machinery fluctuated around 10 percent during 1962–72 but expanded to 16 percent by 1975. On the other hand the share of miscellaneous manufactures declined from about 8 percent in 1962 to 5 percent in 1975. There was a significant increase in the amount of loans allocated to machinery and transport equipment sectors after 1972 which is related in the fairly rapid expansion of the electrical machinery and transport equipment sectors during 1972–75.

As a whole, one may conclude that there was a positive association between the pattern of loan allocations and the shifts in the industrial structure, with the exceptions of the mining sector and, to a lesser extent, the paper, nometallic mineral, basic metal and metal product sectors. These exceptional cases may be explained in terms of Korea's limited mineral endowments and extremely capital intensive production techniques of these sectors.

On the other hand, there was a drastic fall in the share of agricultural and mining products and a rapid increase in the share of manufactures in total exports during 1957–75. Among manufactured exports, the share of food products declined most rapidly while that of electrical machinery (mostly electronic products) and wearing apparel expanded most rapidly. There was a significant expansion in exports of steel products, but there was no matching expansion of their share in total manufacturing outputs, which may reflect the fact that their exports were heavily dependent on imported intermediate input materials such as hot coils for steel sheets and pipes. The share of textiles and miscellaneous manufactures in total manufactures exports increased significantly in the sixties. However, the loans for these products were barely commensurate with their share in total outputs. Their share in total exports started to decline in the seventies. One may say that the expansion of textiles, wearing apparel and miscellaneous manufactures exports can be attributed more to the basic comparative advantage of Korea (i.e., low wages) than to an interest rate subsidy associated with bank loans. The share of basic metals, metal products and electrical machinery sectors in total loans was relatively large and their exports expanded significantly in the early seventies. Among the basic metals, metal and electrical machinery products, steel plates and pipes and various electronic products had an extremely high import content for their intermediate inputs. Since Korea mostly took care of the very labor intensive "final-touch" (or assembling) processes, their export expansion may be attributed to both the low wage level and the availability of subsidized loans.

Although the rapid expansion of the chemical sector's outputs, including petroleum refining and chemical fertilizer manufacturing, in the sixties may be attributed to the allocation of a large amount of subsidized (domestic and foreign) loans, there was no matching expansion of their share in total exports. There was also a relatively large loan allocation to the nonmetallic mineral product sector and their share in exports even declined. Hence, it seems that the allocation of subsidized long-term loans to these extremely capital intensive sectors has contributed mostly to import substitution rather than to export expansion.

Table 8.8. lists 23 major export and import substituting sectors. In 1973, the processed sea food, silk yarn, knit products, wearing apparel, plywood and rubber product sectors exported at least about 40 percent of their total products while imports of these products were negligible. These were all relatively labor intensive sectors with substantial employment effects.

The chemical fibre fabrics, rolled steel, metallic products, electronic products and electrical machinery sectors also exported more than 30 percent of their total products in 1973, but imports of these products amounted to between 28 and 83 percent of the output values of these sectors. The chemical fibre fabrics, metallic product and electronic product sectors were relatively labor intensive while the rolled steel and

Table 8.8. Production and Trade of Selected Commodities

In Million 1970 Dollars & Percent

	1963			1968			1973		
	Output	Exports	Imports	Output	Exports	Imports	Output	Exports	Imports
Fisheries	115	4 (3%)	0 (0%)	190	10 (5%)	1 (1%)	433	100 (23%)	6 (1%)
Processed Sea Foods	24	9(38%)	0 (0%)	71	29 (41%)	0 (0%)	105	59 (56%)	5 (5%)
Silk Yarn	8	5(63%)	0 (0%)	25	20 (80%)	0 (0%)	100	66 (66%)	2 (2%)
Cotton Fabrics	63	5 (8%)	2 (3%)	100	12 (12%)	4 (4%)	168	43 (26%)	15 (9%)
Knit Products	41	4(10%)	0 (0%)	108	52 (48%)	0 (0%)	329	131 (40%)	10 (3%)
Wearing Apparel	90	1 (1%)	0 (0%)	238	61 (26%)	2 (1%)	897	471 (53%)	9 (1%)
Lumber & Plywood	56	7(13%)	1 (2%)	162	64 (40%)	0 (0%)	421	229 (54%)	2 (0%)
Rubber Products	46	1 (2%)	3 (7%)	67	14 (21%)	1 (1%)	202	77 (38%)	3 (1%)
Plastic Products	12	0 (0%)	0 (0%)	45	1 (2%)	0 (0%)	111	24 (22%)	8 (7%)
Chemical Fibre Yarn	8	0 (0%)	14 (175%)	56	1 (2%)	30 (54%)	198	25 (13%)	35 (18%)
Chemical Fibre Fabrics	33	1 (3%)	4 (12%)	66	20 (30%)	21 (32%)	198	97 (49%)	86 (43%)
Rolled Steel	25	2 (8%)	22 (88%)	75	1 (1%)	54 (72%)	370	108 (29%)	178 (48%)
Structural Metallic	16	0 (0%)	4 (25%)	34	1 (3%)	7 (21%)	86	21 (24%)	21 (24%)
Metallic Products	22	0 (0%)	3 (14%)	28	6 (21%)	19 (68%)	92	33 (36%)	26 (28%)
Electronic & Comm. Eq.	4	0 (0%)	7 (175%)	52	13 (25%)	33 (63%)	479	239 (50%)	238 (50%)
Organic Chemicals	6	0 (0%)	14 (233%)	25	0 (0%)	49 (196%)	115	11 (10%)	142(123%)
Chemical Fertilizer	13	0 (0%)	50 (385%)	47	2 (4%)	31 (66%)	105	4 (4%)	13 (12%)
Petroleum Products	3	0 (0%)	30(1,000%)	154	7 (5%)	14 (9%)	581	29 (5%)	21 (4%)
Cement	17	0 (0%)	5 (29%)	73	5 (7%)	3 (4%)	143	13 (9%)	0 (0%)
Industrial Machinery	12	0 (0%)	33 (275%)	23	1 (4%)	176(765%)	68	8 (12%)	185(272%)
Electrical Machinery	9	0 (0%)	11 (122%)	35	4 (11%)	45 (129%)	60	18 (30%)	50 (83%)
Shipbuilding	11	0 (0%)	4 (36%)	30	0 (0%)	66 (220%)	66	7 (11%)	41 (62%)
Motor Vehicles	22	1 (5%)	10 (45%)	154	1 (1%)	68 (44%)	207	3 (1%)	53 (26%)
Sub-Total		40(0.42)			352(0.70)			1,816(0.75)	
All Commodities		96(1.00)			467(1.00)			2,424(1.00)	

Source: The Bank of Korea, *Input-Output Table of Korea* (various issues).

Table 8.9. Direct and Total Factor Coefficients of Selected Sectors: 1970

I-O 117 Sector Classification	Direct Factor-Output Ratios			Total Factor-Output Ratios (A^d)			Total Factor-Output Ratios (A)		
	K	L	K/L	K	L	K/L	K	L	K/L
8. Fisheries	1.59	0.84	1.89	1.89	1.03	1.83	1.97	1.07	1.84
15. Processed Sea Foods	0.26	0.35	0.74	1.30	1.96	1.35	1.36	1.00	1.36
25. Silk Yarn	0.40	0.30	1.33	1.22	1.17	1.04	1.29	1.25	1.03
29. Cotton Fabrics	0.31	0.32	0.97	1.36	0.64	2.13	1.43	0.66	2.17
35. Knit Products	0.42	0.48	0.88	1.27	0.73	1.74	1.61	0.81	1.99
37. Wearing Apparel	0.21	0.35	0.60	0.94	0.67	1.40	1.38	0.82	1.68
39. Lumber & Plywood	0.31	0.16	1.94	0.51	0.24	2.13	0.54	0.28	1.93
48. Rubber Products	0.28	0.29	0.97	0.81	0.49	1.65	0.96	0.53	1.81
91. Plastic Products	0.29	0.19	1.53	0.75	0.35	2.14	0.90	0.39	2.31
28. Chemical Fibre Yarn	1.35	0.18	7.50	1.91	0.35	5.46	2.40	0.45	5.33
33. Chemical Fibre Fabrics	0.69	0.39	1.77	1.51	0.59	2.56	1.99	0.69	2.88
68. Rolled Steel	0.21	0.10	2.10	1.08	0.32	3.38	1.31	0.42	3.12
73. Structural Metallic	0.29	0.28	1.04	0.96	0.51	1.88	1.26	0.62	2.03
74. Metallic Products	0.44	0.40	1.10	1.08	0.61	1.77	1.29	0.70	1.84
83. Electronic & Comm. Eq.	0.27	0.21	1.29	0.57	0.36	1.58	0.90	0.54	1.67
50. Organic Chemicals	0.30	0.21	1.43	0.77	0.51	1.51	0.90	0.60	1.50
58. Chemical Fertilizer	1.15	0.06	19.17	1.99	0.21	9.48	2.02	0.23	8.78
59. Petroleum Products	0.24	0.01	24.00	0.37	0.09	4.11	0.38	0.09	4.22
61. Cement	1.79	0.05	35.80	2.92	0.29	10.07	2.98	0.32	9.31
77. Industrial Machinery	0.38	0.40	0.95	1.03	0.65	1.58	1.26	0.75	1.68
82. Electrical Machinery	0.52	0.23	2.26	1.07	0.45	2.38	1.47	0.60	2.45
86. Shipbuilding	0.59	0.29	2.03	1.07	0.48	2.23	1.39	0.61	2.28
88. Motor Vehicles	0.22	0.14	1.57	0.56	0.31	1.81	0.69	0.37	1.86
13–92. All Manufactures	0.39	0.20	1.95						

Source: The Bank of Korea, *Input-Output Tables of Korea* and Tables B. 32. and B. 33.

electrical machinery sectors were relatively capital intensive. However, by importing a large amount of capital intensive intermediate input materials, their export expansion seems to have also substantially contributed to employment expansion.

In 1963, there were large imports of petroleum products, fertilizer, industrial machinery, organic chemicals, and chemical fibre yearn. In 1973, imports of petroleum products, fertilizer, and chemical fibre yarn were relatively small, though the imports of orgainic chemicals and industrial machinery were still fairly large in terms of the ratio of imports to outputs. There were also substantial increase in the outputs of the shipbuilding and motor vehicles sectors during 1963–73. The exports of all these products amounted to less than 13 percent of the sectoral output values and hence one may regard these as import substituting rather than export industries. The orgainic chemicals, industrial machinery and motor vehicles (assembling) sectors were relatively labor intensive, but the chemical fibre yarn, fertilizer, and petroleum product sectors were extremely capital intensive. Therefore, the employment effect of these import-substituting (and partly exporting) sectors seems to have been relatively small.

We observed that the chemical product, nonmetallic mineral product, basic metal and machinery sectors received very large domestic and foreign loans during 1957–75. Refined petroleum, cement, chemical fertilizer, and chemical fibre yarn are very capital intensive products. On the other hand steel sheets and plates, chemical fibre fabrics, electrical machinery and ships are moderately capital intensive products. Therefore, the fact that there was not only a substantial output expansion in these sectors but also significant increases in their export/output ratios may be attributed to the pattern of loan allocation in Korea during the period 1957–75. Most of these sectors could not be regarded as major export sectors of Korea at this time, and yet, the absolute amount of exports of these (moderately or extremely capital intensive) products has significantly increased over the period which must have accelerated the rising trend in capital intensity of Korea's export commodity bundle. One may safely attribute their failure to become Korea's major export industries to the comparative advantage pattern.

Judging purely on the basis of the output and export pattern, one may conclude that the main objective of government policies was neither to simply maximize GNP nor to maximize employment growth. One may rather say that the main objectives was probably to promote export expansion and import-substitution of selected industries, without paying too much attention to their direct contributions to GNP and employment.

3. Subsidies and Choice of Techniques

A. Aggregated Elasticity of Factor Substitution

It is often argued that wages paid by manufacturing industries are higher than the marginal social cost of labor, while capital tends to be under-priced as a result of credit subsidization, and that these distortions together tend to make the private profitability of capital-intensive production exceed the social profitability.

In order to investigate the impact of factor price distortions on overall employment growth, we also have to estimate the extent to which factor substitutions occur in each sector when there is a change in the factor prices. Our procedure is to compare the trends in the relative use of capital and labor with trends in their cost ratios, although possible independent changes in technology will seriously affect these observations.

We will begin with an investigation of the aggregate association between factor use and factor prices for all industries and also for manufacturing. The observed association will embrace the effect of shifts in the sectoral output pattern as well as the effect of sectoral factor substitutions.

During 1962–76, the GNP and the total capital stock increased at an average annual rate of about 10 percent while the total number of employed persons increased by about 4 percent. Output and capital stock in manufacturing increased by nearly 20 percent per annum while employment in manufacturing increased by about 12 percent per annum.[11] The apparent elasticity of industrial employment with respect to output has not only been low but has also been falling over time in Korea as it has in most other developing countries.[12] A substantial number of

---

[11] See Tables 2.6., 8.2. and B. 21. (for capital stock in manufacturing), and the Bank of Korea, *National Income in Korea*.

[12] Analyzing Korean data for the period 1955–67, G. Ranis arrived at an opposite conclusion. " . . . once the open dualistic economy moves out of its administered price, import-substitution hothouse and into a more market-oriented export-substitution phase, it becomes possible for major efficient changes in output mix and technology—both in a labor-using direction—to take place . . . as can be demonstrated in the cases of Taiwan and Korea . . . to have . . . more output and more employment. . . " "Industrial Sector Labor Absorption," *Economic Development and Cul-*

labor-using innovations must have been introduced in the form of capital stretching on top of the latest vintage machinery imported from the advanced countries. There must also have been double or triple shift utilization of plant capacities, substitution of labor for capital in peripheral activities and a subcontracting system for extremely labor intensive phases of the production process. Yet the Korean experience does not seem to be strong enough to completely eradicate skepticism concerning the possible conflicts between output and employment.

In dealing with the employment problem of developing countries, a number of economists seem to believe that low elasticity of factor substitution is the most important hindrance to rapid growth in employment. However, in this section we can show that, if we were to accept the various sets of assumptions required for estimating procedures of production functions as valid, the lower elasticity of factor substitution would rather raise the employment growth rate in a developing country, though it may result in a slower rate of growth in GNP.[13]

The confusion seems to stem from mixing up static analysis with comparative static (or dynamic) analysis. The argument that modern manufacturing technology tends to be capital intensive and does not permit much substitution between factors, therefore resulting in less employment in an underdeveloped country, is a static proposition. However, any statement based on an observation of slower growth of employment than output or capital stock in a developing country should have been based on a comparative static framework of analysis. In most developing countries, the per capita income and wage rate of workers do increase over time, while the rental rate on capital use may tend to either stay constant or fall with capital formation. If the wage/rental ratio rises over time, the increase in the capital/labor ratio should be larger the larger the elasticity of factor substitution, implying a smaller rate of employment growth for any given rate of capital accumulation.

Most development economists seem to have concentrated their attention on the possible static fact that while the wage level in developing countries is extremely low these countries must continuously add "new capital intensive" processes in their growth process, which does not allow

---

tural Change, April 1973, p. 390. A similar type of optimism was expressed by F. Stewart and P. Streeten in "Conflict between Output and Employment Objectives in Developing Countries," *Oxford Economic Papers,* July 1971, p. 168.

[13] M. Nerlove, "Recent Empirical Studies of the CES and Related Production Functions," in M. Brown, ed., *The Theory and Empirical Analysis of Production,* New York: NBER, 1967, p. 56.

for any substantial substitution of labor for capital. They have not, on the other hand, emphasized the increasing wage/rental ratio and the associated possible factor substitutions leading toward a more capital intensive direction in the growth process.[14] That is, they have mostly emphaized the difficulty in substituting labor for capital and have overlooked the possible fact that the faster growing primary factor in a developing country could be capital rather than labor.

According to Korea's manufacturing census data, the total (gross or net) fixed capital stock in manufacturing increased by an average annual rate of about 19 percent during 1967–73 while employment increased by about 10 percent per annum on the average. As a result, the per worker (gross or net) capital stock increased by about 60–75 percent in this period, implying an average annual growth rate of around 9 percent for the capital/labor ratio in manufacturing. On the other hand, the capital intensity of Korea's exports, which are mostly manufactures, also increased by more than a hundred percent during 1966–73. Having started with a very low capital intensity in the early sixties, the total (direct plus indirect) net capital intensity of Korea's exports was still lower than that of the whole manufacturing industry in the early seventies (2.2 versus 2.8 in 1973). However, the capital intensity of Korea's exports has increased by more than 10 percent per annum since 1966. Hence one may blame the low elasticity of factor substitution in most available modern production technology as a cause of the rapid increases in the capital/labor ratio of the manufacturing industry and in the capital intensity of Korea's exports.

However, one must also examine what has happened in factor prices during the period in order to get a balanced view. According to the manufacturing census data, the average wage rate in manufacturing increased at an average annual rate of about 12 percent during 1967–73. On the other hand, the (weighted average) real interest rate on all loans to the manufacturing sector fell from about 16.2 percent in 1967 to 8.4 percent in 1973 (implying an average annual decline of about 10 percent). Due to severe inflation, the real interest rate fell further to a negative rate in 1974–75.

More than a 9 percent increase in the capital intensity of manufacturing per annum represents, by itself, a very rapid capital deepening. However, if we take account of the fact that the wage/rental ratio increased by about 22 percent per annum on the average during 1967–73, it might well have

---

[14] Cf. H. Pack "The Substitution of Labour for Capital in Kenyan Manufacturing," *Economic Journal*, March 1976.

Table 8.10. Employment and Capital Use in Manufacturing (Manufacturing Census Data)

	Gross Fixed Capital Stock (Million 1970 $)		Net Fixed Capital Stock (Million 1970 $)		Total Number of Workers (1,000 Persons)		Wage Rate in 1970$					Per Worker Capital ($ 1,000)	
								GNP Deflator		Manufacturing Deflator			
	(K)	(dK/K)	(C)	(dC/C)	(L)	(dL/L)	(W)	(dW/W)	(R)	(dR/R)	(gross)	(net)
1966	1,467	—	980	—	567	—	373	—	294	—	2.6	1.7
1967	1,634	11%	1,062	8%	649	14%	405	9%	355	21%	2.5	1.6
1968	1,869	14%	1,205	13%	748	15%	449	11%	409	15%	2.5	1.6
1969	2,286	22%	1,518	26%	829	11%	495	10%	471	15%	2.8	1.8
1970	2,606	14%	1,707	12%	861	4%	532	7%	532	13%	3.0	2.0
1971	2,997	15%	1,950	14%	847	−2%	569	7%	611	15%	3.5	2.3
1967–71 Av.		(15%)		(15%)		(8%)		(9%)		(16%)	2.9	1.9
1972	3,476	16%	2,260	16%	972	15%	563	−1%	608	0%	3.6	2.3
1973	4,579	32%	3,167	40%	1,153	19%	635	13%	687	13%	4.0	2.8
1974	5,392	18%	3,706	17%	1,321	15%	532	0%	694	1%	4.1	2.8
1975	6,437	19%	4,430	20%	1,420	7%	683	8%	771	11%	4.5	3.1
1976	7,921	22%	5,530	25%	1,717	21%	743	9%	870	13%	4.6	3.2
1972–76		(21%)		(24%)		(15%)		(6%)		(8%)	4.2	2.8

Source: Economic Planning Board, *Report on Mining and Manufacturing Census (or Survey)*, various issues, and Table B. 21.

Table 8.11. Weighted Average Interest Rates on Loans to the Manufacturing Sector

In Million 1970 Dollars & Percent

	Total DMB Loans		Total KDB Loans		Private Foreign Borrowings		Gov't Foreign Borrowings		Curb Loans[1]		Total Domestic & Foreign Loans	
	Total Loans	Interest Rate	Total Loans	Interest Rate	Total Loans	Interest Rate	Total Loans	Interest Rate	Total Loans	Interest Rate	Total Loans	Interest Rate
1962	176.8	(4.0%)	129.7	(−1.0%)	1.8	(−1.8%)	2.9	(−1.6%)	—[2]	(—)	388.7	(6.9%)
1963	150.3	(−7.5%)	107.1	(−12.3%)	23.2	(−15.0%)	3.7	(−14.8%)	—[2]	(31.9%)	361.8	(−2.0%)
1964	121.7	(−21.3%)	94.4	(−26.2%)	36.5	(35.5%)	8.0	(33.1%)	77.5	(27.2%)	338.1	(−4.1%)
1965	176.5	(6.2%)	114.1	(−0.8%)	47.9	(19.7%)	7.4	(17.0%)	124.9	(48.9%)	470.8	(17.4%)
1966	237.7	(12.5%)	126.9	(2.9%)	132.6	(−1.3%)	22.9	(−4.6%)	121.1	(49.8%)	641.2	(14.2%)
1967	380.7	(15.4%)	119.6	(6.1%)	237.2	(−0.5%)	35.4	(−4.1%)	182.8	(50.1%)	955.7	(16.2%)
1968	681.8	(13.4%)	136.6	(4.6%)	371.3	(−0.8%)	47.7	(−4.5%)	328.7	(47.9%)	1,566.1	(16.0%)
1969	1,011.2	(13.9%)	156.5	(5.4%)	468.5	(3.1%)	45.8	(−0.8%)	416.3	(44.5%)	2,098.3	(16.6%)
1970	1,044.3	(8.4%)	197.5	(3.3%)	587.9	(5.5%)	71.0	(1.2%)	584.7	(40.6%)	2,485.3	(14.7%)
1971	1,237.3	(7.8%)	200.4	(3.8%)	745.3	(9.7%)	78.2	(5.4%)	630.6	(37.8%)	2,891.8	(14.5%)
1972	1,487.6	(3.7%)	205.0	(−4.1%)	849.0	(6.0%)	113.8	(2.0%)	514.8	(25.0%)	3,170.2	(7.2%)
1973	1,955.0	(7.0%)	279.4	(2.8%)	848.3	(2.8%)	128.6	(−1.8%)	567.1	(26.4%)	3,778.4	(8.4%)
1974	2,551.0	(−28.1%)	292.2	(−32.4%)	917.1	(−31.3%)	119.6	(−36.1%)	588.0	(−1.5%)	4,467.9	(−25.8%)
1975	2,430.9	(−12.9%)	311.5	(−15.3%)	1,152.8	(0.2%)	133.0	(−3.8%)	597.9	(14.8%)	4,626.1	(−6.0%)
1976	2,699.1	(1.6%)	383.7	(−0.8%)	1,348.4	(−4.1%)	129.9	(−7.7%)	—	(28.4%)		

Source: Tables 7.22, and B.23–28, and the Bank of Korea.
Notes: [1] Assuming all curb market loans were allocated to the manufacturing sector.
[2] Applying the 1964 information on curb loans.

been the low (aggregate) elasticity of factor substitution in manufacturing which enabled the approximate 10 percent average annual increase in total manufacturing employment for this period.

Those who emphasize various structural peculiarities of developing countries may be reluctant to accept such an elasticity approach and the associated assumption on causality. However, one cannot deny that the Korean experience does illuminate an aspect which has hitherto been slighted.

We will first estimate the apparent elasticity of factor substitution for whole industry and for manufacturing on the basis of the observed actual association between changes in the wage-rental ratio and changes in the capital-labor ratio in Korea over time. We will then examine a possible employment implication of this observed association. Associative relationships of this type cannot, of course, be used as proof of causality, but the most important implication of our observation will be in the linking of changes in factor supplies, factor prices and employment, in the aggregate, over time. We have not attempted to estimate elasticities of substitution, taking account of technological change, by an econometric means because it has already been well documented that we cannot get very meaningful results.[15]

The so-called elasticity of substitution which we will estimate in this section represents a historical association between wage-rental ratio and capital-labor ratio under the given (but unidentified) pace of technological change. It may be regarded as a "stylized fact" which can be observed, but has yet to be explained by an appropriate analysis. Furthermore, the estimate is based on data for separated points in time *a la* Kendrick, i.e., we will simply compute an arc elasticity of substitution by comparing the capital-labor ratio with the price ratio in the two years 1967 and 1973.[16] Being based on only two years, our estimate is subject to a great deal of uncertainty but is less dominated by special assumptions as to the form of production function. The use of time series data to estimate the elasticity of substitution usually imparts a downward bias that is basically attributable to changes in the quality of labor which, on the hand, tends to be offset by embodied technical change. Our emphasis is on a possible pattern of association, rather than a strict causation, between wage-rental ratio and capital-labor ratio in the process of economic development.

According to the Office of Labor Affairs data on average monthly earn-

---
[15] D. Morawetz, *op. cit.* and M. Nerlove, *op. cit.*
[16] J. W. Kendrick, "Comment on Solow," in *The Behavior of Income Shares*, Princeton University Press for NBER, 1964, pp. 140–142.

Table 8.12. Rate of Change in Wage and Rental: 1967-73

	Real Annual Wage Rate in Manufacturing				Av. Real Interest Rate on Loans to		Wholesale Price Index	
	Office of Labor Data		M & M Census Data					
	GNP Deflator (1970 $)	Manufacturing Deflator (1970 $)	GNP Deflator (1970 $)	Manufacturing Deflator (1970 $)	All Industry (Percent)	Manufacturing (Percent)	All Commodities (1975=100)	Capital Goods (1975=100)
1967	$375	$329	$405	$355	12.5%	16.2%	33.4	44.6
1973	$617	$668	$635	$687	5.5%	8.4%	55.6	70.2
Av. Annual % Change in 1967-73	9%	13%	8%	12%	−12%	−10%	9%	8%

	Fixed Capital Stock (Million 1970 Dollars)				Number of Workers (Thousand Persons)	
	(Han-BOK Data)		(M&M Census Data)			
	All Industries (gross)	Manufacturing (gross) (net)	Manufacturing (gross) (net)		All Industries	Manufacturing
1967	10,217	2,251 1,456	1,634 1,062		8,717	1,021 (649*)
	6,637					
1973	21,315	5,036 2,809	4,579 3,167		11,139	1,774 (1,153*)
	14,252					
Av. Annual % Change in 1967-73	13%	15% 12%	19% 20%		4%	10% (10%*)
	14%					
(in 1969-75)	(12%)	(14%) (9%)	(19%) (20%)		(4%)	10% (10%*)

Source: Bank of Korea, *Economic Statistics Yearbook*, and Tables 7.21, 8.1, 8.2., 8.10. and 8.11.
Note: Figures with asterisk (*) were obtained from the mining and manufacturing census data which cover establishments operating with more than 5 workers. Other employment figures were obtained from the EPB's quarterly survey data.

ings of regular employees in manufacturing industries (deflated by the implicit price deflator for manufacturing output), the average annual growth rate of wages was about 13 percent during 1967–73.[17] At the same time the weighted average interest rates on total KDB, DMB, curb and foreign loans for all industries decreased by about 12 percent per annum on the average during this period. This implies average annual increase in wage/rental ratio for all industries of about 25 percent.[18] On the other hand, according to the total gross fixed capital stock data for all industries (excluding ownership of dwellings) which were obtained by adding (or subtracting) the BOK's annual total gross fixed capital formation figures to Han's 1968 total gross fixed capital stock figure, the gross fixed capital stock increased by about 13 percent annually during 1967–73 on the average, while the total number of employed persons (based on the EPB's quarterly survey data) increased by about 4 percent annually. The increase in net capital stock, which was computed in a similar fashion, was about 14 percent per annum for this period. This implies an average annual increase in the capital/labor ratio for all industries of about 9–10 percent, and an elasticity of factor substitution of around 0.4.

We computed a similar set of statistics for the manufacturing industries. The average annual growth rate of (net or gross) fixed capital in manufacturing was 12 to 15 percent and that of labor was about 10 percent between 1967 and 1973. This implies an average annual growth rate of the capital/labor ratio of 2 to 5 percent. Since the average annual rate of increase in the wage/rental ratio was about 23 percent during this period, the implied elasticity of substitution was between 0.1 and 0.2.

According to the manufacturing census data, in 1968 the net fixed capital stock in the manufacturing industry (covering only establishments with more than 5 workers) was about $1,205 million in 1970 prices. Applying the net-to-gross conversion rate of 1.551 derived from Han's study based on the National Wealth Survey of 1968, we estimated the total

---

[17] The growth rate of wages was about 9 percent during 1967–73 if we apply the GNP deflator which may more closely reflect the change in real purchasing power of wage earners. However, since our concern is on the cost aspect of manufacturers, we took the deflator for manufacturing output.

[18] The exact annual rate of change in the wage/rental ratio itself was not 25 percent. However, considering the quality of the data base for our estimations, we preferred to use rough approximations, using the average growth rates of wage and rental separately. The wholesale price index for all commodities rose at an average annual rate of about 9 percent during 1967–73 and that of capital goods rose at about 8 percent, implying a capital loss of approximately one percent per annum. Since the magnitude of capital loss was rather small, we decided to ignore it in order to simplify the exercise. Substantial capital losses occurred only from 1974 to 1976.

gross fixed capital stock in the manufacturing industry to be $1,869 million in 1968. According to these gross and net fixed capital stock figures for 1968 and the annual (gross and net) investment data of the manufacturing census, the average annual growth rate of fixed capital stock in manufacturing was about 19 percent between 1967 and 1973. Since the total number of workers in manufacturing increased by around 9 percent per annum, the capital/labor ratio increased by around 10 percent per annum, implying an elasticity of substitution of approximately 0.4.[19]

In order to allow for time lags in factor substitutions, we also computed the average annual rate of change in fixed capital stock and employment during 1969-75. But the results were very close to those during 1967-73.

One might argue that there is absolutely no causal relationship between shifts in the wage-rental ratio and shifts in both the aggregate and sectoral capital/labor ratios in a developing country like Korea. However, one would do well to expect some substitutability in the capital/labor ratio in response to changes in the wage/rental ratio. In such a case, one may well presume an (aggregated) elasticity of substitution of around 0.4 for the period 1967-73. Of course the observed association between the capital/labor ratio and the wage/rental ratio is subject to simultaneous equations type problems. We implicitly hypothesize that employment or the capital/labor ratio is a function of the wage/rental ratio. It is indicated that the causation should not be taken as unidirectional, since a higher capital/labor ratio is likely to increase labor productivity, and hence lead to higher wages.[20] In order to avoid, at least on a theoretical level, such problems in interpretation, we may presume a Lewis type economy with an infinite supply of labor where the manufacturing (or urban) wage rate is determined by the average productivity of labor in agriculture (or rural area). That is, we may presume that the increase in the per worker farm income in Korea by an average of 8 percent per annum (or the increase in wage rate for a hired farm employee by 11 percent per annum) during 1966-73 was caused by the capital accumulation and technical progress in the agricultural sector itself which, in turn, caused the upward shifts in the industrial wage floor. Hypothesizing a possible proportional increase in

---

[19] According to the study of Y. C. Kim and J. K. Kwon, the utilization rate of capital equipment in the Korean manufacturing industry increased at an annual average rate of about 8 percent during 1962-71(or during 1967-71). The rate of capacity utilization increased from 13.2 percent in 1962 to 19.8 percent in 1967 and to 26.5 percent in 1971. Therefore, the use of capital in terms of its service flow increased by approximately 27 percent per annum during 1967-71, implying an elasticity of factor substitution of around 0.8. See Y. C. Kim and J. K. Kwon, *op. cit.*

[20] D. Morawetz, *op. cit.*

the compensation premium for the extra costs of urban living, we may rationalize the observed annual increase in the manufacturing wage rate, which amounted to between 8 and 13 percent during 1967–73 depending on the data source and the type deflators applied. Such an approach would at least make the causation sequence unidirectional.

With an increase in the wage/rental ratio of around 25 percent per annum, the capital/labor ratio also has to increase by 25 percent per annum (assuming no time lag) if the elasticity of factor substitution is unity. Since the estimated average annual rate of increase in capital stock in manufacturing was about 20 percent during 1967–73, this implies an average annual rate of "decrease" in employment of roughly 5 percent. Hence one may say that the 10 percent annual increase in employment in manufacturing during this period was possible only because the apparent elasticity of substitution was less than 0.4.[21]

A study of production functions in Korean manufacturing shows that the Cobb-Douglas function may not be a bad approximation of the (aggregated) production process for the whole manufacturing sector.[22] The estimates for manufacturing sub-sectors show that elasticity of substitution is significantly different from zero in all 18 industries and significantly different from unity in only 5 industries. This is far from an unfamiliar result, though it differs from that of some other empirical work.[23] However, the observed actual association between the wage/rental ratio and

---

[21] If elasticity were a policy variable and factor prices were given exogenously, one might have to consider a possible trade-off between GNP and employment growth in terms of a different set of elasticities. However, we consider elasticity of factor substitution as a given datum, and simply examine its employment implications. Employment creation is frequently advocated as a better means of achieving increased equity than income redistribution measures which are politically or administratively more difficult and may impinge on the human dignity of the recipient. See F. Stewart and P. Streeten, *op. cit.*, and E. Thorbecke, "The Employment Problem: A Critical Evaluation of Four ILO Comprehensive Country Reports," *International Labor Review*, May 1973.

[22] C. H. Nam, *Economies of Scale and Production Functions in South Korean Manufacturing* (unpublished Ph.D. dissertation), the University of Minnesota, 1975, pp. 72–75 and 83–90.

[23] For instance, the estimates by Minhas indicated that the elasticity of substitution between capital and labor in manufacturing is generally less than unity. B. S. Minhas, *op. cit.*, Chapter 3. Since the aggregated elasticity of substitution for the whole manufacturing industry includes the effects of shifting output composition as well as the effects of sectoral factor substitutions, the aggregated elasticity should be larger than that for individual manufacturing sub-sectors on the average. It is suggested that the scope for direct substitution in production is greater than that for indirect substitution through changing the output composition. See H. B. Chenery and W. J. Raduchel, "Substitution in Planning Models," in H. Chenery (ed.), *Studies in Development Planning*, (Cambridge: Harvard University Press, 1971). The authors noted however that their results were very sensitive to the assumed parameter values.

the capital/labor ratio in this paper was very far from unity. The relatively high employment growth rate observed in Korea, in spite of the possibly substantial (neutral or labor saving) technical progress, implies that real elasticity of factor substitution in Korea must have been much smaller than unity.

A high elasticity of substitution indicates that a faster growing primary factor can be substituted, with relative ease, for a slower growing one. For an economy where capital is growing more rapidly than the potential labor supply, a higher elasticity has the same effect as capital-using (labor-saving) technical progress which allows a higher rate of output growth by reducing the rapidity with which diminishing returns set in for the faster growing factor—capital.[24] The lower elasticity has an opposite effect and hence lowers the output growth rate but raises the employment growth rate or, in the case of full employment, raises the relative wage rate. What we observed in Korea was very rapid capital accumulation, relatively low elasticity of factor substitution, fairly rapid employment growth (especially in manufacturing) and a high rate of increase in the manufacturing wage rate during 1967–73.[25]

One might argue that the relatively low elasticity we observed was the result of difficulty in obtaining capital financing rather than technical difficulty of factor substitution, indicating that weighted average interest rate was lower than the rate of return on capital. If one carries such an argument to the extreme, one might not be able to identify capital intensive or labor intensive industries in a developing country but only those industries which happened to obtain a large amount of capital and those that could not. On the other hand, one might argue that the observed low elasticity of substitution was due to the rapidly increasing rate of capital utilization since 1966 in Korean manufacturing industries.[26] Furthermore, our result refers to capital and labor inputs as conventionally measured and makes no allowance for growth in the effective stock of capital (or labor force) due to improvements in quality (or investment in human

---

[24] Cf. M. Brown, *On the Theory and Measurement of Technological Change* (Cambridge: Cambridge University Press, 1966), pp.22–3.

[25] Under neoclassical assumptions, if the elasticity of substitution is less than one, increasing the wage will decrease labor use but increase its share in total value added. However, in Korea the labor share in total value added of manufacturing decreased slightly during 1960–73. Therefore, the observed phenomenon may have to be explained in terms of economies of scale, technical progress, absence of labor unions, a Lewis type dual economic structure and a rapidly increasing share of entrepreneurial profits in total value added (i.e., partly in terms of a non-neoclassical framework of income distribution).

[26] Y. C. Kim and J. K. Kwon, *op. cit.*

capital).²⁷ In spite of all such possible problems we may take the observed actual association between the wage/rental ratio and the captial/labor ratio (say, 0.4) as an approximation of the real elasticity of substitution in Korea for the purpose of the following exercises.

We can argue that efficient factor substitution is, to some extent, feasible, but that incorrect market prices of primary factors have conveyed the wrong signals to entrepreneurs in Korea. The weighted average real interest rate on total domestic and foreign loans for all industries fell by about 12 percent per annum during 1967–73. However, suppose that the interest rate did not fall after 1967 and instead remained at the 12.5 percent level for all industries during the period. Then the wage rate (OLA data) might have increased at a rate higher or lower than 13 percent per annum. But let us simply assume that it increased by about 13 percent per annum. Assuming that the total (gross or net) fixed capital stock for all industries increased by around 13 percent annually during this period (as it actually did) the elasticity of substitution of 0.4 implies that employment must have increased by about 9 percent per annum instead of about 4 percent per annum. This implies that total employment in Korea could have increased by nearly 70 percent rather than 30 percent over this period, implying at least an additional 3.0 million extra persons employed.²⁸

If elasticity of substitution is high, the impact of a falling interest rate on employment would be very serious. However, even with limited possibilities for factor substitution, the impact of a rising wage-rental ratio is not insignificant.

The estimated (Type II) real rate of return on capital was about 26 percent for 1967–71 on the average. If the Korean Government had tried to raise the weighted average interest rates on total loans to the manufacturing sector from 16.2 percent in 1967 to 26 percent by 1973, the real interest rate could have increased by about 8 percent per annum instead of falling by 10 percent per annum during 1967–73. This implies only an

---

²⁷ If technical change is primarily of the capital embodied type and there is little or no change in the quality of labor force, conventional measures of inputs may greatly understate the rate of growth in the effective stock of capital. On the other hand, investment in human capital and the consequent growth in the quality of labor force tend to offset the embodied technical change. M. Nerlove, *op. cit.*, p. 57.

²⁸ It should be noted that a homothetic production function was assumed for our exercise. It should also be noted that analysis has ignored the possible distortions in the labor market, as well as any other capital market distortions not in the form of subsidized loans. The omission of the labor market from the analysis was based on our judgement that there are no significant policy-induced distortions in the Korean labor market.

approximate 4 percent increase in the wage/rental ratio per annum instead of 22 percent (applying census data). The annual rate of employment growth could then have been roughly 7 percent larger than the actual rate in manufacturing (assuming an elasticity of 0.4), implying about 50 percent extra employment generation in the manufacturing sector (equivalent to the magnitude of some 0.5 million workers) during 1967–73.[29]

A basic question, however, is whether the wage-rental ratio rose in response to increasing demand for labor, or whether instead, the rise in the wage-rental ratio precluded additional employment and prevented its growth. That the former might be more likely the case can be seen from the above demonstration on extra employment that can be generated by raising real interest rates. That is, if we take the official data on labor force participation rates and unemployment in Korea, such an extra employment could not have happened.

Of course, in reality the wage-rental ratio and employment are simultaneously determined. In econometric terms, the problem posed here is one of "identification"—whether the demand for labor (and capital) shifted in such a way to alter the wage-rental ratio, or whether the wage-rental was altered thereby inducing movements along the demand curve for factors of production. In reality, there must have been some aspect of both, and the argument here goes simply to the relative importance of each.

The real wage rate has been rising since 1965 in the manufacturing sector and since 1967 in the farm sector. Even the difference on urban-rural earning has been declining since 1970. Officially estimated unemployment rates in the early 1970s were very low—generally less than five percent of labor force. With such low unemployment, and a declining rural-urban differential in earnings, one might conclude that the export-led economic growth in Korea led to sufficient increases in the demand for labor so that the wage rate was rising rapidly in response. That is, employment has been relatively full in Korea since the early 1970s, and government policies which have affected the interest rate on loans could not have adversely affected employment itself.[30]

What, then, have been the effects of interest rate subsidies in Korea?

---

[29] There are a few exercises illustrating possible employment implications of freezing technology at its current factor intensity instead of following histroical trends towards increasing capital intensity in developing countries. See summary on V. Tokman and R. Weisskoff in D. Morawetz, *op. cit.*, p. 524, and W. G. Tyler, "Labor Absorption with Import-Substituting Industrialization: An Examination of Elasticities of Substitution in the Brazilian Manufacturing Sector," *Oxford Economic Papers*, March 1974.

[30] Cf. Section 1 of this chapter (pp. 212–215).

The answer lies in the optimum utilization of capital. Our results show that Korea has over-subsidized the use of capital since the late 1960s when the real rates of return on capital began to exceed the real interest rates on loans. It seems evident that, during the early period of the export promotion drive, new investments were primarily in the labor-intensive export industries and the efficiency of allocation of resources was rapidly increasing. By the early 1970s, there is evidence that the overall efficiency of resource allocation had improved markedly. With the large interest rate subsidies, it seems clear that some capital-intensive investments were undertaken which probably were not yet economic, given Korea's factor endowment at that time. Thus, although Korea's resource allocation in the mid-1970s was undoubtedly more economic than it had been before the export drive started, the subsidies to capital encouraged the development of some industries and the use of some processes which were too capital-intensive. In other words, capital was efficiently allocated in the mid-1960s, until the late 1960s and early 1970s when the misallocation of capital began to take place. The empirical evidence supporting this conclusion is the increasing capital intensity of production and exports, as we have shown. Another evidence would lie in the increasing profit rate, which may be deduced from the increasing real rates of return on capital. Insofar as that was the case, the demand for labor might have shifted upward even more, with a higher real wage, had the subsidies to capital been eliminated. In terms of employment, however, the narrowing wage differentials between industry and agriculture, combined with the rapid decline in the unemployment rate, both might suggest that Korea was at, and remained at, full employment during the 1970s. Of course it is questionable whether Korea could have achieved such high rates of growth in GNP and exports during the period if there had not been a fall in interest rates and if Korea had not emphasized capital deepening simply to maximize employment growth or to raise wage rates.

B. Subsidies and Sectoral Factor Use

During 1966–75, the (gross or net) capital intensity of the manufacturing sector as a whole increased by around 80 percent. (See Table 8.10.) Among the manufacturing sectors, the chemical, nonmetallic mineral and steel product sectors could receive very large subsidized domestic and foreign loans during 1966–75. Hence one can expect a more rapid expansion and a more rapid increase in capital intensities of these sectors than in others (for example, the textile and wearing apparel sectors).

Table 8.13. Employment and Capital Use in Selected Manufacturing Sectors

In Thousand 1970 Dollars[1] & Persons

	1955	1960	1966	1968	1970	1973	1975
			(Wearing Apparel)[2]				
Number of Workers[3]	5,129	14,931	36,907	52,674	101,876	101,876	158,837
Gross Capital Stock	—	—	19,555	26,359	38,594	86,629	125,053
Per Worker Capital	—	—	0.5	0.5	0.7	0.9	0.8
Per Worker Value Added	—	0.790	0.655	0.948	0.941	1.303	1.280
Annual Wage Rate	—	0.324	0.227	0.359	0.399	0.491	0.523
			(Weaving & Knitting)				
Number of Workers	70,768	58,165	88,206	123,430	138,360	161,954	167,271
Gross Capital Stock	—	—	69,302	99,007	186,580	425,823	519,396
Per Worker Capital	—	—	0.8	0.8	1.4	2.6	3.1
Per Worker Value Added	—	0.672	0.650	0.779	1.088	1.836	1.957
Annual Wage Rate	—	0.265	0.245	0.307	0.421	0.608	0.625
			(Spinning)				
Number of Workers	15,719	16,449	27,549	47,444	48,041	90,442	101,313
Gross Capital Stock	—	—	97,082	139,182	220,978	426,978	744,305
Per Worker Capital	—	—	3.5	2.9	4.6	4.7	7.3
Per Worker Value Added	—	0.951	1.209	1.360	1.479	2.794	3.105
Annual Wage Rate	—	0.268	0.274	0.401	0.447	0.630	0.763
			(Steel Pipes & Sheets)				
Number of Workers	857	1,024	6,293	15,748	17,855	17,727	23,121
Gross Capital Stock	—	—	4,640	23,599	39,803	401,401	495,271
Per Worker Capital	—	—	0.7	1.5	2.2	22.6	21.4
Per Worker Value Added	—	1.689	1.900	1.452	2.791	9.473	5.755
Annual Wage Rate	—	0.631	0.500	0.443	0.758	1.210	1.259

Table 8.13. (Continued)

In Thousand 1970 Dollars[1] & Persons

	1955	1960	1966	1968	1970	1973	1975
(Synthetic Fiber)							
Number of Workers	—	—	—	8,048	5,812	2,778	5,998
Gross Capital	—	—	—	38,499	85,431	120,160	231,178
Per Worker Capital	—	—	—	4.8	14.7	43.3	38.5
Per Worker Value Added	—	—	—	3.122	4.314	7.998	7.139
Annual Wage Rate	—	—	—	0.399	0.655	2.249	1.006
(Chemical Fertilizer)							
Number of Workers	—	—	2,961	6,342	11,135	8,314	5,160
Gross Capital Stock	—	—	121,875	128,445	140,492	230,678	239,964
Per Worker Capital	—	—	41.2	20.3	12.6	27.8	46.5
Per Worker Value Added	—	—	3.669	7.837	5.024	5.954	15.693
Annual Wage Rate	—	—	1.024	1.243	0.803	1.577	2.214
(Cement)							
Number of Workers	684	1,262	2,500	6,725	5,915	6,170	6,927
Gross Capital Stock	—	—	79,847	190,284	261,647	316,720	389,568
Per Worker Capital	—	—	31.9	28.3	44.2	51.3	56.2
Per Worker Value Added	—	8.105	7.002	5.340	9.188	12.451	16.988
Annual Wage Rate	—	0.804	0.694	0.618	1.519	1.194	2.414
(Petroleum Products)							
Number of Workers	—	—	1,358	2,447	3,176	4,486	4,119
Gross Capital Stock	—	—	8,632	30,397	85,891	303,350	343,073
Per Worker Capital	—	—	6.4	12.4	27.0	67.6	83.3
Per Worker Value Added	—	—	15.165	19.091	39.473	45.955	80.919
Annual Wage Rate	—	—	1.057	0.752	1.925	2.701	2.595

Source: Economic Planning Board, *Report on Mining and Manufacturing Census (or Survey)*.
Notes: [1]Figures in current won were converted into 1970 dollars by applying the BOK's implicit price deflators for fixed capital formation and those for value added in manufacturing.
[2] Including non-rubber footwear manufacturing.
[3] Sum of average number of employees and unpaid workers.

Table 8.14. Differences in Capital Intensity between Small & Large Firms: 1968

Small Firms (5–49 Workers)	Fixed Capital (Incl. Land)		Number of Workers (Annual Av.)	Per Worker Capital: A (1970 $)	A/B
	In Million Won	In Million 1970 $			
All Manufacturing	92,062	333.4	260,627	1,279	53%
Food	13,540	49.0	32,757	1,496	90%
Beverage	5,714	20.7	16,854	1,228	59%
Tobacco	—	—	—	—	—
Textiles	12,854	46.6	39,397	1,183	68%
Wearing Apparel	6,075	22.0	32,349	680	87%
Wood & Cork Products	6,900	25.0	11,094	2,253	137%
Furniture	2,376	8.6	9,747	882	159%
Paper & Paper Products	1,518	5.5	6,731	817	22%
Printing & Publishing	4,389	15.9	10,294	1,545	109%
Leather & Leather Products	427	1.5	993	1,511	48%
Rubber Products	748	2.7	1,480	1,824	227%
Chemicals	4,512	16.3	8,258	1,974	33%
Petroleum & Coal Products	3,607	13.1	8,685	1,508	23%
Clay, Glass & Stone Products	5,196	18.8	24,209	777	9%
Basic Metals	2,613	9.5	4,434	2,143	119%
Metal Products	5,254	19.0	14,042	1,353	126%
Machinery	5,748	20.8	13,288	1,565	127%
Electrical Machinery	1,869	6.8	5,161	1,318	87%
Transport Equipment	5,640	20.4	12,310	1,657	77%
Other Manufactures	3,083	11.2	8,544	1,311	198%

Table 8.14. (Continued)

Large Firms (50 or More Workers)	Fixed Capital (Incl. Land) In Million Won	In Million 1970 $	Number of Workers (Annual Av.)	Per Worker Capital: B (1970 $)	B/A
All Manufacturing	322,605	1,168.3	487,680	2,396	187%
Food	13,394	48.5	29,048	1,670	112%
Beverage	5,075	18.4	8,835	2,083	170%
Tobacco	6,929	25.1	8,771	2,862	—
Textiles	70,940	256.9	146,955	1,748	148%
Wearing Apparel	4,379	15.9	20,325	782	115%
Wood & Cork Products	9,189	33.3	20,279	1,642	73%
Furniture	292	1.1	1,977	556	63%
Paper & Paper Products	11,986	43.4	11,773	3,686	451%
Printing & Publishing	6,158	22.3	15,781	1,413	91%
Leather & Leather Products	1,332	4.8	1,515	3,168	210%
Rubber Products	5,450	19.7	24,473	805	44%
Chemicals	64,132	232.3	38,256	6,072	308%
Petroleum & Coal Products	11,617	42.1	6,309	6,673	443%
Clay, Glass & Stone Products	62,025	224.6	26,360	8,520	1,097%
Basic Metals	12,086	43.8	24,383	1,796	84%
Metal Products	4,297	15.6	14,533	1,073	79%
Machinery	3,708	13.4	10,894	1,230	79%
Electrical Machinery	9,488	34.4	22,613	1,521	115%
Transport Equipment	14,618	52.9	24,443	2,164	131%
Other Manufactures	5,510	20.0	30,157	663	51%

Source: Economic Planning Board, *Report on Mining and Manufacturing Census: 1968.*

The total number of workers in wearing apparel manufacturing increased 4.3 times during 1966–75 (from 37 thousand to 159 thousand persons), and the per workers gross capital stock increased from $500 (in 1970 dollars) to $800. The number of workers in the weaving and knitting industry increased 1.9 times (from 88 thousand to 167 thousand persons) during this period and the per worker gross capital stock increased from $800 to $3,100. The number of workers in the spinning industry, which is the most capital intensive process in textile manufacturing, increased 3.7 times (from 28 thousand to 101 thousand persons) and the per worker capital stock increased from $3,500 to $7,300. In the textile industry, which is regarded as the typically labor intensive sector, not only did the number of employed persons increase by 2 to 4 times in a decade but also the per worker capital stock was more than doubled.

The number of persons employed in manufacturing of steel pipe and sheets, cement, chemical fertilizer and petroleum products also increased 2–4 times during this period. In 1975, the per worker capital stock ranged from $21,400 in steel sheets and pipes to $46,500 in chemical fetilizer, $56,200 in cement and to $83,300 in petroleum products. The per worker capital stock in petroleum products increased from about $6,000 in 1966 to about $83,000 in 1975 and that in steel sheets and pipes increased from about $1,000 in 1966 to about $21,000 in 1975. The number of employed persons in synthetic fiber manufacturing did not increase much but the per worker capital stock increased from about $5,000 in 1968 to about $39,000 in 1975.

What we can observe is a fairly rapid expansion of relatively capital intensive industries and, at the same time, an extremely rapid increase in capital intensity of those sectors during 1966–75. This makes the doubling of capital intensity in, say, textiles production look rather insignificant.

Most empirical works show that small firms tend to use relatively more labor-intensive production techniques than their larger competitors. It is also suggested that small firms tend to use more labor-intensive techniques not because they operate on a small scale, but because they face less distorted capital prices.[31] That is, they tend to be confronted with a capital price which is much closer to the scarcity price than that facing large firms. This lends plausibility to the following type of suggestion:

"If this is the case, the appropriate policy prescription from the point

---

[31] Similar arguments on labor market distortions would indicate higher labor prices for large firms, which would reinforce the tendency for large firms to use less labor-intensive techniques.

of view of short-term employment is not the encouragement of smallness *per se*, but rather promotion of the use of more labor-intensive techniques in firms of all sizes through readjustments of factor prices to reflect real scarcities."[32]

According to the 1968 manufacturing census, the average per worker capital stock of small manufacturing firms was about $1,300 while that of medium and large firms was about $2,400. Apparently, the large firms used nearly twice as much capital per worker on the average.

However, if we examine more detailed sectoral data, we find quite a few irregularities. For instance, the per worker capital stock of small firms manfuacturing wood products, furniture, rubber products, basic metals, metal products, machinery and other miscellaneous goods was larger than that of big firms in 1968. One can only speculate that possible defects in the census data or the primitive stage of development of those sectors in 1968 were plausible causes of such irregularities.

On the other hand, there was no production of synthetic fibers, chemical fertilizers and petroleum products by small firms in 1968. Since these are relatively capital intensive industries and since they were included only in the large industry group, the apparent difference in capital intensity between small and large firms for the entire manufacturing industry would not simply indicate the extent of factor substitution due to differences in factor prices.

During 1960–75, the average per worker capital stock for the manufacturing industries as a whole increased 2.7 times (from about $1,070 in 1960 to $2,920 in 1975 in 1970 prices). However, the capital intensities of the food products, textiles, wearing apparel, leather products and miscellaneous manufacturing sectors, which received less than the average amount of domestic or foreign loans, increased at barely the average rate or at much lower rates.

On the other hand, the capital intensities of the fertilizer, other chemicals, petroleum products and nonmetallic mineral product industries, which received more than an average amount of loans (in terms of sectoral share in total manufactures outputs), were much higher than the average capital intensity of all manufacturing and, in most cases, did increase at a higher rate than the whole manufacturing industry.

The capital intensities of the basic metal, metal products, machinery, electrical machinery and transport equipment industries were very low

---

[32] D. Morawetz, *op. cit.*, p. 526.

Table 8.15. Direct Factor Intensity of Selected Manufacturing Sector: 1960–75
Per Worker Capital Stock (In Thousand 1970 Dollars)

	1960	1963	1966	1968	1970	1973	1975
Food Products	1.38 (1.3)	1.75 (1.7)	1.37 (0.8)	1.32 (0.8)	1.31 (0.7)	2.23 (0.8)	2.72 (0.93)
Textiles	1.01 (0.9)	1.10 (1.1)	2.03 (1.2)	1.78 (1.1)	2.26 (1.2)	3.00 (1.1)	3.51 (1.20)
Wearing Apparel	0.46 (0.4)	0.53 (0.5)	0.65 (0.4)	0.55 (0.3)	0.70 (0.4)	1.27 (0.5)	1.02 (0.35)
Leather Products	0.77 (0.7)	0.67 (0.6)	0.67 (0.4)	0.63 (0.4)	0.69 (0.4)	0.83 (0.3)	0.99 (0.34)
Wood Products	0.65 (0.6)	0.96 (0.9)	0.83 (0.5)	1.02 (0.6)	1.59 (0.8)	1.96 (0.7)	1.98 (0.68)
Paper & Products	1.35 (1.3)	1.11 (1.1)	1.57 (0.9)	1.69 (1.0)	1.86 (1.0)	2.49 (0.9)	2.47 (0.85)
Rubber Products	0.75 (0.7)	0.52 (0.5)	0.50 (9.3)	0.71 (0.4)	0.97 (0.5)	1.38 (0.5)	1.50 (0.51)
Fertilizer	—	1.92 (1.9)	—	21.42(12.6)	19.76(10.2)	22.74 (8.1)	33.72(11.55)
Other Chemicals	2.96 (2.8)	1.41 (1.4)	3.01 (1.7)	2.60 (1.5)	3.32 (1.7)	4.60 (1.6)	5.79 (1.98)
Petroleum & Coal	0.50 (0.5)	0.66 (0.6)	1.75 (1.0)	2.90 (1.7)	5.68 (2.9)	16.92 (6.0)	13.68 (4.68)
Non-Metallic	1.06 (1.0)	1.06 (1.0)	3.12 (1.8)	4.50 (2.7)	4.99 (2.6)	4.82 (1.7)	5.02 (1.72)
Basic Metals	2.83 (2.6)	3.41 (3.3)	1.44 (0.8)	1.07 (0.6)	0.39 (0.2)	3.52 (1.3)	4.04 (1.38)
Metal Products	0.74 (0.7)	1.15 (1.1)	0.94 (0.5)	1.20 (0.7)	1.78 (0.9)	6.20 (2.2)	5.94 (2.03)
Machinery	0.90 (0.8)	1.10 (1.1)	0.87 (0.5)	0.98 (0.6)	1.03 (0.5)	1.30 (0.5)	1.50 (0.51)
Electrical Machinery	0.76 (0.7)	1.30 (1.3)	1.71 (1.0)	1.26 (0.7)	1.42 (0.7)	1.21 (0.4)	2.65 (0.91)
Transport Eq.	1.01 (0.9)	1.03 (1.0)	1.24 (0.7)	1.35 (0.8)	1.49 (0.8)	3.43 (1.2)	5.39 (1.85)
Misc. Manufactures	0.62 (0.6)	0.54 (0.5)	0.71 (0.4)	0.66 (0.4)	0.67 (0.4)	0.75 (0.3)	1.14 (0.39)
All Manufacturing	1.07	1.04	1.75	1.70	1.93	2.80	2.92

Source: Tables B.32. and B.33. and the Bank of Korea, *Input-Output Tables of Korea.*
Note: Figures in the parentheses represent the ratio of capital intensity of each sub-sector to that of all manufacturing.

in the sixties, reflecting the extremely primitive stage of development for those industries during the period. The amount of domestic or foreign loans allocated to these sectors was relatively small in the sixties. It was only with the beginning of the seventies that these sectors started to receive more loan allocations. From 1970 to 1975 we could observe rising capital intensities in basic metal, metal product and transport equipment manufacturing.

The substantial increase in the average capital intensity of the manufacturing sector as a whole may be attributed partly to the rising wage-rental ratio associated with capital accumulation, and partly to the interest rate subsidy associated with domestic and foreign loans. However, the expansion of capital intensive manufacturing sectors as well as the rapid increase in capital intensities of some sectors may have to be attributed mostly to the pattern of subsidized loan allocation during 1957–75.

In 1976, about 21 percent of the total work force in Korea were employed in manufacturing sector. The potential labor force (population of 14 years old and over) is expected to grow at an annual rate of 3 percent during 1977–81 and 2.4 percent during 1982–86. We can also expect a continuous transfer of labor from the agricultural to the industrial sector and a further expansion in the rate of female labor force participation. If Korea is to absorb the increment in the total potential labor force by expanding manufacturing alone, employment in the manufacturing sector must increase by more than 15 percent per year (during 1977–81). Moreover the required rate increase in output must be much greater than 15 percent if increases in labor productivity are taken into account. Although the performance of the manufacturing and service sectors in helping employment growth in Korea has been encouraging over the 1963 to 1975 period, the promotion of heavy and chemical industries during the Fourth Five Year Plan period has to be carried out in the light of these orders of magnitude. That is, more attention has to be paid on the magnitude of subsidized loans and capital intensity of investment projects.

CHAPTER 9

SUMMARY AND CONCLUSION

1

The per capita GNP increased from around $80 in 1910–15 to around $140 in 1936–40 in 1970 prices, implying an average annual growth rate of about 2 percent. Population also grew at approximately 2 percent per annum. The share of agriculture and forestry declined from around two-thirds of GNP in the early 1910s to about half in the late thirties. The share of manufacturing, on the other hand, increased from around 2 percent to more than 10 percent of GNP.

Korea's commodity exports began to increase rapidly after the eighteen-eighties. During the Japanese occupation, the volume of commodity exports almost tripled every ten years to total about one billion yen in 1939 which amounts to approximately one billion dollars in 1970 prices. The gross value of commodity exports was equivalent to between 5 and 10 percent of GNP during 1910–17, but it increased to 17–21 percent during 1921–25 and to around 30 percent of GNP during 1934–40.

Export goods during the colonial period may be classified into three groups: rice and beans, other primary products, and manufactured goods. The single most important manufactured export during 1921–33 was raw silk. Other exports included rice bran, wood, pig iron, cotton tissues, sea weed, pulp, paper and sugar. In the thirties, exports of ammonium sulphate, cement, copper, lead, fish oil, wheat flour and leather were significant. However, since raw silk as well as rice bran, wood, sea weed, fish oil and leather were almost primary products, one may say that

Korea remained essentially an exporter of primary goods during the colonial period.

Heavy industries, electrical power resources and mineral deposits were mostly located in the northern part of Korea while the industries in the southern part consisted mainly of agriculture and light consumption goods manufacturing. The Korean economy, which was initially designed as a colonial economy dependent on Japan and then further crippled by the separation of the North from the South, had to industrialize out of the ruins of the Korean War (1950-53).

2

The years between 1953 and 1977 fall into two distinct phases of growth. During the initial phase—the decade after the end of Korean War—Korea pursued inward-looking policies and experienced a not so impressive growth performance. The reconstruction from the devastation of the Korean War was not completed until the end of the fifties. The economy in the fifties possessed all the familiar characteristics of extremely underdeveloped countries. The next phase of growth from 1962 until 1977 included the First, Second and Third Five Year Plan period and the economy expanded rapidly following aggressive outward-looking policies. A good foundation for industrial modernization was established by the end of the Third Five Year Plan.

In 1940, exports amounted to about 31 percent of the estimated GNP, while imports were about 43 percent. Compared to the pre-World War II period, Korea's exports during 1945-53 were negligible. In 1953, for instance, exports amounted to less than 1 percent of GNP, while imports, which were mostly financed by the U.S. grants-in aid, were about 10 percent. In response to this extreme disparity between exports and imports, various forms of import control emerged during this period and developed into an extremely complicated multiple exchange rate system in the late fifties by adopting import controls not only as a means to reduce deficits in the balance of payments but also as a means of promoting import-substitution-oriented industrialization.

The average annual growth rate of GNP during the nine year period following the war (1953-61) was approximately 4 percent, and about two-thirds of the working population were engaged in agriculture. Commodity exports remained negligible throughout the period, usually amounting to less than 1 percent of GNP. Persistently overvalued domestic currency thwarted the export potential of the Korean economy. The industrial policy pursued during this post-war period may be loosely characterized as a policy of import substitution of non-durable consumer and intermediate goods behind the protective wall of tariffs and quotas. However, any kind of whole-hearted and systematic government effort toward rapid economic growth was conspicuously absent.

The military coup in mid-1961 provided a turning point. The military government started to make systematic efforts to achieve rapid economic growth, and its vigor was maintained by the formulation and energetic execution of a series of five-year economic development plans. Korea achieved one of the highest growth rates in the world during the 1962 to 1977 period. Over that time, per capita GNP in 1977 dollars rose from about $275 to $864, representing an average annual growth rate of nearly 8 percent. Korea's annual commodity exports, which amounted to less than $0.1 billion before 1962, increased at an average annual rate of about 35 percent in constant prices in this period, and the ratio of gross commodity exports to GNP increased from about 2 to 30 percent. Nearly one third of the total workers in manufacturing were employed for export production by 1973.

Although Korea began to intensify its promotion of import substitution in the early sixties, a balance of payments problem in financing various investment projects meant that it had to promote export expansion. The export subsidy policies were not purposely designed to discriminate among industries. However, due to the limited export potential of the primary sector, the share of manufactured products in total commodity exports, which never exceeded the 20 percent level before 1961, steadily increased to more than 80 percent of total commodity exports by 1971. We may say that, as one of the most densely populated countries in the world, Korea possessed a strong potential for production of labor-intensive export manufactures, and this latent potential has been effectively exploited by positive government policies. Export promotion policies gathered momentum as time passed, and as a result people started to identify the period after 1962 as the export-oriented growth phase in Korea's development. However, Korea also achieved a very significant level of import substitution in such products as cement, fertilizer, refined petroleum, textile yarn and fabrics during this period, which in due course began to emerge as a new generation of exportables. Import substitution and export expansion may proceed together, possibly with some time lags.

In 1977, the modernized manufacturing sector contributed about 35 percent of the GNP while the social overhead sectors contributed nearly 10 percent. The once dominant agricultural sector declined to merely 16 percent of GNP, and even the share of the service sectors was reduced to about 36 percent from 43 percent in 1962. The share of agricultural employment had fallen to 40 percent in 1977. The Fourth Five Year Plan (1977–81) aims to expand the share of manufacturing in GNP to about 40 percent and that of SOC sectors to 12 percent by 1981. In addition, according to the Plan, about half of the total manufacturing output and total commodity exports in 1981 will consist of so-called heavy and chemical products.

In consideration of the employment effect of exports, expansion of the traditional mainstay of Korea's exports, the so-called simple labor-intensive manufactures such as textiles, wearing apparel, plywood and other sundry goods will require continuous support. However, there have been more and more protectionist policy measures being taken against such exports, there is increasing competition among developing countries and Korea is experiencing a rapidly rising wage level which is itself the result of successful growth. Therefore, skill intensive and moderately capital intensive industries such as manufacturing of electrical and non-electrical machinery, electronics, ships and other transport equipments, steel products and finished metal products may all require concentrated support from the government during the Fourth Five-Year Plan period (1977–81). Furthermore, in order to promote the export of such products, the government may also have to emphasize diversification of market s to underdeveloped countries in Asia, Latin America and Africa.

3

Commodity exports increased about 35 times (in 1970 constant prices) and the estimated number of persons employed directly and indirectly in export production increased about 8.3 times during 1963–75. This implies average annual growth rates of about 35 percent and 20 percent, respectively, and an export expansion elasticity of employment of about 0.6. The fixed capital stock directly and indirectly employed for export production increased about 37–fold during 1963–75 implying an average annual growth rate of 35 percent and an export expansion elasticity of capital absorption of about 1.0.

Per capita capital stock in Korea increased by only about 30 percent during the fourteen year period from 1953 to 1966, but after 1966 the per capita capital stock began to increase rapidly. Per capita net capital stock increased by nearly 170 percent during 1966–76, but due to rapidly increasing employment, the fixed capital stock per employed person increased by only about 120 percent. However, this still implies that a significant overall capital deepening occurred in Korea during this period.

The annual wage rate in manufacturing increased from $693 in 1966 to $1,381 in 1976 in 1977 prices. On the other hand, possibly due to the rapid capital accumulation and technical progress in the agricultural sector, the per worker farm income increased from about $416 in 1966 to $954 in 1976. Hence one may interpret the rapid rise in the manufacturing wage rate as the result of the capital accumulation in manufacturing and the associated increase in labor productivity and/or the result of the rising minimum wage floor *a la* Lewis via raising the average product of farm workers. On the other hand, the weighted average real interest rates on all types of loans supplied by both formal banking institutions and informal curb markets reached their peak in 1967 and then declined steadily and substantially thereafter. Hence, we can conclude that there has been a rapid and significant capital accumulation and capital deepening in Korea since 1967 which was accompanied by a rapidly rising wage/rental ratio.

The substantial increase in the capital intensity of Korea's exports during 1966–75 was predominantly due to labor-saving factor substitutions in production processes rather than due to shifts in the composition of exports, although the latter effect could have been estimated larger had we employed a more detailed sectoral breakdown. On the other hand, the factor intensity of Korea's competitive import replacements became significantly less capital intensive during 1966–75 due to shifts in the import pattern. However, because of the offsetting increases in sectoral labor-saving factor substitutions we could not find any consistent decline in the capital intensity of competitive import replacements. Instead, the effect of the increase in capital intensity of the competitive import replacement sectors seems to have been more than offset the effect of shifts in the composition of competitive imports in the seventies. As a whole, both exports and competitive import replacements showed the same tendency toward production of more capital-intensive commodities and factor substitution biased toward labor-saving production technology.

The capital intensity of Korea's non-competitive non-natural-resource intensive imports (estimated by using the U.S. and Japanese sectoral factor coefficients) was much higher than that of either her exports or competitive imports. Therefore, Korea's trade appears to have been consistent with the comparative advantage doctrine of Heckscher-Ohlin principally with regard to exports versus non-competitive (non-natural-resource-intensive) imports and export versus non-competitive natural resource intensive imports (such as crude oil, timber, raw cotton, raw sugar, crude rubber, and wool.) That is, the major difference between factor intensities is reflected not between exports and competitive imports but between both these categories and noncompetitive imports.

It appears that while exports were significantly more labor-intensive than competitive imports in the mid-sixties, shifts in Korea's trade pattern, as well as different rates of labor-saving factor substitutions occurred in various production processes, led to the employment implications of export promotion and import substitution being approximately equal in the early seventies. In theory, there is no reason why the capital intensity of exports from Korea should be lower than that of its competitive imports. Throughout the period 1953–76, around 80 percent of Korea's total trade was conducted with developed countries, mostly with the U.S. and Japan. It appears that Korea has had very little to offer other developing countries and *vice versa*, with the exception of natural-resource intensive goods.

4

According to the BOK data on export loans, the share of short-term credit for exports in total bank loans increased from about 3 percent in 1961–66 to about 6–7 percent in 1967–72 and to 12–13 percent in 1973–76. The share of long-term loans for export production increased from about 1–3 percent in 1965–70 to 8–9 percent in 1973–76. It seems that loans for exports were mostly on a short-term basis in the sixties, but the long-term loans for investments in export production began to increase rapidly in the early seventies so that nearly 40 percent of loans for exports were on a long-term basis in the mid-seventies.

According to these BOK data, long-term export loans were mostly loans from small and medium industry export promotion funds and foreign currency loan funds. Hence one may approximate the magnitude of the long-term loans for export production on the basis of the Medium Industry Bank loans and (KFX) foreign currency loans. However, since all KDB and DMB loans have been allocated among industries according to the Regulations on Loan Funds, which gave preferential treatments to export businesses, one may not be able to approximate adequately the "long-term" financial support for export production in Korea on the basis of only these two types of loans.

The development of consumer good industries in the fifties and early sixties seems to owe a lot to the tariff and non-tariff import control system. Non-tariff import restrictions were first introduced mainly to restrain balance of payment deficits. However, they started to serve as one of the principal tools for the government in promoting industrialization in the late fifties. To accelerate investment, however, capital good imports received preferential treatment and, to raise the utilization rate of existing capacities, intermediate good imports also got preferential treatment. As a result, the nontariff import restriction regime seems to have mainly served to encourgae allocation of available domestic resources to protected consumer good sectors. Since the intermediate and capital goods imports were subject to less quantitative controls, their import substitution could not be as profitable as that of consumption goods and hence the development of import substitution for intermediate and capital goods was very slow. It might sound paradoxical, but Korea's relative failure in promoting intermediate and capital good industries in the fifties and early sixties seems to have positively contributed to the rapid expansion of exports in the late sixties and seventies. That is, the manufacturers of export goods were relatively free to use imported intermediate and capital goods instead of high cost domestic products. Low cost imported intermediate and capital goods combined with low cost labor thus helped achieve successful export exapnsion in Korea.

In the mid-seventies, however, the emphasis of the government has clearly shifted to an active development of various intermediate and capital good industries for both domestic consumption and exportation. Should these industries fail to achieve efficiency in terms of international competitiveness because of abuse of tariff and non-tariff protection measures, Korea may face a Latin American style problem in the near future. The impact of high cost intermediate and capital goods may be more serious than high cost consumer goods, and the adverse effect would spread over Korea's entire production activities either for domestic consumption or for exports. However, if Korea is successful in producing a wide range of intermediate and capital goods on a competitive basis in the international market without requiring excessive subsidies over a prolonged period, the most difficult part of the industrialization process will be over and Korea will no longer be classified as an underdeveloped economy. Therefore, the need for more rational and cautious policies on tariff and non-tariff import restrictions may become more urgent in the late seventies and early eighties.

5

Since 1964, the official exchange rate has assumed a more important role in promoting both exports and import substitution. Quantitative import controls were lessened after the 1964 devaluation, and were further relaxed in 1967 when a switch was made in the system of the MCI trade program from a positive list of items that could be imported to a negative list of items that could not be imported without government authorization. However, the (weighted) average legal or actual tariff rates on imports were increased and the import deposit system was continued with its tariff equivalent effects.

There has been no major movement toward import liberalization since 1967 other than slightly lowered tariff rates on imports in 1973. The degree of import liberalization was quite low in 1977 and hence the continued export thrust has quickened the pace of Korea's movement toward an export surplus. However, if the balance of payments position keeps improving in the latter half of the seventies, one should expect more simplified export promotion policies which are likely to lessen some forms of export support, say, the subsidized loans. We can further expect reduced tariff and non-tariff import controls as well as a more important role in resource allocation for the exchange rate. As long as the necessity for massive foreign capital inflows can be economically justified on the basis of the marked difference between the rate of return on capital in Korea and the cost of foreign borrowing, an export surplus and excessive foreign exchange holdings are nothing but an unnecessary waste of resources.

With an average annual growth rate of 10 percent, Korea's GNP has doubled every seven years since 1962. The planned annual growth rate for GNP for the period 1977–91 is about 9 percent which, if attained, will be approximately the same rate of increase. If everything proceeds as planned, GNP will have expanded more than 16 times during the 30 year period since 1962, and Korea will have experienced two major transformations in its industrial structure; a transformation from primary industries to light manufacturing industries in the first half, and a transformation from light manufacturing industries to heavy and chemical industries in the second half. Rapid economic growth can solve many problems by creating new employment, raising the average wage level and enabling an easier adjustment process for declining industries. The kind of transformation which can be expected in the near future might well be a change in the socio-economic structure in terms of improved public services and welfare activities as well as an equitable income distribution.

6

One can observe that the list of aid-financed import commodities corresponds almost exactly with the list of major import substituting investments during the fifties. The U.S. aid financed imports of various finished products and raw materials which were deemed necessary to maintain a decent consumption pattern in Korea and financed the import substitution of such goods in order to eliminate the necessity for (aid-financed) imports.

The total amount of imports financed by the U.S. project assistance as well as the imports of machinery and equipment financed by the non-project assistance were equivalent to 24 percent and 4 percent, respectively, of total gross fixed capital formation in Korea during the period 1954–61. Therefore not only were most of Korea's imports financed by U.S. aid but also nearly 30 percent of total gross fixed capital formation in Korea puring 1954–61 was directly financed by U.S. aid. Furthermore, since the parity exchange rate (1970 = 100) was about twice the size of the official exchange rate during 1953–60, and since the official exchange rate was applied to the U.S. project assistance, the magnitude of the implicit subsidy on imported capital goods may be approximated from the amount of aid-financed capital good imports during 1954–61 (that is, an amount equivalent to about 24 percent of the fixed capital formation). However, only about 18 percent of the U.S. project assistance was allocated to the manufacturing sector during 1954–61. Therefore, as far as the manufacturing sector is concerned, the subsidy element associated with aid-financed underpriced capital goods seems to have been relatively small.

The absolute amount of tariff exemptions on capital good imports was equivalent to approximately 5 percent of the annual gross fixed capital formation in Korea during 1966–74. While the absolute magnitude of tariff exemptions was by no means small we found that the interest rate subsidy associated with loans was large enough to make tariff exemptions look relatively insignificant. The ratio of estimated interest subsidies to annual gross fixed capital formation increased from around 20 percent during 1962–71 to more than 35 percent after 1972.

In terms of money value, the annual net increase in the amount of KDB and DMB loans was equivalent to about 35 percent of the average annual gross domestic capital formation during 1967–76, while the amount of annual government direct investment was equivalent to about 20 percent of the annual gross domestic capital formation. In other words, the government was able to directly influence the allocation of funds equivalent to more than half of the gross domestic capital formation during 1967–76. The annual net foreign borrowing, which amounted to about 25 percent of the gross domestic capital formation during 1967–76 was also subject to government control.

In Korea, interest rates on bank loans (and savings) were kept at an extremely low level compared with those on curb market loans. As a result, there was always a huge excess demand for bank loans in Korea, and hence preferred financing for favored industries served as one of the most powerful tools for pursuing the government strategy of sectoral investment, growth and exports. Monetary policy in this low interest rate system essentially takes the form of a direct control that involves quantitative quotas or ceilings. The government bureaucracies, especially the Ministry of Finance, gained powerful control over the private economy by maintaining a disequilibrium system associated with the low interest rate bank loans.

7

We can observe that the rate of return on capital has been very high in manufacturing, relatively low in agriculture and services and lowest in the social overhead sectors. Artificially low priced SOC services seem to have enhanced the rate of return in other sectors, especially that in the manufacturing sector. In any event, such marked differences in the rate of return on capital among sectors may explain the rapid expansion of manufactruing as well as the moderate decline in the service sector and the drastic decrease in the share of GNP contributed by agriculture. It may further explain the necessity for government direct investment in the social overhead sector.

Among the various sectoral rates of return on (fixed) capital estimated in this paper we decided to take those for manufacturing to represent the (average) real opportunity cost of capital in Korea. However, in order to be on the conservative side, we took the relatively low rates among those estimates for manufacturing, that is, the estimates based on gross incremental-value-added/investment ratios, as the rates of return on capital in computing sectoral subsidies on capital use. If we take account of working capital and capital loss, the estimated rate of return on capital becomes 12 percent for 1954–61, 17 percent during the First Five-Year period, 26 percent during the Second Five-Year Plan period and 27 percent during the Third Five Year Plan period. Since about 10 percent of the gross return on capital was taken away from the entrepreneur in the form of direct taxes, one should subtract approximately 10 percent from these figures in order to get the rates of return on capital to individual entrepreneurs.

The rate of return on capital in Korean industries as a whole increased from around 11 percent in 1954–62 to around 15 percent in 1967–75. The continuous rise in the rate of return on capital in Korea from 1953 to 1975 may reflect the effects of rapidly accumulating social overhead capital stock, internal and external economies of scale, accumulation of skills and other human capital and various forms of technical progress. The extended horizon of business activities towards every part of the international market may have significantly contributed to raising the profitability of doing business in Korea.

The major sources of loans in Korea have consisted of DMB loans, KDB loans, private and government foreign borrowings and curb loans. The DMB loans constituted about 40–50 percent of total loans (year-end balance) during 1964–76. Although the share of KDB loans amounted to about 20–30 percent of total loans during 1964–66, it was reduced to around 10 percent thereafter. The share of foreign loans was negligible until 1962, but after 1966 they increased rapidly to about 30–40 percent of the total outstanding loans in Korea. The share of curb loans, admittedly underestimated, amounted to around 11 percent of total loans during 1964–71, and around 7 percent during 1972–75.

The real interest rate on DMB loans reached a peak of 15 percent in 1967 and then steadily declined to become negative in 1974. Meanwhile the real interest on KDB loans was almost always negative except during 1966–71. Taking account of the devaluation effect, the interest rate on private foreign borrowings was estimated to have been about 8 percent during 1962–66, 3 percent for 1967–71 and −6 percent in 1972–76. The average interest rate on government foreign borrowings was estimated to have been about 5 percent during 1962–66, about zero percent for 1962–71 and about −9 percent for 1972–76.

A most remarkable fact is that, although the absolute amount of interest rate subsidies associated with foreign loans was negligible before 1966, it became equivalent to more than half of the total interest rate subsidies associated with KDB and DMB loans together after 1966. Moreover the ratio of the total interest rate subsidy to the total (gross) capital stock in the manufacturing sector has been steadily increasing from a moderate 3 to 4 percent before 1962 to a rate which exceeds 14 percent in the Third Five Year Plan period. The ratio of interest subsidies to annual gross fixed capital formation in the manufacturing sector increased from around 40 percent during 1962–66, to around 75 percent for 1967–71 and to more than 100 percent since 1972.

If the probability of loan misallocation increases in proportion to the difference between the real interest rate on loans and the real rate of return on capital, the potential danger for such misallocation was the largest during the Third-Year plan period. If the subsidy rate increases further during the Fourth Five-Year Plan period in order to promote capital intensive heavy and chemical industries, the probability for misallocation of available capital may multiply proportionally.

If our estimates for the average rate of return on capital in manufacturing and the associated rates of interest subsidy on capital use in Korea were anywhere near right, then they also suggest that rates of capital accumulation in Korea should be (and have been) considerably higher than they were. Furthermore, they suggest that the government should have taken measures to enhance savings by raising returns to saving, for example, by raising the real rate of interest on bank deposits. After all, in a perfect capital market the only possible equilibrium interest is the one equal to the rate of return on invested capital. Considering the existence of infant industries, the interest rate on every loan may not be raised exactly to the level of the average rate of return on capital, but a movement in this direction would imply an improvement in efficiency. The favorable effect of an increased "availability" of loans may be far more important than the adverse effect of a higher interest rate.

Between 1963 and 1976 the number of employed persons in manufacturing increased by more than 12 percent per annum and that in services and SOC sectors increased by about 5.5 percent. At the same time the growth rate of the potential labor force was only about 3 percent per annum. However, the fact that the growth rate of total employment was only about 1 percent higher than that of the potential labor force during this period is a matter of serious concern for a country like Korea which may still possess a fairly large amount of disguised and seasonal unemployment in rural areas.

The phenomenal growth of manufactured exports was the cause of Korea's rapid employment expansion, especially in manufacturing. However, if we examine the factor intensities of Korea's commodity exports, not only was there an increase in capital intensity due to shifts in the composition of commodity exports but also there was an extremely pronounced increase in capital intensity due to biased factor substitution in production processes. Some of the sectoral capital-labor substitutons and shifts in export composition may be attributed to the increase in per capita capital stock in Korea and the associated rise in the wage-rental ratio. However, a substantial portion of the factor substitutions may have to be attributed to the extensive subsidy on capital use.

8

During 1962–76, the GNP and total capital stock increased by an average annual rate of about 10 percent while the total number of employed persons increased by about 4 percent. Output and capital stock in manufacturing increased by nearly 20 percent per annum while employment in manufacturing increased by about 12 percent per annum. The apparent elasticity of industrial employment with respect to output has not only been low but has actually been falling over time in Korea as in most other developing countries.

With an annual increase in the wage/rental ratio of around 25 percent, the capital/labor ratio also has to increase by 25 percent (assuming no time lag) if the elasticity of factor substitution is unity. Since the estimated average annual rate of increase in the capital stock in manufacturing was about 20 percent (14 percent for all industries) during 1967–73, this implies an average annual rate of "decrease" in employment of roughly 5 percent (or about 10 percent for all industries). Hence one may say that the 10 percent annual increase in employment in manufacturing (or 4 percent for whole industry) for this period was possible only because the elasticity of substitution was about 0.4.

The estimated real rate of return on capital had averaged about 26 percent during 1967–71. If the Korean Government had tried to raise the weighted average interest rates on total loans to the manufacturing sector from 16.2 percent in 1967 to 26 percent by 1973, the real interest rate could have increased by about 8 percent instead of falling 10 percent per annum between 1967 and 1973. This implies an approximate annual increase of 4 percent in the wage/rental ratio instead of 22 percent (applying census data). The annual rate of employment growth could then have been roughly 7 percent larger than the actual rate in manufacturing (assuming an elasticity of 0.4), implying approximately 50 percent extra employment generation in the manufacturing sector (equivalent to the magnitude of some 0.5 million workers) for this period

However, if we take the official data on labor force participation rates and unemployment in Korea, such an extra employment could not have happened. Unemployment rates in the early 1970s were less than five percent of the total labor force. With such low unemployment and a declining rural-urban differential in earnings, one might conclude that employment has been relatively full in Korea since the early 1970s and government policies which have affected the interest rate on loans could not have adversely affected employment. Had the subsidies to capital been eliminated, however, the growth rate of real wages might have been much higher than what we observed in Korea during 1960–76.

9

A notable fact seems to be that the capital intensity of Korea's exports was much lower than that of manufacturing sector as a whole in the sixties, but the difference between the two has become smaller thereafter and in 1975 the former became higher than the latter. This might imply that factor market distortions caused by the export promotion policy were significantly stronger than those caused by the general industrialization policy characterized by extensive subsidized capital financing. We already observed that employment implications of export promotion and import substitution became approximately equal since late sixties.

When the use of a scarce factor, capital, is subsidized in selected firms, one can expect that those firms which could not obtain such subsidies would face higher than equilibrium capital prices and hence would use more labor intensive techniques than if there were no distortions. Therefore, the aggregate capital-labor ratio of the manufacturing sector, for instance, might not be affected at all due to an offsetting of increased and reduced capital intensities among subsidized and non-subsidized firms. That is, for a given amount of labor, the existence of a factor market distortion might not affect the over-all capital-labor ratio of the economy as a whole, unless we assume possible unemployment of capital or labor.

However, in an economy where there is a large amount of disguised unemployment in the rual (as well as in the urban) sector, the interest rate subsidy and the associated expansion of extremely capital intensive sectors (or increased capital intensity of subsidized sectors) will reduce the amount of capital available to non-subsidized sectors. Since the latter sectors face higher capital prices, they are expected to use more labor intensive techniques, presuming the existence of ample opportunities for capital-labor substitution. However, instead of having many non-subsidized manufacturing firms with extremely low capital intensities, the economy might simply end up with a small number of workers in the industrial sector. That is, a selective subsidy on capital use may imply reduced employment opportunities in the industrial sector.

Conclusions on employment implications of the export-led growth in Korea are as follows: First, there has been a continuous shift in employment from the farm sector to the manufacturing sector, due to the rapid export-led growth of manufacturing production. In the farm sector, this has helped raising the real wage rate since about 1967, and reducing the difference between urban-rural earnings since about 1970. Second, within the manufacturing sector, capital intensity has been increasing since the early 1960s, with the rate of increase at first higher in import-competing industries than in exports', until the early 1970s when capital intensity began to rise faster in exports. This has been attributed to the higher rate of capital subsidization in export industries, resulting in the differential increase in the wage/rental ratios. Thus, with this extensive capital subsidization, manufactured exports have not been creating employment as much as they would otherwise have. A similar conclusion is drawn with respect to the manufacturing sector as a whole *vis-a-vis* other sectors. Furthermore, on the basis of official employment data, one may conclude that Korea began to have full employment since about 1970, implying that the growth in total employment could not have been higher even though the wage/rental ratios did not increase as much at they could have. That is, the effect of export promotion on employment in Korea was a rapid growth in total employment in the 1960s, a relatively full employment since about 1970, and a change in the sectoral distribution of employment.

It should also be noted that deducing the employment effects of trade and subsidy policies in terms of employment growth would not provide an adequate basis to judge the overall efficiency of such policies. For instance, Korea's exports might have been less capital intensive if there had been no subsidy on capital use, but one might question whether Korea could have expanded its exports (and GNP) so rapidly if it had insisted upon using less capital-intensive production techniques. Slower growth in export earnings might also have resulted in slower growth of the Korean economy as a whole, thus reducing overall employment growth rates.

Subsidization and expansion of export industries can remove possible foreign exchange bottlenecks and result in a more rapid growth of an economy as a whole. The employment growth might not be as high as that of an economy without factor market distortions, but it might be higher than a "slow" growth economy (caused by foreign exchange bottlenecks) with a distortion-free factor market. Of course there remains the question of whether it is possible to expand exports without distorting capital prices, even when there is no alternative but export expansion for removing the foreign exchange bottlenecks. Our study does not conclusively answer the question of whether (and to what extent) the rising capital intensity of Korea's industries and exports was unavoidable for maintainence of a high rate of growth in GNP and exports.

To some extent, the increase in capital intensity of Korea's exports beyond a level justifiable by the shifts in factor supply conditions and associated changes in real opportunity cost of capital may, if it actually occurred, be attributable to the protectionist policies of developed countries. Quite frequently, after Korea had achieved success in exporting a certain labor intensive good the developed countries imposed various tariff and/or non-tariff restrictions against this import so that there was no other choice but to try to expand other more capital intensive exports.[1] For instance, Korea's exports of non-rubber footwear to the U.S. amounted to about 8 million pairs in 1972. They rose to 16 million pairs in 1975 and to 44 million pairs in 1976. The total number of workers directly employed in footwear manufacturing was about 54 thousand persons

---

[1] For example, the U.S. has imposed various tariff and non-tariff import restrictions on textiles, footwear, stainless tablewares, stainless steel alloy tools, steel silicon, electrical steel, handbags and ginseng products exported from Korea. The U.S. is expected to impose import restrictions on TV sets, leather clothes, electronic watches, saccharine, fishing net and cast-iron-cookware in the late seventies. Import restrictions by OECD countries as a whole are extended to such items as socks, gloves, albums, canned mushrooms, radio, umbrellas, pp bags, tape recorders, ceramics, tires and tubes, steel plates, refrigerator, plywood and hand-tools.

in 1974 and the number increased to nearly 100 thousand persons in 1976. By 1976 the annual production capacity of non-rubber footwear reached 60 million pairs. In 1977, the U.S. imposed an (average) annual quota of 36 million pairs for the period 1977–80 which amounts to only 82 percent of the base year export amount. The U.S. textile quota imposed in 1972 allowed an annual increase of 7.5 percent of the base year export amount for synthetic textiles (and 1 percent for woolen textiles), implying that the practice of import controls in the U.S. has become more heavy-handed and malignant.[2]

The Kennedy Round of trade negotiations under the GATT in the sixties was successful in reducing tariffs on those manufactured goods which were mostly exported by developed countries. However, it practically did nothing to reduce non-tariff barriers against goods exported by developing countries. The so-called General Scheme of Preferential Tariffs for underdeveloped countries introduced in the seventies seems to be a deceptive device more or less designed for international public relations of advaned countries rather than as a measure which gives any substantial help to developing countries. Instead of waging a futile war against these import restrictions, it may be more efficient for Korea to shift its export pattern towards those goods which are mostly exported by developed countries as soon as the shifts in factor supply conditions allow such movements.

In advanced countries, such costs of import controls as inflation, hardships for the unorganized and misled consumers and poor resource allocation, are not perceived clearly enough by the masses to correct the distorted public opinion which regards imports of labor-intensive goods as an international philanthropism based on the sacrifice of the workers in developed countries. The problem is so heavily loaded with political difficulties arising from the vested interests of large and politically power-

---

[2]In 1961, the Kennedy Administration requested that GATT meet to seek an international understanding on textile trade, which led to the Long Term Arrangement Regarding International Trade in Cotton Textiles (LTA) on October 1, 1962. Annual investments in textile plants had doubled and by 1968, U.S. textile employment had increased to about 10 percent above its 1961 level. The textile imports from all sources in 1970 supplied less than 5 percent of the U.S. market for textiles, and yet the Nixon administration forced new limitations on imports of textiles of man-made and wool fibres from Japan, Hong Kong, Korea and Taiwan, which became effective as of October 1, 1971. See P. Isard, "Employment Impacts of Textile Imports and Investment: A Vintage-Capital Model," *American Economic Review*, June 1973, pp. 409–410. Korea signed a five-year textile trade agreement (covering 140 categories of cotton, woolen and synthetic textiles) with the U.S. on January 4, 1972, which became effective retroactively from October 1, 1971.

ful groups within the developed countries that the only option left for a developing country like Korea seems to be a continuous shift in the output and export pattern. These shifts must even be made somewhat prematuredly in view of given factor supply conditions. Furthermore, the system of countervailing duties in advanced countries and GATT regulations both tend to tolerate the existence of export subsidization either in the form of preferential access to credit at low interest rates or in accelerated depreciation (which favors capital-intensive production methods) instead of a general income tax exemption which has a less biased impact on the factor intensity of production technology. Perhaps the developed countries are unintentionally improving the long-run growth prospects of the underdeveloped countries by not allowing the latter to indulge in simple labor intensive production for an excessively long period of time.

10

One may argue that artificially low interest rates not only serve as an investment stimulus and indirect export subsidy but also provide a necessary dynamism to a backward economy by amplifying the profit incentives for potential entrepreneurs. One may be able to justify temporary support, in the form of subsidized loans, for new export efforts in an effort to offset the uncertainties in the early development phase (i.e., the transitional phase from primary exports to light manufactures exports and that from light manufactures to heavy industrial products). However, even if it is possible to justify interest rate subsidies on selected investment activities for one reason or the other, it may not be possible to justify the scope of the current interest rate subsidies in Korea. We would therefore like to suggest a desirable direction for change. In 1975, the total outstanding DMB loan balance was about 2,750 billion won. The net increase in DMB loans in 1975 (about 450 billion won) was equivalent to about 18 percent of the total gross capital formation in 1975 while the net increase in bank notes (about 100 billion won), net government revenue surplus (about 320 billion won) and net foreign borrowing (about 900 billion won) amounted to about 4 percent, 13 percent and 37 percent of the gross capital formation respectively. If the government were to allow the operation of a completely free market system in DMB activities on savings and loans, the interest rate on DMB loans would increase substantially and furthermore it would lose its control of DMB loan allocations. However, the government can still maintain complete control over the sectoral allocation of funds generated by the (non-inflationary) annual increase in bank notes and government revenue surplus, as well as an indirect control on the sectoral allocation of foreign loan funds, which together amounted to more than half of the gross capital formation in 1975. As far as the first two types of funds are concerned, the government may apply interest rates which are as low as it pleases. The real interest rates on foreign borrowings are already fairly low. The government can, in principle, restrict its interest rate subsidy activities for strategic industrial projects within the limit of these three types of funds. It still possesses the tax incentive mechanism which is, potentially, no less powerful than the interest-rate-incentive mechanism. On the other hand, in return for the loss of government control and elimination of interest rate subsidies on DMB loans, there will be more efficiency in capital use and, probably most important, a vastly increased supply of DMB loan funds through increased savings resulting from higher interest rates. Korea has already experienced a rapid expansion of DMB loans based on rapidly increasing savings during the high interest rate period on bank savings and loans (1966–71). A rational interest rate policy may allow a repeat of this experience thus helping to raise the average propensity to save from around 20 percent of GNP to more than 30 percent, as in Japan. Even to an individual firm, the expanded availability of loan funds may more than offset the adverse effect of higher interest rates on DMB loans.

BIBLIOGRAPHY

1. Baldwin, R.E., "Determinants of the Commodity Structure of U.S. Trade," *American Economic Review*, March 1971.
2. Balassa, B., "Trade Policy and Planning in Korea," in *Basic Documents and Selected Papers of Korea's Third Five-Year Economic Development Plan (1972–76)*, ed. by S.H. Jo and S.Y. Park, Seoul: Sokang University, 1972.
3. Bhagwati, J.N. and Eckaus, R.S., eds., *Development and Planning*, Cambridge, Mass., 1973.
4. Bhagwati, J.N. and Krueger, A.O., "Exchange Control, Liberalization, and Economic Growth," *American Economic Review Papers and Proceedings*, May 1973.
5. Brown, M., *On the Theory and Measurement of Technological Change*, Cambridge: Cambridge University Press, 1966.
6. Bruton, H.J., "Productivity Growth in Latin America, "*American Economic Review*, December 1967.
7. Chenery, H.(ed.), *Studies in Development Planning*, Cambridge: Harvard University Press, 1971.
8. Cole, D.C. and Lyman, P.N., *Korean Development*, Cambridge: Harvard University Press, 1971.
9. Frank, C.R., Kim, K.S. and Westphal, L.E., *Foreign Trade Regimes and Economic Development: South Korea*, New York: NBER, 1975.
10. Hall, C.A., "Direct Shifting of the Corporation Income Tax in Manufacturing," *American Economic Review*, May 1964.
11. Han, K.C., *Estimates of Korean Capital and Inventory Coefficients in 1968*, Seoul: Younsei University, 1970.
12. Harberger, A.C. and Wisecarver, D.L., "Private and Social Rates of Return to Capital in Uruguay," *Economic Development and Cultural Change*, April 1977.
13. Harberger, A.C., "The Incidence of the Corporation Tax" *Journal of Political Economy*, June 1962.

14. Harris, J.R., "Migration, Unemployment and Development: A Two-Sector Analysis," *American Economic Review*, March 1970.
15. Harris, J.R. and Todaro, M.P., "Wages, Industrial Employment and Labor Productivity: the Kenyan Experience," *Eastern Africa Economic Review*, June 1969.
16. Hong, Wontack, "Distortions and Static Negative Marginal Gains from Trade," *Journal of International Economics*, June 1976.
17. _____, *Factor Supply and Factor Intensity of Trade in Korea*, Seoul: KDI Press, 1976.
18. Hong, W. and Krueger, A.O., *Trade and Development in Korea*, Seoul: KDI Press, 1975.
19. Ichimura, S and Tatemoto, M., "Factor Proportions and Foreign Trade: The Case of Japan, "*Review of Economics and Statistics,*" November 1959.
20. Isard, P., "Employment Impacts of Textile Imports and Investment: A Vintage-Capital Model," *American Economic Review*, June 1973.
21. Kendrick, J.W., "Comment on Solow," in *The Behavior of Income Shares*, Princeton University Press for NBER, 1964.
22. Kim, Y.C. and Kwon, J.K., "The Utilization of Capital and the Growth of Output in a Developing Economy: Case of South Korean Manufacturing," *Journal of Development Economics*, 4, 1977.
23. Kim, Y.C. and Winston, G.C., "The Optimal Utilization of Capital Stock and the Level of Economic Development," *Economica*, November 1974.
24. Krueger, A.O., *Growth, Distortions, and Pattern of Trade Among Many Countries*, International Finance Section, Princeton University, February 1977.
25. Krueger, A.O., *Project on Alternative Trade Strategies and Employment*, Project Working Paper No 1, New York: NBER, 1976. (mimeographed)
26. Krueger, A.O., *The Role of the Foreign Sector and Aid in Korea's Development*, Seoul: KDI, 1977. (mimeographed)
27. Leff, N.H., "Rates of Return to Capital, Domestic Savings, and Investment in the Developing Countries," *Kyklos*, Vol 28, 1975.
28. Leontief, W., "Domestic Production and Foreign Trade: The American Capital Position Re-Examined," *Proceedings of the American Philosophical Society*, September 1953.
29. Leontief, W., "Factor Proportions and the Structure of American Trade: Further Theoretical and Empirical Analysis," *Review of*

Economics and Statistics, November 1956.
30. Lewis, A., "Economic Development with Unlimited Supplies of Labor," *The Manchester School,* May 1954.
31. Magee, S.P., *International Trade and Distortions in Factor Markets,* New York: Marcel Dekker, 1976.
32. Minhas, B.S., *An International Comparison of Factor Costs and Factor Use,* Amsterdam: North Holland, 1963.
33. Morawetz, D., "Employment Implications of Industrialization in Developing Countries: A Survey," *Economic Journal,* September 1974.
34. Nam, C.H., *Economies of Scale and Production Functions in South Korean Manufacturing,* (unpublished Ph. D. dissertation), the University of Minnesota, 1975.
35. Nerlove, M., "Recent Empirical Studies of the CES and Related Production Functions," in M. Brown, ed., *The Theory and Empirical Analysis of Production,* New York: NBER, 1967.
36. Park, Y.C., *The Unorganized Financial Sector in Korea, 1945–75,* Korea Development Institute, 1976. (mimeographed)
37. Pack H., "The Substitution of Labour for Capital in Kenyan Manufacturing," *Economic Journal,* March 1976.
38. Prebisch, R., "Commercial Policy in the Developing Countries," *American Economic Review Papers and Proceedings,* May 1959.
39. Ranis, G., "Industrial Sector Labor Absorption," *Economic Development and Cultural Change,* April 1973.
40. Ranis, G.R. and Fei, J.H., "A Theory of Economic Development," *American Economic Review,* September 1961.
41. Rybczynski, T.N., "Factor Endowments and Relative Commodity Prices," *Economica,* New Series, November 1955.
42. Sen, A.K., *Choice of Techniques,* Blackwell: Oxford, 1962.
43. Solomon, E., "Alternative Rate of Return Concepts and Their Implications for Utility Regulation," *The Bell Journal of Economics & Management Science,* Spring 1970.
44. Solow, R.M., *Capital Theory and the Rate of Return,* Amsterdam: North-Holland, 1963.
45. Stewart, F. and Streeten, P., "Conflict between Output and Employment Objectives in Developing Countries," *Oxford Economic Papers,* July 1971.
46. Stigler, G., *Capital and Rates of Return in Manufacturing Industries,* Princeton University Press: New Jersey, 1963.
47. Stolper, W.F. and Samuelson, P.A., "Protection and Real Wages,"

Review of Economic Studies, November 1941.
48. Suh, S.T., *Import Substitution and Economic Development in Korea,* Seoul: KDI, 1977. (mimeographed)
49. Thorbecke, E., "The Employment Problem: A Critical Evaluation of Four ILO Comprehensive Country Reports," *International Labor Review,* May 1973.
50. Tyler, W.G., "Labor Absorption with Import-Substituting Industrialization: An Examination of Elasticities of Substitution in the Brazilian Manufacturing Sector," *Oxford Economic Papers,* March 1974.
51. Watanabe, S. "Exports and Employment: The Case of the Republic of Korea," *International Labor Review,* December 1972.
52. Westphal, L.E. and Kim, K.S., *Industrial Policy and Development in Korea,* Washington D.C.: IBRD, 1974. (mimeographed)

STATISTICAL REFERENCES

1. Bank of Chosun, *Annual Economic Review of Korea: 1948.*
2. Bank of Korea, *Annual Economic Review: 1957 & 1958.*
3. _____, *Economic Statistics Yearbook*(various issues).
4. _____, *Final Report on Revenues and Expenditure*(various issues).
5. _____, *Financial Statements Analysis*(various issues).
6. _____, *Flow of Funds in Korea: 1971.*
7. _____, *Input-Output Table of Korea*(various issues).
8. _____, *Monetary Statistics in Korea: 1960–73.*
9. _____, *Monthly Economic Statistics*(various issues).
10. _____, *Monthly Research Review,* December 1959.
11. _____, *National Income in Korea*(various issues).
12. _____, *National Income Statistics Yearbook*(various issues).
13. _____, *Summary of Financial Statistics*(various issues).
14. Bureau of Taxation, *Major Taxation Statistics,* April 1976. (mimeographed)
15. Economic Planning Board, *Annual Report on the Economically Active Population: 1977.*
16. _____, *Annual Report on the Family Income and Expenditure Survey*(various issues).
17. _____, *Korea Population Projection (1975–85).*
18. _____, *Korea Statistical Yearbook*(various issues).
19. _____, *Report on Mining and Manufacturing Census (or Survey).* (various issues)
20. _____, *Report on National Wealth Survey* (as of December 31, 1968), Seoul, 1972.
21. _____, *1960 Population and Housing Census of Korea.*
22. _____, *1966 Population Census Report of Korea.*
23. _____, *1970 Population and Housing Census Report.*
24. _____, *1975 Population and Housing Census Report.*
25. Government General of Chosen, *Chosen Sotokufu Tokei Nenpo*

(various issues).
26. Government of Korea, *First Five-Year Economic Development Plan (1962–66)*, January 1962.
27. _____, *Second Five-Year Economic Development Plan (1967–71)*, July 1966.
28. _____, *Third Five-Year Economic Development Plan (1972–76)*, February 1971.
29. _____, *Fourth Five-Year Economic Development Plan (1977–81)*, December 1976.
30. Hong-Moon-Gwan, *A Complete Collection of Revised Tax Laws* (in Korean), 1972, 1974 & 1977.
31. International Monetary Fund, *Exchange Restrictions* (various issues).
32. Korea Law Editing Association, *Korean Statute Chronicle* (in Korean), 1971.
33. Korean Traders Association, *Foreign Trade Yearbook* (various issues).
34. _____, *Statistical Yearbook of Foreign Trade* (1973–76).
35. _____, *Trade Yearbook* (various issues).
36. Ministry of Agriculture & Fisheries, *Report on the Results of Farm Household Economy Survey* (various issues).
37. Ministry of Finance, *Yearbook of Foreign Trade Statistics* (1966–69).
38. Ministry of Reconstruction, *Monthly Reconstruction Survey & Statistics*, October 1957.
39. Office of Customs Administration, *Statistical Yearbook of Foreign Trade* (1970–72).
40. Office of National Tax Administration, *Statistical Yearbook of National Tax* (various issues).

STATISTICAL APPENDIX

CONTENTS

B. 1. Sectoral Gross Output Value and Estimated Value Added: 1910–40 281
B. 2. Population and Estimated GNP: 1910–40 285
B. 3. Exports/GNP and Imports/GNP Ratios: 1910–39 286
B. 4. Commodity Trade of Korea: 1886–1939 287
B. 5. Commodity Trade by Country: 1910–1935..................289
B. 6. Exports by Commodity: 1910–35 291
B. 7. Imports by Commodity: 1910–35 295
B. 8. Output and Exports of Major Manufactures: 1935..........307
B. 9. Rice Production and Exports: 1910–40 308
B.10. Gross Output Value of Manufacturing Sectors: 1930–40 309
B.11. Output Composition of Korean Manufacturing Industry: 1939 310
B.12. Employment by Industrial Sectors: 1917–42 311
B.13. U.S. Aid to Korea: 1954–75 313
B.14. U.S. Non-Project Assistance by Sectors: 1954–72 315
B.15. U.S. Project Assistance by Sectors: 1954–75 318
B.16. Sectoral Weighted Average Legal Tariff Rates..............322
B.17. Number of Items Subject to Import Control: 1967(2/2)–1976(2/2) 350
B.18. Wastage Allowances on Imported Raw Materials for Exports 357
B.19. Composition of Value Added in Manufacturing: 1962–76..361
B.20. Labor Share in Value Added: Manufacturing 362
B.21. Employment and Capital Formation in Manufacturing 363
B.22. Composition of Sectoral Value Added: 1970 & 1973.........365

B.23. Balance of Private Foreign Borrowing: 1959-76 366
B.24. Sectoral Interest Rates on Private Foreign Borrowing 370
B.25. Private Foreign Borrowing: Loan Balance, Principal
   Repayments and Interest Rates by Source (1959-76) 374
B.26. Balance of Government Foreign Borrowing: 1959-76 377
B.27. Sectoral Interest Rates on Government Foreign Borrowing
   Weighted by Loan Balance 379
B.28. Government Foreign Borrowing: Loan Balance, Principal
   Repayments and Interest Rates by Source (1959-76) 381
B.29. Inflow of Foreign Loans (1959-76) 384
B.30. Foreign Loans by Interest Rates and Terms of Repayment:
   1959-76 385
B.31. Exports, Competitive Imports and Non-Competitive Imports
   (I-O Data): 1960-75 386
B.32. Sectoral Direct Labor Coefficients 387
B.33. Sectoral Direct Capital Coefficients 393
B.34. Sectoral Net Fixed Capital Stock (1953-76)................399
B.35. Sectoral Gross Fixed Capital Stock (1953-76) 400

Table B.1. Sectoral Gross Output Value and Estimated Value Added: 1910–40

In Million Yen & Percent

	Gross Output Value					
	Agri-culture (A)	Forestry (B)	Fishery (C)	Mining (D)	Manufac-turing (E)	Total (O)
1910	221 (82%)	19 (7%)	8 (3%)	6 (2%)	(16) (6%)	(270)
1911	330 (87%)	20 (5%)	9 (2%)	6 (2%)	16 (4%)	381
1912	404 (88%)	20 (4%)	13 (3%)	7 (2%)	17 (4%)	461
1913	472 (86%)	22 (4%)	17 (3%)	8 (1%)	28 (5%)	547
1914	416 (84%)	23 (5%)	19 (4%)	9 (2%)	29 (6%)	496
1915	376 (77%)	23 (5%)	21 (4%)	11 (2%)	55 (11%)	486
1916	461 (79%)	24 (4%)	26 (4%)	14 (2%)	60 (10%)	585
1917	634 (80%)	26 (3%)	34 (4%)	17 (2%)	85 (11%)	796
1918	1,000 (80%)	28 (2%)	52 (4%)	31 (2%)	144 (11%)	1,265
1919	1,235 (78%)	29 (2%)	72 (5%)	25 (2%)	229 (14%)	1,590
1920	1,327 (81%)	30 (2%)	61 (4%)	24 (1%)	234 (12%)	1,646
1921	958 (74%)	57 (4%)	71 (5%)	16 (1%)	201 (15%)	1,303
1922	1,051 (73%)	74 (5%)	75 (5%)	15 (1%)	223 (16%)	1,438
1923	1,033 (72%)	77 (5%)	83 (6%)	17 (1%)	234 (16%)	1,444
1924	1,152 (73%)	74 (5%)	85 (5%)	19 (1%)	251 (16%)	1,581
1925	1,214 (74%)	54 (3%)	86 (5%)	21 (1%)	269 (16%)	1,644

Table B.1. (Continued)

In Million Yen & Percent

	Gross Output Value					
	Agriculture (A)	Forestry (B)	Fishery (C)	Mining (D)	Manufacturing (E)	Total (O)
1926	1,140 (71%)	60 (4%)	90 (6%)	24 (1%)	300 (19%)	1,614
1927	1,123 (69%)	64 (4%)	107 (7%)	24 (1%)	303 (19%)	1,621
1928	1,023 (66%)	65 (4%)	114 (7%)	26 (2%)	319 (21%)	1,547
1929	964 (64%)	74 (5%)	113 (8%)	27 (2%)	327 (22%)	1,505
1930	724 (62%)	63 (5%)	83 (7%)	25 (2%)	281 (24%)	1,176
1931	703 (63%)	59 (5%)	78 (7%)	22 (2%)	253 (23%)	1,115
1932	832 (64%)	55 (4%)	76 (6%)	34 (3%)	311 (24%)	1,308
1933	921 (61%)	94 (6%)	90 (6%)	48 (3%)	367 (24%)	1,520
1934	1,020 (59%)	106 (6%)	106 (6%)	69 (4%)	438 (25%)	1,739
1935	1,147 (55%)	114 (5%)	134 (6%)	88 (4%)	608 (29%)	2,091
1936	1,209 (52%)	118 (5%)	164 (7%)	110 (5%)	731 (31%)	2,332
1937	1,561 (52%)	139 (5%)	188 (6%)	150 (5%)	959 (32%)	2,997
1938	1,575 (48%)	157 (5%)	190 (6%)	202 (6%)	1,143 (35%)	3,267
1939	1,644 (42%)	193 (5%)	327 (8%)	241 (6%)	1,498 (38%)	3,903
1940	2,053 (43%)	237 (5%)	373 (8%)	(241) (5%)	1,874 (39%)	(4,778)

Table B.1. (Continued)

In Million Yen & Percent

	Estimated Value Added					
	Agriculture (A×0.77)	Forestry (B×0.98)	Fishery (C×0.56)	Mining (D×0.76)	Manufacturing (E×0.31)	Total (V)
1910	170 (83%)	19 (9%)	5 (2%)	5 (2%)	5 (2%)	204
1911	254 (88%)	20 (7%)	5 (2%)	5 (2%)	5 (2%)	289
1912	311 (89%)	20 (6%)	7 (2%)	5 (1%)	5 (1%)	348
1913	363 (89%)	22 (5%)	10 (2%)	6 (1%)	9 (2%)	410
1914	320 (86%)	23 (6%)	11 (3%)	7 (2%)	9 (2%)	370
1915	290 (83%)	23 (7%)	12 (3%)	8 (2%)	17 (5%)	350
1916	355 (84%)	24 (6%)	15 (4%)	11 (3%)	19 (4%)	424
1917	488 (85%)	26 (5%)	19 (3%)	13 (2%)	26 (5%)	572
1918	778 (86%)	27 (3%)	29 (3%)	24 (3%)	45 (5%)	903
1919	951 (86%)	28 (3%)	40 (4%)	19 (2%)	71 (6%)	1,109
1920	1,022 (88%)	29 (2%)	34 (3%)	18 (2%)	63 (5%)	1,166
1921	738 (81%)	56 (6%)	40 (4%)	12 (1%)	62 (7%)	908
1922	809 (81%)	73 (7%)	42 (4%)	11 (1%)	69 (7%)	1,004
1923	795 (79%)	76 (8%)	47 (5%)	13 (1%)	73 (7%)	1,004
1924	887 (81%)	73 (7%)	48 (4%)	14 (1%)	78 (7%)	1,100
1925	935 (82%)	53 (5%)	48 (4%)	16 (1%)	83 (7%)	1,135

Table B.1. (Continued)

In Million Yen & Percent

	Estimated Value Added					
	Agriculture (A×0.77)	Forestry (B×0.98)	Fishery (C×0.56)	Mining (D×0.76)	Manufacg-turin (E×0.31)	Total (V)
1926	878 (80%)	59 (5%)	50 (5%)	18 (2%)	93 (8%)	1,098
1927	865 (79%)	63 (6%)	60 (5%)	18 (2%)	94 (9%)	1,100
1928	788 (76%)	64 (6%)	64 (6%)	20 (2%)	99 (10%)	1,035
1929	742 (74%)	73 (7%)	63 (6%)	21 (2%)	101 (10%)	1,000
1930	558 (72%)	62 (8%)	47 (6%)	19 (2%)	87 (11%)	773
1931	541 (73%)	58 (8%)	44 (6%)	17 (2%)	78 (11%)	738
1932	641 (75%)	54 (6%)	43 (5%)	26 (3%)	96 (11%)	860
1933	709 (71%)	92 (9%)	50 (5%)	37 (4%)	114 (11%)	1,002
1934	785 (69%)	104 (9%)	59 (5%)	52 (5%)	136 (12%)	1,136
1935	883 (67%)	112 (8%)	75 (6%)	67 (5%)	189 (14%)	1,326
1936	931 (64%)	116 (8%)	92 (6%)	84 (6%)	227 (16%)	1,450
1937	1,202 (65%)	136 (7%)	105 (6%)	114 (6%)	297 (16%)	1,854
1938	1,213 (61%)	154 (8%)	106 (5%)	154 (8%)	354 (18%)	1,981
1939	1,266 (55%)	189 (8%)	183 (8%)	183 (8%)	464 (20%)	2,285
1940	1,581 (57%)	232 (8%)	209 (8%)	183 (7%)	581 (21%)	2,786

Source: Government General of Chosen, *Chosen Sotokufu Tokei Nenpo: 1939 & 1941* (Government General of Chosen Statistics Yearbook), Seoul, 1941 & 1943, and The Bank of Korea, *Interindustry Relations Tables for 1960*, Seoul, 1964.

Table B.2.   Population and Estimated GNP: 1910-40

	Population (Thousand Persons)		Wholesale Price Indexes (1970 = 100)	Value of One Yen in 1970 Dollar (R)	Estimated GNP		Per Capita GNP in 1970 Dollar
	Korean	Japa-nese			Million Current Yen (G =V/0.7)	Million 1970 Dollars (G×R)	
1910	13,129	172	—	($2.62)	291	762	57
1911	13,832	211	0.124	$2.62	413	1,082	77
1912	14,567	244	0.130	$2.48	497	1,233	83
1913	15,170	272	0.133	$2.42	586	1,418	92
1914	15,621	291	0.125	$2.58	529	1,365	86
1915	15,958	304	0.118	$2.73	500	1,365	84
1916	16,309	321	0.138	$2.33	606	1,412	85
1917	16,617	333	0.191	$1.69	817	1,381	82
1918	16,697	337	0.261	$1.23	1,290	1,587	93
1919	16,784	347	0.327	$0.98	1,584	1,552	91
1920	16,916	348	0.339	$0.95	1,666	1,583	92
1921	17,059	368	0.255	$1.26	1,297	1,634	94
1922	17,208	389	0.253	$1.27	1,434	1,821	104
1923	17,447	403	0.250	$1.29	1,434	1,850	104
1924	17,620	412	0.269	$1.20	1,571	1,885	105
1925	18,543	425	0.286	$1.13	1,621	1,832	97
1926	18,615	442	0.259	$1.24	1,569	1,946	102
1927	18,632	455	0.243	$1.32	1,571	2,074	109
1928	18,667	469	0.238	$1.35	1,479	1,997	104
1929	18,784	489	0.230	$1.40	1,429	2,001	104
1930	19,686	502	0.200	$1.61	1,104	1,777	88
1931	19,710	515	0.161	$2.00	1,054	2,108	104
1932	20,037	524	0.160	$2.01	1,229	2,471	120
1933	20,206	543	0.178	$1.82	1,431	2,604	126
1934	20,514	561	0.180	$1.79	1,623	2,905	138
1935	21,249	583	0.199	$1.62	1,894	3,068	141
1936	21,374	609	0.211	$1.53	2,071	3,169	144
1937	21,683	630	0.246	$1.31	2,649	3,470	156
1938	21,951	633	0.294	$1.10	2,830	3,113	138
1939	22,098	650	0.345	$0.93	3,264	3,036	134
1940	22,955	690	0.380	$0.85	3,980	3,383	143

Source: Government General of Chosen, *Chosen Sotokufu Tokei Nenpo: 1941*, the Bank of Korea, *Price Statistics Summary: 1970*, Seoul, 1971 and Table B. 1.

Note: The assumption that 30 percent of GNP consists of non-commodity was based on K. Ohkawa's study on Japan, *The Growth Rate of the Japanese Economy Since 1878* (Tokyo: Kinokuniya, 1957).

Table B.3. Exports/GNP and Imports/GNP Ratios: 1910–39

	Commodity Exports			Commodity Imports		
	Million Current Yen (X)	Export Output Ratio (X/O)	Export GNP Ratio (X/G)	Million Current Yen (M)	Import Output Ratio (M/O)	Import GNP Ratio (M/G)
1910	19.9	7%	7%	39.8%	15%	14%
1911	18.6	5%	5%	54.1%	14%	13%
1912	21.0	5%	4%	67.1%	15%	14%
1913	31.2	6%	5%	72.1%	13%	12%
1914	35.0	7%	7%	63.7%	13%	12%
1915	50.2	10%	10%	59.7%	12%	12%
1916	57.8	10%	10%	75.1%	13%	12%
1917	85.0	11%	10%	104.1%	13%	13%
1918	155.9	12%	12%	160.4%	13%	12%
1919	222.0	14%	14%	283.1%	18%	18%
1920	197.0	12%	12%	249.3%	15%	15%
1921	218.3	17%	17%	232.4%	18%	18%
1922	215.4	15%	15%	256.1%	18%	18%
1923	261.7	18%	18%	265.8%	18%	19%
1924	329.0	21%	21%	309.6%	20%	20%
1925	341.6	21%	21%	340.0%	21%	21%
1926	363.0	23%	23%	372.2%	23%	24%
1927	358.9	22%	23%	383.4%	24%	24%
1928	366.0	24%	25%	414.0%	27%	28%
1929	345.7	23%	24%	423.1%	28%	30%
1930	266.6	23%	24%	367.1%	31%	33%
1931	261.8	24%	25%	270.5%	24%	26%
1932	311.4	24%	25%	320.4%	25%	26%
1933	368.6	24%	26%	404.2%	27%	28%
1934	465.4	27%	29%	519.2%	30%	32%
1935	550.8	26%	29%	659.4%	32%	35%
1936	593.3	25%	29%	762.4%	33%	37%
1937	685.5	23%	26%	863.6%	29%	33%
1938	879.6	27%	31%	1,055.9%	32%	37%
1939	1,006.8	26%	31%	1,388.5%	36%	43%

Source: The same as Tables B.1. and B.2.

Table B.4. Commodity Trade of Korea: 1886–1939

In Million Yen & Percent

	Exports		Imports			Net*			Exports		Imports			Net*	
	Total (E)	To Japan	Total (M)	From Japan	E-M	Gold Exports			Total (E)	To Japan	Total (M)	From Japan	E-M	Gold Exports	
1886	0.6	—	2.5	—	−2.0	(—)	1901		8.5	87%	14.8	62%	−6.2	(4.3)
1887	0.8	—	2.8	—	−2.0	(1.3)	1902		8.5	79%	13.7	63%	−5.2	(5.5)
1888	0.9	—	3.1	—	−2.2	(1.3)	1903		9.7	80%	18.4	63%	−8.7	(5.2)
1889	1.3	—	3.4	—	−2.1	(1.1)	1904		7.5	78%	27.4	70%	−19.9	(4.7)
1890	3.6	—	4.8	—	−1.2	(0.3)	1905		7.9	71%	33.0	73%	−25.1	(4.4)
1891	3.4	—	5.3	—	−1.9	(0.2)	1906		8.9	81%	30.3	77%	−21.4	(4.7)
1892	2.5	—	4.6	—	−2.2	(0.6)	1907		17.0	76%	41.6	71%	−24.6	(3.6)
1893	1.7	—	3.9	—	−2.2	(0.6)	1908		14.1	78%	41.0	59%	−26.9	(1.8)
1894	2.4	—	5.9	—	−3.5	(0.5)	1909		16.3	74%	36.7	60%	−20.4	(6.0)
1895	2.7	—	8.3	—	−5.6	(0.6)	1910		19.9	77%	39.8	64%	−19.9	(7.3)
1896	4.9	—	6.7	—	−1.8	(0.9)	1911		18.6	71%	54.1	63%	−35.2	(8.1)
1897	9.1	—	10.2	—	−1.1	(0.2)	1912		21.0	73%	67.1	61%	−46.1	(8.7)
1898	5.8	—	11.9	—	−6.1	(3.4)	1913		31.2	81%	72.1	56%	−40.8	(10.7)
1899	5.1	—	10.3	—	−5.2	(4.2)	1914		35.0	82%	63.7	61%	−28.7	(10.5)
1900	9.6	—	11.1	—	−1.5	(3.7)	1915		50.2	81%	59.7	70%	−9.5	(10.9)

Table B.4. (Continued)

In Million Yen & Percent

	Exports		Imports			Net*		Exports		Imports			Net*	
	Total (E)	To Japan	Total (M)	From Japan	E-M	Gold Exports		Total (E)	To Japan	Total (M)	From Japan	E-M	Gold Exports	
1916	57.8	74%	75.1	70%	−17.3	(14.5)	1931	261.8	95%	270.5	81%	−8.7	(17.6)
1917	85.0	76%	104.1	70%	−19.1	(9.2)	1932	311.4	91%	320.4	81%	−9.0	(17.7)
1918	155.9	88%	160.4	73%	−4.5	(5.7)	1933	368.6	86%	404.2	84%	−35.6	(20.6)
1919	222.0	90%	283.1	65%	−61.1	(2.8)	1934	465.4	88%	519.2	85%	−53.8	(36.0)
1920	197.0	86%	249.3	57%	−52.3	(4.6)	1935	550.8	88%	659.4	85%	−108.6	(137.4)
1921	218.3	90%	232.4	67%	−14.4	(4.8)	1936	593.3	87%	762.4	85%	−169.1	
1922	215.4	92%	256.1	63%	−40.6	(3.0)	1937	685.5	84%	863.6	85%	−178.0	
1923	261.7	92%	265.8	63%	−4.1	(5.5)	1938	879.6	81%	1,055.9	87%	−176.3	
1924	329.0	93%	309.6	68%	19.5	(4.2)	1939	1,006.8	73%	1,388.5	89%	−381.7	
1925	341.6	93%	340.0	69%	1.6	(3.6)							
1926	363.0	93%	372.2	67%	−9.2	(7.0)							
1927	358.9	92%	383.4	70%	−24.5	(4.7)							
1928	366.0	91%	414.0	71%	−48.0	(3.1)							
1929	345.7	90%	423.1	75%	−77.4	(5.2)							
1930	266.6	90%	367.1	76%	−100.5	(15.1)							

Source: Oriental Economist, *Foreign Trade of Japan: A Statistical Survey*, (Tokyo, 1935) and Government General of Chosen, *Table of Trade and Shipping*.
*Consists of gold and silver coins & bullion.

Table B.5. Commodity Trade by Country: 1901–1935

In MillionYen

	Trade with Japan Proper				Trade with Other Foreign Countries			
	Exports (X)	Imports (M)	(X-M)	Net Gold Exports	Exports (X)	Imports (M)	(X-M)	Net Gold Exports
1901	7.5	9.1	−1.7	4.1	1.1	5.7	−4.6	0.2
1902	6.7	8.7	−2.0	5.1	1.8	5.0	−3.2	0.4
1903	7.7	11.7	−4.0	5.3	2.0	6.7	−4.8	−0.1
1904	5.9	19.3	−13.4	4.9	1.7	8.2	−6.5	−0.2
1905	5.6	24.0	−18.4	4.9	2.3	8.9	−6.6	−0.6
1906	7.2	23.3	−16.0	4.2	1.7	7.1	−5.4	0.6
1907	13.0	29.6	−16.6	3.4	4.0	12.1	−8.0	0.2
1908	11.0	24.0	−13.1	2.4	3.2	17.0	−13.8	−0.7
1909	12.1	21.9	−9.8	5.8	4.2	14.8	−10.6	0.2
1910	15.4	25.4	−10.0	7.2	4.5	14.4	−9.9	0.2
1911	13.3	34.1	−20.7	8.1	5.5	20.0	−14.5	0.0
1912	15.4	40.8	−25.4	8.8	5.6	26.4	−20.7	−0.1
1913	25.3	40.4	−15.1	10.8	5.9	31.6	−25.7	−0.1
1914	28.6	39.1	−10.5	10.7	6.5	24.7	−18.2	−0.2
1915	40.9	41.5	−0.6	11.2	9.3	18.2	−8.8	−0.3
1916	43.0	52.5	−9.5	15.8	14.9	22.7	−7.8	−1.3
1917	64.7	72.7	−8.0	9.7	20.2	31.4	−11.2	−0.1
1918	137.2	117.3	19.9	5.7	18.7	43.2	−24.5	−0.1
1919	199.9	184.9	14.9	2.8	22.1	98.2	−76.1	0.0

Table B.5. (Continued)

In Million Yen

	Trade with Japan Proper				Trade with Other Foreign Countries			
	Exports (X)	Imports (M)	(X-M)	Net Gold Exports	Exports (X)	Imports (M)	(X-M)	Net Gold Exports
1920	169.4	143.1	26.3	22.4	27.6	106.2	−78.5	−17.8
1921	197.4	156.5	40.9	7.1	20.9	75.9	−55.0	−2.3
1922	197.9	160.3	37.7	3.3	17.5	95.8	−78.3	−0.2
1923	241.3	167.5	73.8	5.7	20.4	98.3	−77.9	−0.1
1924	306.7	211.8	94.8	4.2	22.4	97.8	−75.4	0.0
1925	317.3	234.6	82.7	3.8	24.3	105.4	−81.0	−0.3
1926	338.2	248.2	89.9	7.2	24.8	123.9	−99.2	−0.2
1927	330.8	269.5	61.3	4.9	28.1	113.9	−85.8	−0.2
1928	333.8	295.8	38.0	3.2	32.2	118.2	−86.0	−0.1
1929	309.9	315.3	−5.4	5.5	35.8	107.8	−72.0	−0.3
1930	240.7	278.2	−37.5	26.7	25.9	88.9	−63.0	−11.6
1931	249.0	217.8	31.3	39.5	12.8	52.7	−39.9	−21.9
1932	292.1	258.7	23.5	18.4	29.2	61.9	−32.5	−0.7
1933	315.9	339.8	−24.0	20.6	52.8	64.4	−11.6	0.0
1934	407.7	439.6	−31.9	36.0	57.7	79.5	−21.8	−0.1
1935	485.9	558.8	−72.9	206.7	64.9	100.6	−35.7	−69.4

Source: The same as Table B.4.

Table B.6. Exports by Commodity: 1910–35

In Million Yen & Percent

	1910		1911		1912		1913		1914		1915		1916	
Rice	6.3	(32%)	5.2	(28%)	7.5	(36%)	14.5	(46%)	17.1	(49%)	24.5	(49%)	19.4	(34%)
Beans	5.7	(29%)	4.6	(25%)	5.2	(25%)	5.7	(18%)	4.2	(12%)	5.3	(11%)	6.4	(11%)
Other Foodstuffs[1]	0.5	(3%)	0.2	(1%)	0.3	(1%)	0.7	(2%)	0.8	(2%)	1.4	(3%)	1.8	(3%)
Cotton & Cocoons	0.2	(1%)	0.3	(2%)	0.4	(2%)	0.9	(3%)	1.4	(4%)	1.9	(4%)	3.2	(6%)
Bulls, Hide & Furs	1.7	(9%)	1.8	(10%)	1.3	(6%)	1.6	(5%)	2.2	(6%)	4.0	(8%)	4.2	(7%)
Fish, fresh & salted	0.3	(2%)	0.3	(2%)	0.4	(2%)	0.8	(3%)	0.9	(3%)	0.9	(2%)	1.4	(2%)
Iron & Gold Ore	0.9	(5%)	0.5	(3%)	0.6	(3%)	0.7	(2%)	1.0	(3%)	1.4	(3%)	0.8	(1%)
Coal & Graphite	0.5	(3%)	0.5	(3%)	0.5	(2%)	0.6	(2%)	0.7	(2%)	0.8	(2%)	1.0	(2%)
Sea Weed & Porphyra	0.1	(1%)	0.1	(1%)	0.3	(1%)	0.3	(1%)	0.3	(1%)	0.4	(1%)	0.5	(1%)
Fish Oil	—		—		—		—		—		—		—	
Wheat Flour	—		—		—		—		—		—		—	
Sugar	—		—		—		—		—		—		—	
Cotton Tissues	—		—		—		—		—		0.1	(0%)	—	
Wood	0.1	(1%)	0.1	(1%)	0.2	(1%)	0.2	(1%)	0.1	(0%)	0.2	(0%)	0.2	(0%)
Pulp & Paper	—		—		—		—		—		—		—	
Leather	—		—		—		—		0.1	(0%)	0.1	(0%)	0.1	(0%)
Ammonium Sulphate	—		—		—		—		—		—		0.1	(0%)
Cement	—		—		—		—		—		—		—	
Pig Iron	—		—		—		—		—		—		—	
Copper & Lead	—		—		—		—		—		—		—	
Rice Bran & Manures	0.4	(2%)	0.5	(3%)	0.7	(3%)	0.8	(3%)	0.9	(3%)	0.9	(2%)	0.9	(2%)
Sub-Total	16.8	(84%)	14.1	(76%)	17.4	(83%)	25.5	(82%)	29.7	(85%)	41.9	(83%)	40.0	(69%)
Manufactured Exports	0.7	(4%)	0.7	(4%)	1.2	(6%)	1.3	(4%)	1.4	(4%)	1.7	(3%)	1.8	(3%)
Total Exports	19.9	(100%)	18.6	(100%)	21.0	(100%)	31.2	(100%)	35.0	(100%)	50.2	(100%)	57.8	(100%)

Table B.6. (Continued)

In Million Yen & Percent

	1917	1918	1919	1920	1921	1922	1923
Rice	27.4 (32%)	61.5 (39%)	109.0 (49%)	77.0 (39%)	92.8 (43%)	95.8 (44%)	113.9 (44%)
Beans	10.2 (12%)	11.7 (8%)	23.1 (10%)	17.9 (9%)	24.4 (11%)	22.9 (11%)	22.2 (8%)
Other Foodstuffs[1]	3.6 (4%)	3.8 (2%)	3.8 (2%)	4.1 (2%)	7.9 (4%)	3.9 (2%)	4.4 (2%)
Cotton & Cocoons	7.4 (9%)	11.1 (7%)	12.0 (5%)	8.4 (4%)	6.0 (3%)	6.4 (3%)	16.4 (6%)
Bulls, Hide & Furs	3.2 (4%)	3.9 (3%)	7.0 (3%)	8.6 (4%)	6.5 (3%)	5.7 (3%)	6.1 (2%)
Fish, fresh & salted	2.5 (3%)	8.4 (5%)	11.9 (5%)	12.4 (6%)	13.2 (6%)	13.6 (6%)	15.8 (6%)
Iron & Gold Ore	0.9 (1%)	2.7 (2%)	3.7 (2%)	4.7 (2%)	4.3 (2%)	3.3 (2%)	3.0 (1%)
Coal & Graphite	2.0 (2%)	1.8 (1%)	1.2 (1%)	2.2 (1%)	1.8 (1%)	2.2 (1%)	1.8 (1%)
Sea Weed & Porphyra	0.8 (1%)	1.3 (1%)	2.2 (1%)	1.4 (1%)	2.4 (1%)	3.1 (1%)	4.1 (2%)
Fish Oil	—	—	—	—	—	—	—
Wheat Flour	—	—	—	—	0.1 (0%)	0.0 (0%)	0.0 (0%)
Sugar	—	—	—	—	—	0.8 (0%)	2.6 (1%)
Cotton Tissues	—	—	—	—	—	—	—
Silk	0.1 (0%)	0.7 (0%)	2.1 (1%)	2.5 (1%)	1.6 (1%)	1.5 (1%)	1.4 (1%)
Wood	—	—	—	—	13.1 (6%)	13.8 (6%)	22.9 (9%)
Pulp & Paper	0.3 (0%)	0.4 (0%)	0.8 (0%)	1.6 (1%)	3.6 (2%)	4.8 (2%)	7.5 (3%)
Leather	—	—	1.1 (1%)	3.4 (2%)	2.0 (1%)	2.2 (1%)	0.4 (0%)
	0.1 (0%)	0.4 (0%)	0.2 (0%)	0.1 (0%)	0.0 (0%)	0.0 (0%)	0.0 (0%)
Ammonium Sulphate	0.1 (0%)	0.3 (0%)	0.4 (0%)	0.6 (0%)	0.2 (0%)	0.1 (0%)	0.0 (0%)
Cement	—	—	—	—	0.9 (0%)	0.5 (0%)	0.2 (0%)
Pig Iron	—	15.4 (10%)	10.2 (5%)	6.1 (3%)	4.1 (2%)	6.3 (3%)	5.7 (2%)
Copper & Lead	5.1 (4%)	3.9 (3%)	2.0 (1%)	1.6 (1%)	0.2 (0%)	0.1 (0%)	0.0 (0%)
Rice Bran & Mannures	1.3 (2%)	1.6 (1%)	2.7 (1%)	2.6 (1%)	7.4 (3%)	6.1 (3%)	7.8 (3%)
Sub-Total	63.0 (74%)	128.9 (83%)	193.4 (87%)	155.2 (79%)	192.5 (88%)	187.1 (87%)	236.2 (90%)
Manufactured Exports	5.8 (7%)	24.0 (15%)	21.7 (10%)	19.9 (10%)	35.6 (16%)	33.3 (15%)	52.6 (20%)
Total Exports	85.0 (100%)	155.9 (100%)	222.0 (100%)	197.0 (100%)	218.3 (100%)	215.4 (100%)	261.7 (100%)

Table B.6. (Continued)

In Million Yen & Percent

	1924	1925	1926	1927	1928	1929	1930
Rice	164.5 (50%)	173.2 (51%)	192.6 (53%)	191.6 (26%)	183.7 (50%)	148.8 (43%)	109.7 (41%)
Beans	26.2 (8%)	21.1 (6%)	25.3 (7%)	23.0 (7%)	24.6 (7%)	23.3 (7%)	18.4 (7%)
Other Foodstuffs[1]	5.4 (2%)	6.1 (2%)	4.1 (1%)	4.4 (1%)	4.2 (1%)	6.0 (2%)	6.1 (2%)
Cotton & Cocoons	20.9 (6%)	21.6 (6%)	12.0 (3%)	9.2 (3%)	10.0 (3%)	11.2 (3%)	9.7 (4%)
Bulls, Hide & Furs	8.1 (2%)	8.4 (2%)	6.9 (2%)	6.3 (2%)	8.6 (2%)	7.1 (2%)	4.8 (2%)
Fish, fresh & salted	17.5 (5%)	14.1 (4%)	15.2 (4%)	13.5 (4%)	13.9 (4%)	14.5 (4%)	11.8 (4%)
Iron & Gold Ore	3.5 (1%)	2.3 (1%)	2.1 (1%)	2.5 (1%)	3.4 (1%)	3.6 (1%)	2.5 (1%)
Coal & Graphite	2.3 (1%)	2.8 (1%)	3.1 (1%)	3.4 (1%)	3.9 (1%)	4.1 (1%)	3.3 (1%)
Sea Weed & Porphyra	4.5 (1%)	4.3 (1%)	3.5 (1%)	4.0 (1%)	4.1 (1%)	5.7 (2%)	2.9 (1%)
Fish Oil	—	—	—	3.9 (1%)	4.5 (1%)	5.9 (2%)	2.7 (1%)
Wheat Flour	0.1 (0%)	0.1 (0%)	0.2 (0%)	0.1 (0%)	0.1 (0%)	0.1 (0%)	0.1 (0%)
Sugar	6.0 (2%)	4.5 (1%)	2.3 (1%)	6.0 (2%)	5.7 (2%)	5.6 (2%)	4.8 (2%)
Cotton Tissues	1.1 (0%)	1.3 (0%)	2.5 (1%)	3.1 (1%)	2.5 (1%)	2.9 (1%)	2.7 (1%)
Silk	19.6 (6%)	27.1 (8%)	27.1 (7%)	25.9 (7%)	28.8 (8%)	29.5 (9%)	23.9 (9%)
Wood	6.3 (2%)	3.7 (1%)	5.1 (1%)	3.2 (1%)	4.9 (1%)	4.1 (1%)	2.3 (1%)
Pulp & Paper	0.3 (0%)	0.8 (0%)	2.4 (1%)	2.1 (1%)	3.0 (1%)	2.8 (1%)	3.6 (1%)
Leather	0.1 (0%)	0.2 (0%)	0.2 (0%)	0.1 (0%)	0.3 (0%)	0.2 (0%)	0.2 (0%)
Ammonium Sulphate	0.0 (0%)	0.0 (0%)	0.0 (0%)	0.0 (0%)	0.0 (0%)	0.0 (0%)	2.9 (1%)
Cement	0.5 (0%)	0.4 (0%)	0.5 (0%)	0.8 (0%)	0.8 (0%)	2.0 (1%)	1.8 (1%)
Pig Iron	4.5 (1%)	4.6 (1%)	5.4 (1%)	5.4 (2%)	7.2 (2%)	7.1 (2%)	5.5 (2%)
Copper & Lead	0.2 (0%)	0.6 (0%)	1.3 (0%)	0.6 (0%)	0.9 (0%)	1.3 (0%)	1.2 (0%)
Rice Bran & Mannures	6.1 (2%)	5.5 (2%)	8.8 (2%)	7.2 (2%)	7.2 (2%)	10.0 (3%)	6.8 (3%)
Sub-Total	297.7 (90%)	302.7 (89%)	320.6 (88%)	316.3 (88%)	322.2 (88%)	295.8 (86%)	227.7 (85%)
Manufactured Exports	49.3 (15%)	53.1 (16%)	59.3 (16%)	62.4 (17%)	69.9 (19%)	77.2 (22%)	61.4 (23%)
Total Exports	329.0 (100%)	341.6 (100%)	363.0 (100%)	358.9 (100%)	366.0 (100%)	345.7 (100%)	266.6 (100%)

Table B.6. *(Continued)*

In Million Yen & Percent

	1931	1932	1933	1934	1935
Rice	138.5 (53%)	145.3 (47%)	154.7 (42%)	224.3 (48%)	244.7 (44%)
Beans	14.4 (6%)	22.2 (7%)	20.7 (6%)	19.1 (4%)	18.8 (3%)
Other Foodstuffs[1]	3.1 (1%)	4.5 (1%)	6.7 (2%)	5.2 (1%)	5.7 (1%)
Cotton & Cocoons	4.2 (2%)	4.8 (2%)	8.3 (2%)	8.9 (2%)	14.7 (3%)
Bulls, Hide & Furs	4.7 (2%)	5.4 (2%)	6.2 (2%)	6.2 (1%)	6.8 (1%)
Fish, fresh & salted	10.6 (4%)	11.8 (4%)	13.1 (4%)	13.8 (3%)	12.4 (2%)
Iron & Gold Ore	2.3 (1%)	2.4 (1%)	3.8 (1%)	3.4 (1%)	7.7 (1%)
Coal & Graphite	3.7 (2%)	4.5 (1%)	5.6 (2%)	7.6 (2%)	9.0 (2%)
Sea Weed & Porphyra	3.3 (2%)	3.0 (1%)	4.6 (1%)	4.8 (1%)	3.8 (1%)
Fish Oil	1.4 (1%)	1.2 (0%)	1.2 (0%)	1.2 (0%)	5.5 (1%)
Wheat Flour	0.1 (0%)	0.4 (0%)	0.7 (0%)	0.7 (0%)	0.9 (0%)
Sugar	2.7 (1%)	3.5 (1%)	2.5 (1%)	2.5 (1%)	3.2 (1%)
Cotton Tissues	2.5 (1%)	6.5 (2%)	6.2 (2%)	6.5 (1%)	4.7 (1%)
Silk	19.0 (7%)	19.4 (6%)	23.2 (6%)	18.0 (4%)	19.9 (4%)
Wood	2.2 (1%)	2.6 (1%)	5.8 (2%)	7.3 (2%)	8.1 (1%)
Pulp & Paper	3.3 (1%)	2.8 (1%)	5.2 (1%)	5.2 (1%)	4.2 (1%)
Leather	0.3 (0%)	0.5 (0%)	0.8 (0%)	1.0 (0%)	1.1 (0%)
Ammonium Sulphate	4.1 (2%)	9.4 (3%)	13.6 (4%)	15.0 (3%)	16.2 (3%)
Cement	1.3 (0%)	0.6 (0%)	1.6 (0%)	1.8 (0%)	3.7 (1%)
Pig Iron	3.1 (1%)	6.2 (2%)	5.1 (1%)	7.3 (2%)	7.3 (1%)
Copper & Lead	1.7 (1%)	2.9 (1%)	6.5 (2%)	12.2 (3%)	24.0 (4%)
Rice Bran & Mannures	4.4 (2%)	9.1 (3%)	9.0 (2%)	14.1 (3%)	16.9 (3%)
Sub-Total	230.9 (88%)	269.0 (86%)	305.1 (83%)	386.1 (83%)	439.3 (80%)
Manufactured Exports	49.4 (19%)	68.1 (22%)	86.0 (23%)	97.6 (21%)	119.5 (22%)
Total Exports	261.8 (100%)	311.4 (100%)	386.6 (100%)	465.4 (100%)	550.8 (100%)

Source: Oriental Economist Inc., *Foreign Trade of Japan: A Statistical Survey*, (Tokyo, 1935) and the Government General of Chosen, *Table of Trade and Shipping*.

Notes: [1] Consist of wheat, leaf tobacco, apple, chestnut, and ginseng.

Table B.7. Imports by Commodity: 1910–35

In Million Yen & Percent

	1910		1911		1912		1913		1914	
Rice, Barley & Wheat	—		0.2	(0%)	0.2	(0%)	2.9	(4%)	2.7	(4%)
Millet, Corn & Bean	—		—		0.3	(0%)	3.9	(5%)	1.1	(2%)
Vegetable, Fruits & Tobacco	0.5	(2%)	0.7	(1%)	1.0	(1%)	1.2	(2%)	1.1	(2%)
Cotton Ginned & Wadding	0.4	(1%)	0.5	(1%)	0.7	(1%)	0.7	(1%)	0.5	(1%)
Crude India-Rubber	—		—		—		—		—	
Coal	0.8	(2%)	1.3	(2%)	1.5	(2%)	1.8	(3%)	1.7	(3%)
Salt	0.4	(1%)	0.6	(1%)	0.8	(1%)	0.8	(1%)	0.6	(1%)
Fish, Dried or Preserved	0.3	(1%)	0.3	(1%)	0.3	(0%)	0.4	(1%)	0.4	(1%)
Wheat Flours	0.3	(1%)	0.7	(1%)	1.3	(2%)	2.0	(3%)	1.2	(2%)
Confectioneries, Soy & Milk	0.3	(1%)	0.3	(1%)	0.4	(1%)	0.3	(0%)	0.3	(0%)
Sugar & Molasses	0.9	(2%)	1.3	(2%)	1.6	(2%)	1.9	(3%)	1.5	(2%)
Beverages	1.0	(3%)	3.9	(7%)	4.9	(7%)	5.2	(7%)	4.5	(7%)
Cotton Yarn & Thread	1.8	(5%)	2.2	(4%)	2.4	(4%)	2.0	(3%)	2.2	(3%)
Textile Fabrics[1]	9.1	(23%)	11.6	(21%)	11.3	(17%)	13.0	(18%)	11.7	(20%)
Textile Products[2]	0.9	(2%)	1.0	(2%)	1.2	(2%)	1.2	(2%)	1.3	(2%)
Other Textile Materials	—		4.4	(8%)	9.2	(14%)	6.1	(9%)	4.6	(7%)
Wood & Wood Products	1.2	(3%)	1.5	(3%)	2.5	(4%)	2.0	(3%)	1.9	(3%)
Paper	0.7	(2%)	1.0	(2%)	1.2	(2%)	1.4	(2%)	1.3	(2%)
Leather & Leather Products	—		—		0.1	(0%)	0.1	(0%)	0.1	(0%)
Rubber Products[3]	—		—		—		—		—	

Table B.7. (Continued)

In Million Yen & Percent

	1910		1911		1912		1913		1914	
Caustic Soda; Calcium Carbide	—		—		—		—		—	
Chemical Fertilizer[4]	—		—		—		—		—	
Other Chemicals[5]	0.8	(2%)	1.0	(2%)	1.2	(2%)	1.3	(2%)	1.2	(2%)
Petroleum Products	1.3	(3%)	1.5	(3%)	1.9	(3%)	2.1	(3%)	1.6	(3%)
Cement & Stone Powder	0.4	(1%)	0.6	(1%)	0.7	(1%)	0.8	(1%)	0.6	(1%)
Plate or Sheet Glass	—		0.1	(0%)	0.2	(0%)	0.1	(0%)	0.2	(0%)
Porcelain	0.3	(1%)	0.5	(1%)	0.6	(1%)	0.5	(1%)	0.4	(1%)
Iron & Steel	1.0	(3%)	2.1	(4%)	3.0	(4%)	2.7	(4%)	2.4	(4%)
Metal Products[6]	0.2	(1%)	0.3	(1%)	0.6	(1%)	0.5	(1%)	0.5	(1%)
Machine Tools & Pumps	0.1	(0%)	0.2	(0%)	0.3	(0%)	0.3	(0%)	0.4	(1%)
Electrical & Comm. Equipment[7]	0.3	(1%)	0.3	(1%)	0.3	(0%)	0.2	(0%)	0.3	(0%)
Transport Equipment	—		0.3	(1%)	0.4	(1%)	0.6	(1%)	0.7	(1%)
Oil-Cake & Other Manures	—		—		—		0.2	(0%)	0.2	(0%)
Misc. Manufactures[8]	0.4	(1%)	0.6	(1%)	0.7	(1%)	0.7	(1%)	0.6	(1%)
Unclassifiable[9]	16.4	(41%)	15.1	(28%)	16.3	(24%)	15.1	(21%)	15.7	(25%)
Manufactured Imports	21.5	(54%)	35.7	(66%)	46.3	(69%)	45.6	(63%)	39.8	(62%)
Total Imports	39.8	(100%)	54.1	(100%)	67.1	(100%)	72.0	(100%)	63.7	(100%)

Table B.7. (Continued)

In Million Yen & Percent

	1915		1916		1917		1918		1919	
Rice Barley & Wheat	0.3	(1%)	0.2	(0%)	0.9	(1%)	1.6	(1%)	1.3	(0%)
Millet, Corn & Bean	0.8	(1%)	—		1.3	(1%)	3.3	(2%)	16.0	(6%)
Vegetable, Fruits & Tobacco	0.9	(2%)	1.4	(2%)	1.3	(1%)	1.6	(1%)	2.8	(1%)
Cotton Ginned & Wadding	0.7	(1%)	0.7	(1%)	0.8	(1%)	1.5	(1%)	3.9	(1%)
Crude India-Rubber	—		—		—		—		—	
Coal	1.8	(3%)	1.8	(2%)	3.6	(3%)	8.4	(5%)	14.4	(5%)
Salt	0.9	(2%)	1.1	(1%)	1.0	(1%)	1.5	(1%)	3.3	(1%)
Fish, Dried or Preserved	0.3	(1%)	0.4	(1%)	0.4	(0%)	0.6	(0%)	1.0	(0%)
Wheat Flours	0.7	(1%)	0.9	(1%)	1.0	(1%)	1.9	(1%)	3.6	(1%)
Confectioneries, Soy & Milk	0.3	(1%)	0.3	(0%)	0.4	(0%)	0.4	(0%)	0.7	(0%)
Sugar & Molasses	1.6	(3%)	1.9	(3%)	2.2	(2%)	3.4	(2%)	4.9	(2%)
Beverages	4.4	(7%)	5.1	(7%)	5.1	(5%)	6.4	(4%)	11.4	(4%)
Cotton Yarn & Thread	2.6	(4%)	3.4	(5%)	5.4	(5%)	4.3	(3%)	6.5	(2%)
Textile Fabrics[1]	11.7	(20%)	16.5	(22%)	20.3	(20%)	27.8	(18%)	65.4	(23%)
Textile Products[2]	1.4	(2%)	1.7	(2%)	2.4	(2%)	3.0	(2%)	4.7	(2%)
Other Textile Materials	3.8	(6%)	4.2	(5%)	7.0	(7%)	8.9	(5%)	17.1	(6%)
Wood & Wood Products	1.6	(3%)	1.2	(2%)	1.7	(2%)	3.1	(2%)	4.0	(1%)
Paper	1.5	(3%)	2.0	(3%)	2.6	(3%)	4.3	(3%)	4.5	(2%)
Leather & Leather Products	0.8	(1%)	1.6	(2%)	0.4	(0%)	0.2	(0%)	0.5	(0%)
Rubber Products[3]	—		—		—		—		—	

Table B.7. (Continued)

In Million Yen & Percent

	1915		1916		1917		1918		1919	
Caustic Soda & Calcium Carbide	—		0.2	(0%)	0.2	(0%)	0.4	(0%)	0.4	(0%)
Chemical Fertilizer[4]	—		—		—		—		—	
Other Chemicals[5]	1.3	(2%)	1.9	(3%)	2.5	(2%)	3.1	(2%)	3.6	(1%)
Petroleum Products	1.8	(3%)	2.5	(3%)	2.9	(3%)	3.2	(2%)	8.9	(3%)
Cement & Stone Powder	0.7	(1%)	0.9	(1%)	1.8	(2%)	1.9	(1%)	1.8	(1%)
Plate or Sheet Glass	0.2	(0%)	0.2	(0%)	0.2	(0%)	0.3	(0%)	0.5	(0%)
Porcelain	0.4	(1%)	0.6	(1%)	0.7	(1%)	0.9	(1%)	1.5	(1%)
Iron & Steel	2.1	(4%)	2.7	(4%)	5.2	(5%)	9.1	(6%)	11.7	(4%)
Metal Products[6]	0.5	(1%)	0.8	(1%)	1.1	(1%)	1.4	(1%)	2.1	(1%)
Machine Tools & Pumps	0.4	(1%)	0.5	(1%)	0.7	(1%)	1.1	(1%)	1.7	(1%)
Electrical & Comm. Equipment[7]	0.4	(1%)	0.5	(1%)	0.7	(1%)	1.7	(1%)	2.0	(1%)
Transport Equipment	0.3	(1%)	0.5	(1%)	0.6	(1%)	1.2	(1%)	2.0	(1%)
Oil-Cake & Other Manures	0.1	(0%)	—		0.2	(0%)	0.4	(0%)	1.5	(1%)
Misc. Manufactures[8]	0.5	(1%)	0.6	(1%)	0.7	(1%)	0.8	(1%)	1.2	(0%)
Unclassifiable[9]	14.9	(25%)	18.8	(25%)	28.8	(28%)	52.7	(33%)	78.2	(28%)
Manufactured Imports	39.4	(66%)	51.1	(68%)	66.4	(64%)	89.8	(56%)	163.2	(58%)
Total Imports	59.7	(100%)	75.1	(100%)	104.1	(100%)	160.4	(100%)	283.1	(100%)

Table B.7. (Continued)

In Million Yen & Percent

	1920		1921		1922		1923		1924	
Rice, Barley & Wheat	3.2	(1%)	1.0	(0%)	4.9	(2%)	4.3	(2%)	15.7	(5%)
Millet, Corn & Bean	23.6	(9%)	1.6	(1%)	9.8	(4%)	16.5	(6%)	24.5	(8%)
Vegetable, Fruits & Tobacco	3.7	(1%)	3.9	(2%)	4.9	(2%)	3.0	(1%)	5.4	(2%)
Cotton Ginned & Wadding	1.3	(1%)	2.3	(1%)	3.6	(1%)	4.5	(2%)	2.4	(1%)
Crude India-Rubber	—		—		—		—		—	
Coal	17.0	(7%)	8.8	(4%)	8.0	(3%)	9.6	(4%)	8.1	(3%)
Salt	1.4	(1%)	1.2	(1%)	1.4	(1%)	2.5	(1%)	2.6	(1%)
Fish, Dried or Preserved	1.1	(0%)	1.3	(1%)	1.0	(0%)	1.2	(0%)	1.4	(0%)
Wheat Flours	3.7	(2%)	2.1	(1%)	2.3	(1%)	3.0	(1%)	4.9	(2%)
Confectioneries, Soy & Milk	1.0	(0%)	0.9	(0%)	1.1	(0%)	1.3	(0%)	1.8	(1%)
Sugar & Molasses	4.3	(2%)	4.6	(2%)	4.5	(2%)	5.2	(2%)	7.2	(2%)
Beverages	10.9	(4%)	11.1	(5%)	11.9	(5%)	13.3	(5%)	14.9	(5%)
Cotton Yarn & Thread	4.3	(2%)	5.3	(2%)	4.1	(2%)	4.7	(2%)	8.0	(3%)
Textile Fabrics[1]	35.7	(15%)	46.7	(20%)	44.6	(17%)	48.9	(18%)	61.8	(20%)
Textile Products[2]	4.6	(2%)	5.0	(2%)	5.7	(2%)	8.6	(3%)	10.7	(3%)
Other Textile Materials	10.7	(5%)	18.5	(8%)	12.9	(5%)	21.3	(8%)	26.3	(8%)
Wood & Wood Products	4.1	(2%)	9.4	(4%)	14.7	(6%)	12.2	(5%)	11.9	(4%)
Paper	4.5	(2%)	5.2	(2%)	5.5	(2%)	5.2	(2%)	6.3	(2%)
Leather & Leather Products	1.1	(0%)	0.9	(0%)	0.8	(0%)	1.1	(0%)	1.5	(0%)
Rubber Products[3]	—		—		2.6	(1%)	4.5	(2%)	5.7	(2%)

Table B.7. (Continued)

In Million Yen & Percent

	1920		1921		1922		1923		1924	
Caustic Soda & Calcium Carbide	0.2	(0%)	0.4	(0%)	0.4	(0%)	0.5	(0%)	0.6	(0%)
Chemical Fertilizer[4]	—		—		—		0.1	(0%)	1.0	(0%)
Other Chemicals[5]	3.3	(1%)	3.8	(2%)	3.6	(1%)	4.3	(2%)	4.4	(1%)
Petroleum Products	8.9	(4%)	5.1	(2%)	5.8	(2%)	6.3	(2%)	6.9	(2%)
Cement & Stone Powder	1.9	(1%)	2.4	(1%)	2.8	(1%)	4.5	(2%)	2.0	(1%)
Plate or Sheet Glass	0.5	(0%)	0.6	(0%)	0.6	(0%)	0.6	(0%)	0.6	(0%)
Porcelain	1.4	(1%)	1.3	(1%)	1.5	(1%)	1.6	(1%)	1.8	(1%)
Iron & Steel	9.6	(4%)	6.7	(3%)	8.7	(3%)	9.4	(4%)	7.5	(2%)
Metal Products[6]	1.6	(1%)	1.8	(1%)	2.4	(1%)	2.0	(1%)	2.6	(1%)
Machine Tools & Pumps	1.9	(1%)	1.2	(1%)	1.4	(1%)	1.3	(0%)	1.6	(1%)
Electrical & Comm. Equipment[7]	1.8	(1%)	2.3	(1%)	1.8	(1%)	1.5	(1%)	2.0	(1%)
Transport Equipment	2.9	(1%)	1.7	(1%)	2.0	(1%)	2.4	(1%)	3.0	(1%)
Oil-Cake & Other Manures	5.0	(2%)	6.5	(3%)	6.0	(2%)	8.2	(3%)	6.0	(2%)
Misc. Manufactures[8]	1.6	(1%)	1.7	(1%)	2.1	(1%)	2.7	(1%)	3.5	(1%)
Unclassifiable[9]	72.5	(29%)	67.1	(29%)	72.6	(28%)	49.5	(19%)	45.0	(15%)
Manufactured Imports	126.6	(51%)	146.5	(63%)	150.8	(59%)	175.9	(66%)	205.7	(66%)
Total Imports	249.3	(100%)	232.4	(100%)	256.0	(100%)	265.8	(100%)	309.6	(100%)

Table B.7. (Continued)

In Million Yen & Percent

	1925	1926	1927	1928	1929
Rice, Barley & Wheat	24.7 (7%)	21.4 (6%)	22.7 (6%)	12.8 (3%)	15.4 (4%)
Millet, Corn & Bean	32.4 (10%)	34.9 (9%)	35.7 (9%)	30.8 (7%)	26.1 (6%)
Vegetable, Fruits & Tobacco	6.5 (2%)	9.8 (3%)	9.4 (2%)	9.0 (2%)	7.6 (2%)
Cotton Ginned & Wadding	3.9 (1%)	5.0 (1%)	6.4 (2%)	6.5 (2%)	7.2 (2%)
Crude India-Rubber	—	—	—	1.7 (0%)	1.6 (0%)
Coal	7.7 (2%)	8.6 (2%)	10.7 (3%)	10.4 (3%)	10.2 (2%)
Salt	2.6 (1%)	2.8 (1%)	2.4 (1%)	2.1 (1%)	1.5 (0%)
Fish, Dried or Preserved	1.5 (0%)	1.5 (0%)	2.3 (1%)	2.7 (1%)	2.9 (1%)
Wheat Flours	6.7 (2%)	6.4 (2%)	6.2 (2%)	6.9 (2%)	6.9 (2%)
Confectioneries, Soy & Milk	2.2 (1%)	2.6 (1%)	2.8 (1%)	2.8 (1%)	3.0 (1%)
Sugar & Molasses	6.8 (2%)	6.6 (2%)	9.3 (2%)	10.7 (3%)	11.6 (3%)
Beverages	15.5 (5%)	17.0 (5%)	17.4 (5%)	19.1 (5%)	19.6 (5%)
Cotton Yarn & Thread	10.8 (3%)	10.8 (3%)	8.7 (2%)	9.9 (2%)	10.3 (2%)
Textile Fabrics[1]	69.6 (20%)	64.4 (17%)	57.0 (15%)	61.9 (15%)	53.8 (13%)
Textile Products[2]	12.1 (4%)	14.1 (4%)	13.8 (4%)	16.4 (4%)	18.6 (4%)
Other Textile Materials	24.1 (7%)	26.5 (7%)	28.1 (8%)	35.3 (8%)	35.9 (8%)
Wood & Wood Products	10.0 (3%)	11.8 (3%)	12.6 (3%)	13.2 (3%)	11.3 (3%)
Paper	6.5 (2%)	7.0 (2%)	7.3 (2%)	8.1 (2%)	7.7 (2%)
Leather & Leather Products	1.6 (0%)	1.8 (0%)	1.7 (0%)	1.6 (0%)	1.3 (0%)
Rubber Products[3]	4.7 (1%)	6.6 (2%)	5.7 (1%)	5.6 (1%)	7.1 (2%)

Table B.7. (Continued)

In Million Yen & Percent

	1925		1926		1927		1928		1929	
Caustic Soda & Calcium Carbide	0.6	(0%)	0.8	(0%)	0.8	(0%)	1.1	(0%)	1.1	(0%)
Chemical Fertilizer[4]	3.0	(1%)	5.7	(2%)	5.1	(1%)	8.5	(2%)	10.7	(3%)
Other Chemicals[5]	4.6	(1%)	4.9	(1%)	4.9	(1%)	6.2	(1%)	5.9	(1%)
Petroleum Products	8.7	(3%)	7.4	(2%)	11.1	(3%)	10.7	(3%)	14.0	(3%)
Cement & Stone Powder	1.9	(1%)	2.9	(1%)	3.5	(1%)	4.7	(1%)	3.7	(1%)
Plate or Sheet Glass	0.5	(0%)	0.6	(0%)	0.5	(0%)	0.5	(0%)	0.7	(0%)
Porcelain	2.3	(1%)	2.4	(1%)	2.4	(1%)	2.9	(1%)	2.9	(1%)
Iron & Steel	7.4	(2%)	9.9	(3%)	13.4	(3%)	16.9	(4%)	19.6	(5%)
Metal Products[6]	2.5	(1%)	2.8	(1%)	2.8	(1%)	3.8	(1%)	4.3	(1%)
Machine Tools & Pumps	1.5	(0%)	1.9	(1%)	1.9	(0%)	2.1	(1%)	2.5	(1%)
Electrical & Comm. Equipment[7]	1.4	(0%)	2.3	(1%)	1.9	(0%)	3.6	(1%)	3.5	(1%)
Transport Equipment	3.2	(1%)	4.6	(1%)	5.6	(1%)	7.5	(2%)	10.1	(2%)
Oil-Cake & Other Manures	5.6	(2%)	11.5	(3%)	11.1	(3%)	11.0	(3%)	13.2	(3%)
Misc. Manufactures[8]	3.5	(1%)	4.2	(1%)	4.3	(1%)	5.1	(1%)	5.7	(1%)
Unclassifiable[9]	37.0	(11%)	50.7	(14%)	53.9	(14%)	61.9	(15%)	65.5	(15%)
Manufactured Imports	225.3	(66%)	239.0	(64%)	242.2	(63%)	278.8	(67%)	288.0	(68%)
Total Imports	340.1	(100%)	372.2	(100%)	383.4	(100%)	414.0	(100%)	423.1	(100%)

Table B.7. (Continued)

In Million Yen & Percent

	1930		1931		1932		1933		1934	
Rice, Barley & Wheat	11.3	(3%)	1.3	(0%)	3.0	(1%)	3.8	(1%)	5.1	(1%)
Millet, Corn & Bean	25.4	(7%)	11.6	(4%)	21.1	(7%)	18.0	(4%)	21.0	(4%)
Vegetable, Fruits & Tobacco	6.8	(2%)	5.9	(3%)	5.9	(2%)	5.9	(1%)	10.4	(2%)
Cotton Ginned & Wadding	5.5	(1%)	4.7	(2%)	6.9	(2%)	9.6	(2%)	14.1	(3%)
Crude India-Rubber	1.5	(0%)	1.0	(0%)	1.3	(0%)	2.1	(1%)	4.4	(1%)
Coal	10.3	(3%)	8.5	(3%)	7.9	(2%)	10.7	(3%)	13.2	(3%)
Salt	1.2	(0%)	1.4	(1%)	2.3	(1%)	2.8	(1%)	2.6	(1%)
Fish, Dried or Preserved	2.8	(1%)	2.1	(1%)	2.4	(1%)	3.6	(1%)	4.1	(1%)
Wheat Flours	5.9	(2%)	3.8	(1%)	3.8	(1%)	4.0	(1%)	5.4	(1%)
Confectioneries, Soy & Milk	2.7	(1%)	2.8	(1%)	3.5	(1%)	4.0	(1%)	5.4	(1%)
Sugar & Molasses	9.0	(2%)	6.7	(2%)	8.9	(3%)	7.4	(2%)	6.8	(1%)
Beverages	17.4	(5%)	16.0	(6%)	18.2	(6%)	21.3	(5%)	25.4	(5%)
Cotton Yarn & Thread	8.1	(2%)	6.1	(2%)	7.3	(2%)	9.8	(2%)	14.3	(3%)
Textile Fabrics[1]	44.3	(12%)	35.5	(13%)	41.9	(13%)	56.7	(14%)	56.0	(11%)
Textile Products[2]	14.9	(4%)	12.1	(4%)	16.9	(5%)	21.3	(5%)	28.3	(5%)
Other Textile Materials	31.0	(8%)	23.5	(8%)	28.8	(9%)	41.6	(10%)	54.3	(10%)
Wood & Wood Products	7.8	(2%)	6.7	(2%)	6.0	(2%)	8.7	(2%)	12.2	(2%)
Paper	6.9	(2%)	5.8	(2%)	6.9	(2%)	8.6	(2%)	10.3	(2%)
Leather & Leather Products	1.3	(0%)	1.2	(0%)	1.4	(0%)	1.9	(0%)	2.6	(1%)
Rubber Products[3]	5.4	(1%)	2.7	(1%)	3.6	(1%)	3.1	(1%)	5.2	(1%)

Table B.7. (Continued)

In Million Yen & Percent

	1930		1931		1932		1933		1934	
Caustic Soda & Calcium Carbide	1.2	(0%)	1.0	(0%)	0.8	(0%)	1.3	(0%)	1.5	(0%)
Chemical Fertilizer[4]	6.7	(2%)	3.4	(1%)	2.8	(1%)	4.0	(1%)	12.2	(2%)
Other Chemicals[5]	5.4	(1%)	4.9	(2%)	6.0	(2%)	7.8	(2%)	9.6	(2%)
Petroleum Products	11.0	(3%)	9.8	(4%)	14.6	(5%)	14.8	(4%)	20.1	(4%)
Cement & Stone Powder	3.1	(1%)	2.3	(1%)	2.7	(1%)	4.0	(1%)	6.2	(1%)
Plate or Sheet Glass	0.5	(0%)	0.5	(0%)	0.5	(0%)	0.7	(0%)	0.9	(0%)
Porcelain	2.3	(1%)	2.1	(1%)	2.3	(1%)	2.9	(1%)	3.9	(1%)
Iron & Steel	16.1	(4%)	11.8	(4%)	15.0	(5%)	20.5	(5%)	28.3	(5%)
Metal Products[6]	4.3	(1%)	3.1	(1%)	3.5	(1%)	5.0	(1%)	6.7	(1%)
Machine Tools & Pumps	2.0	(1%)	1.8	(1%)	1.8	(1%)	2.3	(1%)	3.1	(1%)
Electrical & Comm. Equipment[7]	4.0	(1%)	2.5	(1%)	2.6	(1%)	3.8	(1%)	4.3	(1%)
Transport Equipment	6.4	(2%)	5.8	(2%)	5.9	(2%)	11.1	(3%)	14.7	(3%)
Oil-Cake & Other Manures	12.3	(3%)	5.2	(2%)	4.9	(2%)	7.5	(2%)	8.3	(2%)
Misc. Manufactures[8]	5.6	(2%)	5.3	(2%)	5.5	(2%)	6.4	(2%)	8.3	(2%)
Unclassifiable[9]	66.6	(18%)	51.6	(19%)	52.9	(17%)	67.2	(17%)	89.9	(17%)
Manufactured Imports	238.4	(65%)	184.5	(68%)	219.1	(68%)	284.1	(70%)	358.4	(69%)
Total Imports	367.0	(100%)	270.5	(100%)	320.4	(100%)	404.2	(10%)	519.1	(100%)

Table B.7. (Continued)

In Million Yen & Percent

1935			1935		
Rice, Barley & Wheat	16.7	(3%)	Rubber Products[3]	5.6	(1%)
Millet, Corn & Bean	26.2	(4%)	Caustic Soda & Calcium Carbide	1.6	(0%)
Vegetable, Fruits & Tobacco	15.4	(2%)	Chemical Fertilizer[4]	14.3	(2%)
Cotton Ginned & Wadding	16.8	(3%)	Other Chemicals[5]	11.2	(2%)
Crude India-Rubber	5.4	(1%)	Petroleum Products	26.1	(4%)
Coal	14.6	(2%)	Cement & Stone Powder	5.6	(1%)
Salt	2.7	(0%)	Plate or Sheet Glass	1.2	(0%)
Fish, Dried or Preserved	4.1	(1%)	Porcelain	5.3	(1%)
Wheat Flours	11.0	(2%)	Iron & Steel	42.4	(6%)
Confectioneries, Soy & Milk	6.5	(1%)	Metal Products[6]	7.9	(1%)
Sugar & Molasses	8.9	(1%)	Machine Tools & Pumps	4.5	(1%)
Beverages	27.7	(4%)	Electrical & Comm. Equipment[7]	8.5	(1%)
Cotton Yarn & Thread	14.3	(2%)	Transport Equipment	18.5	(3%)
Textile Fabrics[1]	47.1	(7%)	Oil-Cake & Other Manures	11.8	(2%)
Textile Products[2]	32.5	(5%)	Misc. Manufactures[8]	9.0	(1%)
Other Textile Materials	69.2	(10%)	Unclassifiable[9]	132.9	(20%)
Wood & Wood Products	17.4	(3%)			
Paper	12.4	(2%)	Manufactured Imports	428.7	(65%)
Leather & Leather Products	4.1	(1%)	Total Imports	659.4	(100%)

Source & Notes to Table B. 7.

Source: Oriental Economist, *Foreign Trade of Japan: A Statistical Survey*, (Tokyo: 1935) and Government General of Chosen, *Table of Trade and Shipping of Chosen: 1935.*

Notes: [1] Consist of tussah silk, fujiginu, cotton flannel, shirtings gray, shirting bleached, white sheeting, imitation nankeens, populin, kokuraori, muslins, jeans, drills, cotton satins, imitated grass cloths, cotton crapes, china grass cloths, woolen cloths, damasks, Habutae and capes.

[2] Consist of cordages & ropes, Meisen, towels, fishing nets, gunny bags, undershirts, Japanese clothing, European clothing, Tabi and hats.

[3] Consist of boots and Chikatabi.

[4] Consist of ammonium sulphate and superphospate of lime.

[5] Consist of soaps, perfume, prepared medicines, explosives and matches.

[6] Consist of nails, electric wire, stoves & parts and enamelled iron wares.

[7] Consist of telegraphic instruments, electric motors and lamps & parts.

[8] Consist of umbrellas & parasols, toys, phonographs and books.

[9] Consist of misc. manufacturing, parcel post (excluding textiles) and travelling effects.

Table B.8. Output and Exports of Major Manufactures: 1935

In Thousand Yen

	Domestic Output Value (A)	Exports		Re-Exports of Japanese Products (D)	Total Exports (E)	Net Exports (F=E−D)	Exports-Output Ratio (F/A)
		To Japan Proper (B)	To Foreign Countries (C)				
Cotton Tissues	19,815	1,188	2,097	1,435	4,720	3,285	17%
Cotton Yarns	15,022	—	14	571	585	14	0%
Raw Silk	12,795	14,189	—	—	14,189	14,189	111%
Tussah Silk	—	5,715	—	—	5,715	5,715	—
Sugar	8,522	89	3,185	7	3,281	3,274	38%
Cement	9,545	2,797	763	179	3,739	3,560	37%
Paper & Pulp	—	4,032	574	217	4,823	4,606	—
Paper Products	279	—	55	160	215	55	20%
Ammonium Sulphate	28,226	11,132	1	1	11,134	11,133	39%
Pig Iron	2,231	7,276	—	2	7,278	7,276	—
Total	46,418	6,689		2,572	55,679	53,107	—

Source: Government General of Chosen, *Table of Trade and Shipping for 1935* and *Chosen Sotokufu Tokei Nenpo: 1935.*

Table B.9. Rice Production and Exports: 1910–40

In Thousand ⅛ or Acres

	Rice Production		Rice Exports to Japan		Imports of Millet	Imports of Beans
	Acreage	Output[1] (O)	(E)	(E/O)		
1910	1,965	1,119	—	—	—	—
1911	2,404	1,222	—	(—)	—	—
1912	3,472	1,511	37	(2%)	11	—
1913	3,570	1,628	44	(3%)	108	—
1914	3,636	1,817	154	(8%)	19	—
1915	3,658	2,120	281	(13%)	15	—
1916	3,722	1,927	200	(10%)	2	—
1917	3,746	2,090	179	(9)	19	—
1918	3,793	2,053	260	(13%)	32	2
1919	3,768	2,287	421	(18%)	137	4
1920	3,810	1,906	248	(13%)	160	4
1921	3,753	2,232	436	(20%)	6	4
1922	3,817	2,149	470	(22%)	105	10
1923	3,800	2,252	518	(23%)	163	30
1924	3,861	2,276	682	(30%)	202	47
1925	3,883	1,983	664	(33%)	252	22
1926	3,891	2,216	782	(35%)	323	26
1927	3,925	2,295	886	(39%)	371	42
1928	3,719	2,595	1,060	(41%)	293	55
1929	3,998	2,027	807	(40%)	229	53
1930	4,072	2,877	775	(27%)	245	44
1931	4,104	2,381	1,199	(50%)	167	76
1932	4,025	2,452	1,080	(44%)	243	43
1933	4,403	2,729	1,130	(41%)	162	42
1934	4,194	2,508	1,343	(54%)	205[2]	50[3]
1935	4,153	2,683	1,265	(47%)	150[2]	29[3]
1936	3,923	2,912	1,346	(46%)		
1937	4,016	4,020	1,010	(25%)		
1938	4,067	3,621	1,522	(42%)		
1939	3,026	2,153	854	(40%)		
1940	4,021	3,229	59	(2%)		

Source: H. Ouchi, ed., *Nihon Keizai Tokei Shu* (Tokyo: Nihon Tokei Kenkyujo, 1958) and Oriental Economist, *Foreign Trade of Japan: A Statistical Survey* (Tokyo, 1935).

Notes: [1] 1 MT of rice is 6.67 suk.
[2] Excluding kao-liang.
[3] Excluding red or white small beans (Soja bean only).

Table B.10. Gross Output Value of Manufacturing Sectors: 1930–40

In Million Yen & Percent

	Food Products	Textiles	Wood & Products	Nonmetallic Mineral	Chemical Products	Metal Products	Machinery & Equip.	Misc. Manufactures	Total
1930	82.2	45.7	5.6	10.5	42.1	6.0	10.1	72.5	281.0
1931	81.0	32.9	4.8	9.0	42.6	6.6	7.9	52.0	236.8
1932	104.3	47.2	5.0	9.8	49.6	6.2	8.3	69.4	299.8
1933	122.7	55.3	6.0	11.1	70.5	9.1	7.5	73.9	356.3
1934	137.7	67.8	7.3	12.5	91.2	9.7	9.5	90.1	425.6
1935	169.4	82.3	8.2	17.6	147.8	27.0	11.5	103.8	567.7
1936	199.9	99.5	9.9	21.9	195.4	33.7	13.5	117.0	690.8
1937	238.0	141.2	11.7	25.1	305.0	50.8	16.6	131.0	919.2
1938	274.4	162.8	15.7	35.9	354.5	90.9	26.7	181.8	1,142.6
1939	328.4	201.4	21.1	43.3	501.8	136.1	53.2	213.1	1,498.3
1940	373.4	232.2	35.0	61.7	699.4	129.7	76.7	265.6	1,873.6
1930	29%	16%	2%	4%	15%	2%	4%	26%	100%
1931	34%	14%	2%	4%	18%	3%	3%	22%	100%
1932	35%	16%	2%	3%	17%	2%	3%	23%	100%
1933	34%	16%	2%	3%	20%	3%	2%	21%	100%
1934	32%	16%	2%	3%	21%	2%	2%	21%	100%
1935	30%	14%	1%	3%	26%	5%	2%	18%	100%
1936	29%	14%	1%	3%	28%	5%	2%	17%	100%
1937	26%	15%	1%	3%	33%	6%	2%	14%	100%
1938	24%	14%	1%	3%	31%	8%	2%	16%	100%
1939	22%	13%	1%	3%	33%	9%	4%	14%	100%
1940	20%	12%	2%	3%	37%	7%	4%	14%	100%

Source: Government General of Chosen, *Chosen Sotokufu Tokei Nenpo.*

Note: Excluding electricity & gas, and repairing & processing fee. Due to differences in classification, the sectoral output values presented in this table do not agree with those in Tables B.11 and B.12, which are based on I-O sectoral classification.

Table B.11. Output Composition of Korean Manufacturing Industry: 1939

In Million Yen & Percent

I-O 43 Sector	South Korea	North Korea	Total
7. Processed Foods	118.0 (59%)	83.2 (41%)	201.2 (13%)
8. Beverages	96.2 (69%)	42.8 (31%)	139.0 (9%)
9. Tobacco	57.2 (83%)	11.4 (17%)	68.7 (5%)
10. Fibre Spinning	73.8 (88%)	9.6 (12%)	83.4 (6%)
11. Textile Fabrics	87.0 (85%)	15.0 (15%)	102.0 (7%)
12. Textile Products	61.3 (67%)	30.6 (33%)	91.9 (6%)
13–14. Wood & Furniture	13.3 (62%)	8.2 (38%)	21.5 (1%)
15. Paper Products	6.8 (25%)	20.9 (75%)	27.7 (2%)
16. Printing & Publishing	17.2 (89%)	2.2 (11%)	19.4 (1%)
17. Leather & Products	2.8 (65%)	1.5 (35%)	4.3 (0%)
18. Rubber Products	12.7 (71%)	5.3 (29%)	18.0 (1%)
19. Basic Chemicals	9.5 (5%)	177.8 (95%)	187.3 (13%)
20. Other Chemicals	31.9 (28%)	80.7 (72%)	112.6 (8%)
21. Chemical Fertilizer	0.7 (1%)	76.8 (99%)	77.5 (5%)
23. Coal Products	4.3 (45%)	5.2 (55%)	9.5 (1%)
24. Nonmetallic Minerals	12.5 (28%)	32.5 (72%)	45.0 (3%)
25. Iron & Steel	3.5 (3%)	105.1 (97%)	108.6 (7%)
26. Steel Products	4.4 (52%)	4.1 (48%)	8.5 (1%)
28. Metal Products	6.8 (34%)	13.1 (66%)	19.9 (1%)
29. Machinery	29.9 (70%)	13.0 (30%)	42.9 (3%)
30. Electrical Machinery	0.9 (100%)	—	0.9 (0%)
31. Transport Equipment	6.0 (75%)	2.0 (25%)	8.0 (1%)
32. Misc. Manufactures	18.5 (20%)	75.9 (80%)[1]	94.4 (6%)
All Manufacturing	675.3 (45%)	816.9 (55%)	1,492.2 (100%)[2]

Source: Government General of Chosen, *Chosen Sotokufu Tokei Nenpo: 1939*.
Notes: [1] Including non-chemical manures (animal or vegetable origin).
[2] Excluding 6.1 million yen worth of charcoal.

Table B.12. Employment by Industrial Sectors: 1917–42

Household Basis

In Thousand Persons

Year End	Agriculture & Forestry	Fishery (Incl. Salt)	Manu-facturing	Commerce & Transportation	Gov't & Services	Other Employed	Total
1917	6,949 (19)	76 (5)	116 (17)	338 (41)	70 (32)	166 (16)	7,715 (130)
1918	7,131 (19)	85 (6)	110 (16)	365 (41)	75 (34)	187 (16)	7,953 (132)
1919	7,290 (22)	88 (7)	119 (15)	373 (43)	79 (36)	186 (17)	8,135 (140)
1920	7,193 (19)	75 (5)	117 (21)	352 (42)	95 (38)	114 (6)	7,946 (131)
1921	7,196 (20)	85 (5)	115 (21)	356 (44)	100 (42)	139 (6)	7,991 (138)
1922	7,293 (19)	84 (5)	127 (23)	365 (47)	105 (46)	173 (9)	8,147 (149)
1923	7,323 (19)	85 (5)	125 (20)	369 (47)	109 (49)	189 (10)	8,200 (150)
1924	7,377 (18)	89 (5)	133 (21)	390 (52)	111 (49)	208 (9)	8,308 (154)
1925	7,737 (19)	98 (5)	144 (23)	430 (52)	128 (55)	239 (9)	8,776 (163)
1926	7,807 (19)	104 (6)	141 (23)	421 (54)	126 (55)	252 (11)	8,851 (168)
1927	7,784 (19)	104 (5)	139 (23)	429 (56)	129 (58)	273 (12)	8,858 (173)
1928	7,681 (19)	104 (5)	135 (23)	430 (57)	129 (59)	282 (11)	8,761 (174)
1929	7,687 (18)	113 (5)	137 (24)	433 (57)	140 (62)	300 (12)	8,810 (178)
1930	7,772 (18)	113 (5)	143 (27)	445 (56)	148 (63)	347 (11)	8,968 (180)
1931	7,555 (18)	112 (5)	138 (26)	439 (56)	158 (64)	393 (12)	8,795 (181)
1932	7,278 (19)	93 (4)	122 (19)	359 (44)	148 (68)	510 (11)	8,510 (165)
1933	7,049 (15)	88 (3)	132 (22)	392 (49)	92 (66)	422 (6)	8,175 (161)
1934	7,155 (15)	101 (3)	146 (24)	428 (55)	159 (66)	440 (7)	8,429 (170)
1935	7,519 (15)	103 (3)	169 (26)	449 (55)	152 (68)	479 (8)	8,871 (175)
1936	7,367 (14)	110 (3)	184 (29)	464 (58)	163 (74)	501 (9)	8,789 (187)
1937	7,413 (14)	110 (3)	203 (31)	478 (55)	166 (76)	501 (8)	8,871 (187)

Table B.12. (Continued)

In Thousand Persons

Year End	Agriculture	Fishery	Mining	Manu-facturing	Trans-portation	Commerce	Gov't & Services	Other Employed	Total
1938	7,398 (13)	117 (3)	103 (6)	172 (32)	50 (10)	461 (48)	175 (72)	504 (6)	8,980 (190)
1939	7,275 (13)	120 (3)	130 (7)	176 (33)	59 (11)	475 (47)	178 (75)	499 (8)	8,912 (197)
1940	7,136 (12)	120 (3)	144 (8)	193 (33)	58 (13)	461 (45)	177 (77)	555 (9)	8,844 (200)
1941	7,294 (12)	132 (3)	173 (9)	250 (39)	70 (13)	465 (45)	209 (80)	555 (10)	9,148 (211)
1942	7,377 (11)	169 (3)	197 (9)	312 (45)	84 (17)	486 (42)	251 (88)	706 (11)	9,582 (226)

Source: Government General of Chosen, *Chosen Sotokufu Tokei Nenpo* (various issues).
Note: Figures in the parentheses represent Japanese residents. Excludes partially employed persons who were also engaged in other profession on part-time basis.

Table B.13. U.S. Aid to Korea: 1954–75

In Thousand U.S. Dollars

CY	Supporting Assistance		Technical Support	PL 480 Title I		PL 480 Title II & III	Development Loan	Total
	Non-Project	Project*		Sale	Loan			
1954	74,340	6,046	—	0	—	—	0	80,385
1955	168,337	34,801	112	9,986	—	15,900	0	229,135
1956	220,803	53,116	1,214	37,536	—	16,800	0	329,468
1957	207,170	92,553	2,842	30,433	—	28,278	0	361,281
1958	163,038	67,218	3,362	38,613	—	22,300	0	294,532
1959	148,235	68,790	3,084	12,544	—	16,900	0	249,553
1960	160,044	56,330	3,416	32,601	—	15,140	1,289	268,819
1961	113,582	30,939	2,872	36,075	—	28,626	3,161	215,254
1962	126,614	22,029	1,753	62,666	—	—	10,473	223,535
1963	102,724	13,023	1,256	94,729	—	24,038	20,038	255,809
1964	72,824	5,520	847	54,346	—	21,140	4,546	159,224
1965	79,208	4,159	1,002	62,328	—	27,561	2,630	176,888
1966	54,833	3,999	1,186	35,038	—	28,457	49,690	173,203

Table B.13. (Continued)

In Thousand U.S. Dollars

CY	Supporting Assistance		Technical Support	PL 480 Title I		PL 480 Title II & III	Development Loan	Total
	Non-Project	Project*		Sale	Loan			
1967	59,827	4,361	1,252	58,025	—	31,578	74,750	229,791
1968	43,705	8,661	1,320	58,545	—	42,291	37,991	197,512
1969	16,747	6,269	1,255	64,972	78,705	39,841	31,887	239,677
1970	14,214	5,299	1,078	54,667	45,853	21,929	38,763	181,804
1971	9,422	4,158	922	30,810	68,897	16,071	55,666	185,946
1972	568	2,465	919	3,665	185,453	11,572	36,776	241,417
1973	—	2,477	848	0	60,392	634	27,706	92,057
1974	—	1,754	345	0	—	0	44,118	46,216
1975	—	868	—	0	83,975	0	192,183	277,025
Total	1,836,234	494,838	30,885	777,578	523,275	414,053	631,666	4,708,531

Source: USAID to Korea.
*Including aids under Technical Cooperation, Defense Support and Development Grant Projects.

Table B.14. U.S. Non-Project Assistance by Sectors: 1954-72

In Thousand U.S. Dollars

I-O 43 Sectors	1954	1955	1956	1957	1958	1959	1960	1961	1962
1. Agriculture	4,579	9,087	14,086	27,389	5,879	7,295	1,234	5,656	–
2. Other Agriculture	17,887	32,240	26,603	19,511	18,108	18,374	27,797	9,639	46
3. Forestry	2,284	1,000	5,884	3,658	3,774	5,509	4,745	3,367	10,732
4. Fishery	–	–	522	942	330	666	1,545	–	–
5. Coal	1,213	3,211	3,025	2,901	9,569	1,070	2,138	586	–
6. Other Mineral	793	71	–	573	265	749	905	1,157	3,028
7. Processed Foods	1,428	2,109	6,978	9,539	4,572	1,336	2,780	1,672	793
10. Fibre Spinning	6,500	12,190	21,721	20,922	18,136	14,289	9,062	3,041	3,895
12. Textile Products	1,026	572	–	–	–	–	–	–	–
13. Lumber & Plywood	3,501	3,217	2,503	4,359	4,044	5,093	7,769	4,213	374
14. Wood Products	–	500	–	–	–	356	99	1,037	–
15. Paper Products	510	513	7,686	5,802	8,402	3,799	4,437	2,645	9,575
17. Leather & Products	200	334	1,515	612	506	504	407	–	322
18. Rubber Products	975	139	532	783	179	–	929	467	13
19. Basic Chemicals	–	478	1,523	2,330	1,550	1,146	1,025	254	–

Table B.14. (Continued)

In Thousand U.S. Dollars

I-O 43 Sectors	1954	1955	1956	1957	1958	1959	1960	1961	1962
20. Other Chemicals	2,400	4,223	11,145	10,795	10,453	9,550	7,265	6,097	9,581
21. Chemical Fertilizer	16,520	50,792	65,187	50,555	30,652	39,617	39,580	29,702	48,868
22. Petroleum Products	10,499	27,215	30,162	19,357	15,667	15,379	21,385	19,530	27,274
23. Coal Products	—	593	171	995	1,940	2,143	1,541	1,197	—
24. Nonmetallic Mineral	760	2,293	4,455	4,113	1,183	—	1,202	1,258	9
25. Iron & Steel	207	2,210	2,796	5,542	4,604	2,763	4,402	3,284	4,416
27. Nonferrous Metals	483	693	1,494	2,433	2,979	1,872	2,189	1,832	20
29. Machinery	616	3,727	3,764	5,820	9,739	8,698	12,193	9,590	2,694
30. Electrical Machinery	79	3,470	1,508	2,214	2,777	1,654	287	612	55
31. Transport Equipment	337	1,439	1,376	1,630	650	127	1	—	—
32. Misc. Manufacturing	144	700	371	1,949	3,804	2,655	3,741	598	3
39. Transportation	—	377	141	709	2	—	49	322	—
42. Scrap	50	—	—	—	—	—	—	—	—
43. Unclassifiable	1,346	4,943	6,177	2,679	3,604	4,257	2,881	5,827	4,916
Total	74,337	168,336	220,802	207,170	163,038	148,235	160,043	113,582	126,614

Table B.14. (Continued)

In Thousand U.S. Dollars

I-O 43 Sectors	1963	1964	1965	1966	1967	1968	1969	1970	1971	1972
3. Forestry	5,898	6,030	8,338	3,311	2,288	7,817	4,065	664	406	—
6. Other Mineral	1,136	1,786	580	68	56	19	—	576	394	—
7. Processed Foods	—	—	2,498	6,634	—	—	—	—	34	—
10. Fibre Spinning	9,050	598	2,152	2,020	3,240	3,508	169	—	1,077	—
13. Lumber & Plywood	9,032	4,443	298	—	—	—	—	—	—	—
15. Paper Products	50	8,622	8,084	10,355	12,632	14,233	2,562	21	—	—
17. Leather & Products	249	206	200	10	106	550	—	—	—	—
18. Rubber Products	—	—	—	—	3	72	—	—	—	—
19. Basic Chemicals	—	358	308	4	—	—	—	—	—	—
20. Other Chemicals	10,723	7,095	10,182	1,273	1,535	3,206	2,515	7,523	6,693	568
21. Chemical Fertilizer	25,016	29,641	35,882	25,421	39,776	10,611	824	—	—	—
22. Petroleum Products	26,573	8,243	—	1,042	—	—	—	—	—	—
25. Iron & Steel	4,725	1,758	903	1,042	—	—	—	—	—	—
27. Nonferrous Metals	5,040	2,047	4,501	1,074	67	1,290	—	—	—	—
29. Machinery	102	—	203	125	—	80	3,531	5,184	735	—
30. Electrical Machinery	—	—	324	79	—	—	—	—	—	—
31. Transport Equipment	—	—	641	863	—	—	—	—	—	—
32. Misc. Manufacturing	—	—	2,929	1,552	4	—	—	—	—	—
43. Unclassifiable	5,101	1,995	1,182	999	117	2,318	3,079	245	27	—
Total	102,722	72,822	79,205	54,830	59,824	43,704	16,745	14,213	9,366	568

Source: USAID to Korea.

Table B.15. U.S. Project Assistance by Sectors: 1954-75

In Thousand U.S. Dollars

I-O 43 Sectors	1954	1955	1956	1957	1958	1959	1960	1961
1, 2. Agriculture	43	1,828	3,659	5,217	3,022	5,167	2,487	1,351
3. Forestry	–	–	7	520	187	22	–	–
4. Fishery	–	–	–	235	934	2,332	749	189
5. Coal	71	36	132	28	841	395	2,070	1,098
6. Other Mineral	–	–	–	–	15	621	107	520
7. Processed Foods	–	90	824	669	10	2	135	–
10. Fibre Spinning	–	–	238	977	376	–	–	–
11. Textile Fabrics	–	–	–	464	1,746	–	13	–
12. Textile Products	–	–	237	236	249	39	–	–
13. Lumber & Plywood	–	–	–	–	–	227	273	–
15. Paper Products	–	–	–	771	552	867	62	–
16. Printing	–	–	–	201	1	1	–	–
17. Leather & Products	–	–	217	3	–	–	–	–
18. Rubber Products	85	281	182	126	469	148	–	–
19. Basic Chemicals	–	–	225	170	7	6	2	–
20. Other Chemicals	12	215	565	106	208	4	–	–
21. Chemical Fertilizer	1,238	3,139	4,421	5,347	4,771	6,009	5,449	4,231
22. Petroleum Products	–	–	646	364	–	–	–	–
24. Nonmetallic Mineral	–	–	943	88	655	79	3	–
25. Iron & Steel	–	–	984	1,011	–	–	–	–

26. Steel Products	—	—	—	267	—	—	—	—	—
27. Nonferrous Metals	—	4	95	—	—	—	—	—	—
28. Metal Products	—	—	200	—	232	—	—	—	—
29. Machinery	—	—	394	297	29	—	—	—	—
30. Electrical Machinery	124	811	947	770	927	1,578	1,617	344	
31. Transport Equipment	—	68	340	341	400	—	—	—	
32. Misc. Manufacturing	—	—	74	47	1,326	945	4,713	3,873	
33. Building	—	—	—	23	2,290	324	1,830	79	
34. Other Construction	—	—	45	34	41	10	—	—	
35. Electricity	2,896	2,937	5,502	11,092	7,278	7,152	9,691	5,079	
36. Banking	—	—	—	9	50	78	68	72	
37. Water & Sanitary Service	317	1,808	806	3,235	3,137	2,134	1,362	336	
38. Communication	134	1,053	1,711	1,099	811	1,367	2,144	524	
39. Transportation	1,312	19,261	24,470	46,957	24,866	27,862	10,740	6,725	
41. Other Services	43	639	2,347	8,182	7,636	9,774	12,480	6,119	
43. Unclassifiable	—	2,504	2,690	3,667	4,126	1,644	329	393	
Total	6,275	34,674	52,901	92,553	67,192	68,787	56,324	30,933	

Table B.15. (Continued)

In Thousand U.S. Dollars

I-O 43 Sectors	1962	1963	1964	1965	1966	1967	1968
1, 2. Agriculture	445	255	187	289	487	687	721
4. Fishery	224	—	—	—	—	—	—
5. Coal	1,169	246	456	673	270	31	168
6. Other Mineral	987	1,170	690	643	703	453	141
7. Processed Foods	—	56	—	—	—	—	—
16. Printing	1	—	—	—	—	—	—
18. Rubber Products	52	—	—	—	—	—	—
21. Chemical Fertilizer	3,529	43	—	−61	—	—	—
24. Nonmetallic Mineral	—	—	−27	—	—	—	—
30. Electrical Machinery	189	—	—	—	—	—	—
31. Transport Equipment	−6	7	—	—	—	—	—
32. Misc. Manufacturing	1,386	291	−77	—	—	—	—
33. Building	11	12	1	−74	—	—	—
35. Electricity	5,534	5,315	2,388	1,438	177	29	—
36. Banking	—	21	40	25	183	192	99
37. Water & Sanitary Service	1,111	1,211	111	7	1	—	—
38. Communication	234	41	36	30	11	—	—
39. Transportation	2,439	1,794	223	132	279	135	38
40. Trade	—	—	—	—	6	33	121
41. Other Services	4,153	2,526	1,455	1,056	1,876	2,757	7,372
43. Unclassifiable	258	347	35	—	6	39	—
Total	21,716	13,335	5,518	4,158	3,999	4,356	8,661

Table B.15.   (Continued)

In Thousand U.S. Dollars

I-O 43 Sectors	1969	1970	1971	1972	1973	1974	1975
1, 2. Agriculture	817	745	765	683	576	254	157
5. Coal	75	1	–	–	–	–	–
6. Other Mineral	90	42	7	–	–	–	–
35. Electricity	–	9	–	–	–	–	–
36. Banking	53	98	87	58	–	–	–
39. Transportation	42	28	28	9	–	–	–
40. Trade	149	37	–	–	–	32	–
41. Other Services	5,043	4,337	3,271	1,714	1,902	1,468	711
43. Unclassifiable	–	–	–	–	2	–	–
Total	6,269	5,297	4,158	2,464	2,480	1,754	868

Source: USAID to Korea.
Note: Includes aids under technological cooperation, defense support and development grant projects.

Table B.16. Sectoral Weighted Average Legal Tariff Rates (1958–75)

In Thousand Dollars and Percent

I-O 43 Sectors	SITC	1958 Imports	1958 Tariff Rates	1959–60 Imports	1959–60 Tariff Rates	1961 Imports	1961 Tariff Rates	1962 Imports	1962 Tariff Rates
1.									
Wheat & Meslin, Unmilled	041.0	26,362	15%	33,872	25%	24,019	10%	26,053	10%
Rice	042.1,2	527	10%	1	20%	41	25%	—	25%
Barley, Unmilled	043.0	18,464	10%	16	20%	5,237	25%	—	25%
Sub-Total		(43,353)	(13%)	(33,889)	(25%)	(29,297)	(13%)	(26,053)	(10%)
2.									
Raw Cotton	263.1	31,686	10%	59,399	10%	29,423	10%	34,179	10%
Sheeps & Lamb's Wool, carded	262.7,8	6,187	10%	20,110	20%	7,063	40%	2,296	40%
Soybeans	221.4	3	15%	89	25%	441	25%	32	25%
Maize, Unmilled	044	404	25%	1,381	25%	714	25%	1,593	25%
Sheeps and Lamb's Wool	262.1	303	10%	1	10%	18	10%	2,892	10%
Sub-Total		(38,583)	(10%)	(80,980)	(13%)	(37,659)	(16%)	(40,992)	(12%)
3.									
Natural Rubber & Gums	231.1	4,463	10%	12,950	10%	5,184	10%	5,477	10%
Wood & Lumber	242,243	11,053	10%	14,233	10%	7,168	10%	18,381	10%
Bamboo	292.32	270	25%	809	25%	273	25%	83	25%
Plants, mainly for Medicines	292.4	1,042	10%	1,945	15%	786	10%	1,021	10%
Sub-Total		(16,828)	(10%)	(29,937)	(11%)	(13,411)	(10%)	(24,962)	(10%)
5.									
Bituminous Coal	321.412	15,362	10%	9,578	10%	4,331	10%	2,213	10%

	Code								
6. Natural Phosphates & Crude Minerals	27	244	F	865	F	473	F	1,718	F
Metalliferous Ores & Metal Scrap	28	465	F	15	F	13	F	1,406	F
Crude Oil	331.0	—	—	—	—	—	—	539	—
Sub-Total		(709)	(F)	(880)	(F)	(486)	(F)	(3,663)	(F)
7. Raw Sugar	061.1	6,833	40%	11,391	50%	5,577	65w/kg	3,802	7.6w/kg
Molasses	061.5	3,187	30%	4,668	50%	2,551	80%	631	100%
Raw Hides & Skins	261.1,2	629	15%	965	15%	326	15%	397	25%
Flour of Wheat & Meslin	046.0	1,776	25%	5	35%	—	35%	2,773	35%
Milk, evaporated or condensed	022.1	346	25%	1,208	30%	416	50%	442	50%
Milk, dried	022.2	1,363	25%	1,200	30%	724	50%	2,011	50%
Sub-Total		(14,134)	(33%)	(19,437)	(46%)	(9,594)	(63%)	(10,056)	(58%)
8. Alcoholic Beverages	11	4,104	100%	38	100%	34	180%	82	180%
9. Manufactured Tobacco	12	1	100%	—	100%	—	250%	6	250%
10. Synthetic Fiber Yarns, n.e.s.	651.6,7	—	20%	6,623	20%	1,210	20%	13,156	40%

Table B.16. (Continued)

In Thousand Dollars and Percent

I-O 43 Sectors	SITC	1958 Imports	1958 Tariff Rates	1959-60 Imports	1959-60 Tariff Rates	1961 Imports	1961 Tariff Rates	1962 Imports	1962 Tariff Rates
14.									
Furniture	82	469	80%	6	80%	9	90%	130	90%
Wood and Cork Manufactures	63	158	60%	218	60%	144	70%	107	70%
Sub-Total		(627)	(75%)	(224)	(60%)	(153)	(71%)	(237)	(81%)
15.									
Mechanical Wood Pulp	251.2	619	10%	2,284	10%	1,538	10%	1,019	F
Chemical Wood Pulp	251.5,6,7,8,9	1,015	15%	3,706	10%	3,444	15%	7,135	10%
Newsprint	641.1	3,994	15%	4,787	15%	1,413	30%	450	30%
Printing Paper, n.e.s.	641.2	835	20%	21	30%	1	40%	823	30%
Kraft Paper	641.3	76	35%	879	35%	388	50%	221	50%
Cigarette Paper	641.4	4,797	35%	57	35%	41	50%	13	50%
Packing and Wrapping Paper	641.595	279	35%	672	35%	244	50%	145	—
Sub-Total		(11,615)	(24%)	(12,558)	(15%)	(7,069)	(20%)	(9,661)	(13%)
16.									
Books and Pamphlets, Printed	892	806	F	1,202	F	666	F	1,083	F
17.									
Leather, Leather Manufactures,	61	10	60%	18	60%	5	60%	16	60%
18.									
Rubber Manufactures, n.e.s.	62	191	50%	146	50%	128	60%	334	60%

19.

Beef Tallow	411.321	2,026	20%	3,997	20%	2,301	20%	2,737	20%
Methanol	512.21	52	10%	227	10%	155	25%	484	25%
Menthol	512.232	47	10%	32	10%	—	40%	—	40%
Glycerine	512.26	111	35%	771	35%	313	35%	353	35%
Acetic Acid	512.511	251	10%	231	10%	162	15%	129	15%
Oxalic Acid	512.521	50	10%	100	10%	92	15%	63	15%
Titanium Oxide	513.55	249	15%	594	15%	370	15%	526	15%
Aqua Ammonia	513.61	16	10%	59	10%	15	15%	4	15%
Sodium Hydroxide	513.62,3	1,066	10%	1,116	20%	819	25%	757	25%
Lard	091.31	1,072	20%	22	30%	43	40%	5	40%
Coal Tar Dyestuffs	531.011–15	2,102	25%	5,168	25%	2,921	25%	1,730	25%
Color Lakes	531.02	104	20%	423	20%	178	20%	152	20%
Vegetable Tanning Extracts	532.4	313	10%	550	15%	270	15%	206	15%
Synthetic Perfume	551.2	207	50%	461	50%	316	60%	648	80%
Sub-Total		(7,666)	(20%)	(13,751)	(23%)	(7,955)	(24%)	(7,794)	(30%)

325

Table B.16. (Continued)

In Thousand Dollars and Percent

I-O 43 sectors	SITC	1958 Imports	1958 Tariff Rates	1959-60 Imports	1959-60 Tariff Rates	1961 Imports	1961 Tariff Rates	1962 Imports	1962 Tariff Rates
20.									
Antibiotics	541.3	—	15%	1,453	15%	999	15%	1,508	15%
Synthetic Plastic Materials, n.e.s.	581.2	3,155	20%	5,758	20%	2,754	30%	3,209	30%
Antioxidants	599.75,6	152	10%	566	10%	214	15%	560	15%
Activated Carbon	599.92	46	20%	184	20%	142	20%	242	20%
Staple Fibers	266.2	1,660	15%	2,178	20%	1,290	20%	3,718	30%
Synthetic Fibers	266.3,4	5,785	20%	5,050	25%	2,797	25%		
Rayon Yarns	651.71	8,488	20%	20,352	25%	6,627	25%	11,008	30%
Carbon Black	513.27	156	15%	763	15%	278	25%	563	25%
Antibiotic Preparations	541.71	3,804	15%	3,056	15%	649	15%	715	15%
Synthetic Fiber Yarns, n.e.s.	651.6,7	—	40%	6,623	40%	1,210	50%	13,156	50%
Cellulose Acetate	581.321	100	10%	324	20%	260	30%	311	30%
Cellophane Sheets	581.322	410	35%	500	35%	233	50%	109	50%
Celluloid	581.323	136	25%	220	35%	78	40%	85	40%
Sub-Total		(23,892)	(19%)	(47,027)	(25%)	(17,531)	(27%)	(35,184)	(36%)
21.									
Urea	561.121	—	10%	—	10%	—	10%	9,469	10%
Ammonium Sulphate	561.122	27,022	10%	42,076	10%	20,950	10%	27,373	10%
Ammonium Nitrate	561.123	2,192	10%	4,127	10%	200	10%	1,288	10%
Calcium Superphosphate	561.211	10,075	10%	10,508	10%	3,118	F	2,294	F
Potassium Chloride	561.321	395	10%	480	15%	0	10%	572	10%
Sub-Total		(39,684)	(10%)	(57,191)	(10%)	(24,268)	(9%)	(40,996)	(9%)

22.									
Heavy Oil	332.4	5,691	10%	13,602	10%	6,999	20%	10,296	20%
Pitch and Asphalt	332.9	2,112	10%	3,561	10%	1,696	10%	3,359	10%
Vaseline	332.61	41	20%	202	20%	325	25%	184	20%
Parafin Wax	332.62	964	10%	1,550	10%	34	30%	43	25%
Sub-Total		(8,808)	(10%)	(18,915)	(10%)	(9,054)	(18%)	(13,882)	(18%)
23.									
Coal Tar	521.1	20	15%	33	15%	38	15%	122	15%
24.									
Cement	661.2	6,516	25%	2,201	30%	1,489	15%	3,595	15%
Refractory Bricks	662.3	87	35%	500	50%	252	15%	179	10%
Sub-Total		(6,603)	(25%)	(2,701)	(34%)	(1,741)	(15%)	(3,774)	(15%)
25.									
Steel Ingots and Blooms	672	88	10%	1,067	10%	1,874	10%	199	10%
26.									
Railway Pails	676.1	1,388	10%	538	10%	279	10%	1,286	F
Steel Wire Rods	673.1	434	20%	228	20%	57	25%	253	25%
Steel Bars, Shapes & Angles	673.2,4,5	1,663	20%	2,634	20%	617	20%	2,689	20%
Steel Plates and Sheets	674	5,494	15%	10,136	15%	2,732	20%	63,480	20%
Steel Hoops and Strips	675	238	20%	963	20%	690	20%	2,754	20%
Steel Tubes, Pipes and Fittings	678	2,735	10%	2,299	10%	468	25%	2,179	25%
Sub-Total		(11,952)	(14%)	(16,798)	(15%)	(4,843)	(25%)	(72,641)	(20%)

327

Table B.16. (Continued)

In Thousand Dollars and Percent

I-O 43 Sectors	SITC	1958 Imports	1958 Tariff Rates	1959-60 Imports	1959-60 Tariff Rates	1961 Imports	1961 Tariff Rates	1962 Imports	1962 Tariff Rates
27.									
Aluminium	684	1,781	10%	3,800	10%	1,766	10%	4,444	10%
Zinc	686	1,018	30%	1,546	30%	1,056	30%	1,255	30%
Tin	687	386	35%	834	35%	344	35%	660	35%
Brass Bronze and Other Alloys	682.2	583	30%	240	30%	104	30%	462	30%
Sub-Total		(3,768)	(21%)	(6,420)	(19%)	(3,270)	(20%)	(6,821)	(18%)
28.									
Materials for Construction	691.11	294	15%	422	15%	150	15%	4	15%
Hand Tools, Tools for Machines	695	242	40%	582	40%	451	40%	1,381	40%
Wire Ropes and Twistd Wire	693.1	181	35%	268	35%	180	35%	281	35%
Sub-Total		(717)	(28%)	(1,272)	(31%)	(781)	(34%)	(1,666)	(40%)
29.									
Textile Machinery, Parts	717.1	5,984	10%	11,369	10%	4,422	5%	6,542	5%
Construction Machinery	718.41	609	10%	429	10%	700	5%	24	5%
Mining Machinery	718.42	722	10%	1,096	10%	1,376	5%	233	5%
Machine Tools for Working Metals	715.1	1,160	10%	2,304	10%	1,520	5%	1,234	5%
Metal Working Machinery	715.2	252	10%	246	10%	309	5%	292	5%
Paper Mill and Pulp Machinery	718.1	627	10%	2,480	10%	799	5%	394	5%
Printing Machines & Parts	718.2	351	10%	867	10%	595	10%	580	10%
Compression Filters, Vacuum Filters	719.14	81	10%	201	10%	76	5%	342	5%

Cranes	719.31	108	10%	247	10%	263	5%	67	5%
Sewing Machines & Parts	717.3	655	20%	600	20%	245	20%	1,531	60%
Ball Bearing Parts	719.7	41	15%	49	15%	37	30%	296	30%
Air Conditioning Equipment	719.15	108	60%	147	50%	11	80%	146	80%
Gas Compressors	719.221–225	228	10%	235	10%	293	5%	504	5%
Centrifugal Separators	719.23	122	10%	98	10%	80	5%	368	5%
Hoists, Capstans, Winches	719.32	128	20%	243	20%	263	20%	67	20%
Steam Generating Boilers	711.1	274	20%	335	15%	374	25%	626	25%
Engines	711.521–24	383	35%	1,661	30%	3,398	30%	7,232	30%
Internal Combustion Parts	711.525–29	384	25%	737	25%	421	15%	364	15%
Sub-Total		(12,217)	(12%)	(23,344)	(13%)	(15,182)	(12%)	(20,752)	(20%)
30.									
Generators	722.111	1,307	20%	1,049	20%	5,537	10%	124	10%
Motors	722.129	485	20%	1,042	20%	305	10%	25	10%
Transformers and Converters	722.141	87	30%	481	30%	625	35%	240	35%
Switchgear, Switchboards, Circuit	722.2	295	25%	1,029	25%	1,009	35%	6,187	35%
Telephonic Apparatus	724.91	1,319	20%	1,164	30%	813	30%	5,447	30%
Loudspeaker Apparatus	724.92	178	30%	379	35%	170	35%	533	35%
Radio Telegraphic and TV	724.99	113	15%	276	15%	724	15%	4,027	15%
Electrothermic Apparatus	725.0	225	60%	264	60%	116	80%	347	80%
Apparatus for Medical Purposes	726.1	414	20%	433	20%	314	20%	63	20%
Electric Fluorescent Lamp	729.25	134	30%	254	30%	42	40%	323	40%
Condensers for Telegraphic & TV	729.95	86	50%	433	50%	347	50%	548	50%
Electric Apparatus	724.2	346	60%	1,002	60%	361	80%	255	80%
Sub-Total		(4,989)	(26%)	(7,806)	(32%)	(10,363)	(22%)	(18,119)	(31%)

Table B.16. (Continued)

In Thousand Dollars and Percent

I-O 43 Sectors	SITC	1958 Imports	1958 Tariff Rates	1959-60 Imports	1959-60 Tariff Rates	1961 Imports	1961 Tariff Rates	1962 Imports	1962 Tariff Rates
31.									
Railway Locomotives	731.1–3	3,203	F	107	F	61	F	496	F
Railway Vehicles, n.e.s.	731.4–6	874	F	358	F	113	F	557	F
Ships and Boats	735	733	20%	6,908	20%	368	25%	294	25%
Parts of Railway Vehicles	731.7	799	F	171	F	169	F	291	F
Automotive Passanger Cars	732.1	429	100%	16	100%	5	250%	1,226	250%
Automotive Trucks	732.3	896	40%	86	50%	4	50%	518	50%
Parts for Road Motor Vehicles	732.6	788	60%	150	60%	85	35%	—	—
Sub-Total		(7,727)	(18%)	(7,796)	(20%)	(805)	(17%)	(3,382)	(100%)
32.									
Watches and Clocks, and Parts thereof	864	110	60%	2,213	60%	1,058	50%	1,254	50%
Measuring and Testing Instruments	861.9	1,107	15%	911	15%	651	15%	1,358	30%
Microscopes and Parts	861.3	71	15%	117	15%	68	15%	112	15%
Cameras, Including for Movie	861.4	219	80%	80	60%	94	60%	44	60%
Parts of Cameras	861.5	85	60%	207	60%	70	60%	152	60%
Sub-Total		(1,592)	(29%)	(3,528)	(47%)	(1,951)	(38%)	(2,920)	(40%)
41.									
Cinematographic Films, not Exposed	862.41	333	30%	666	40%	222	40%	122	40%
Films, Unexposed, n.e.s.	862.42	105	25%	205	15%	144	40%	1,069	40%
Sensitized	862.43	275	60%	404	60%	106	80%	248	80%
Sub-Total		(713)	(41%)	(1,275)	(42%)	(472)	(49%)	(1,439)	(47%)

42.

Metalliferous Ores and Metal Scrap	28	465 10%	15 10%	13 10%	1,406 10%
Agriculture, Fishery & Forestry		98,764 11%	144,806 15%	80,367 14%	92,007 11%
Mining		16,071 10%	10,458 9%	4,817 9%	5,876 4%
Manufacturing		162,389 20%	249,185 20%	119,000 22%	265,728 25%
All Commodities (A)		277,224 16%	404,449 18%	204,184 19%	363,611 21%
Total Commodity Imports (B)		378,165	647,334	316,142	415,234
A/B (%)		73%	63%	65%	88%

Table B.16. (Continued)

Percentage Rate on CIF & Thousand Dollars

I-O 43 Sectors	SITC	1963-67 Imports	1963-67 Tariff Rates	1968-72 Imports	1968-72 Tariff Rates	1973-74 Imports	1973-74 Tariff Rates	1975 Imports	1975 Tariff Rates
1.									
Wheat & Meslin, Unmilled	041	225,945	10%	475,890	10%	554,183	10%	293,651	F
Rice	042	45,521	25%	561,790	25%	237,077	25%	195,118	F
Barley, Unmilled	043	35,016	25%	46,561	25%	138,659	25%	106,575	F
Sub-Total		(306,486)	(14%)	(1,084,241)	(18%)	(929,919)	(16%)	(595,344)	(F)
2.									
Milk Cow & Cattles	011,(2)	1,597	10%	7,256	10%	11,511	F	914	F
Other Bovine Species	(0019)	—	—	—	—	522	10%	12	20%
Raw Cotton	2631	208,384	10%	333,423	10%	301,876	10%	248,992	F
Other Sheep's Wool	262222	3,161	20%	14,676	20%	—	—	—	—
Carbonized Wool	(26224)	—	—	—	—	6,108	50%	4,353	40%
Scoured Wool	(26225)	—	—	—	—	9,273	50%	1,247	40%
Soya Beans	2214	4,353	25%	21,917	25%	30,426	20%	14,770	9%
Maize, Unmilled	044	2,848	50%	68,879	50%	107,817	15%	87,104	15%
Sub-Total		(220,343)	(11%)	(446,151)	(17%)	(467,533)	(13%)	(357,392)	(5%)
3.									
Natural Rubber & Gums	2311	33,475	10%	65,492	10%	89,754	10%	42,819	20%
Sawlogs, Coniferous	2422	29,664	10%	68,026	10%	86,427	10%	31,038	5%
Sawlogs, Nonconiferous	242313	125,094	10%	—	—	—	—	—	—
Lauwans	(242311)	—	—	537,515	10%	555,973	10%	233,886	5%
Sub-Total		(188,233)	(10%)	(671,033)	(10%)	(732,154)	(10%)	(307,743)	(7%)

4.									
Other Fish, Frozen	03114,(9)	68	35%	1,850	35%	14,140	30%	7,330	30%
Other Veg. Products, n.e.s.	292999,(5)	1,875	35%	96	35%	24	20%	28	20%
Rubber of Konyaku	(292996)	–	–	–	–	27	50%	67	50%
Other	292999	–	–	–	–	25	40%	19	40%
Other Coral & Shells	291153	185	25%	1,574	25%	2,172	60%	1,032	60%
Shells of Abalone	(291159)	–	–	496	20%	680	60%	407	60%
Coral	291152	977	15%	1,839	60%	1,070	60%	510	60%
Shells & Waste	(291154)	–	–	–	–	–	60%	3	60%
Sub-Total		(3,105)	(28%)	(5,855)	(39%)	(18,138)	(37%)	(9,396)	(36%)
5.									
Anthracite Coal	321411	141	15%	36	10%	14	10%	–	F
Bituminous Coal	321412	7,993	10%	2,168	10%	42,933	10%	37,539	F
Sub-Total		(8,134)	(10%)	(2,204)	(10%)	(42,947)	(10%)	(37,539)	(F)
6.									
Natural Phosphates	2713	1,262	F	38,640	F	35,242	F	52,794	F
Iron Ore & Concentrates	281	13	F	1,794	F	29,132	F	24,414	F
Copper Ore	28311	217	F	20,274	F	16,745	F	9,040	F
Crude Oil	33101	101,391	F	656,928	5%	1,236,726	5%	1,267,593	F
Copper Waste	284022	4,531	10%	15,394	10%	62,620	15%	27,983	5%
Asbestos	2764	6,726	15%	31,165	15%	29,900	15%	18,111	10%
Salt	2763	807	30%	11,745	40%	–	–	–	–
For Chemical Products	(27632)	–	–	–	–	10,769	10%	5,792	5%
Other	(27639)	–	–	–	–	582	40%	496	40%
Sub-Total		(121,157)	(1%)	(775,940)	(6%)	(1,421,716)	(5%)	(1,406,223)	(F)

333

Table B.16. (Continued)

Percentage Rate on CIF & Thousand Dollars

I-O 43 Sectors	SITC	1963–67		1968–72		1973–74		1975	
		Imports	Tariff Rates	Imports	Tariff Rates	Imports	Tariff Rates	Imports	Tariff Rates
7.									
Prepared Forage	08199	9,139	20%	74,678	20%	2,847	20%	1,439	20%
Denatured Molasses	06154	1,530	20%	8,342	20%	15,108	20%	9,876	30%
Raw Hides & Skins	211	2,467	25%	20,897	25%	52,451	25%	50,951	25%
Flour of Wheat	046011	23,893	35%	45,768	35%	6,978	30/35%	3,582	30%
Flour of Meslin	(046012)	—	—	—	—	—	—	—	—
Powdered Milk	02222	7,076	50%	—	—	—	30%	—	—
Skimmed, n.e.s.	022229	—	—	13,790	80%	193	60%	26	60%
Not Skimmed									
Sugared	02221	—	—	5,957	150%	19	80%	8	80%
Other	(02229)	—	—	—	—	157	60%	123	60%
Skimmed & Sugared	022222	—	—	7,473	150%	78	80%	32	80%
Raw Sugar	06111	25,397	7.6 w/kg	118,573	7.6 w/kg	194,410	7.6 w/kg	185,387	7.6 w/kg
Molasses	06152	984	100%	12,817	100%	10,538	40%	9,940	40%
Other Molasses	(06151,9)	—	—	—	—	238	80%	—	80%
Sub-Total		(70,486)	(37%)	(308,295)	(35%)	(293,555)	(12%)	(261,364)	(11%)

335

8. Alcoholic Beverages	112	1,068	180%	2,357	150%	1,595	150%	3,918	150%
9.									
Manufactured Tobacco	122[2]	132	250%	843	150%	176	150%	207	150%
Other Manufactured Tobacco	12232	18	35%	778	35%	47	35%	—	—
Sub-Total		(150)	(224%)	(1,621)	(95%)	(223)	(126%)	(207)	(150%)
10.									
Greasy Wool	2621	19,207	10%	48,213	10%	60,003	35%	30,923	40%
Other Sheep's Wool, Dyed	26282	3,576	35%	7,337	35%	7,534	60%	1,286	60%
Cotton Yarn, not for Retail Sale	65141	351	40%	3,748	40%	2,379	30/10%	471	10%
Cotton Yarn, for Retail Sale	65142	1,183	60%	—	—	711	50%	128	50%
Embroidery Thread	(651426)	—	—	86	90%	—	—	—	—
Other	(651429)	—	—	1,626	80%	—	—	—	—
Yarn, Craped or Stretched	651619	1,768	50%	13,001	60%	4,241	60%	928	40%
Yarn of Wool	6512	507	70%	3,521	80%	8,348	70%	2,396	70%
Yarn of Discont. Synthetic Fibres	651642	—	50%	13,790	80%	19,914	70%	2,080	70%
Yarn of Polyester Fibres	(651641)	—	—	44,472	80%	24,979	70%	5,109	70%
Yarn of Discont. Synthetic Fibres	651651	3,953	50%	9,889	80%	70	70%	—	—
Yarn of Regenerated Fibres	651752	10,568	50%	2,011	80%	658	70%	143	70%
Yarn of Continuous Regenerated	65171	20,538	30%	—	—	—	—	—	—
Sub-Total		(61,651)	(30%)	(147,694)	(64%)	(128,837)	(52%)	(43,464)	(47%)

Table B.16. (Continued)

Percentage Rate on CIF & Thousand Dollars

I-O 43 Sectors	SITC	1963-67		1968-72		1973-74		1975	
		Imports	Tariff Rates	Imports	Tariff Rates	Imports	Tariff Rates	Imports	Tariff Rates
11.									
Tire Cord Fabrics	653511	2,939	35%	3,950	40%	4,025	50/40%	2,238	40%
Other Fabrics, Regenerated	653619	1,738	80%	5,122	40%	7,731	80%	3,289	40%
Woolen Fabrics	65321	385	80%	17,231	103%	21,360	80%	12,709	80%
Woven Fabrics of Jute	6534	7	80%	1,746	103%	454	80%	23	80%
Woven Fabrics, Synthetic	653521	2,566	80%	151,598	103%	157,785	80%	51,786	80%
Other Fabrics, Synthetic	653519	10,080	80%	26,839	100%	32,507	80%	48,323	80%
Silk Fabrics	653519	7,195	80%	23,210	150%	19,594	100%	8,061	100%
Sub-Total		(24,910)	(75%)	(229,696)	(98%)	(243,456)	(81%)	(126,429)	(80%)
12.									
Felt	655834	1,181	30%	3,108	20%	3,636	20%	1,555	20%
Elastic Fabrics	6555	76	80%	2,140	80%	3,938	80%	264	60%
Knitted Fabrics	65372	32	80%	9,671	103%	18,388	80%	7,431	80%
Tulle, Lace & the Like	65401	580	80%	7,585	103%	12,444	80%	7,515	80%
Embroidery	65406	2	100%	123	103%	687	100%	474	100%
Bonded Fibre Fabrics	655411	9	80%	2,776	103%	2,524	80%	1,429	80%
Textile Fabrics	65543	48	80%	1,915	103%	6,020	80%	12,966	80%
Sub-Total		(1,928)	(49%)	(27,318)	(89%)	(47,637)	(75%)	(31,634)	(77%)
13.									
Railway Sleepers of Wood	2431	2,887	10%	5,613	10%	—	F	—	—
Lumber, Coniferous Species	24321	674	15%	1,746	25%	1,692	30/25%	263	25%
Other Lumber, Plane	243329	34	15%	222	25%	107	30/25%	17	25%
Other Lumber, Sawn	243319	620	15%	1,339	25%	183	30/25%	118	25%
Sub-Total		(4,125)	(12%)	(8,920)	(16%)	(1,982)	(30/25%)	(398)	(25%)

337

14.

Seats & Parts	82101	89	80%	1,351	100%	1,565	80%	356	80%
Spools, Cops of Jurned Wood	63282,(1)	18	35%	700	50%	463	50%	67	30%
Other Articles of Wood	632899	200	70%	625	100%	616	80%	169	40%
Other Articles of Cork	633022	35	50%	426	40%	168	40%	2	40%
Mattresses & Matt. Supports	(82103)	—	—	393	100%	52	80%	27	80%
Of Beddings	821031	193	100%	—	—	—	—	—	—
Other	821032	19	80%	—	—	—	—	—	—
Furniture & Parts	821093	154	80%	3,302	100%	2,669	80%	1,544	80%
Sub-Total		(708)	(80%)	(6,797)	(91%)	(5,533)	(76%)	(2,165)	(75%)

15.

Wood Pulp	2512	4,218	F	6,438	F	6,456	F	4,846	F
Semi-Bleached Kraft Pulp	251721	8,449	F	26,639	F	12,192	F	3,296	20%
Waste of Paper	2511	4,251	10%	8,734	10%	34,899	10%	22,278	10%
Other Pulp	2515	2,034	10%	3,523	10%	213	10%	70	10%
Chemical Wood Pulp	2516	133	10%	8,547	10%	8,129	10%	5,036	10%
Soda Wood Pulp	25171	13,415	10%	41,828	10%	22,385	10%	23,501	10%
Other Sulphated Wood Pulp	251722	7,608	10%	46,207	10%	79,383	10%	32,879	20%
Sulphite Wood Pulp	251827	16,770	10%	16,934	10%	12,259	10%	3,619	20%
Newsprint Paper	64111	4,938	30%	8,448	30%	867	30%	—	—
Other Kraft Paper & Paperboard	64132	901	50%	—	—	7,295	50%	2,494	50%
Kraft Paper	(641311)	—	—	2,125	50%	—	—	—	—
Kraft Paperboard	(641319)	—	—	1,029	60%	—	—	—	—
Sub-Total		(62,717)	(10%)	(170,452)	(10%)	(184,078)	(11%)	(98,019)	(15%)

Table B.16. (Continued)

Percentage Rate on CIF & Thousand Dollars

I-O 43 Sectors	SITC	1963–67 Imports	1963–67 Tariff Rates	1968–72 Imports	1968–72 Tariff Rates	1973–74 Imports	1973–74 Tariff Rates	1975 Imports	1975 Tariff Rates
16.									
Other Books & Pamphlets	892112	3,406	F	13,094	F	5,318	F	3,062	F
Newspapers & Periodicals	8922	1,214	F	3,387	F	1,802	F	1,299	F
Postage, Stamps & Stock	89293	33	F	4,000	F	8	F	39	F
Other Printed Matter	892999	87	F	7,032	F	786	F	341	F
Sub-Total		(4,380)	(F)	(27,513)	(F)	(7,914)	(F)	(4,741)	(F)
17.									
Bovine Cattle Leather	6113	181	60%	265	60%	1,052	60%	364	60%
Equine Leather	6114	13	60%	6,091	60%	28,221	60%	37,261	60%
Parts of Footwear	6123	644	80%	1,628	100%	1,436	80%	657	80%
Sub-Total		(838)	(75%)	(7,984)	(68%)	(30,709)	(61%)	(38,282)	(60%)
18.									
Taps, Cocks & Valves, n.e.s.	71992	7,194	40%	25,109	50%	17,489	50%	12,883	50%
Parts	(719929)	—	—	8,158	50%	1,418	30%	1,200	30%
Automatic Control Type	(719921)	—	—	3,123	50%	7,625	30%	7,591	20%
Vacanized Rubber Thread	62103	145	80%	1,228	80%	780	60%	113	60%
Sub-Total		(7,339)	(41%)	(37,618)	(51%)	(27,312)	(44%)	(21,787)	(38%)

19.

Beef Tallow	411321	20,041	20%	54,906	10/30%	73,641	20/30%	40,209	30%
Other Halogenated Derivatives	512139	653	25%	17,109	15%	13,393	F	10,081	F
Other Hydrocarbons	512129	70	15%	1,585	20%	17,851	15%	14,188	15%
Methanol	512211	4,091	15%	8,138	15%	2,824	20/15%	39	15%
Other Acyclic Compounds	512515	2,176	15%	9,492	15%	9,753	15%	6,311	20%
Polyhydric Alcohols	512225	1,490	35%	5,790	20%	26,098	20%	26,580	10%
Saturated Monohydric Alcohols	512222	1,935	25%	6,846	20%	5,958	20%	6,598	10%
Cyclic Compounds	512523	3,260	15%	—	—	—	—	—	—
Dioctyl Phthalate	(5125271)	—	—	1,373	50%	5,883	50%	1,395	30%
Dimethyl Telephthalate	(5125274)	—	—	22,021	15%	59,102	15%	54,140	20%
Other Esters of Mineral Acids	512692	1,481	15%	5,938	20%	5,328	5%	5,438	F
Nitrile-Function Compounds	51276	758	15%	30,449	15%	19,639	30%	29,539	20%
Other Organo Sulphur Compounds	512812	1,034	15%	5,266	20%	7,333	20%	853	5%
Heterocyclic Compounds	51285	3,174	15%	—	—	—	—	—	—
Caprolactam	(5128571)	—	—	46,093	15%	59,882	15%	31,855	30%
Other	(5128599)	—	—	12,649	20%	13,795	20%	6,175	20%
Meat, Meal & Fish Meal	0815	—	20%	—	—	—	—	—	—
Fish Flour & Meal	(08141)	—	—	10,718	20%	472	20%	8	15%
Titanium Oxides	51355	3,294	15%	9,085	20%	2,840	40/30%	2,655	30%
Nonmetal Oxides	513399	478	15%	3,728	20%	4,690	40%	3,108	30%
Sodium Hydroxides	513621	5,150	25%	5,111	35%	9,221	30%	2,469	30%
Aluminium Oxides	513651	375	15%	1,749	20%	6,182	5%	4,314	5%
Other Aluminium Oxides	(513613)	—	—	8,766	20%	2,649	20%	—	—
Lard & Pig Fat	09131	323	40%	8,427	40%	1,460	40%	1,258	30%
Acid Dyes	531013	2,162	40%	6,776	60%	5,866	60%	1,168	30%

Table B.16. (Continued)

Percentage Rate on CIF & Thousand Dollars

I-O 43 Sectors	SITC	1963–67 Imports	1963–67 Tariff Rates	1968–72 Imports	1968–72 Tariff Rates	1973–74 Imports	1973–74 Tariff Rates	1975 Imports	1975 Tariff Rates
Other Synthetic Dyestuff	531019	6,333	40%	3,564	20%	5,024	40%	4,105	30%
Vat & Disperse Dyes	531016	2,035	40%	12,574	60%	22,635	60%	18,487	30%
Fatty Acids	431311	299	40%	5,834	20%	5,324	30%	405	15%
Odoriferous Substances	55123	2,108	35%	4,676	60%	5,080	60%	2,503	60%
Sub-Total		(62,720)	(23%)	(308,663)	(24%)	(391,923)	(24%)	(273,881)	(21%)
20.									
Sulphur	2741	3,934	10%	21,793	10%	15,947	10%	16,455	10%
Synthetic Rubber	2312	8,001	15%	14,972	15%	10,122	15%	531	15%
Block of Phenol Resins	581121	71	10%	19,411	15%	6,307	30%	—	—
Block of Vinylchloride Resins	581221	697	10%	—	—	—	—	—	—
Polyvinyl Alcohol	(5812191)	—	—	619	15%	1,766	15%	—	F
Antibiotics	5413	9,070	15%	25,115	20%	19,643	20%	15,125	F
Other Blocks of Polyethylene	581229	19,584	30%	67,668	20%	31,348	30/25%	8,060	30%
Anti-knock Preparations	59975	2,382	15%	10,368	20%	9,630	20%	5,277	30%
Compound Catalysts	599991	2,690	15%	9,428	20%	911	F	602	F
Other	(5999913,9)	—	—	—	—	3,588	20%	2,502	20%
Other Chemical Products	599999,(8)	995	25%	11,033	20%	16,493	30%	10,176	20%
Regenerated Discont. Fibers	26631	9,159	20%	21,318	30%	16,414	30%	16,140	30%
Continuous Filament Tow	266322	60	30%	—	—	—	—	—	—
Acetate Fibres	(266321)	—	—	10,694	30%	4,684	40/30%	2,447	30%
Acetate Rayon Yarn	65171	18,051	30%	17,074	30%	19,914	30%	3,675	30%

Surface-Acting Agents	5542	4,211	35%	14,038	40%	14,595	40%	12,029	30%
Carbon Black	51327	4,342	25%	4,710	35%	2,365	40%	1,572	30%
Other Medicaments	54179	8,519	25%	12,890	50%	4,598	60%	2,908	60%
Raw Filament Yarn	651612	19,166	20%	69,951	60%	18,744	60%	1,247	40%
Synthetic Fibres, Discont.	266211	12,782	20%	31,423	60%	34,948	60%	1,413	50%
Polyacrylonitrile Fibres	(26211)	—		5,287	60%	13,357	70%	2,324	40%
Raw Filament Yarn	651613	54,908	30%	84,992	60%	19,798	30%	—	
Of Polyamide Fibres	(6516113)	—		—		49,897	60%	2,076	40%
Styrene	512111	1,159	15%	6,915	15%	18,287	15%	7,734	10%
Continuous Filament Tow	26622	1,323	30%	7,502	60%	43,258	60%	21,936	50%
Polyacrylonitrile Fibres	(266221)	—		53,129	60%	9,419	70%	307	50%
Synthetic Fibres, Discont.	26623	—		9,627	60%	728	60%	93	60%
Polyacrylonitrile Fibres	266231	28,655	30%	24,438	60%	34,014	70%	1,518	60%
Other Plastic Materials	58119	368	40%	4,853	60%	6,482	60%	—	
Other Resins	58129	570	40%	8,022	50%	14,727	60%	1,387	60%
Copolymerisation Products	(581239)	—		8,062	20%	15,921	50%	6,150	25%
Sub-Total		(210,697)	(26%)	(575,332)	(47%)	(457,905)	(45%)	(143,684)	(27%)
21.									
Chemical Fertilizer, Nitro.	5611	162,824	10%	27,344	F	2,831	F	10,464	F
Phosphatic Fertilizer	5612	108,022	F	7,195	F	41,687	F	63,909	F
Disintegrated Phosphate Lime	(561292)	—		—		596	20%	30	F
Potassic Fertilizer	5613	20,139	F	22,326	F	23,107	F	64,913	F
Fertilizers, n.e.s.	5619	11,494	F	8,003	F	1,135	F	565	F
Sub-Total		(302,479)	(5%)	(64,868)	(F)	(69,356)	(F)	(139,881)	(F)

Table B.16. (Continued)

Percentage Rate on CIF & Thousand Dollars

I-O 43 Sectors	SITC	1963–67 Imports	1963–67 Tariff Rates	1968–72 Imports	1968–72 Tariff Rates	1973–74 Imports	1973–74 Tariff Rates	1975 Imports	1975 Tariff Rates
22.									
Raw Petroleum, Topped	331025	4,022	F	10,384	20%	6,507	20%	3,622	20%
Residual Fuel Oils	3324	30,815	20%	8,442	20%	21,162	20%	31,832	20%
Non-Lubricating Oils, n.e.s.	332919	422	25%	9,945	20%	—	—	—	—
Mineral Oils, Bituminous	(332512–9)	—		—		3,272	20%	—	
Sub-Total		(35,259)	(18%)	(28,771)	(20%)	(30,941)	(20%)	(35,454)	(20%)
23.									
Cokes & Semi-Cokes	3218	2,889	20%	10,462	5%	7,540	5%	10,258	5%
24.									
Cement	6612	18,913	15%	3,295	15/30%	1,810	15/30%	137	15%
Refractory Bricks	662321	1,999	10%	12,086	20%	10,255	20%	99	20%
Other Electrical Carbons	729961	1,354	20%	6,000	20%	7,233	10%	8,072	10%
Carbon Electrodes	(729962)	—		—		837	20%	821	20%
Asbestos Board	66381	465	50%	3,921	50%	1,499	50%	1,110	50%
Electrical Insulators	72321	1,298	35%	7,028	40%	25	20%	168	60%
Of Ceramics	(7232112)	—		—		6,310	50%	8,005	30%
Sub-Total		(24,029)	(17%)	(32,330)	(29%)	(27,969)	(26%)	(18,412)	(22%)

343

25.										
Pig Iron & Cast Iron	6712	6,438	10%	16,574	10%	22,958	10%	11,214	10%	
Billets of Iron or Steel	67251	13,986	10%	8,362	20%	7,934	20%	3,517	20%	
Slabs	(672513)	—	—	20,369	10%	58,000	10%	30,847	20%	
Sub-Total		(20,424)	(10%)	(45,305)	(12%)	(88,892)	(11%)	(45,578)	(18%)	
26.										
Rails of Iron or Steel	67611	11,038	F	20,191	F	17,718	F	2,370	F	
Wire Rods of High Carbon Steel	673121	1,882	10%	10,966	10%	20,329	10%	16,552	10%	
Bars of Alloy Steel	673232	1,650	10%	11,289	10%	9,909	10%	8,927	10%	
Plates & Sheets of Alloy Steel	674333	12,591	10%	52,187	10%	13,520	15%	8,310	20%	
Hoops & Strip of Alloy Steel	675033	1,344	10%	10,815	10%	22,764	15%	12,337	20%	
Angles & Shapes of Iron or Steel	67341	6,750	20%	17,957	25%	26,467	25%	15,535	20%	
Iron or Steel Coils	67271	1,590	10%	205,040	35%	322,649	30%	69,542	20%	
Heavy Plates of Iron or Steel	67411	20,247	20%	16,352	35%	74,559	35%	58,409	20%	
Plates & Sheets of Iron or Steel	674313	30,583	20%	15,203	40%	18,331	40%	—	—	
Tubes & Pipes of Steel	678335	1,846	35%	—	—	—	—	—	—	
Coated Metal	(67839)	—	—	12,290	50%	3,825	50%	2,177	30%	
Sub-Total		(89,521)	(16%)	(372,290)	(28%)	(530,071)	(28%)	(194,159)	(19%)	
27.										
Ingots or Lumps of Aluminium	684111	18,967	10%	17,819	10%	20,937	10%	14,142	10%	
Tin & Tin Alloys, Unwrought	68711	2,784	10%	8,036	10%	9,420	10%	6,045	10%	
Blister Copper	682119	2,202	10%	—	—	—	—	—	—	
Copper Lumps (Refined)	(68212)	—	—	18,096	25%	32,425	20%	8,972	20%	
Plates & Sheets of Aluminium	68422	275	30%	6,560	40%	10,513	30%	6,302	20%	
Zinc & Zinc Alloys	68611	10,666	15%	11,765	50%	18,795	40%	2,495	40%	
Sub-Total		(34,894)	(12%)	(62,276)	(25%)	(92,090)	(22%)	(37,956)	(16%)	

Table B.16. (Continued)

Percentage Rate on CIF & Thousand Dollars

I-O 43 Sectors	SITC	1963–67 Imports	1963–67 Tariff Rates	1968–72 Imports	1968–72 Tariff Rates	1973–74 Imports	1973–74 Tariff Rates	1975 Imports	1975 Tariff Rates
28.									
Construction Materials	69113	13,784	15%	—	—	15,840	40%	7,165	40%
For Bridges, Towers & Vessels	(691111)	—	—	17,532	40%	—	—	—	—
Other	(69119)	—	—	62,576	40%	—	—	—	—
Vats	(719811,2)	—	—	10,816	20%	8,921	20%	2,774	20%
Tube & Pipe Fittings of Steel	(6785)	—	—	11,672	50%	9,438	40%	7,799	40%
Those Not Coated	67851	1,707	30%	—	—	—	—	—	—
Those Coated	67852	1,295	35%	—	—	—	—	—	—
Reservoirs & Tanks of Steel	69211	3,746	40%	14,075	50%	2,401	50%	1,489	50%
Other Casks, Drums, Can, etc.	692212	6,292	40%	6,455	50%	4,414	50%	1,621	50%
Articles of Iron or Steel, n.e.s.	698919	6,349	15%	19,778	50%	11,351	50%	3,417	50%
Other Tools for Hand Tools	695242	1,926	25%	10,289	50%	3,298	30%	—	—
Dies for Press Working	(6952443)	—	—	—	—	6,308	50%	2,767	50%
Wire & Cables of Aluminium	69313	110	40%	740	40%	6,001	40%	67	40%
Other Wire of Base Metal	698872	967	35%	2,589	40%	2,019	30%	694	60%
Other	(698875)	—	—	—	—	2,900	40%	1,881	40%
Bolt, Nuts & Rivets of Steel	69421	1,638	60%	5,119	50%	6,153	50%	4,426	50%
Hand Tools	69522	881	40%	2,889	50%	2,973	50%	1,421	30%
Other Nettings of Aluminium	693339	—	50%	4,720	50%	27	50%	51	50%
Articles of Aluminium, n.e.s.	69894	5,265	80%	13,450	50%	7,571	30%	8,398	30%
Articles of Copper, n.e.s.	69829	180	70%	6,999	70%	405	70%	81	70%
Sub-Total		(44,140)	(33%)	(189,699)	(45%)	(90,020)	(40%)	(44,051)	(40%)

29.

Steam Turbins & Parts	711321	5,160	5%	40,267	5%	6,758	5%	18,173	5%
Other Parts of Office Machine	714922	6	50%	21,877	5%	28,731	5%	10,484	20%
Spinning & Extruding Machines	71711	43,076	5%	181,282	5%	228,294	5%	108,463	5%
Other Construction Machinery	718429	5,595	5%	—	—	—	—	—	—
Bulldozers	(718421)	—	—	32,080	5%	9,571	5%	11,250	5%
Others	7184289	—	—	33,927	10%	5,918	10%	2,490	10%
Grinding Machines, etc.	715116	3,080	5%	9,901	10%	7,706	10%	10,101	10%
Pressing Machines	715121	1,755	5%	12,863	10%	9,261	10%	14,791	10%
Rolling Mills & Rolls	715221,2	2,316	5%	24,810	10%	19,794	10%	5,897	10%
Machinery for Paper or Pulp	71811	3,924	5%	19,172	10%	5,953	10%	4,340	10%
Printing Machinery & Parts	71829l(−5)	5,235	10%	24,572	10%	8,009	10%	5,184	10%
Furnaces	71914	5,846	5%	33,887	10%	14,018	10%	3,750	10%
Lifting & Loading Machinery	719311	5,363	5%	28,759	10%	100,394	10%	—	—
Lathes, Planners, etc.	715111	3,530	5%	14,007	20%	12,728	20%	11,750	20%
Weaving Machines	717121	9,835	20%	40,190	20%	26,573	20%	14,044	20%
Knitting Machines	717123	5,320	20%	19,228	20%	13,920	20%	6,369	60%
Machinery for Cleaning	717152	13,045	20%	51,693	20%	29,993	20%	324,963	20%
Other Sewing Machines	71732	5,491	20%	12,681	20%	14,779	30%	6,261	30%
Refrigerating Machines	719152	2,873	20%	10,760	20%	11,750	20%	2,838	20%
Machinery for Laboratory	719191	857	15%	19,155	20%	651	20%	568	20%
Machinery for Other Use	719199	15,219	20%	81,910	20%	51,868	20%	9,000	20%
Other Air Compressors	719225	4,072	25%	23,527	20%	3,900	20%	3,147	20%
Others	(7192249)	—	—	—	—	5,110	50%	2,878	30%
Fans & Blowers	719226	2,177	30%	12,078	20%	4,108	20%	3,842	20%
Centrifuges & Filtering Machinery	719232	2,193	25%	15,331	20%	15,613	20%	9,040	20%
Motor Operated	(7192329)	—	—	10,123	50%	—	—	—	—

Table B.16. — (Continued)

Percentage Rate on CIF & Thousand Dollars

I-O 43 Sectors	SITC	1963–67 Imports	1963–67 Tariff Rates	1968–72 Imports	1968–72 Tariff Rates	1973–74 Imports	1973–74 Tariff Rates	1975 Imports	1975 Tariff Rates
Lifting Machinery	719319	9,549	20%	45,086	20%	12,949	20%	11,584	20%
Steam Generating Boilers	71111	6,471	25%	43,236	50%	4,671	10%	4,857	10%
Heated Water Boilers	(71113,5)	—	—	—	—	21,926	30%	3,926	20%
Parts of Boilers	71112	17,114	20%	41,101	50%	3,380	10%	68	10%
Others	(71119)	—	—	—	—	815	30%	114	30%
Gasoline Engines	711524	4,032	60%	5,338	50%	5,885	50%	5,797	50%
Other Combustion Engines	711525	5,928	15%	9,079	50%	7,686	50%	14,842	50%
Machinery for Sorting, Separating	71851,(1)	12,269	5%	26,174	50%	920	50%	742	30%
Other Crushing Machines	(718512)	—	—	—	—	3,743	30%	6,954	30%
Other Air Conditioning Machines	719122	2,960	30%	11,511	50%	5,081	80%	12	80%
Parts	(719129)	—	—	—	—	532	50%	54	50%
Other Liquid Pumps	719212	8,534	30%	31,517	50%	9,131	50%	11,481	40%
Appliances for Projecting	719643	1,105	20%	7,699	50%	3,116	50%	5,164	30%
Single Needle Sewing Machines	71731–3	510	60%	10,676	70%	13,113	60%	5,903	60%
Other Machines	71983–9	26,139	20%	96,938	20%	54,977	20%	5,120	20%
Sub-Total		(240,579)	(16%)	(1,102,435)	(20%)	(783,325)	(15%)	(666,241)	(18%)
30.									
Electrical Generators	722111	2,283	10%	6,764	10%	6,111	30%	2,500	30%
Electrical Generators	722112	2,351	5%	9,186	F	1,757	10%	1,827	10%
Electrical Generators	722113	10,701	F	42,937	F	13,593	F	9,354	F
Electric Furnaces & Parts	729921	1,938	F	12,225	F	11,077	F	3,709	20%
Other Electrical Generators	(7299291)	—	—	11,841	10%	1,322	10%	157	5%

346

347

Transformers	722149	6,609	5%	—	—	—	20%	328	10%
Measuring Instruments	(722151)	—	—	13,713	20%	2,127	60%	983	20%
Others	(7221612-9)	—	—	11,058	70%	4,819	20%	1,410	60%
Other Electrical Line Telephone	724919	764	30%	11,758	20%	7,995	10%	2,568	20%
Other Equipment & Parts	7249981,5	5,188	15%	16,857	20%	3,584	10%	7,389	10%
Others	(7149908)	—	—	3,709	20%	791	20%	714	10%
Other Thermionic, etc.	72934	4,479	15%	146,113	20%	372,588	50%	25,650	20%
Other Measuring Instruments	729522	7,757	15%	32,023	20%	6,769	20%	1,871	20%
Other Electrical Apparatus	72229	16,978	35%	56,612	40%	18,065	50%	19,382	30%
Other Insulated Wire & Cable	72314	3,657	40%	10,316	50%	3,057	60%	493	30%
Parts of Television Receivers	724129	728	30%	11,891	50%	21,545	50%	12,836	30%
Parts of Radio Receivers	724213	788	70%	9,036	50%	16,705	50%	4,190	30%
Other Sound Recorders	891116	146	50%	11,056	50%	54,592	50%	15,054	80%
Apparatus, Electrical Circuits	722249	1,565	40%	34,137	70%	16,652	50%	22,952	50%
Radio Receivers	724212	2,768	70%	13,802	100%	16,074	80%	9,849	30%
Sub-Total		(68,701)	(21%)	(465,034)	(29%)	(579,223)	(28%)	(143,216)	(33%)
31.									
Railway Locomotives	7312	662	F	18,471	F	56,268	F	63	F
Other Railway Locomotives	7313	11,523	F	22,537	F	1,012	F	23,102	F
Railway Passanger Cars	7315	121	F	16,356	F	—	F	5,890	F
Railway Goods Wagons	73162	11,612	F	32,315	F	2,533	F	3,695	F
Aircraft	7341	11,100	F	86,152	F	167,873	F	146	F
Steel Vessels	735349	6,481	F	126,518	F	196,057	F	83,336	F
Steel Vessels	735341	11,904	10%	18,442	10%	149,353	F	97,336	F
Fork-Lift Trucks & Tractors	719322	3,047	25%	7,323	20%	2,807	50%	1,898	50%

Table B.16. (Continued)

Percentage Rate on CIF & Thousand Dollars

I-O 43 Sectors	SITC	1963–67 Imports	1963–67 Tariff Rates	1968–72 Imports	1968–72 Tariff Rates	1973–74 Imports	1973–74 Tariff Rates	1975 Imports	1975 Tariff Rates
Other Fork-Lift & Tractors	(719322)	—	—	—	—	3,393	30%	3,580	30%
Steel Vessels	73532	14,583	20%	15,672	20%	5,220	F	1,063	F
Steel Vessels	735323	—	—	66,496	50%	41,322	10%	4,215	F
Other Lorries & Trucks	732323	14,991	50%	98,550	50%	60,587	50%	39,109	50%
Special Purpose Lorries & Vans	7324	2,623	25%	13,334	50%	7,656	30%	4,971	30%
Other Chassis	73272	1,168	50%	28,650	50%	10,875	40/50%	3,108	40%
Other Parts for Motor Vehicles	732899	3,656	35%	13,572	50%	13,230	30%	14,803	40%
Steel Vessels, Tankers	(735332)	25,332	10%	16,266	50%	19,010	5%	23,137	5%
Cargo Vessels	(735342)	—	—	25,078	50%	1,316	10%	8,315	5%
Other Passenger Motor Cars	732112	8,880	250%	10,642	80%	702	80%	236	80%
General Motor Vehicles	732229	1,521	50%	68,150	150%	7,814	100/150%	5,843	150%
Others	(73219)	—	—	—	—	8,858	150%	5	100%
Tri-Cycles	732322	2,494	50%	17,539	80%	1,519	50/80%	—	—
Pick-Up Trucks & Similar Trucks	732321	961	80%	8,151	80%	60,587	50%	39,109	50%
Small Motor Vehicles	732111	56	180%	2,456	150%	2,376	60/150%	1,497	100%
Small Motor Vehicles	(73215)	—	—	—	—	7,697	100/150%	—	—
Sub-Total		(133,583)	(32%)	(712,670)	(38%)	(828,065)	(15%)	(364,457)	(17%)
32.									
Human Hair	89994	652	30%	29,586	35%	1,860	40/35%	443	35%
Watch Movement Assembled	86413	1,748	50%	19,473	40%	13,228	40%	5,739	40%
Articles of Plastic Materials	89302	3,387	50%	18,053	100%	2,367	80%	7,459	60%
For Machine	(89301)	—	—	—	—	15,079	50%	1,882	30%

Bottoms & Parts	89952	606	70%	7,175	100%	13,764	80%	7,475	80%
Slide Fasteners & Parts	899531	978	80%	10,811	100%	14,706	80%	7,616	80%
Instruments for Measuring	86197	1,317	15%	8,718	20%	5,377	30%	4,930	30%
For Refrigerators	(8619751)	—	—	86	70%	596	50%	1,010	30%
Of Bourdon Tube Type	(8619712)	—	—	—	—	86	60%	62	60%
Instruments for Analysis	86198	1,493	15%	5,736	20%	2,827	20%	2,000	20%
Parts & Accessories, n.e.s.	86199	1,607	15%	5,527	20%	5,749	20%	4,790	20%
Sub-Total		(24,105)	(19%)	(105,165)	(55%)	(75,639)	(55%)	(43,406)	(52%)
41.									
Cinematographic Film	863096	2,081	500w/m	8,835	600w/m	3,247	715w/m	3,197	720w/m
42.									
Iron & Steel Scrap	282	41,689	5%	206,304	5%	246,134	5%	17,152	F
Waste & Scrap of Paper	2511	4,251	10%	8,734	10%	34,899	10%	22,278	10%
Old Clothing & Waste	26701	11,660	80%	8,879	50%	5,641	30%	512	30%
Sub-Total		(57,600)	(21%)	(223,917)	(7%)	(286,494)	(6%)	(39,942)	(6%)
Agriculture, Fishery & Forestry		718,167	13%	2,207,280	15%	2,147,744	13%	1,269,875	3%
Mining		129,191	2%	778,144	6%	1,464,663	5%	1,443,762	F
Manufacturing		1,593,253	20%	5,284,317	34%	5,315,531	26%	2,836,181	23%
All Commodities (A)		2,440,611	17%	8,269,741	26%	8,927,938	20%	5,549,818	12%
Total Commodity Imports (B)		3,141,414		10,192,384		11,086,158		7,264,166	
A/B		77.7%		81.1%		80.5%		76.4%	

350

Table B.17. Number of Items Subject to Import Control: 1967 (2/2) – 1976 (2/2)

Based on 1,312 Basic (5-digit) SITC Items

	1967 (2/2)						1968 (1/2)						1968 (2/2)					
	X	Q	R	L	V	T	X	Q	R	L	V	T	X	Q	R	L	V	T
Total	104	110	163	6	174	557	78	158	52	1	259	548	76	66	34	3	376	555
Agriculture	2		1		33	36	2		7		25	34	2		1		33	36
Forestry					6	6					8	8					8	8
Fishery					1	1					1	1					4	4
Mining	2		1			3	1					3	1	1				3
Manufacturing	100	110	161	6	134	511	75	157	45	0	225	502	73	65	32	3	331	504
Food Products	6	2	4		44	56	7	4	1		45	57	7		1		59	66
Yarns & Fabrics	40	6	6		1	53	19	23	3		2	47	19	1	2		30	51
Textile Products	21	16	7		2	46	20	15	1		5	41	20		1		25	46
Wood & Products	1	2			8	11	1	2			8	11	1	2			7	8
Furniture	2	4			3	9	2	4			5	11	2	1			5	8
Paper & Products	5	10	5		3	23	5	8	2		7	22	5	6	1		9	21
Printing & Publishing		2	1		3	6	1	2			6	9	1	1			4	6
Leather & Products	2	11	1		1	15	2	11	1		2	16	2		1			3
Rubber Products	4	6	1		1	12	4	7			1	12	4	7				11
Chemical Products	6	4	12	5	36	63	2	15	8		35	60	2	9	5	3	44	63
Fertilizer				1		1					3	3					3	3
Petroleum Products					4	4		2			3	5		2	1		2	5
Non-Metallic Products	9	6			2	7		3	3		3	9		4	3		2	9
Basic Metal	2	18	1		4	25	1	7	7		12	27	1	7	4		10	22
Metal Products	2	12	19		7	40	4	18	3		17	42	10	1			26	37
Machinery			11		2	13		3	1		11	15	3	2			12	17
Electrical Machinery	2		20		1	23		7	1		15	23	4	2			21	27
Transportation Equip.			8		4	12		1	2	1	13	17					20	20
Railway Equipment																	1	1
Misc. Manufactures	8				8	76	7	21	10		31	69	8	9	9		50	76
Plastic Products	1	4	1			6		4	1		1	6	1	2			1	4

Table B.17. (*Continued*)

	1969 (1/2)						1969 (2/2)						1970 (1/2)					
	X	Q	R	L	V	T	X	Q	R	L	V	T	X	Q	R	L	V	T
Total	77	58	56	0	386	577	77	68	53	0	395	593	78	64	78	21	371	612
Agriculture	2				32	34	2				31	33			6		32	38
Forestry			1		10	10					10	10				1	7	8
Fishery				1	3	4					4	4				1	4	5
Mining	1	1				3			1	3		5	1	1			8	11
Manufacturing	74	57	54		341	526	74	67	50	0	350	541	77	63	71	19	320	550
Food Products	7	2			58	67	7	2			58	67	7		4	1	56	68
Yarns & Fabrics	18	4			29	51	18	2	3		26	49	19	2	6		24	51
Textile Products	20	1			23	44	20	1			21	42	19	1	2		20	42
Wood & Products	1				8	9	1				8	9	1				8	9
Furniture	2	1			6	9	2	1			6	9	2	1			5	8
Paper & Products	5	6	2		8	21	5	6	2		7	20	5	6	2		8	21
Printing & Publishing	1	1			7	9	1	1			8	9	1				8	9
Leather & Products	2				12	14	2	9			12	23	2	9			3	14
Rubber Products	4	7				11	4	6				11		6			1	3
Chemical Products	2	7	6		46	61	2	8	5		50	65	2	6	11		49	68
Fertilizer					3	3					2	3						3
Petroleum Products	1	1			4	6	2	2			2	4	2	2	3	1	2	4
Non-Metallic Products		4	3		2	9		2	3		5	10		3	3	2	4	11
Basic Metal	1	6	11		9	27	1	6	11		10	28	2	6	12	2	10	32
Metal Products	2	11	1		26	40	2	13	2		26	43	2	11	4	2	33	40
Machinery		3	3		13	19		3	5		15	20		3	7	2	13	25
Electrical Machinery		2	5		19	26		2	4		20	26		2	3	2	19	26
Transportation Equip.					20	20					20	20					21	22
Railway Equipment						1					1	1			1			1
Misc. Manufactures	8	6	14		46	74	8	6	13		48	75	8	5	15	10	42	80
Plastic Products	1	2			2	5	1				3	4	1			1	4	6

352

Table B.17. (Continued)

	1970 (2/2)						1971 (1/2)						1971 (2/2)					
	X	Q	R	L	V	T	X	Q	R	L	V	T	X	Q	R	L	V	T
Total	72	65	82	20	357	596	69	42	60	26	370	567	70	44	62	30	370	576
Agriculture			6		32	38			6		31	37			6		32	38
Forestry				1	7	8				1	7	8				1	7	8
Fishery		1		1	4	5				1	2	3					2	3
Mining	1	1	1		8	11	1	1			10	11	1		1		10	11
Manufacturing	71	64	75	18	306	534	69	41	54	24	320	508	70	43	56	28	319	516
Food Products	7		4		56	67	6		4	1	57	68	6		5		56	67
Yarns & Fabrics	18	2	6		25	51	16	2	5		27	50	16	2	4		28	50
Textile Products	19	2	3		17	41	19	1	1		22	43	19	1	1		22	43
Wood & Products	1				8	9	1				7	8	1				7	9
Furniture	2	1			5	8	2				5	7	2				5	7
Paper & Products	5	6	2		8	21	5	5			8	18	5	5			7	17
Printing & Publishing	1				8	9	1		1		7	8	1		1		7	9
Leather & Products	2	9			3	14	9		1		4	15	3	9	1		3	16
Rubber Products	4	6			1	11	4				7	7	3	3				6
Chemical Products	2	6	11		48	67	6		9		51	69	3	6	9		55	73
Petroleum Products	2				2	4	2				3	5	2				3	5
Non-Metallic Products	3	3	1		4	11	3		1	1	7	11	3		1	1	7	11
Basic Metal	2	6	14	2	9	33		14		6	9	29		12		6	11	29
Metal Products	11	4			22	37	2	3	4	6	12	27	2	5	4	5	16	32
Machinery	3	7	2		10	22	2	2	6	1	14	23	2	2	5	1	14	22
Electrical Machinery	2	3	2		19	26	2	2	1	2	21	26	2	2	1	2	21	26
Transportation Equip.	2				16	18	2	1	2	1	14	17	1		2	1	14	17
Railway Equipment	1					1	1					1						1
Misc. Manufactures	7	5	15	11	40	78	8	2	5	5	51	72	8	3	8	11	51	81
Plastic Products	1		3			4	1		1		2	4	1		1	1	2	5

Table B.17. (Continued)

	1972 (1/2)						1972 (2/2)						1973 (1/2)					
	X	Q	R	L	V	T	X	Q	R	L	V	T	X	Q	R	L	V	T
Total	67	31	109	53	372	632	69	29	112	49	388	647	66	25	135	22	383	631
Agriculture				6	38	44				6	39	45			5		37	42
Forestry				1	7	8				1	7	8			2		7	9
Fishery				1	2	3				1	2	3				1	2	3
Mining		1	2	2	3	8		1	3	1	2	7			2		3	6
Manufacturing	67	30	107	43	322	569	69	28	109	41	337	584	66	24	126	21	334	571
Food Products	6		3	3	60	72	6		2	3	60	71	6		3	2	66	77
Yarns & Fabrics	16	2	3	1	31	53	16	2	3	1	31	53	14	2	5		29	50
Textile Products	19		3		21	43	19		3		22	44	18		3		22	43
Wood & Products	1		1		7	9	1		1		7	9	1		1		7	9
Furniture	1				5	6	2				6	8	2				5	7
Paper & Products	6	2	1		13	22	5	2	1		12	20	5		3		11	19
Printing & Publishing	1				4	6			1		4	6	1		1		4	6
Leather & Products	2	9			2	13	2	9			2	13	1	9		1	1	12
Rubber Products	4	3			2	9	4	2			2	8	4	2			2	8
Chemical Products	2	5	18	1	50	76	2	5	18	1	51	77	2	4	24	1	46	77
Petroleum Products	2		4		3	9				1	3	4				1	4	5
Non-Metallic Products	4			1	9	14			5	1	10	16			5	1	10	16
Basic Metal			17	6	12	35			17	6	15	38			22		13	35
Metal Products	2	5	8	5	20	40	2	5	8	5	19	39	2	5	12		19	38
Machinery		1	23	3	7	34		1	23	3	7	34		1	19		9	29
Electrical Machinery			6	16	6	28			6	14	8	28			5	14	6	25
Transportation Equip.			2	1	15	18			2		16	18			4		10	14
Railway Equipment					1	1					1	1			1			1
Misc. Manufactures	6	1	11	5	52	75	8	1	17	5	59	90	8	1	16	2	66	93
Plastic Products	1		1	1	2	5	1		1	2	3	7	1		2	1	3	7

353

354

Table B.17.——(Continued)

	1973 (2/2)						1974 (1/2)						1974 (2/2)					
	X	Q	R	L	V	T	X	Q	R	L	V	T	X	Q	R	L	V	T
Total	70	25	138	21	379	633	69	24	161	18	376	648	68	24	162	21	383	658
Agriculture			5		37	42			8		35	43			8		35	43
Forestry			2		7	9			2	1	7	9			2	1	7	9
Fishery				1	2	3				1	2	3					2	3
Mining		1	3		2	6			2		3	5			2		8	10
Manufacturing	70	24	128	20	331	573	69	24	149	17	329	588	68	24	150	20	331	593
Food Products	6		3	2	66	77		5	5		67	78	5		5		67	77
Yarns & Fabrics	16	2	5		29	52		1	4		28	50	16		4		28	50
Textile Products	19		3		21	43	2		4		22	45	18	2	3		23	44
Wood & Products	1		1		7	9			2		6	9	1		2		6	9
Furniture	2				5	7			2		5	7	2				5	7
Paper & Products	5		3		11	19	6		10		16	32	6		10		16	32
Printing & Publishing	1		1		4	6				1		1				1		
Leather & Products	4	9	1		3	7	3	9	1		3	16	3	9	1		3	16
Rubber Products	3	2			1	6	3	2			1	6	3	2			1	6
Chemical Products	2	4	25		45	76	2	4	29		40	75	2	4	29	1	38	74
Petroleum Products					5	5					4	4					4	4
Non-Metallic Products			5	1	10	16			4	1	11	16			5	1	10	16
Basic Metal			20		12	32			20		9	29			20		10	30
Metal Products	2	5	10		21	38	2	5	11		18	36	3	5	11	2	18	37
Machinery		1	25		11	37		1	24	1	8	34		1	27		9	39
Electrical Machinery			7	14	7	28			11	12	6	29			9	12	8	29
Transportation Equip.			5		9	14			9		10	19			10		10	20
Railway Equipment			1			1			1		1	1						1
Misc. Manufactures	8	1	11	2	61	83	1	1	12	2	72	95	8	1	12	2	72	95
Plastic Products	1	2	2	1	3	7			2	1	3	7	1		2	1	3	7

Table B.17. (Continued)

	1975 (1/2)						1975 (2/2)						1976 (1/2)				
	X	Q	R	L	V	T	X	Q	R	L	V	T	X	Q	L	V	T
Total	68	24	164	26	354	636	69	21	184	20	369	663	61	221	19	402	703
Agriculture			11		29	40			9		38	47		9		35	44
Forestry			1		7	8				4	4	8		1		11	12
Fishery			2		1	3			1		2	3		1		3	4
Mining			5		9	14			10		10	20			1	9	17
Manufacturing	68	24	147	25	307	571	69	21	165	19	315	589	61	203	18	344	626
Food Products		5	1	52	6	64	6		5		69	80	8	6		66	80
Yarns & Fabrics	18	2	4	23	13	47	4		4	28		49	7	6		30	43
Textile Products	18		5	16	22	39	5		5	16		43	22	3		23	48
Wood & Products	1		1	7	1	9	1		2		5	8	3	2		5	10
Furniture	2			6		8	2		2		5	7	1			4	5
Paper & Products	4		13	10		27	6		14		7	27	4	14		8	26
Printing & Publishing	1			5		6	1				5	6	1			2	3
Leather & Products	2	9		2		13	2	6	2		2	10	2	8		2	12
Rubber Products	4	2		1		7	4	2	2		2	8	3	2		2	7
Chemical Products	1	4	34	1	33	73	1	2	30	1	39	73	1	41	1	33	76
Coal Products														1			1
Petroleum Products					4	4					4	4				10	10
Non-Metallic Products		5		11		16			6		12	18	8	8		13	21
Basic Metal		15		12		27			22		9	31		22		31	53
Metal Products	3	5	8	18		34	2	5	11		15	33	2	17		21	40
Machinery		1	28	13		48	1		36	5	6	48		36	3	5	44
Electrical Machinery			7	14	8	29			4	12	11	27		10	13	7	30
Transportation Equip.			6		13	19			8		12	20		7		12	19
Railway Equipment			1			1			1			1		1			1
Misc. Manufactures	7	1	13		70	93			15		61	85	8	16	1	68	93
Plastic Products	1	2		3		7	1		2	1	7	11	1	1		2	4

355

Table B.17. (Continued)

	1976 (2/2)					1976 (2/2)			
	X	R	L	V	T		X	R	L	V	T
Total	60	164	18	450	692	Chemical Products	1	48	1	32	82
Agriculture		8		35	43	Coal Products		1			1
Forestry		1		11	12	Petroleum Products				10	10
Fishery			1	3	4	Non-Metallic Products		7		14	21
Mining		7		10	17	Basic Metal		22		31	53
Manufacturing	60	148	17	391	616	Metal Products	2	6		31	39
Food Products	6	10		64	80	Machinery		2	2	32	36
Yarns & Fabrics	6	6		30	42	Electrical Machinery		1	12	14	27
Textile Products	22	3		23	48	Transportation Equip.		3	1	17	21
Wood & Products	3	2		5	10	Railway Equipment				1	1
Furniture	1			4	5	Misc. Manufactures	8	12	1	67	88
Paper & Products	4	14		8	26	Plastic Products	1	1		2	4
Printing & Publishing	1			2	3						
Leather & Products	2	8		2	12						
Rubber Products	3	2		2	7						

Source: Korean Traders Association, *Trade Yearbook*.
Notes: X; Imports Prohibited. V; Other Restricted Items. L; Link Import Items.
Q; Quota Item. R; MCI Recommendation Required. T; Total Number of Items.

Table B.18. Wastage Allowances on Imported Raw Materials for Exports

In Thousand Dollars or Percent

Raw Materials for Exports	Imports in 1971	Final Export Product	Wastage Allowances					
			1966–70	1971	1972	1973	1974	1975
Textile Material	91,307							
Raw Cotton		Cotton Fabrics	—	15%	15%	15%	14%	14%
Raw Cotton (Combed)	43,154	Cotton Sewing Thread	—	35%	35%	35%	35%	29%
Raw Cotton		Polyestel/Cotton Yarn	—	—	12%	12%	12%	12%
Cotton Fabrics	3,965	Underclothes	—	13%	13%	13%	13%	13%
Raw Silk	1,375	Silk Woven Fabrics	—	—	30%	30%	30%	30%
Greasy Wool	1,090	Wool Top Dyed	—	13%	13%	13%	13%	13%
Greasy Wool		Worsted Yarn	24%	24%	24%	24%	24%	24%
Woolen Fabrics	1,821	Wool Shirts	—	12%	12%	10%	10%	10%
Viscos Rayon Yarn	2,627	Viscos Fabrics	12%	12%	12%	10%	10%	10%
Acetate Staple Fiber		Spun Rayon Yarn	—	6%	6%	6%	6%	6%
Acetate Flakes	2,315	Acetate F Yarn	—	16%	15%	15%	15%	15%
Acrylic Fiber		Sweater	20%[1]	19%	19%	19%	19%	19%
Nylon F Yarn		Nylon Net	—	—	11%	11%	11%	11%
Nylon Strech Yarn	19,679	Nylon Socks	20%[2]	18%	14%	14%	14%	14%
Nylon F Yarn		Nylon Fabrics	—	—	12%	12%	10%	10%
Other Synthetic Yarn		Tricot Fabrics	15%[3]	14%	14%	14%	14%	14%
Other Synthetic Yarn	2,311	Raschel Lace Fabrics	16%	15%	15%	15%	15%	15%
Other Synthetic Yarn		Carpet	—	—	22%	22%	22%	22%
Polyester Fabrics	1,429	Men's & Sports Wear	—	13%	12%	12%	12%	11%
Polyester Chip		Polyestel Fiber	—	—	18%	18%	18%	15%
Caprolactam	3,452	Nylon F Yarn	31%	31%	28%	27%	25%	21%

Table B.18. (Continued)

Raw Materials for Exports	Imports in 1971	Final Export Product	Wastage Allowances (In Thousand Dollars or Percent)					
			1966–70	1971	1972	1973	1974	1975
Acrylonitrile ⎤	3,252	Exlan & Cashmilon	—	—	26%	26%	17%	17%
Acrylonitrile ⎦		Acrylic Fibre	—	29%	29%	29%	29%	29%
Polyester Yarn	4,837	Polyester Fabrics	—	—	13%	13%	13%	13%
Synthetic Resin	2,352							
P.V.C. Resin		Vinyl Leather	12%	11%	9%	9%	8%	8%
P.V.C. Resin		P.V.C. Pipe			6%	6%	6%	6%
P.V.C. Resin	494	Vinyl Sheet		11%	8%	8%	8%	8%
P.V.C. Resin		Footwear			11%	11%	11%	11%
P.V.C. Resin		P.V.C. Hose			5%	5%	5%	5%
Polyethylene Resin ⎤	1,858	Synthetic Products (Tools)		5%	4%	4%	4%	4%
Polyethylene Resin ⎦		Polyethylene Tube			3%	3%	3%	3%
Paper	4,488							
Kraft Paper	268	Cement	40%	37%	37%	37%	37%	37%
Paper Board	3,272	Individual Box	—	—	18%	18%	18%	18%
Paper Pulp	948	Printing Paper	—	—	19%	19%	19%	19%
Leather	1,979							
Leather ⎤		Shoes	—	—	10%	10%	10%	10%
Leather ⎦	1,979	Base Ball Glove	—	—	10%	10%	10%	10%
Synthetic Leather		Bag	—	—	—	14%	14%	14%
Vinyl Leather		Clothes	—	12%	12%	10%	10%	10%

Rubber									
	5,020								
Natural & Synthetic Rubber		Automobile Tire	—	12%	—	9%	9%	8%	
Natural & Synthetic Rubber		Automobile Tube	—	10%	10%	10%	10%	10%	
Natural & Synthetic Rubber		Bicycle Tire	16%	12%	9%	9%	9%	8%	
Natural & Synthetic Rubber		Shoes	—	9%	9%	9%	8%	8%	
Natural Rubber	5,020	Rubber Hose & Conveyer Belt	—	6%	6%	6%	6%	6%	
Natural Rubber		Rubber Floats	—	—	12%	12%	12%	12%	
Natural Rubber		Rubber Packing	—	17%	17%	17%	17%	17%	
Natural Rubber		Rubber Board	—	11%	11%	11%	11%	11%	
Steel Products									
	28,483								
Steel Scrap		Steel Ingot	12%	12%	12%	12%	12%	12%	
Steel Scrap		Angle Bar	21%[4]	20%	20%	20%	20%	18%	
Steel Scrap		Billet & Sheet Bar	17%	17%	17%	17%	17%	14%	
Steel Scrap		Wire Rod	22%	22%	22%	22%	22%	19%	
Steel Ingot	317	Billet & Sheet Bar	7%	7%	7%	7%	7%	4%	
Steel Ingot		Wire Rod & Steel Bar	10%	10%	10%	10%	10%	7%	
Billets & Slabs	2,358	Angle Bar	5%	5%	5%	5%	5%	4%	
Coil for Re-rolling of Steel		Steel Pipe	—	—	7%	7%	7%	7%	
Coil for Re-rolling of Steel		Steel Plate	—	—	6%	6%	6%	6%	
Coil for Re-rolling of Steel	25,516	Cold Rolled Steel Sheet (1.6mm)	—	14%	13%	13%	13%	13%	
Coil for Re-rolling of Steel		Cold Rolled Steel Sheet in Coil	—	—	11%	11%	11%	11%	
Coil for Re-rolling of Steel		Hot Rolled Steel Sheet in Coil	—	4%	4%	4%	4%	4%	
Coil for Re-rolling of Steel		Galvanized Steel Scaffolding	—	—	—	—	10%	10%	
Steel Wire Rod	292	Galvanized Wire Rope	—	6%	6%	6%	6%	6%	
Mild Steel Wire Rod		Common Nails or Box Nails	—	—	—	10%	10%	10%	

359

Table B.18. (Continued)

In Thousand Dollars or Percent

Raw Materials for Exports	Imports in 1971	Final Export Product	Wastage Allowances					
			1966–70	1971	1972	1973	1974	1975
Logs	110,773							
Veneer Logs		Plywood (1/8" AA AB)	48%	48%	48%	48%	48%	48%
Veneer Logs	110,773	Plywood (BB Printing Grade)	48%	44%	44%	44%	44%	44%
Veneer Logs		Plywood (CC Printing Grade)	48%	50%	50%	50%	50%	50%
Human Hair	2,722							
Human Hair	2,722	Wigs	48%	47%	47%	47%	47%	47%
Nylon & Yarn		Wigs	31%	31%	31%	31%	31%	31%
Modacrylic Tow		Artificial Eyebrows	—	9%	9%	9%	9%	9%
Sub-Total	247,124	(Total Raw Material Imports for Exports in 1971: 506,301)						

Source: Korea Trade Service Center, *Bulletin of Raw Material Requirements in Export Production*, and the Ministry of General Affairs, *Official Gazette*.

Notes: [1] 19 percent since 1968.
[2] 18 percent since 1969.
[3] 14 percent since 1968.
[4] 20 percent since 1969.

Table B.19. Composition of Value Added in Manufacturing: 1962–76

In percent (%)

	Wages & Salaries	Interest & Rent	Net Profit	(Direct Tax)	Public Imports[1]	Sub-Total	Depreciation	Bad Debt	Total
1962	41.9 (46%)	13.3 (14%)	28.6 (31%)	(—)	8.0 (9%)	91.8 (100%)	8.1	—	100.0%
1963	39.6 (45%)	10.4 (12%)	31.6 (36%)	(—)	6.9 (8%)	88.5 (100%)	11.4	—	100.0%
1964	35.8 (43%)	14.9 (18%)	26.5 (32%)	(—)	6.7 (8%)	83.9 (100%)	16.1	—	100.0%
1965	37.9 (44%)	14.2 (17%)	29.3 (34%)	(—)	4.2 (5%)	85.6 (100%)	14.0	0.5	100.0%
1966	35.9 (41%)	19.9 (23%)	27.3 (31%)	(—)	4.5 (5%)	87.6 (100%)	11.8	0.5	100.0%
1967	38.8 (44%)	19.3 (22%)	25.9 (29%)	(8.3) (9%)	5.1 (6%)	89.1 (100%)	10.4	0.5	100.0%
1968	36.0 (43%)	20.8 (25%)	23.0 (27%)	(6.6) (8%)	4.6 (5%)	84.4 (100%)	15.0	0.5	100.0%
1969	38.6 (45%)	24.5 (29%)	15.6 (18%)	(5.1) (6%)	6.4 (8%)	85.1 (100%)	14.3	0.6	100.0%
1970	39.9 (47%)	27.8 (33%)	11.9 (14%)	(3.8) (4%)	5.6 (7%)	85.2 (100%)	14.2	0.5	100.0%
1971	41.2 (49%)	32.2 (38%)	4.6 (5%)	(1.6) (2%)	5.7 (7%)	83.7 (100%)	15.8	0.5	100.0%
1972	38.1 (47%)	22.8 (28%)	15.5 (19%)	(3.9) (5%)	4.8 (6%)	81.2 (100%)	18.1	0.7	100.0%
1973	32.8 (42%)	13.9 (18%)	28.1 (36%)	(7.9) (10%)	4.1 (5%)	78.9 (100%)	20.5	0.6	100.0%
1974	37.7 (47%)	16.4 (20%)	22.0 (27%)	(5.4) (7%)	4.7 (6%)	80.8 (100%)	18.5	0.7	100.0%
1975	41.2 (50%)	18.7 (23%)	15.6 (19%)	(3.8) (5%)	6.8 (8%)	82.3 (100%)	16.8	0.8	100.0%
1976	42.5 (51%)	18.2 (22%)	17.5 (21%)	(5.8) (7%)	6.3 (8%)	84.5 (100%)	15.0	0.6	100.0%
Annual Averages									
1962–66	38.2 (44%)	14.5 (17%)	28.7 (33%)	(—) (—)	6.1 (7%)	87.5 (100%)	12.3	0.5	100.0%
1967–71	38.9 (46%)	24.9 (29%)	16.2 (19%)	(5.1) (6%)	5.5 (7%)	85.5 (100%)	13.9	0.5	100.0%
1972–76	38.5 (47%)	18.0 (22%)	19.7 (24%)	(5.4) (7%)	5.3 (6%)	81.7 (100%)	17.8	0.7	100.0%

Source: The Bank of Korea, *Financial Statements Analysis* (various issues).
Note: [1] Public imposts represent various taxes related with business operation, such as business tax, wealth tax and automobile tax, and public imposts but exclude corporation tax.

Table B.20. Labor Share in Value Added: Manufacturing (Mining & Manufacturing Census Data)

In Million Won or Persons

	Employee Remuneration (A)	Average No. of Employee (B)	Average Wage Rate (C = A/B)	Unpaid Workers (D)	Total Imputed Wages (E = A+CD)	Gross Value Added (I)[1] (F)	Net Value Added (II)[2] (G)	Labor Share Gross(I) (E/F)	Labor Share Net(II) (E/G)
1960	6,765	247,572	0.0273	25,682	7,466	21,866	18,586	34%	40%
1963	16,148	381,649	0.0423	20,332	17,008	61,534	52,304	28%	33%
1966	37,821	540,951	0.0699	25,714	39,618	156,174	132,748	25%	30%
1967	53,423	620,753	0.0861	28,058	55,839	207,220	176,137	27%	32%
1968	77,053	721,685	0.1068	26,622	79,896	301,433	256,218	27%	31%
1969	106,786	800,674	0.1334	28,255	110,555	426,030	362,126	26%	31%
1970	137,798	833,246	0.1654	27,795	142,395	549,793	467,324	26%	31%
1971	161,545	819,673	0.1971	27,021	166,871	690,535	586,955	24%	28%
1972	211,453	946,538	0.2234	25,281	217,101	899,408	764,497	24%	28%
1973	310,588	1,126,413	0.2757	26,061	317,773	1,380,014	1,173,012	23%	27%
1974	451,270	1,298,384	0.3476	22,223	458,995	1,867,177	1,587,101	25%	29%
1975	651,615	1,396,105	0.4667	24,039	662,834	2,828,149	2,403,927	23%	28%
1976	1,009,092	1,691,047	0.5967	26,261	1,024,762	4,075,056	3,463,798	25%	30%

Source: Economic Planning Board (and Korea Development Bank), *Report on Mining and Manufacturing Survey or Census* (various issues).

Notes: [1] M & M Survey (or Census) covers manufacturing establishments operating with five or more workers only. Value added includes allowance for the depreciation of fixed capital stock.

[2] According to the BOK's *Financial Statement Analysis*, the depreciation allowance amounted to about 15 percent of value added (inclusive of depreciation) in manufacturing on the average during 1967–73. Value added figures in M & M Census were reduced by 15 percent in order to approximate the value added exclusive of the depreciation allowance.

Table B.21. Employment and Capital Formation in Manufacturing (Mining & Manufacturing Census Data)[1]

	Number of Employees (Year End)		Unpaid Workers	Average Number of Employees	Average Number of Workers	Employee Remuneration (million won)	Gross Output (million won)
	Total	Female					
1955	—	—	—	—	221,200	—	—
1958	—	—	—	—	260,427	5,765	—
1960	249,572	92,175	25,682	238,723	264,405	6,765	59,735
1961	—	—	—	—	326,528	—	69,319
1962	—	—	—	—	361,275	—	108,320
1963	381,649	144,788	20,332	360,726	381,058	16,148	166,858
1964	—	—	—	—	372,748	—	195,133
1965	—	—	—	—	460,525	—	297,284
1966	540,951	203,522	25,714	543,045	568,759	37,821	417,370
1967	738,515	—	28,058	620,753	648,811	53,423	550,989
1968	711,551	—	26,622	721,685	748,307	77,058	769,077
1969	812,720	—	28,255	800,674	828,929	106,792	1,047,658
1970	786,532	—	27,795	833,246	861,041	137,798	1,334,515
1971	818,715	—	27,021	819,673	846,694	161,545	1,672,740
1972	989,519	451,854	25,281	946,538	971,819	211,453	2,241,608
1973	1,188,728	554,955	26,061	1,126,413	1,152,474	310,588	3,695,328
1974	1,242,481	575,629	22,223	1,298,384	1,320,607	451,270	5,706,216
1975	1,478,815	701,731	24,039	1,396,105	1,420,144	651,615	8,169,953
1976	1,462,365	834,940	26,261	1,691,047	1,717,308	1,009,092	11,677,230

Table B.21. (Continued)

	Gross Investment		Depreciation		Net Investment		Total Fixed Capital		Total Fixed Capital (1968 Basis)	
	(million won)	(million 1970 $)[2]	(million won)	(million 1970 $)[2]	(million won)	(million 1970 $)[2]	(million won)	(million 1970 $)[2]	gross[3]	net[4]
1960	2,647	33	—	—	—	—	24,132	304	—	—
1963	11,167	85	—	—	—	—	—	—	—	—
1966	19,984	81	85	85	—	−4	136,106	553	1,467	980
1967	44,564	167	85	85		82			1,634	1,062
1968	64,903	235	92	92		143	332,789	1,205	1,869	1,205
1969	117,241	417	104	104		313			2,286	1,518
1970	99,403	320	131	131		189			2,606	1,707
1971	132,120	391	148	148		243			2,997	1,950
1972	179,153	479	169	169		310			3,476	2,260
1973	486,933	1,103	196	196		907	1,504,055	3,408	4,579	3,167
1974	506,514	813	274	274		539			5,392	3,706
1975	746,712	1,045	321	321		724			6,437	4,430
1976	1,051,183	1,484	384	384		1,100			7,921	5,530

Source: Economic Planning Board (& Korea Development Bank), *Report on Mining and Manufacturing Census* in 1960, 1963, 1966, 1968, and 1973, *Report on Mining and Manufacturing Survey* in 1967, 1969, 1970, 1971, 1972, 1974, 1975 and 1976, and *Report on Sample Survey for Mining and Manufacturing Establishments* in 1961, 1962, 1964, and 1965.

Notes: [1] The census or survey data cover all manufacturing establishments with more than five workers. The report on sample survey covers all (medium &) large establishments and stratified samples of small establishments.
[2] Implicit price deflator (1970=100) for gross domestic fixed capital formation (in manufacturing) and the exchange rate of 310.6 won per dollar were used to get 1970 dollar figures.
[3] The total net fixed capital stock in 1968 was converted into gross stock value by applying Han's gross-to-net conversion rate.
[4] The 1968 rate of depreciation for fixed capital stock in manufacturing was applied to other years.

Table B.22. Composition of Sectoral Value Added: 1970 & 1973 (Based on Imputed Wage Payments)

In Billion Won & Percent

	Primary Sectors	Manu-facturing	SOC Sectors	Service Sectors
1970				
1. Compensation of Employees	337.8 (47%) (48%)	220.8 (39%) (42%)	97.9 (42%) (51%)	876.0 (80%) (82%)
2. Other Value Added	365.5 (51%) (52%)	188.5 (33%) (36%)	68.1 (29%) (35%)	142.4 (13%) (13%)
3. Indirect Taxes less Subsidy	3.7 (1%) (1%)	120.7 (21%) (23%)	26.7 (11%) (14%)	44.8 (4%) (4%)
Net Value Added (1 + 2 + 3)	707.0 —(100%)	530.0 —(100%)	192.8 —(100%)	1,063.2 —(100%)
4. Consumption of Fixed Capital	15.9 (2%) —	42.6 (7%) —	42.8 (18%) —	29.6 (3%) —
Gross Value Added	722.9(100%) —	572.6(100%) —	235.6(100%) —	1,092.9(100%) —
Total Output	993.9 —	1,785.5 —	367.3 —	1,616.8 —
1973				
1. Compensation of Employees	533.0 (43%) (44%)	446.8 (35%) (40%)	167.0 (40%) (49%)	1,515.9 (75%) (78%)
2. Other Value Added	658.1 (53%) (55%)	482.9 (38%) (44%)	127.1 (37%) (37%)	363.7 (18%) (19%)
3. Indirect Taxes less Subsidy	8.1 (1%) (1%)	175.6 (14%) (16%)	45.4 (11%) (13%)	71.4 (4%) (4%)
Net Value Added (1 + 2 + 3)	1,199.1 —(100%)	1,105.3 —(100%)	339.5 —(100%)	1,951.0 —(100%)
4. Consumption of Fixed Capital	39.9 (3%) —	172.8 (14%) —	78.5 (19%) —	73.8 (4%) —
Gross Value Added	1,239.0(100%) —	1,278.1(100%) —	418.0(100%) —	2,024.8(100%) —
Total Output	1,703.8 —	4,296.6 —	753.7 —	2,915.9 —

Source: The Bank of Korea, Report on 1970 Input-Output Table, Report on 1973 Input-Output Table, Tables on Employment for 1970 and Tables on Employment for 1973, and Ministry of Agriculture & Fisheries, Report on the Results of Farm Household Economy Survey (various issues).

Table B.23. Balance of Private Foreign Borrowing: 1959–76

In Thousand U.S. Dollars

Arrival Basis	1959	1960	1961	1962	1963	1964	1965	1966	1967
2. Other Agriculture	—	—	—	—	—	—	—	—	—
4. Fishery	—	—	—	—	−28	3,428	13,553	35,341	37,410
6. Other Minerals	—	—	—	—	—	—	—	—	1,500
7. Processed Foods	—	—	—	—	—	—	—	—	250
8. Beverages	—	—	—	—	—	—	—	296	540
10. Textile Fibres	—	—	—	—	2,100	6,912	8,596	22,415	52,561
11. Textile Fabrics	—	—	—	−53	383	5,867	9,533	9,421	8,592
12. Textile Products	—	—	—	—	—	—	—	—	—
13. Lumber & Plywood	—	—	—	—	—	—	—	375	2,156
15. Paper & Products	—	—	—	121	233	635	454	273	3,260
16. Printing & Publishing	—	—	—	—	—	—	—	—	—
18. Rubber Products	—	—	—	—	—	—	—	—	200
19. Basic Chemicals	—	—	—	—	—	—	—	3,600	11,220
20. Other Chemicals	—	—	—	—	—	—	—	40,045	49,228
21. Chemical Fertilizer	—	—	—	—	—	—	—	—	—
22. Petroleum Products	—	—	—	—	6,000	7,021	9,036	16,702	20,159
24. Nonmetallic Mineral	2,130	1,993	1,728	1,449	10,042	9,946	9,482	14,333	32,597
25. Iron & Steel	—	—	—	—	—	—	—	—	14,311
26. Steel Products	—	—	—	—	—	—	—	3,629	7,732
27. Nonferrous Metals	—	—	—	—	—	—	—	—	—

28. Metal Products	—	—	—	—	—	—	—	124	404
29. Machinery	—	—	—	—	—	—	—	44	1,260
30. Electrical Machinery	—	—	—	1,063	900	4,525	5,987	2,586	5,975
31. Transport Equipments	—	—	—	—	—	304	—	—	3,202
32. Misc. Manufacturing	—	—	—	—	—	—	—	—	1,208
33. Building & Maintenance	—	—	—	—	—	—	—	—	—
34. Other Construction	—	—	—	—	—	—	—	—	—
35. Electricity	—	—	—	—	—	—	—	2,100	8,203
36. Banking & Dwelling	—	—	—	—	—	—	—	—	410
37. Water & Sanitary Service	—	—	—	—	—	—	—	—	—
39. Transportation	—	—	—	—	1,327	997	—	661	23,031
41. Other Services	—	—	—	—	—	—	3,800	3,800	3,325
43. Unclassifiable	—	—	—	—	—	—	—	—	—
1–6. Primary Sectors	2,130	—	—	—	−28	3,428	13,553	35,341	38,910
7–32. Manufacturing	—	1,993	1,728	1,517	19,821	31,281	41,930	119,830	214,855
35, 37, 39. SOC Sectors	—	—	—	—	1,327	997	—	2,761	31,234
33, 34, 36, 41. Service Sectors	—	—	—	—	—	—	3,800	3,800	3,735
1–43. All Sectors	2,130	1,993	1,728	1,517	19,793	36,036	60,280	161,732	288,734

Table B.23. (Continued)

In Thousand U.S. Dollars

Arrival Basis	1968	1969	1970	1971	1972	1973	1974	1975	1976
2. Other Agriculture	—	—	—	—	989	1,367	1,225	1,715	2,909
4. Fishery	36,102	41,085	33,819	39,282	37,983	33,403	52,153	55,618	62,851
6. Other Minerals	1,500	1,500	1,500	1,500	1,372	3,100	3,000	3,000	2,321
7. Processed Foods	4,938	7,873	16,300	22,260	21,201	22,803	24,781	23,864	26,622
8. Beverages	602	352	152	—	—	—	—	—	—
10. Textile Fibres	74,599	95,703	87,649	79,349	72,497	92,034	191,144	218,256	310,907
11. Textile Fabrics	10,330	15,143	18,215	20,001	17,521	26,194	29,001	65,056	91,629
12. Textile Products	—	—	—	—	—	—	5,614	5,614	6,351
13. Lumber & Plywood	2,020	13,277	16,157	13,396	11,350	8,635	10,483	8,996	5,998
15. Paper & Products	7,856	12,184	13,698	13,108	10,163	9,979	6,931	4,617	19,457
16. Printing & Publishing	—	—	474	905	2,837	1,786	322	109	2
18. Rubber Products	456	1,065	852	639	426	16,004	23,896	23,537	21,683
19. Basic Chemicals	1,038	3,477	17,266	22,279	41,989	47,837	71,363	75,902	85,288
20. Other Chemicals	26,027	35,644	64,960	103,737	131,493	150,591	228,594	241,144	224,631
21. Chemical Fertilizer	47,548	44,773	38,902	33,038	30,684	26,699	54,594	127,074	215,180
22. Petroleum Products	56,562	78,590	136,763	199,015	224,566	213,309	208,608	200,293	182,719
24. Nonmetallic Mineral	61,913	76,069	85,314	109,305	124,916	120,728	102,471	126,457	154,505
25. Iron & Steel	14,295	14,044	19,491	18,705	41,314	40,067	69,620	185,983	227,798
26. Steel Products	14,278	19,872	21,240	59,391	101,091	103,729	100,022	153,044	224,556
27. Nonferrous Metals	3,843	12,653	13,487	13,487	11,801	11,874	11,965	10,579	21,457

Table B.23. (Continued)

In Thousand U.S. Dollars

Arrival Basis	1968	1969	1970	1971	1972	1973	1974	1975	1976
28. Metal Products	348	470	1,391	1,244	1,100	966	828	1,032	949
29. Machinery	2,617	2,525	2,223	2,085	1,774	1,522	1,102	787	14,592
30. Electrical Machinery	6,357	7,781	10,131	14,226	13,107	19,087	24,570	38,411	49,641
31. Transport Equipments	7,690	9,404	22,179	42,108	55,498	120,613	162,641	314,089	349,160
32. Misc. Manufacturing	1,208	1,162	1,070	878	765	461	1,259	1,248	1,175
33. Building & Maintenance	—	2,773	2,551	2,029	1,507	985	463	0	0
34. Other Construction	13,054	17,878	15,663	15,222	19,870	16,411	14,533	14,377	15,366
35. Electricity	43,711	170,969	222,235	248,971	256,202	345,950	369,332	384,996	355,447
36. Banking & Dwelling	789	1,132	863	594	4,525	8,556	8,500	8,500	8,500
37. Water & Sanitary Service	—	—	—	—	5,132	5,132	4,766	5,859	13,023
39. Transportation	74,030	132,672	154,298	158,710	141,493	224,804	238,098	337,931	293,153
41. Other Services	3,424	9,268	20,766	20,727	16,663	12,776	7,731	6,876	29,504
43. Unclassifiable	—	—	—	—	10,618	33,215	96,311	121,868	162,946
1–6. Primary Sectors	37,602	42,585	35,319	40,782	40,344	37,770	56,378	60,333	68,081
7–32. Manufacturing	344,525	452,061	587,914	969,156	916,093	1,034,918	1,329,809	1,826,092	2,234,300
35, 37, 39. SOC Sectors	117,741	303,641	376,533	407,681	402,827	575,886	612,196	728,786	661,623
33, 34, 36, 41. Service Sectors	17,267	31,051	39,843	38,572	42,565	38,728	31,227	29,753	53,370
1–43. All Sectors	517,135	829,338	1,039,609	1,256,191	1,412,447	1,720,517	2,125,921	2,766,932	3,180,320

Table B.24. *Sectoral Interest Rates on Private Foreign Borrowing Weighted by Loan Balance: 1959-76*

In Percent

Arrival Basis	1959	1960	1961	1962	1963	1964	1965	1966	1967
2. Other Agriculture	—	—	—	—	—	—	—	—	—
4. Fishery	—	—	—	—	7.0	5.5	5.7	5.6	5.6
6. Other Minerals	—	—	—	—	—	—	—	—	7.0
7. Processed Foods	—	—	—	—	—	—	—	—	6.2
8. Beverages	—	—	—	—	—	—	—	6.2	6.1
10. Textile Fibres	—	—	—	—	7.5	4.2	4.5	5.2	6.0
11. Textile Fabrics	—	—	—	—	—	5.7	5.9	6.0	6.0
12. Textile Products	—	—	—	—	—	—	—	—	—
13. Lumber & Plywood	—	—	—	—	—	—	—	6.0	6.8
15. Paper & Products	—	—	—	7.0	7.0	7.0	7.0	7.0	6.0
16. Printing & Publishing	—	—	—	—	—	—	—	—	—
18. Rubber Products	—	—	—	—	—	—	—	—	—
19. Basic Chemicals	—	—	—	—	—	—	—	—	6.0
20. Other Chemicals	—	—	—	—	—	—	—	6.0	5.5
21. Chemical Fertilizer	—	—	—	—	—	—	—	5.6	5.6
22. Petroleum Products	—	—	—	—	4.5	4.5	4.5	4.5	4.6
24. Nonmetallic Mineral	5.3	5.3	5.3	5.3	5.9	6.0	5.9	5.7	5.6
25. Iron & Steel	—	—	—	—	—	—	—	—	7.2
26. Steel Products	—	—	—	—	—	—	—	6.0	6.3
27. Nonferrous Metals	—	—	—	—	—	—	—	—	—

28. Metal Products	—	—	—	—	—	—	5.8	6.3
29. Machinery	—	—	—	—	—	—	5.8	5.6
30. Electrical Machinery	—	—	—	6.5	—	6.3	6.2	6.1
31. Transport Equipments	—	—	—	—	—	6.0	6.0	6.0
32. Misc. Manufacturing	—	—	—	—	—	—	—	6.3
33. Building & Maintenance	—	—	—	—	—	—	—	—
34. Other Construction	—	—	—	—	—	—	—	—
35. Electricity	—	—	—	—	—	—	6.0	5.7
36. Banking & Dwelling	—	—	—	—	—	—	—	5.8
37. Water & Sanitary Service	—	—	—	—	—	—	—	—
39. Transportation	—	—	—	—	6.0	6.0	6.0	5.5
41. Other Services	—	—	—	—	—	6.0	6.0	6.0
43. Unclassifiable	—	—	—	—	—	—	—	—
1–6. Primary Sectors	—	—	5.6	7.0	5.5	5.7	5.6	5.7
7–32. Manufacturing	5.3	5.3	5.6	5.6	5.2	5.4	5.5	5.8
35, 37, 39. SOC Sectors	—	—	—	—	6.0	6.0	6.0	5.6
33, 34, 36, 41. Service Sectors	—	—	—	—	—	6.0	6.0	6.0
1–43. All Sectors	5.3	5.3	5.3	5.6	5.3	5.5	5.5	5.8

371

Table B.24. *(Continued)*

In Percent

Arrival Basis	1968	1969	1970	1971	1972	1973	1974	1975	1976
2. Other Agriculture	—	—	—	—	7.0	7.0	7.1	7.9	7.7
4. Fishery	5.8	5.8	5.9	5.8	5.8	6.0	6.5	6.5	6.4
6. Other Minerals	7.0	7.0	7.0	7.0	8.5	8.5	8.5	8.5	8.5
7. Processed Foods	7.3	7.4	7.2	7.8	7.9	8.4	8.4	8.0	7.6
8. Beverages	6.1	6.0	6.0	—	—	—	—	—	—
10. Textile Fibres	6.2	6.4	6.5	6.7	6.9	8.0	10.4	8.1	7.3
11. Textile Fabrics	6.0	6.0	6.0	6.1	6.2	7.7	8.5	8.0	7.4
12. Textile Products	—	—	—	—	—	—	11.5	8.0	6.7
13. Lumber & Plywood	6.9	7.8	8.0	8.0	8.0	8.6	11.4	8.1	6.6
15. Paper & Products	6.4	6.3	6.2	6.2	6.2	6.1	6.1	6.0	8.6
16. Printing & Publishing	—	—	6.5	6.5	6.4	5.6	6.5	6.5	6.5
18. Rubber Products	6.1	6.1	6.1	6.1	6.1	8.4	8.6	7.3	6.8
19. Basic Chemicals	6.7	7.1	7.5	7.3	7.1	8.8	8.5	7.3	6.9
20. Other Chemicals	5.9	6.1	6.9	6.7	6.5	7.9	9.4	7.7	6.9
21. Chemical Fertilizer	5.6	5.6	5.6	5.6	5.7	6.0	8.5	7.5	7.0
22. Petroleum Products	5.0	5.2	6.7	6.7	7.0	8.6	8.9	7.7	7.1
24. Nonmetallic Mineral	5.9	6.1	6.4	6.6	6.8	7.7	8.0	7.2	6.8
25. Iron & Steel	7.2	7.1	7.3	6.9	6.5	6.4	7.4	6.9	6.8
26. Steel Products	6.8	7.3	7.7	7.1	6.9	7.3	7.2	7.1	7.0
27. Nonferrous Metals	5.8	5.8	5.8	5.8	5.8	6.1	7.0	6.6	7.3

28. Metal Products	6.2	6.5	7.9	8.0	8.1	8.2	7.9	7.9	8.2
29. Machinery	5.7	5.7	5.6	5.8	5.8	5.8	5.8	5.8	7.0
30. Electrical Machinery	6.1	6.2	6.4	6.9	7.0	7.6	8.1	8.2	8.4
31. Transport Equipments	4.2	4.5	6.3	6.7	6.8	8.9	9.1	7.5	6.9
32. Misc. Manufacturing	6.3	6.3	6.3	6.3	6.4	6.5	7.9	7.8	7.8
33. Building & Maintenance	—	6.0	6.2	6.2	6.2	6.1	6.0	—	—
34. Other Construction	6.0	5.9	5.9	6.2	6.6	6.7	6.8	7.1	6.8
35. Electricity	6.2	6.5	6.5	6.4	6.4	6.3	6.4	6.4	6.4
36. Banking & Dwelling	5.8	6.8	6.8	6.8	8.3	12.7	12.6	9.0	7.6
37. Water & Sanitary Service	—	—	—	—	7.0	7.0	7.0	7.1	7.4
39. Transportation	5.8	5.8	6.1	6.3	6.2	7.5	7.8	7.5	7.1
41. Other Services	6.0	6.3	6.4	6.4	6.6	7.2	7.7	8.1	7.0
43. Unclassifiable	—	—	—	—	6.2	6.2	8.3	7.1	7.2
1–6. Primary Sectors	5.8	5.9	5.9	5.9	5.9	6.3	6.6	6.6	6.5
7–32. Manufacturing	5.9	6.1	6.6	6.7	6.8	8.0	8.9	7.5	7.1
35, 37, 39. SOC Sectors	5.9	6.2	6.3	6.4	6.3	6.8	6.9	6.9	7.0
33, 34, 36, 41. Service Sectors	6.0	6.1	6.2	6.3	6.8	8.0	9.0	8.0	7.0
1–43. All Sectors	5.9	6.1	6.5	6.5	6.6	7.5	8.2	7.3	7.0

Table B.25. Private Foreign Borrowing: Loan Balance, Principal Repayments and Interest Rates by Source
(Loan Balance)

In Thousand U.S. Dollars

Arrival Basis	1959	1960	1961	1962	1963	1964	1965	1966	1967
1. United States	2,130	1,993	1,728	1,449	7,155	14,166	21,489	40,045	61,960
2. Japan	—	—	—	—	—	—	4,246	66,792	119,328
3. IBRD	—	—	—	—	—	—	—	—	—
4. IDA	—	—	—	—	—	—	—	—	—
5. ADB	—	—	—	—	—	—	—	—	—
6. IFC	—	—	—	—	—	—	—	—	—
7. Germany	—	—	—	121	10,183	18,251	23,516	23,392	38,120
8. Others	—	—	—	−53	2,455	3,619	11,029	31,503	69,326
Total	2,130	1,993	1,728	1,517	19,793	36,036	60,280	161,732	288,734

Arrival Basis	1968	1969	1970	1971	1972	1973	1974	1975	1976
1. United States	158,689	272,823	365,628	446,629	471,675	614,708	818,701	1,056,570	1,141,089
2. Japan	183,675	254,166	273,492	314,721	360,544	372,692	425,278	540,727	519,909
3. IBRD	—	—	—	—	—	—	—	—	350
4. IDA	—	—	—	—	—	—	—	—	—
5. ADB	—	—	—	4,422	6,438	6,925	5,346	4,399	3,491
6. IFC	—	—	406	768	1,295	1,401	1,261	23,200	49,624
7. Germany	60,336	82,157	102,191	104,630	101,671	122,181	118,752	144,507	913,841
8. Others	114,435	220,192	297,892	385,021	470,824	602,610	756,583	997,529	1,276,016
Total	517,135	829,338	1,039,609	1,256,191	1,412,447	1,720,517	2,125,921	2,766,932	3,180,320

Table B.25. — Continued (Principal Repayments)

In Thousand U.S. Dollars

Arrival Basis	1959	1960	1961	1962	1963	1964	1965	1966	1967
1. United States	10	137	265	279	294	1,203	203	1,487	3,429
2. Japan	—	—	—	—	—	—	—	76	2,336
3. IBRD	—	—	—	—	—	—	—	—	—
4. IDA	—	—	—	—	—	—	—	—	—
5. ADB	—	—	—	—	—	—	—	—	—
6. IFC	—	—	—	—	—	—	—	—	—
7. Germany	—	—	—	—	125	1,003	1,528	1,955	3,827
8. Others	—	—	—	53	142	493	1,994	4,474	7,907
Total	10	137	265	332	561	2,699	3,725	7,992	17,499

Arrival Basis	1968	1969	1970	1971	1972	1973	1974	1975	1976
1. United States	7,981	14,796	29,868	38,264	57,171	61,918	69,369	83,714	147,663
2. Japan	6,278	14,561	31,274	30,687	45,516	52,930	53,889	55,465	69,179
3. IBRD	—	—	—	—	—	—	—	—	—
4. IDA	—	—	—	—	—	—	—	—	—
5. ADB	—	—	—	—	517	1,109	1,119	851	912
6. IFC	—	—	—	—	—	—	140	280	1,903
7. Germany	3,985	6,892	8,350	12,351	18,965	23,628	27,194	24,280	21,926
8. Others	9,599	15,896	22,787	33,998	49,824	85,592	97,549	79,337	99,833
Total	27,843	52,145	92,279	115,300	171,993	225,177	249,260	243,927	340,606

Table B.25. Continued (Interest Rates Weighted by Loan Balance)

In Percent

	1959	1960	1961	1962	1963	1964	1965	1966	1967
1. United States	5.3	5.3	5.3	5.3	4.6	4.1	4.7	4.9	5.2
2. Japan	—	—	—	—	—	—	6.0	5.7	5.6
3. IBRD	—	—	—	—	—	—	—	—	—
4. IDA	—	—	—	—	—	—	—	—	—
5. ADB	—	—	—	—	—	—	—	—	—
6. IFC	—	—	—	—	—	—	—	—	—
7. Germany	—	—	—	7.0	6.1	6.0	6.0	6.0	6.2
8. Others	—	—	—	—	6.3	6.4	5.8	5.6	6.3
Total	5.3	5.3	5.3	5.6	5.6	5.3	5.5	5.5	5.8

	1968	1969	1970	1971	1972	1973	1974	1975	1976
1. United States	5.7	6.4	7.1	7.2	7.3	8.8	9.2	7.8	7.1
2. Japan	5.6	5.5	5.6	5.7	5.8	6.2	6.7	6.7	6.7
3. IBRD	—	—	—	—	—	—	—	—	8.5
4. IDA	—	—	—	—	—	—	—	—	—
5. ADB	—	—	—	6.9	6.9	6.9	6.9	6.9	6.9
6. IFC	—	—	8.5	8.5	8.5	8.5	8.5	9.6	10.0
7. Germany	6.2	6.2	6.2	6.3	6.4	6.6	6.7	7.0	6.9
8. Others	6.5	6.4	6.7	6.6	6.7	7.3	8.3	7.2	6.8
Total	5.9	6.1	6.5	6.6	6.6	7.5	8.2	7.3	7.0

Table B.26. Balance of Government Foreign Borrowing: 1959-76

In Thousand U.S. Dollars

Arrival Basis	1960	1961	1962	1963	1964	1965	1966	1967
1. Rice, Barley & Wheat	—	—	—	—	—	—	—	—
2. Other Agriculture	—	—	—	—	—	—	—	—
4. Fishery	—	—	—	—	—	—	—	—
5. Coal	—	—	—	—	1,441	3,987	8,669	10,788
7. Processed Foods	—	—	—	—	—	—	—	—
10. Textile Fibres	—	—	2,475	3,130	2,864	2,250	2,856	5,260
19. Basic Chemicals	—	—	—	—	—	—	—	—
21. Chemical Fertilizer	—	—	—	—	—	—	13,876	19,867
24. Nonmetallic Mineral	—	—	—	—	3,987	3,987	3,987	6,964
25. Iron & Steel	—	—	—	—	—	—	—	—
29. Machinery	—	—	—	—	—	—	—	—
34. Other Construction	—	—	—	—	—	—	6,457	9,740
35. Electricity	1,095	1,010	2,566	3,706	3,141	5,287	9,528	15,988
36. Banking & Dwelling	—	—	—	—	—	—	—	—
37. Water & Sanitary Service	—	—	—	—	—	7	157	1,339
38. Communication	—	1,008	2,752	6,269	9,878	11,603	14,458	15,883
39. Transportation	—	—	—	18,437	20,268	23,265	42,598	70,810
41. Other Services	—	—	—	—	—	—	210	742
42. Agricultural Products	—	—	—	—	—	—	—	—
43. Unclassifiable	—	63	263	510	1,462	3,101	11,681	30,711
1-6. Primary Sectors	—	—	—	—	1,441	3,987	8,669	10,788
7-32. Manufacturing	—	—	2,475	3,130	6,851	6,507	20,719	32,091
35, 37, 38, 39. SOC Sectors	1,095	2,018	5,318	28,412	33,287	40,162	66,741	104,020
34, 36, 41. Service Sectors	—	—	—	—	—	—	6,667	10,482
1-43. All Sectors	1,095	2,081	8,056	32,052	43,041	53,757	114,477	188,092

Table B.26. (Continued)

In Thousand U.S. Dollars

Arrival Basis	1968	1969	1970	1971	1972	1973	1974	1975	1976
1. Rice, Barley & Wheat	—	—	—	—	13,621	14,575	41,640	50,011	111,168
2. Other Agriculture	407	902	956	989	2,672	5,365	7,558	7,617	7,903
4. Fishery	—	115	3,378	4,627	4,922	11,224	17,467	17,165	16,126
5. Coal	11,790	12,387	12,385	12,275	12,278	12,551	12,301	11,793	11,051
7. Processed Foods	—	—	996	2,378	2,699	3,054	2,851	2,965	4,031
10. Textile Fibres	7,159	6,729	6,283	5,810	5,810	5,810	5,810	5,810	5,810
19. Basic Chemicals	4,889	4,889	5,131	5,626	10,641	29,989	31,945	33,147	31,342
21. Chemical Fertilizer	24,200	24,200	48,800	48,800	48,800	48,800	48,800	48,800	47,200
24. Nonmetallic Mineral	6,964	6,964	6,964	6,964	6,964	6,898	6,765	6,632	6,450
25. Iron & Steel	—	—	—	8,253	44,250	54,062	61,291	93,620	93,569
29. Machinery	1,052	1,413	2,826	2,901	3,624	8,263	15,884	19,676	26,914
34. Other Construction	9,784	9,843	9,849	10,110	11,453	12,959	11,232	10,183	9,342
35. Electricity	28,614	59,260	78,030	95,699	114,561	119,982	128,823	159,615	212,117
36. Banking & Dwelling	—	—	—	—	—	8,900	28,000	55,000	70,000
37. Water & Sanitary Service	5,275	9,169	13,453	14,621	17,543	24,995	28,083	42,137	57,424
38. Communication	22,777	28,177	36,016	39,746	46,758	66,087	72,306	93,987	115,530
39. Transportation	82,430	102,739	111,327	158,233	233,878	314,857	395,047	480,894	577,255
41. Other Services	1,352	1,632	4,653	7,799	16,091	55,096	92,893	138,347	199,128
42. Agricultural Products	40,549	97,040	137,760	331,289	559,695	726,664	748,224	746,019	861,859
43. Unclassifiable	45,582	68,247	97,872	130,456	178,854	260,078	355,046	524,767	704,165
1–6. Primary Sectors	12,197	13,404	16,719	17,891	33,493	43,715	78,966	86,586	146,248
7–32. Manufacturing	44,264	44,195	71,000	80,732	122,788	156,876	173,346	210,650	215,316
35, 37, 38, 39. SOC Sectors	139,096	199,345	238,826	308,299	412,707	525,921	624,259	776,633	962,326
34, 36, 41. Service Sectors	11,136	11,475	14,502	17,909	27,544	76,955	132,125	203,530	278,470
1–43. All Sectors	292,824	433,706	576,679	886,576	1,335,114	1,790,209	2,111,966	2,548,185	3,168,384

Table B.27. *Sectoral Interest Rates on Government Foreign Borrowing Weighted by Loan Balance: 1959–76*

In Percent

Arrival Basis	1959	1960	1961	1962	1963	1964	1965	1966	1967
1. Rice, Barley & Wheat	—	—	—	—	—	—	—	—	—
2. Other Agriculture	—	—	—	—	—	—	—	—	—
4. Fishery	—	—	—	—	—	—	—	1.8	1.6
5. Coal	—	—	—	—	—	3.0	2.4	—	—
7. Processed Foods	—	—	—	—	—	—	—	—	—
10. Textile Fibres	—	—	—	5.8	5.8	5.8	5.8	5.0	3.6
19. Basic Chemicals	—	—	—	—	—	—	—	—	—
21. Chemical Fertilizer	—	—	—	—	—	—	—	2.0	2.0
24. Nonmetallic Mineral	—	—	—	—	—	0.8	0.8	0.8	1.5
25. Iron & Steel	—	—	—	—	—	—	—	—	—
29. Machinery	—	—	—	—	—	—	—	—	—
34. Other Construction	—	—	—	—	—	—	—	3.5	3.5
35. Electricity	—	3.1	3.1	6.4	7.0	7.0	4.3	2.3	1.7
36. Banking & Dwelling	—	—	—	—	—	—	—	—	—
37. Water & Sanitary Service	—	—	—	—	—	—	2.0	2.2	2.3
38. Communication	—	—	3.5	3.5	3.7	3.8	3.9	3.9	3.8
39. Transportation	—	—	—	—	0.8	0.8	0.8	1.7	2.2
41. Other Services	—	—	—	—	—	—	—	3.0	3.0
42. Agricultural Products	—	—	—	—	—	—	—	—	—
43. Unclassifiable	—	—	0.8	0.8	0.8	0.8	0.8	1.9	2.4
1–6. Primary Sectors	—	—	—	—	—	3.0	2.4	1.8	1.6
7–32. Manufacturing	—	—	—	5.8	5.8	2.8	2.7	2.2	2.2
35, 37, 38, 39. SOC Sectors	—	3.1	3.3	4.9	2.3	2.3	2.2	2.3	2.4
34, 36, 41. Service Sectors	—	—	—	—	—	—	—	3.5	3.5
1–43. All Sectors	—	3.1	3.2	5.0	2.5	2.3	2.1	2.3	2.4

Table B.27. (Continued)

In Percent

	1968	1969	1970	1971	1972	1973	1974	1975	1976
1. Rice, Barley & Wheat	—	—	—	—	3.0	2.9	4.1	3.9	4.8
2. Other Agriculture	3.0	3.0	3.0	3.0	1.6	1.2	1.0	1.0	1.0
4. Fishery	—	6.9	6.9	6.9	6.9	7.3	7.4	7.4	7.4
5. Coal	1.4	1.4	1.4	1.3	1.3	1.4	1.3	1.3	1.3
7. Processed Foods	—	—	3.5	3.5	3.5	3.5	3.5	3.7	4.8
10. Textile Fibres	3.1	2.9	2.7	2.5	2.5	2.5	2.5	2.5	2.5
19. Basic Chemicals	2.5	2.5	2.5	2.6	3.4	6.0	6.0	6.1	6.0
21. Chemical Fertilizer	2.0	2.0	2.3	2.3	2.3	2.3	2.3	2.3	2.3
24. Nonmetallic Mineral	1.5	1.5	1.5	1.5	1.5	1.5	1.5	1.5	1.5
25. Iron & Steel	—	—	—	3.5	3.5	3.5	3.5	3.5	3.5
29. Machinery	3.5	3.5	3.5	3.5	3.5	3.2	3.1	3.1	4.7
34. Other Construction	3.5	3.5	3.5	3.5	3.5	3.5	3.5	3.5	3.5
35. Electricity	1.6	1.6	1.9	2.1	2.3	2.4	2.9	3.3	4.3
36. Banking & Dwelling	—	—	—	—	—	8.0	8.5	9.0	9.1
37. Water & Sanitary Service	2.9	2.9	2.9	2.9	2.6	3.0	3.5	4.5	5.1
38. Communication	3.3	3.8	4.2	4.1	4.2	4.1	4.0	4.0	4.6
39. Transportation	2.1	2.6	2.7	3.2	4.2	4.5	4.7	5.2	5.6
41. Other Services	3.0	3.0	3.0	4.5	4.7	6.0	5.5	5.0	4.8
42. Agricultural Products	3.0	3.0	3.0	3.0	3.0	3.0	3.0	3.0	3.0
43. Unclassifiable	2.6	2.7	3.0	3.5	3.9	4.3	4.7	5.9	6.4
1-6. Primary Sectors	1.5	1.5	2.6	2.9	2.9	3.4	4.1	4.0	4.6
7-32. Manufacturing	2.2	2.2	2.3	2.4	2.8	3.4	3.5	3.5	3.7
35, 37, 38, 39. SOC Sectors	2.2	2.5	2.7	3.0	3.6	3.9	4.2	4.6	5.2
34, 36, 41. Service Sectors	3.4	3.4	3.3	3.9	4.2	5.8	6.0	6.0	5.8
1-43. All Sectors	2.4	2.6	2.8	3.0	3.3	3.6	3.9	4.4	4.8

Table B.28. Government Foreign Borrowing: Loan Balance, Principal Repayments and Interest Rates by Source

(Loan Balance)

In Thousand U.S. Dollars

Arrival Basis	1959	1960	1961	1962	1963	1964	1965	1966	1967
1. United States	—	1,095	2,081	8,056	16,880	20,857	25,115	62,992	114,724
2. Japan	—	—	—	—	—	—	—	17,436	30,846
3. IBRD	—	—	—	—	—	—	—	—	—
4. IDA	—	—	—	—	12,049	13,880	16,873	16,873	16,873
5. ADB	—	—	—	—	—	—	—	—	—
6. Germany	—	—	—	—	3,123	8,304	11,769	16,931	24,364
7. Others	—	—	—	—	—	—	—	245	1,285
Total	—	1,095	2,081	8,056	32,052	43,041	53,757	114,477	188,092

Arrival Basis	1968	1969	1970	1971	1972	1973	1974	1975	1976
1. United States	197,033	308,554	411,122	548,678	804,445	955,046	1,003,805	1,072,761	1,319,168
2. Japan	44,283	63,262	80,644	182,617	273,677	412,502	530,892	577,051	619,027
3. IBRD	—	—	9,483	40,781	96,643	164,198	245,750	424,784	609,752
4. IDA	24,076	27,345	29,810	44,941	48,719	57,839	77,859	92,100	102,088
5. ADB	—	4,974	9,707	18,337	25,859	71,584	114,473	188,113	253,974
6. Germany	25,829	27,532	32,553	40,049	51,780	75,409	89,480	129,101	150,583
7. Others	1,603	2,039	3,360	11,173	33,991	53,631	49,707	64,275	113,792
Total	292,824	433,706	576,679	886,576	1,335,114	1,790,209	2,111,966	2,548,185	3,168,384

Table B.28. Continued (Principal Repayments)

In Thousand U.S. Dollars

Arrival Basis	1959	1960	1961	1962	1963	1964	1965	1966	1967
1. United States	—	20	145	294	255	1,067	1,154	1,184	1,227
2. Japan	—	—	—	—	—	—	—	—	—
3. IBRD	—	—	—	—	—	—	—	—	—
4. IDA	—	—	—	—	—	—	—	—	—
5. ADB	—	—	—	—	—	—	—	—	—
6. Germany	—	—	—	—	—	—	—	263	711
7. Others	—	—	—	—	—	—	—	—	—
Total	—	20	145	294	255	1,067	1,154	1,447	1,938

Arrival Basis	1968	1969	1970	1971	1972	1973	1974	1975	1976
1. United States	1,251	1,710	2,248	2,999	2,359	3,166	3,638	5,557	10,650
2. Japan	—	—	—	—	—	86	5,011	7,170	9,624
3. IBRD	—	—	42	546	2,044	2,532	7,431	7,640	13,055
4. IDA	—	—	—	—	—	153	169	169	169
5. ADB	—	—	—	—	440	1,814	3,234	6,694	11,002
6. Germany	1,001	1,409	1,827	2,727	4,835	6,382	6,773	8,603	9,012
7. Others	—	57	115	117	3,686	4,948	5,105	6,280	9,674
Total	2,252	3,176	4,232	6,389	13,364	19,081	31,361	42,113	63,186

Table B.28. Continued (Interest Rates Weighted by Loan Balance)

In Percent

	1959	1960	1961	1962	1963	1964	1965	1966	1967
1. United States	—	3.1	3.2	5.0	3.6	2.8	2.3	1.9	2.0
2. Japan	—	—	—	—	—	—	—	3.5	3.5
3. IBRD	—	—	—	—	—	—	—	—	—
4. IDA	—	—	—	—	0.8	0.8	0.8	0.8	0.8
5. ADB	—	—	—	—	—	—	—	—	—
6. Germany	—	—	—	—	4.0	3.8	3.7	3.7	3.5
7. Others	—	—	—	—	—	—	—	7.5	7.5
Total	—	3.1	3.2	5.0	2.5	2.3	2.1	2.3	2.4

	1968	1969	1970	1971	1972	1973	1974	1975	1976
1. United States	2.2	2.4	2.5	2.6	2.7	2.8	3.0	3.3	3.6
2. Japan	3.5	3.5	3.5	3.3	3.4	3.5	3.8	3.8	3.9
3. IBRD	—	—	6.5	6.8	6.9	7.0	7.1	7.4	7.6
4. IDA	0.8	0.8	0.8	0.8	0.8	0.8	0.8	0.8	0.8
5. ADB	—	6.9	6.9	6.9	7.0	7.3	7.4	7.6	7.8
6. Germany	3.5	3.6	3.8	4.1	4.4	4.3	4.1	3.7	3.8
7. Others	6.4	5.5	5.7	6.0	5.8	5.7	5.7	5.9	6.7
Total	2.4	2.6	2.8	3.0	3.3	3.6	3.9	4.4	4.8

Table B.29. Inflow of Foreign Loans (1959–76)
Arrival Basis

In Million Dollars & Percent

	Government Borrowing							Private Borrowing						
	New Borrowing			Net Indebtedness				New Borrowing			Net Indebtedness			
	Total	U.S.	Japan	Total	U.S.	Japan		Total	U.S.	Japan	Total	U.S.	Japan	
1959	—	—	—	—	—	—		2.1	100%	—	2.1	100%	—	
1960	1.1	100%	—	1.1	100%	—		—	—	—	2.0	100%	—	
1961	1.1	100%	—	2.1	100%	—		—	—	—	1.7	100%	—	
1962	6.3	100%	—	8.1	100%	—		—	—	—	1.5	100%	—	
1963	24.3	37%	—	32.1	53%	—		18.8	32%	—	19.8	36%	—	
1964	12.0	42%	—	43.0	48%	—		18.9	43%	—	36.0	39%	—	
1965	11.9	45%	—	53.8	47%	—		28.0	27%	15%	60.3	36%	—	
1966	62.2	63%	28%	114.5	55%	15%		109.5	18%	57%	161.7	25%	7%	
1967	75.5	70%	18%	188.1	61%	16%		144.4	18%	38%	288.7	21%	41%	
1968	107.0	78%	12%	292.8	67%	15%		256.3	41%	28%	517.1	31%	36%	
1969	143.3	79%	13%	433.7	71%	15%		363.4	35%	24%	829.3	33%	31%	
1970	145.0	72%	12%	576.7	71%	14%		298.0	41%	17%	1,039.6	35%	26%	
1971	312.5	45%	32%	886.6	62%	21%		325.4	37%	22%	1,256.2	36%	25%	
1972	433.5	60%	15%	1,335.1	60%	20%		306.8	27%	29%	1,412.4	33%	26%	
1973	425.3	36%	24%	1,790.2	53%	23%		492.8	42%	13%	1,720.5	36%	22%	
1974	379.1	14%	40%	2,112.0	48%	25%		666.3	41%	16%	2,125.9	39%	20%	
1975	480.4	16%	13%	2,548.2	42%	23%		868.0	37%	20%	2,766.9	38%	20%	
1976	689.4	37%	7%	3,168.4	42%	20%		808.9	29%	5%	3,180.3	36%	16%	

Source: Economic Planning Board.

Table B 30. Foreign Loans by Grace Period and Repayment Period: 1959–76

No. of Years	Private Borrowing			Government Borrowing		
	No. of Cases	Million Dollars	Percentage Share	No. of Cases	Million Dollars	Percentage Share
(Grace Period)						
1	366	1,146.8	(24%)	26	103.7	(3%)
2	304	1,148.0	(24%)	33	229.2	(7%)
3	208	1,395.6	(30%)	34	322.3	(10%)
4	56	285.7	(6%)	12	140.2	(4%)
5	39	315.1	(7%)	19	479.4	(14%)
6	16	224.3	(5%)	9	88.1	(3%)
7	8	27.0	(1%)	48	483.4	(15%)
8	5	75.4	(2%)	0	0	(0%)
9	3	10.2	(0%)	1	6.1	(0%)
10	6	59.0	(1%)	81	1,451.3	(44%)
11–15	7	20.8	(0%)	1	6.1	(0%)
16–20	0	0	(0%)	0	0	(0%)
21–25	0	0	(0%)	0	0	(0%)
26 & Over	0	0	(0%)	0	0	(0%)
Weighted Average		(2.8 Years)			(7.0 Years)	
(Repayment Period)						
1	32	122.9	(3%)	0	0	(0%)
2	33	108.1	(2%)	3	4.1	(0%)
3	97	314.6	(7%)	8	7.4	(0%)
4	122	353.8	(8%)	7	66.6	(2%)
5	200	672.3	(14%)	6	4.8	(0%)
6	91	254.5	(5%)	9	14.6	(0%)
7	139	575.5	(12%)	4	10.0	(0%)
8	130	828.4	(18%)	14	27.1	(0%)
9	42	367.2	(8%)	1	1.1	(0%)
10	73	457.2	(10%)	17	173.2	(5%)
11–15	51	550.5	(12%)	75	1,053.2	(32%)
16–20	5	94.1	(2%)	46	556.6	(17%)
21–25	1	2.2	(0%)	8	160.5	(5%)
26 & Over	2	6.6	(0%)	66	1,230.9	(37%)
Weighted Average		(7.4 Years)			(20.4 Years)	

Table B.31. Exports, Competitive Imports and Non-Competitive Imports (I-O Data): 1960–75

		1960	1963	1966	1968	1970	1973	1975
Exports								
Commodity	(In Milion Won)	5,804	13,103	70,223	130,228	270,239	1,221,548	2,347,039
Non-Commodity		4,163	8,247	43,292	87,026	105,196	350,296	477,374
Commodity	(In Thousand Dollars)	40,051	77,044	258,820	470,801	870,057	3,066,911	4,849,254
Non-Commodity		38,291	48,509	159,562	314,626	338,686	879,480	986,310
Commodity	(In Thousand 1970 Dollars)	46,571	95,470	276,813	467,065	870,057	2,424,444	3,267,691
Non-Commodity		44,524	60,110	170,655	312,129	338,686	695,241	664,629
Competitive Imports								
Commodity	(In Million Won)	13,147	45,143	116,390	213,007	379,798	1,182,864	2,219,873
Non-Commodity		2,168	4,118	11,372	37,745	38,029	64,242	67,913
Commodity	(In Thousand Dollars)	107,579	324,767	428,716	770,875	1,222,787	2,969,776	4,856,515
Non-Commodity		26,331	30,717	41,534	135,664	122,442	161,291	140,316
Commodity	(In Thousand 1970 Dollars)	125,092	334,122	437,912	787,411	1,222,787	2,196,580	2,120,442
Non-Commodity		30,617	31,602	42,425	138,574	122,442	119,298	64,871
Non-Competitive Imports								
Commodity	(In Million Won)	27,859	34,509	80,751	173,850	214,769	499,896	1,411,776
Non-Commodity		0	172	419	1,141	0	0	0
Commodity	(In Thousand Dollars)	227,965	222,763	297,656	628,524	691,467	1,255,071	2,916,893
Non-Commodity		0	1,322	1,544	4,124	0	0	0
Commodity	(In Thousand 1970 Dollars)	265,076	229,180	304,041	642,006	691,467	928,307	1,348,541
Non-Commodity		0	1,360	1,577	4,213	0	0	0

Source: The Bank of Korea, *Input-Output Tables of Korea* 1960, 1963, 1968, 1970, 1973 & 1975.

Note: Commodity sectors consist of sectors 1–92 and non-commodity sectors consist of sectors 93–117. In order to get 1970 dollar values, 1963–75 figures were deflated by BOK's export and import unit value indexes, and 1960 figures were deflated by the U.S. wholesale price index. Non-competitive imports include natural resource intensive goods.

Table B.32. Sectoral Direct Labor Coefficients

In Person per $1,000 (1970 Prices) of Output

	1960	1963	1966	1968	1970	1973	1975
(1) Rice, Barley & Wheat							
1. Rice, Barley & Wheat	0.9317[1]	0.9317	1.0549	1.0543	0.9563	0.7588	0.5612
(2) Other Agriculture							
2. Other Cereals	2.6650[1]	2.6650	2.4420	2.7719	2.1123	2.1980	1.6774
3. Vegetables	1.4310[1]	1.4310	1.5534	1.4909	1.2653	1.4729	0.9217
4. Fruit	2.8583[1]	2.8583	2.1336	1.6048	1.6733	1.0661	2.0258
5. Industrial Crops	2.8583[1]	2.8583	2.1336	1.6048	1.6733	1.0661	2.0258
6. Livestock & Sericulture	2.7983[1]	2.7983	1.5719	0.8982	0.8053	0.7914	0.7490
(3) Forestry							
7. Forestry	0.7363[4]	0.7363[4]	0.7363[4]	0.7363[4]	0.7363	0.7363[4]	0.7363[4]
(4) Fishery							
8. Fishery	2.5190	2.2029	1.2791	0.9620	0.8408	0.3988	0.3988[5]
(5) Coal							
9. Coal	0.7520	0.5331	0.4712	0.4246	0.3751	0.2957	0.4069
(6) Other Minerals							
10. Metallic Ores	0.7967	0.7180	0.5024	0.4362	0.2824	0.2232	0.2449
11. Nonmetallic Minerals	1.5092	0.9842	0.6229	0.5808	0.5640	0.3403	0.3781
12. Salt	3.2043[2]	3.2043[2]	3.2043	2.3048	1.5050	0.9196	1.1368
(7) Processed Foods							
13. Meat & Dairy Products	0.2099	0.3398	0.1727	0.1589	0.1177	0.0531	0.0542
14. Veg. & Fruit Processing	0.4982	0.2400	0.7738	0.3506	0.3682	0.2939	0.3388
15. Processing of Sea Food	1.0015	0.8834	0.7610	0.7328	0.4023	0.1972	0.2118
16. Grain Milling	0.2128	0.2092	0.3241	0.2970	0.1269	0.0583	0.0451
17. Bakery & Confectionery	0.5025	0.2944	0.4030	0.3530	0.2627	0.1862	0.1341
18. Sugar Refining	0.0192	0.0271	0.0351	0.0281	0.0247	0.0136	0.0058
19. Seasonings	0.3419	0.1907	0.2891	0.2280	0.1664	0.0812	0.0640
20. Other Processed Foods	0.3537	0.2431	0.3478	0.2436	0.1425	0.0746	0.0730

Table B.32. (Continued)

In Person per $1,000 (1970 Prices) of Output.

	1960	1963	1966	1968	1970	1973	1975
(8) Beverages							
21. Alcoholic Beverages	0.2884	0.1818	0.1758	0.1370	0.1092	0.0716	0.0524
22. Soft Drinks	0.2592[1]	0.2592	0.3244	0.1938	0.1691	0.0775	0.0563
(9) Tobacco							
23. Tobacco	0.0795[1]	0.0795	0.0977	0.0583	0.0490	0.0480	0.0292
(10) Fibre Spinning							
24. Cotton Yarn	0.3126	0.3018	0.2674	0.2651	0.2536	0.1499	0.1218
25. Silk Yarn	0.7119	0.5528	0.4576	0.2799	0.2974	0.1261	0.1280
26. Woolen Yarn	0.2249	0.2545	0.2018	0.2439	0.5150	0.1775	0.3123
27. Hemp & Flax Yarn	0.2249	0.5833[2]	0.5833	0.2439	0.5150	0.1775	0.3123
28. Chemical Fibre Yarn	0.2249	0.5833[2]	0.5833	0.1951	0.1595	0.0779	0.0870
(11) Textile Fabrics							
29. Cotton Fabrics	0.4619	0.4726	0.4000	0.4378	0.3235	0.1475	0.1951
30. Silk Fabrics	0.7259	0.4909	0.5264	0.4161	0.2385	0.2736	0.1892
31. Woolen Fabrics	0.1744	0.2980	0.5502	0.3229	0.1908	0.1726	0.1579
32. Hemp Fabrics	0.4270	0.6962	1.1017	0.8125	0.4346	0.2471	0.3846
33. Chemical Fibre Fabrics	0.4020	0.4020[3]	0.4020[3]	0.4020	0.3910	0.1494	0.1892
34. Dyeing & Finishing	0.3398	0.3455	0.3796	0.3400	0.2578	0.1341	0.1165
(12) Textile Products							
35. Knit Products	0.4256	0.4481	0.5255	0.4505	0.4669	0.2690	0.1996
36. Rope & Fishing Nets	0.4136	0.3587	0.4161	0.3545	0.3397	0.2200	0.0744
37. Apparels & Accessories	0.4019	0.5422	0.5200	0.4982	0.3963	0.2918	0.2406
38. Misc. Textile Product	0.7274	1.0137	0.9217	0.6006	0.4270	0.3254	0.2629
(13) Lumber & Plywood							
39. Lumber & Plywood	0.2452	0.1856	0.1826	0.1754	0.1576	0.0787	0.0921
(14) Wood & Furniture							
40. Wood Products	0.5439	0.8277	0.8677	1.1800	0.8276	0.3311	0.3364
41. Furniture	0.6382	0.6055	0.7146	0.5547	0.5174	0.3352	0.3150

(15) Paper Products							
42. Pulp	0.4097[1]	0.2127	0.2067	0.1761	0.1356	0.0796	0.0725
43. Paper	0.4097[1]	0.2127	0.2067	0.1761	0.1356	0.0796	0.1477
44. Paper Products	0.4626	0.2948	0.3837	0.3131	0.2850	0.1729	0.1477
(16) Printing & Publishing							
45. Printing & Publishing	0.4742	0.3972	0.4329	0.3607	0.3225	0.2268	0.2012
(17) Leather Products							
46. Leather & Fur	0.1649	0.2828	0.2451	0.2548	0.3182	0.1413	0.0728
47. Leather Products	0.5803	0.6471	0.5560	0.4274	0.4505	0.1722	0.2304
(18) Rubber Products							
48. Rubber Products	0.2501	0.3717	0.4239	0.3618	0.2872	0.1952	0.1928
(19) Basic Chemicals							
49. Inorganic Chemicals	0.2277	0.1812	0.3025	0.2233	0.1696	0.1053	0.0909
50. Organic Chemicals	0.2866	0.1520	0.2718	0.2413	0.2091	0.0615	0.0375
(20) Other Chemical Product							
51. Explosives	0.2215[1]	0.2215	0.2146	0.1897	0.1266	0.2943	0.1846
52. Paint	0.1001	0.1247	0.1417	0.1069	0.0890	0.1013	0.0706
53. Drugs	0.2610	0.2579	0.2219	0.1864	0.1479	0.1057	0.0834
54. Soap	0.1193	0.1166	0.1686	0.1541	0.1230	0.0700	0.0645
55. Cosmetics	0.2833[1]	0.2833	0.2747	0.1814	0.1383	0.0992	0.0946
56. Pesticides	0.1961[1]	0.1961	0.2246	0.1812	0.2285	0.1441	0.0695
57. Other Chemical Product	0.4509	0.3448	0.4354	0.2172	0.1517	0.0879	0.0599
(21) Chemical Fertilizer							
58. Chemical Fertilizer	0.1967[1]	0.1967	0.1593	0.0629	0.0582	0.0680	0.0195
(22) Petroleum Products							
59. Petroleum Products	0.0827[1]	0.0827	0.0227	0.0183	0.0117	0.0079	0.0027
(23) Coal Products							
60. Coal Products	0.3266	0.2666	0.2167	0.1579	0.1183	0.0606	0.0717

Table B.32. (Continued)

In Person per $1,000 (1970 Prices) of Output

	1960	1963	1966	1968	1970	1973	1975
(24) Non-Metallic Mineral							
61. Cement	0.0657	0.0812	0.0695	0.0931	0.0519	0.0494	0.0285
62. Ceramic Products	0.8450	0.6505	0.8716	0.5582	0.4210	0.1919	0.1880
63. Glass Products	0.3408	0.3720	0.4197	0.3401	0.2868	0.1765	0.1353
64. Pottery	1.1389	1.3178	1.3690	1.2365	0.9199	0.4374	0.4599
65. Other Stone & Clay	0.6694	0.5312	0.3759	0.5689	0.5992	0.3028	0.1503
(25) Iron & Steel							
66. Pig Iron	0.2196	0.1212	0.1843	0.2479	0.2919	0.0890	0.1089
67. Steel Ingots	0.2196	0.1212	0.1843	0.2479	0.2919	0.0890	0.1089
(26) Steel Products							
68. Rolled Steel	0.2009	0.1324	0.1508	0.1807	0.1009	0.0318	0.0400
69. Pipes & Plated Steel	0.1584	0.1111	0.1006	0.1271	0.0542	0.0381	0.0546
70. Cast & Forged Steel	0.5767	0.4043	0.2997	0.1947	0.2854	0.1169	0.1896
(27) Non-Ferrous Metals							
71. Non-Ferrous Smelting	0.2230[1]	0.2230	0.1332	0.1198	0.1037	0.0727	0.0473
72. Primary Non-Ferrous	0.2524	0.2111	0.3192	0.2756	0.2521	0.1226	0.1064
(28) Finished Metal Products							
73. Structural Metallic	0.3032	0.4095	0.5775	0.3939	0.2794	0.1812	0.1524
74. Other Metallic Product	0.5321	0.5075	0.5426	0.4610	0.4006	0.2684	0.2156
(29) Machinery							
75. Prime Movers & Boilers	0.5402	0.5296	0.4289	0.4098	0.3342	0.2417	0.1902
76. Working Machinery	0.4754	0.6869	0.6207	0.5419	0.4056	0.2642	0.2266
77. Industrial Machinery	0.7097	0.5616	0.5277	0.4147	0.3974	0.1736	0.1898
78. Other Machinery	0.2838	0.5435	0.4377	0.3861	0.2796	0.2479	0.1392
79. Office Machines	0.6565	0.5026	0.5910	0.4905	0.3658	0.1447	0.1425
80. Household Machines	0.6565	0.5026	0.5910	0.4905	0.3658	0.1447	0.1425
81. Machine Spare Parts	0.7350	0.6290	0.5726	0.4124	0.4160	0.2000	0.1753

(30) Electrical Machinery						
82. Electrical Machinery	0.5361	0.2804	0.3252	0.2135	0.2520	0.2123	0.1798
83. Electronic & Comm. Eq.	0.5285	0.4821	0.3250	0.2664	0.2063	0.1489	0.1516
84. Household Elec. Appl.	0.6624	0.4732	0.3717	0.4612	0.2366	0.2434	0.2071
85. Other Electric Equip.	0.1320	0.1936	0.2034	0.1767	0.2144	0.1120	0.0928
(31) Transport Equipment						
86. Shipbuilding	0.5282	0.3994	0.3525	0.4084	0.3137	0.1606	0.0813
78. Railroad Transport Eq.	0.4396	0.3688	0.1800	0.1574	0.3064	0.1685	0.1152
88. Motor Vehicles	0.6654	0.5736	0.3597	0.1653	0.1422	0.0960	0.0755
89. Other Transport Eq.	0.5998	0.4501	0.4366	0.7253	0.1431	0.2090	0.1844
(32) Misc. Manufacturing						
90. Measuring & Optical	0.4940	0.5840	0.5964	0.2905	0.3372	0.2257	0.1971
91. Synthetic Resin Product	0.3813[1]	0.3813	0.3006	0.2257	0.1942	0.1351	0.1813
92. Other Manufactures	0.5978	0.5459	0.7354	0.5516	0.4625	0.3485	0.3069
(33) Building & Maintenance						
93. Residential Building	0.5346	0.4427	0.2414	0.2281	0.2033	0.1712	0.1802
94. Non-Residential Building	0.5346	0.4427	0.2414	0.2281	0.2033	0.1712	0.1802
95. Building Maintenance	0.5346	0.4427	0.2414	0.2281	0.2033	0.1712	0.1802
(34) Other Construction						
96. Public Construction	0.7654	0.5803	0.3415	0.2678	0.2696	0.2624	0.2326
97. Other Construction	0.7654	0.5803	0.3415	0.2678	0.2696	0.2624	0.2326
(35) Electricity						
98. Electricity	0.1776	0.2121	0.1527	0.0950	0.0710	0.0376	0.0192
(36) Banking & Dwelling						
99. Banking & Insurance	0.0982	0.1343	0.1248	0.1503	0.1384	0.1242	0.1822
100. Dwelling & Real Estate	0.0982	0.1343	0.1248	0.1503	0.1384	0.1242	0.1822

Table B.32. (Continued)

In Person per $1,000 (1970 Prices) of Output

	1960	1963	1966	1968	1970	1973	1975
(37) Water & Sanitary Service							
101. Water & Sanitary Service	0.9174	0.9174	0.9627	0.4841	0.4899	0.3067	0.1099
(38) Communication							
102. Communication	0.6520	0.6520	0.4838	0.4218	0.3700	0.2649	0.1997
(39) Transportation							
103. Railroad Transportation	0.7760	0.7405	0.4529	0.4422	0.3530	0.2741	0.2213
104. Other Transportation	0.7760	0.7405	0.4529	0.4422	0.3530	0.2741	0.2213
105. Storage	0.7760	0.7405	0.4929	0.4422	0.3530	0.2741	0.2213
(40) Trade							
106. Trade	1.1583	0.8911	1.1376	0.8600	0.7258	0.5345	0.5249
(41) Other Services							
107. Education	0.8163	0.6720	0.8803	1.0050	0.8186	0.6849	0.7729
108. Medical Service	0.8163	0.6720	0.8803	1.0050	0.8186	0.6849	0.7729
109. Social Service	0.8163	0.6720	0.8803	1.0050	0.8186	0.6849	0.7729
110. Agricultural Service	0.8163	0.6720	0.8803	1.0050	0.8186	0.6849	0.7729
111. Business Service	0.8163	0.6720	0.8803	1.0050	0.8186	0.6849	0.7729
112. Recreation	0.8163	0.6720	0.8803	1.0050	0.8186	0.6849	0.7729
113. Personal Service	0.8163	0.6720	0.8803	1.0050	0.8186	0.6849	0.7729
114. Office Supplies	0	0	0	0	0	0	0
(42) Scrap							
115. Iron Scrap	0	0	0	0	0	0	0
116. Other Scrap	0	0	0	0	0	0	0
(43) Unclassifiable							
117. Unclassifiable	0	0	0	0	0	0	0

Source: See Hong, *op. cit.*, Chapter 7.
Notes: [1] 1963 coefficient.
[2] 1966 coefficient.
[3] 1968 coefficient.
[4] 1970 coefficient.
[5] 1973 coefficient

Table B.33. Sectoral Direct Capital Coefficients

	1960	1963	1966	1968	1970	1973	1975
(1) Rice, Barley & Wheat							
1. Rice, Barley & Wheat	0.2538[3]	0.2538[2]	0.2538	0.3252	0.3421	0.4246	0.3779
(2) Other Agriculture							
2. Other Cereals	0.2720[2]	0.2720[2]	0.2720	0.3450	0.3278	0.5254	0.4828
3. Vegetables	0.2208[2]	0.2208[2]	0.2208	0.2835	0.2812	0.3782	0.3594
4. Fruit	1.0324[2]	1.0324[2]	1.0324	1.8030	2.4989	1.4264	1.1717
5. Industrial Crops	0.2162[2]	0.2162[2]	0.2162	0.2497	0.2762	0.3041	0.2923
6. Livestock & Sericulture	0.8435[2]	0.8435[2]	0.8435	0.7474	0.6829	0.8396	0.4836
(3) Forestry							
7. Forestry	0.1777[3]	0.1777[3]	0.1777[3]	0.1777	0.1777[3]	0.1777[3]	0.1777[3]
(4) Fishery							
8. Fishery	1.5933[3]	1.5933[3]	1.5933[3]	1.5933	1.5933[3]	1.5933[3]	1.5933[3]
(5) Coal							
9. Coal	0.3081	0.1940	0.5478	0.4913	0.6217	0.3573	0.5335
(6) Other Minerals							
10. Metallic Ores	0.4111	0.6306	0.4113	0.5437	0.5006	0.5631	0.5632
11. Nonmetallic Minerals	0.2506	0.3991	0.2781	0.3913	0.3416	0.3414	0.3961
12. Salt	0.6698[2]	0.6698[2]	0.6698	0.4565	0.2516	0.2981	0.3491
(7) Processed Foods							
13. Meat & Dairy Products	0.4779[2]	0.4779[2]	0.4779	0.2070	0.1845	0.1135	0.2169
14. Veg. & Fruit Processing	0.2687	0.2993	0.8120	0.4517	0.3175	0.2262	0.3074
15. Processing of Sea Food	0.5238	0.5475	0.4105	0.5765	0.2895	0.2393	0.3905
16. Grain Milling	0.3990	0.4502	0.4098	0.3972	0.1791	0.2066	0.1820
17. Bakery & Confectionery	0.1987	0.1987[1]	0.2783	0.1766	0.1534	0.2082	0.2075
18. Sugar Refining	0.1984	0.1984[1]	0.2456	0.1248	0.1129	0.1083	0.0611
19. Seasonings	0.4072	0.3038	0.3925	0.3637	0.6042	0.5625	0.3631
20. Other Processed Foods	0.5292	0.4103	0.4464	0.3662	0.2022	0.1527	0.1500

Table B.33. (Continued)

	1960	1963	1966	1968	1970	1973	1975
(8) Beverages							
21. Alcoholic Beverages	0.3126	0.2370	0.2387	0.1575	0.1302	0.1524	0.1322
22. Soft Drinks	0.1557	0.2642	0.6651	0.3145	0.1480	0.4230	0.3609
(9) Tobacco							
23. Tobacco	0.2592	0.2592	0.2592	0.1543	0.1102	0.1381	0.1295
(10) Fibre Spinning							
24. Cotton Yarn	0.5473	0.4285	1.5424	0.7253	1.1374	0.4788	0.7899
25. Silk Yarn	0.5176	0.3895	0.4181	0.3103	0.3662	0.2104	0.2348
26. Woolen Yarn	0.4906	0.8315	0.5347	0.6352	1.6506	0.9098	2.3422
27. Hemp & Flax Yarn	0.4906	0.5347[2]	0.5347	0.6352	1.6506	0.9098	
28. Chemical Fibre Yarn	0.4906	1.6540[3]	1.6540[3]	1.6540[3]	1.3101	0.4727	0.5384
(11) Textile Fabrics							
29. Cotton Fabrics	0.2907	0.2492	0.1433	0.3879	0.3138	0.2976	0.5966
30. Silk Fabrics	0.5501	0.3791	0.6235	0.2913	0.4869	0.8018	0.4376
31. Woolen Fabrics	0.2948	0.5743	0.5743[1]	0.4359	0.3803	0.4082	0.3799
32. Hemp Fabrics	0.1017[2]	0.1017[2]	0.1017	0.2086	0.2103	0.5802	4.1779
33. Chemical Fibre Fabrics	0.4093[3]	0.4093[3]	0.4093[3]	0.4093[3]	0.5640	0.3805	0.4376
34. Dyeing & Finishing	0.4755	0.5284	0.6264	0.4181	0.3378	0.2415	0.0921
(12) Textile Products							
35. Knit Products	0.2743	0.4526	0.4462	0.3927	0.4434	0.3332	0.2382
36. Rope & Fishing Nets	0.1950	0.4104	0.1623	0.2346	0.2866	0.2423	0.2790
37. Apparels & Accessories	0.1285	0.1310	0.3400	0.2343	0.2498	0.3649	0.2279
38. Misc. Textile Product	0.4151	0.2817	0.5031	0.4707	0.4266	0.5106	0.3407
(13) Lumber & Plywood							
39. Lumber & Plywood	0.2056	0.2101	0.2007	0.2583	0.3173	0.1863	0.2385
(14) Wood & Furniture							
40. Wood Products	0.1610	0.6392	0.3621	0.2342	0.4093	0.1600	0.1454
41. Furniture	0.2574	0.4584	0.3252	0.2266	0.2776	0.2456	0.2446

(15) Paper Products						
42. Pulp	0.4534[1]	0.4228	0.5929	0.4618	0.4405	0.3767	0.3618
43. Paper	0.4534[1]	0.4228	0.5929	0.4618	0.4405	0.3767	
44. Paper Products	0.2768	0.2472	0.3240	0.6163	0.3754	0.2612	0.1911
(16) Printing & Publishing							
45. Printing & Publishing	0.7621	0.3119	0.5168	0.4047	0.4457	0.4091	0.4089
(17) Leather Products							
46. Leather & Fur	0.2914	0.2838	0.2180	0.4196	0.2715	0.1467	0.1057
47. Leather Products	0.1668	0.3350	0.3153	0.1911	0.2875	0.1376	0.1795
(18) Rubber Products							
48. Rubber Products	0.1883	0.1915	0.2111	0.2583	0.2773	0.2692	0.2892
(19) Basic Chemicals							
49. Inorganic Chemicals	0.9163	0.4070	1.9599	1.5252	1.1778	0.7372	0.5996
50. Organic Chemicals	0.4017	0.4456	0.4412	0.4154	0.3818	0.6380	0.4132
(20) Other Chemical Product							
51. Explosives	0.3374[2]	0.3374[2]	0.3374	0.2450	0.4051	0.4209	0.3052
52. Paint	0.1620	0.4151	0.2011	0.1389	0.1708	0.1201	0.1437
53. Drugs	0.2673	0.2463	0.2262	0.1674	0.1378	0.1486	0.1347
54. Soap	0.2582	0.1488	0.2222	0.2216	0.2137	0.1464	0.1833
55. Cosmetics	0.2311[1]	0.2311	0.2783	0.1745	0.1105	0.1006	0.1050
56. Pesticides	0.1529	0.1529	0.1463	0.1227	0.1370	0.1426	0.0896
57. Other Chemical Products	0.6596[1]	0.6596	0.9349[3]	0.9349	1.2625	0.9280	0.7502
(21) Chemical Fertilizer							
58. Chemical Fertilizer	1.3476[3]	1.3476[3]	1.3476[3]	1.3476	1.1502	1.5465	0.6575
(22) Petroleum Products							
59. Petroleum Products	0.2628[1]	0.2628	0.2717	0.2405	0.2700	0.4127	0.1428
(23) Coal Products							
60. Coal Products	0.1626	0.1646	0.1499	0.1430	0.1430	0.1100	0.1218

Table B.33. (Continued)

	1960	1963	1966	1968	1970	1973	1975
(24) Non-Metallic Mineral							
61. Cement	3.1199[2]	3.1199[2]	3.1199	2.7880	1.7949	1.4232	0.8261
62. Ceramic Products	0.2607	0.3460	0.5250	0.3334	0.3397	0.2207	0.3835
63. Glass Products	0.5321	0.4941	0.3855	0.3003	0.6561	0.5254	0.4009
64. Pottery	0.4729	0.4851	0.3672	0.4063	0.5778	0.3974	0.4089
65. Other Stone & Clay	0.8042	0.3262	0.1473	0.3944	0.3304	0.3782	0.1577
(25) Iron & Steel							
66. Pig Iron	0.3939	0.3367	0.2819[3]	0.2819	0.2013	0.6615	0.4396
67. Steel Ingots	0.3939	0.3367	0.2819[3]	0.2819	0.2013	0.6615	
(26) Steel Products							
68. Rolled Steel	0.3939	0.3367	0.2819[3]	0.2819	0.2013	0.6615	0.7025
69. Pipes & Plated Steel	0.2936	0.0923	0.1301	0.2885	0.3101	0.0660	0.1058
70. Cast & Forged Steel	0.4997	0.3378	0.7050	0.2543	0.5609	0.1767	0.4184
(27) Non-Ferrous Metals							
71. Non-Ferrous Smelting	0.4581	0.5716	0.2292	0.2854	0.2213[4]	0.2336	0.2385
72. Primary Non-Ferrous	0.3856	0.6113	0.3188[3]	0.3188	1.1529	1.1529	0.5745
(28) Finished Metal Products							
73. Structural Metallic	0.3361	0.4251	0.4589	0.3073	0.2829	0.2519	0.3682
74. Other Metallic Product	0.2687	0.3736	0.4502	0.4130	0.4064	0.2974	0.2406
(29) Machinery							
75. Prime Movers & Boilers	0.4172	0.4003[3]	0.4003[3]	0.4003	0.4325	0.5277	0.6154
76. Working Machinery	0.7185	0.5997	0.8354	0.6040	0.4465	0.1433	0.3016
77. Industrial Machinery	0.6299	0.4160	0.5051	0.3907	0.3449	0.2610	0.2577
78. Other Machinery	0.3717	0.5756	0.5188	0.4075	0.3709	0.3701	0.1290
79. Office Machines	0.3961	0.3713	0.3764	0.3760	0.5590	0.1721	0.2040
80. Household Machines	0.3961	0.3713	0.3764	0.3760	0.5590	0.1721	
81. Machine Spare Parts	0.6990	0.4866[2]	0.4866	0.4797	0.4130	0.3665	0.8171

(30) Electrical Machinery						
82. Electrical Machinery	0.4607	0.5941	0.3208[3]	0.3208	0.4948	0.2857	0.2516
83. Electronic & Comm. Eq.	0.3232	0.2806[3]	0.2806[3]	0.2806	0.2715	0.1652	0.4278
84. Household Elec. Appl.	0.2787	0.3356	0.1614	0.3719	0.1773	0.2143	0.4598
85. Other Electric Equip.	0.2032	0.1419	0.4298	0.3017	0.4126	0.2876	0.3475
(31) Transport Equipment						
86. Shipbuilding	0.9416	0.9089	0.4946	0.6728	0.6040	1.0125	0.6001
87. Railroad Transport Eq.	0.4764	0.2518[2]	0.2518	0.2801	0.4105	0.7385	0.5994
88. Motor Vehicles	0.4936	0.5989	0.4658	0.1985	0.2208	0.2051	0.3151
89. Other Transport Eq.	0.3676	0.2928	0.1807	0.4192	0.2648[4]	0.2648[4]	0.2259
(32) Misc. Manufacturing						
90. Measuring & Optical	0.5016	0.4190	0.8696	0.2789	0.3053	0.1750	0.1634
91. Synthetic Resin Product	0.4655	0.2508	0.4748	0.3806	0.2923	0.1682	0.3977
92. Other Manufactures	0.3386	0.2612	0.3412	0.2379	0.2248[4]	0.2095	0.2066
(33) Building & Maintenance						
93. Residential Building	0.2564	0.1463	0.0822	0.0656	0.0550	0.0630	0.0479
94. Non-Residential Bldng	0.1391	0.0794	0.0446	0.0356	0.0299	0.0342	0.0260
95. Building Maintenance	0.0293	0.0167	0.0094	0.0075	0.0063	0.0072	0.0055
(34) Other Construction						
96. Public Construction	0.9025	0.5148	0.2894	0.2309	0.1937	0.2218	0.1687
97. Other Construction	0.7684	0.4383	0.2464	0.1966	0.1649	0.1889	0.1436
(35) Electricity						
98. Electricity	1.7973	4.1881	3.5900	3.5117	4.5680	4.5572	4.5572[4]
(36) Banking & Dwelling						
99. Banking & Insurance	0.3124	0.2682	0.2204	0.2291	0.1666	0.1379	0.4244
100. Dwelling & Real Estate	31.3454	26.9174	22.1216	22.9906	16.7188	13.8426	11.1780

Table B.33. (Continued)

		1960	1963	1966	1968	1970	1973	1975
(37)	Water & Sanitary Service							
101.	Water & Sanitary Service	1.8049	4.2057	3.6051	3.5265	4.5873	6.5772	6.5772[4]
(38)	Communication							
102.	Communication	1.8009	1.9352	1.5133	1.7179	1.6523	1.6926	1.6842
(39)	Transportation							
103.	Railroad Transportation	5.4288	5.8338	4.5619	5.1787	4.9809	5.1026	5.0772
104.	Other Transportation	3.1157	3.3481	2.6181	2.9721	2.8586	2.9284	2.9139
105.	Storage	0.4989	0.5361	0.4192	0.4759	0.4577	0.4689	0.4666
(40)	Trade							
106.	Trade	1.0050	0.6778	0.4836	0.3330	0.3189	0.2035	0.1942
(41)	Other Services							
107.	Education	2.6574	2.4430	2.4953	2.8744	2.4478	2.6542	2.9031
108.	Medical Service	0.8350	0.7676	0.7841	0.9032	0.7692	0.8340	0.9122
109.	Social Service	0.7926	0.7286	0.7442	0.8573	0.7301	0.7916	0.8659
110.	Agricultural Service	8.3691[3]	8.3691[3]	8.3691[3]	8.3691	8.3691[3]	8.3691[3]	8.3691[3]
111.	Business Service	0.3937	0.3620	0.3697	0.4259	0.3627	0.3933	0.4302
112.	Recreation	0.6230	0.5727	0.5850	0.6739	0.5739	0.6223	0.6806
113.	Personal Service	1.3673	1.2570	1.2839	1.4790	1.2595	1.3657	1.4938
114.	Office Supplies	0	0	0	0	0	0	0
(42)	Scrap							
115.	Iron Scrap	0	0	0	0	0	0	0
116.	Other Scrap	0	0	0	0	0	0	0
(43)	Unclassifiable							
117.	Unclassifiable	0	0	0	0	0	0	0

Source: See Hong, *op. cit.*, Chapter 7.
Notes: [1] 1963 coefficient.
[2] 1966 coefficient.
[3] 1968 coefficient.
[4] 1973 coefficient.

Table B.34. Sectoral Net Fixed Capital Stock: 1953–76
(Applying Sectoral Implicit Price Deflator for Fixed Capital Formation)

In Million 1970 Dollars

	1953	1954	1955	1956	1957	1958	1959	1960	1961	1962	1963	1946
Agriculture & Fishery*	290.3	299.2	313.9	329.4	353.6	371.0	392.3	416.7	452.2	473.6	515.8	553.8
Mining & Quarrying	93.3	91.4	91.7	95.3	100.3	101.6	100.5	96.4	91.2	86.9	85.1	81.1
Manufacturing	477.7	496.8	537.5	591.8	646.8	697.2	735.1	772.0	813.2	869.2	935.7	986.5
Construction	92.4	88.6	82.1	79.4	76.7	75.4	72.4	74.2	74.8	83.4	87.0	87.0
Electricity & Sanitary	78.2	81.4	89.9	94.2	98.1	106.8	113.7	120.1	138.3	174.1	233.1	261.6
Transportation & Comm.	402.2	431.6	457.2	485.1	540.3	585.3	634.3	669.5	725.4	796.3	882.8	948.1
Trade	549.9	539.8	532.3	521.2	506.1	496.6	487.7	478.6	466.7	462.0	449.5	433.1
Banking & Real Estate	44.0	43.8	43.7	44.5	45.1	46.0	47.1	47.5	46.2	45.5	45.1	45.4
Public Administration	487.3	493.2	498.1	503.2	508.7	514.5	520.3	525.7	527.9	529.9	534.1	537.0
Other Services	777.2	797.1	823.3	841.3	855.3	867.8	888.4	908.9	932.6	973.8	1,015.5	1,067.8
Ownership of Dwellings	4,356.8	4,372.2	4,384.8	4,401.6	4,413.5	4,424.0	4,445.4	4,492.6	4,527.8	4,563.4	4,605.1	4,659.3
Whole Industry	7,649.3	7,735.1	7,854.5	7,987.0	8,144.5	8,286.2	8,437.2	8,602.2	8,796.3	9,058.1	9,388.8	9,660.7

	1965	1966	1967	1968	1969	1970	1971	1972	1973	1974	1975	1976
Agriculture & Fishery*	606.8	695.0	765.2	843.4	927.6	1,046.7	1,166.9	1,329.6	1,489.7	1,717.4	1,916.6	2,142.8
Mining & Quarrying	80.7	81.8	81.7	84.7	84.6	78.5	76.7	76.0	78.2	88.4	102.7	121.8
Manufacturing	1,071.5	1,273.2	1,456.0	1,681.6	1,918.4	2,137.8	2,350.5	2,457.8	2,808.5	2,993.5	3,189.6	3,507.9
Construction	89.1	94.8	95.8	125.0	148.0	151.6	160.0	166.5	182.7	171.6	185.0	165.3
Electricity & Sanitary	287.9	323.3	406.1	565.8	791.3	1,005.6	1,169.9	1,261.3	1,352.7	1,520.3	1,721.3	2,030.4
Transportation & Comm.	1,033.6	1,226.3	1,514.8	1,868.6	2,412.9	2,881.6	3,375.5	3,925.4	4,483.1	5,158.4	5,938.4	6,740.5
Trade	426.3	405.2	389.1	405.7	452.0	506.1	566.8	534.8	495.7	480.0	528.4	567.0
Banking & Real Estate	46.5	49.4	50.8	61.6	75.5	90.3	98.9	104.3	114.3	126.6	159.5	183.3
Public Administration	542.9	548.9	566.0	599.6	632.0	664.0	721.5	778.4	823.6	845.4	883.8	944.5
Other Services	1,137.9	1,211.4	1,311.9	1,431.1	1,612.9	1,812.4	2,022.5	2,189.1	2,424.4	2,627.3	2,847.4	3,150.3
Ownership of Dwellings	4,723.9	4,816.4	4,926.2	5,115.1	5,317.3	5,575.8	5,857.8	6,117.8	6,477.3	7,013.7	7,592.3	8,061.5
Whole Industry	10,047.1	10,725.7	11,563.6	12,782.2	14,372.5	15,950.4	17,567.0	18,941.0	20,730.2	22,742.7	25,065.3	27,614.5

* Includes capital stock for agricultural service sector.

Table B.35. Sectoral Gross Fixed Capital Stock: 1953–76

In Million 1970 Dollars

	1953	1954	1955	1956	1957	1958	1959	1960	1961	1962	1963	1964
Agriculture & Fishery	513.7	530.9	552.7	577.6	610.4	637.3	667.8	703.5	749.5	785.6	841.8	903.8
Mining & Quarrying	36.1	37.4	41.0	46.8	56.0	62.3	66.0	71.4	73.1	76.5	82.5	86.5
Manufacturing	727.1	−760.0	818.4	892.2	972.0	1,047.4	1,109.8	1,176.5	1,242.5	1,331.1	1,446.5	1,560.4
Construction	63.3	64.2	66.1	68.5	72.2	76.8	79.9	83.3	87.2	100.5	111.4	119.1
Electricity & Sanitary	−20.0	−14.1	−1.2	7.0	14.3	28.8	39.4	50.1	76.4	121.4	190.5	229.1
Transportation & Comm.	993.7	1,034.7	1,071.8	1,114.9	1,187.6	1,250.0	1,323.5	1,378.4	1,455.2	1,554.7	1,679.6	1,778.4
Trade	222.4	234.3	252.1	265.4	277.8	295.3	316.4	335.0	350.3	376.1	403.4	429.6
Banking & Real Estate	61.6	61.9	62.2	63.5	64.6	66.0	67.7	68.8	69.0	69.8	70.4	71.7
Public Administration	763.8	771.2	777.6	784.6	792.3	801.0	810.0	818.7	824.2	829.3	837.0	843.6
Other Services	1,386.9	1,415.6	1,451.1	1,478.0	1,502.6	1,526.6	1,560.2	1,592.5	1,627.7	1,681.1	1,735.8	1,799.5
Ownership of Dwellings	6,762.7	6,824.7	6,867.6	6,912.9	6,954.9	6,995.8	7,045.8	7,120.7	7,180.1	7,238.2	7,305.8	7,382.6
Whole Industry	11,511.2	11,720.6	11,958.4	12,211.4	12,504.7	12786.2	13,086.5	13,398.8	13,735.1	14,164.5	14,704.7	15,204.1

	1965	1966	1967	1968	1969	1970	1971	1972	1973	1974	1975	1976
Agriculture & Fishery	980.2	1,093.1	1,194.5	1,308.2	1,436.6	1,605.3	1,784.9	2,016.6	2,259.8	2,576.7	2,874.0	3,239.2
Mining & Quarrying	93.9	104.2	115.5	131.3	144.8	156.0	171.8	185.5	203.4	228.1	263.7	307.5
Manufacturing	1,717.6	1,985.3	2,251.2	2,608.2	3,013.4	3,427.8	3,852.3	4,268.5	5,036.4	5,662.8	6,360.9	7,301.4
Construction	128.6	139.8	150.4	193.8	237.4	262.9	292.8	320.4	365.2	391.4	433.0	480.4
Electricity & Sanitary	265.9	316.4	414.8	592.0	840.8	1,078.7	1,271.8	1,399.7	1,531.2	1,737.1	1,983.4	2,371.7
Transportation & Comm.	1,897.8	2,137.8	2,475.8	2,898.2	3,514.0	4,053.3	4,625.7	5,258.6	5,940.5	6,746.2	7,667.3	8,619.7
Trade	474.0	512.5	563.8	629.3	737.6	862.0	1,003.5	1,104.8	1,222.4	1,375.5	1,566.2	1,784.5
Banking & Real Estate	73.9	78.0	81.5	95.5	114.0	135.1	151.0	164.7	183.6	208.2	248.7	279.7
Public Administration	854.1	865.9	888.9	929.9	971.5	1,013.5	1,082.2	1,152.8	1,211.5	1,261.5	1,315.0	1,395.0
Other Services	1,879.3	1,965.2	2,081.2	2,219.7	2,424.0	2,649.9	2,890.2	3,089.2	3,361.4	3,600.1	3,865.9	4,235.6
Ownership of Dwellings	7,468.0	7,582.5	7,717.9	7,933.6	8,163.6	8,446.7	8,756.0	9,044.0	9,432.0	9,983.2	10,592.1	11,096.6
Whole Industry	15,833.2	16,780.7	17,935.3	19,539.6	21,597.7	23,691.1	25,882.5	28,004.6	30,747.3	33,770.7	37,170.2	41,111.3